The Perrin-Smith Handbook of Current English is the composition handbook in the Scott, Foresman College English Program—Frances Remus, Directing Editor. It was prepared under the editorial supervision of:

Kenneth Bennett, Staff Editor
The College Composition Series

For special criticism and help in the final processing of the Handbook, grateful acknowledgment is made to:

Delmer Rodabaugh, University of Minnesota
Powell Stewart, University of Texas
John C. Sherwood, University of Oregon
Benjamin P. Atkinson, Hobart and William Smith Colleges

Art direction, Hal Kearney
Design, Catherine Hinkle

The Perrin-Smith Handbook of Current English

by Porter G. Perrin and George H. Smith
University of Washington

Scott, Foresman and Company
Chicago Atlanta Dallas Palo Alto Fair Lawn, N.J.

Subject of Gerund is in the possessive case.

To be = uses nominative case
Subject of infinitive is in objective case.

But preposition when it means except

expository paragraphs
1. Give examples
2. Enumerate details
3.

a like
Comparison & Contrast differ

1. Food in cafeteria & at home
2. Architecture of classroom building & Caldwell Hall,

Preface

This *Handbook of Current English* is designed to help college students increase their skill in writing to meet the expectations of educated readers. It describes our language as it is actually used in American books and periodicals and shows why some kinds of expression are considered more effective than others. If a student's problems come from lack of knowledge, the information is here; if they are from faulty habits previously formed, there are suggestions for change with reasons for making the change; and if they come from uncertainty in choosing between words or forms contained in the language, principles are given for choosing the more appropriate ones.

The basis of Good English and the governing principles of appropriateness are discussed in the early sections. Section two, a description of the levels of English usage, and sections three and four, on standards of Good English, are needed to interpret the specific recommendations made in the later Handbook sections, and students need to read them to understand corrections made on their papers. "General English" is the type encouraged for most writing, but the Formal English expected in some college writing is fully presented and an instructor can select the level that he wishes to emphasize.

Students should also become familiar at the beginning of a course with section five, "Writing a paper," which will give them an answer to their inevitable question "How am I supposed to write a paper?"

The Handbook is arranged in sections that treat single, definite topics. Each section includes grammatical definitions where needed rather than in a separate list. Particular matters of usage are treated at the point where they are related to general principles that apply to them rather than in a separate glossary of usage. Frequent tables summarize the terms and main points of a topic. An especially full index provides an easy way of finding both general and particular matters, and students should be encouraged to form a habit of using it in revising their papers.

Themes can be marked either by the use of abbreviations that are keyed to section numbers (a list is on the back end papers), or if an instructor prefers, by the section numbers themselves. Abbreviations are recommended because they carry directly the point being made, and if the student needs information on it he can easily refer to the section concerned.

The exercises emphasize and develop certain points through specific drill, through practice in applying the principles given, and through discussion to develop further understanding of ideas presented in the sections. (A key to the exercises is available to instructors.)

Published sources that treat more fully many of the topics of the Handbook are listed in the General Bibliography (pages xxii, xxiii) and more specific references are given at the end of many sections.

P.G.P.
G.H.S.

Contents

Good English

Composition

Grammar and usage

General Bibliography

The following authoritative books and magazines on current English have been the most useful in gathering material for this book. They are frequently referred to in specific sections, usually by author's name only. They will give further details on subjects treated in the Handbook and reliable information on other topics of English usage.

American Speech, New York, Columbia University Press. A periodical, founded in 1925, containing much direct observation of current American usage, especially vocabularies of particular regions and occupations

Bryant, Margaret M., *Modern English and Its Heritage,* New York, Macmillan, 1948. Discussion of current English, especially of the sentence, with historical background

Curme, George O., *Syntax,* Boston, Heath, 1931; and *Parts of Speech and Accidence,* Boston, Heath, 1935. A very full grammar of modern English with much historical material

Fowler, H. W., *A Dictionary of Modern English Usage,* Oxford University Press, 1926. Though based on British usage and now somewhat dated, still a readable and often illuminating discussion of particular points of usage

Fries, C. C., *American English Grammar* (NCTE Monograph No. 10), New York, Appleton-Century-Crofts, 1940. A number of points of grammar and usage discussed with special attention to differences between levels of usage

Government Printing Office Style Manual, Washington, Government Printing Office, revised edition, 1953. Referred to as *GPO Style Manual*

Jespersen, Otto, *Essentials of English Grammar,* New York, Holt, 1933. An abridgment of Jespersen's four-volume *Modern English Grammar,* the most important description of current English

Kenyon, John S., and Thomas A. Knott, *A Pronouncing Dictionary of American English*, Springfield, G. & C. Merriam Company, 1944. The most reliable guide to American pronunciation

Marckwardt, Albert H., and Fred G. Walcott, *Facts About Current English Usage* (NCTE Monograph No. 7), New York, Appleton-Century-Crofts, 1938. Includes the data of the Sterling A. Leonard study (1932) of debatable and divided usage

Mencken, H. L., *The American Language*, 4th edition, New York, Knopf, 1936; *Supplement I* (1945) and *Supplement II* (1948). A mass of material on American usage, with commentary and references to further sources

Pooley, Robert C., *Teaching English Usage* (NCTE Monograph No. 16), New York, Appleton-Century-Crofts, 1946. Discussion of a number of debatable expressions, with evidence and recommendations for teaching

Roberts, Paul, *Understanding Grammar*, New York, Harper, 1954. A good brief systematic English grammar

Robertson, Stuart, *The Development of Modern English*, New York, Prentice-Hall, 1934 (2nd ed., revised by Frederick G. Cassidy, 1954). Gives the background of many points of current usage

Skillin, Marjorie, and Robert M. Gay, *Words into Type*, New York, Appleton-Century-Crofts, 1948. A detailed manual of publishers' style

Summey, George, Jr., *American Punctuation*, New York, Ronald, 1949. The authoritative treatment of punctuation, with material bearing on sentences and traits of usage

More specialized works are cited in the various sections to which they apply. Dictionaries are listed in §48, Using a dictionary.

Articles and notes on specific matters of usage are found frequently in these periodicals: *College English, The English Journal, Inside the ACD, Language, Language Learning, PADS* (Publications of the American Dialect Society), *Quarterly Journal of Speech, Word Study.*

... language is a means to an end, and that end is specifically to grasp, to possess, to communicate experience. Accordingly, that is good language, good English, which, on the one hand, most fully realizes one's own impressions, and, on the other, is most completely adapted to the purposes of any particular communication.—C. C. Fries

The circle of the English language has a well-defined centre but no discernible circumference.—Oxford English Dictionary

... standard English is an ever-changing, never-fully-realized ideal toward which the entire English speaking race is steadily striving, but good English—or may we change the term to better English?—is the aim and goal of every intelligent speaker of the language, just as better thinking is always the desire of such a person.—Arthur G. Kennedy

Language is not something we can disembody; it is an ethical as well as mechanical matter, inextricably bound up in ourselves, our positions, and our relations with those about us.—William S. Whyte, Jr.

It takes a great deal of experience to become natural.—Willa Cather

Good English

1 Studying current English

This is a book about the English language we use: the language that we hear in conversation, in public talks, and over the radio, the language that we read in newspapers, magazines, and books. It is the language that we speak and write as we tell others of our experiences, knowledge, ideas, feelings, desires. This book is especially about what is usually called Good English, the English that is used by educated people in carrying on the affairs of business, science, literature, government—the language of public affairs in general.

1.1 English as a language A language consists of a system of sounds, a collection of words, some changes in word forms, some patterns into which the words fit to convey meaning; it may or may not also have a system of writing and printing to record the spoken language on paper. In the hundreds of years that English has been a separate language, the usage of millions of people has developed the vast and varied language we speak and write today.

Sounds—English has between forty and fifty sounds, about twenty of them vowel sounds and the rest consonants. Each sound is used with slight variations in actual speech; for example, some people have a full *r* and others a very slight indication of the sound. The pronunciation of words varies considerably among the different regions in which English is used, so that we can easily identify some people as Englishmen or as Southerners or Westerners.

Words—English has a vocabulary, counting everything from slang and local words to rarely used words and scientific terms, of probably well over two million words. Many of these are used in several different senses—one dictionary gives

1

forty different meanings for the word *check*. A college size
dictionary has about 130,000 entries, and a college student
probably uses or recognizes over 50,000 basic words, not including derivatives made by adding syllables like *-ed, -ly.*

Word forms—Compared with Latin or German or Russian,
English uses very few changes in word forms: only a few
endings, like the *-s* or *-es* of nouns (*boys, churches*), the *-s,
-ed, -ing* of verbs, *-er* and *-est* for comparing adverbs and adjectives, and a few internal changes, like *man—men, sing—
sang.* This small number of word forms makes it possible for
a youngster to master English in a shorter time than he could
learn a highly inflected language. There are many elements
that can be used to make new words: prefixes (*in-, mega-, re-,
super-*), suffixes (*-er, -ish, -ship, -teria*). And English makes
compounds freely by putting two or more words together
(*bookcase, streamlined*).

Constructions—English has two basic ways of combining
words into groups: by phrases centered on nouns (*in the
morning, a clear picture*) and by clauses centered on verbs
(*he runs the forty-yard dash; when she bought the blouse*).
We interpret the meaning of these familiar patterns very
largely from the order in which the words stand, an order that
fortunately we pick up unconsciously and rarely make a mistake in. Out of these simple word groups we build sentences
of varying length and complexity. Describing these typical
constructions and the exceptions to them is the principal job
of English grammar.

Writing practices—English, which like other languages first
developed in speech, is represented in writing and printing
by the twenty-six letters of the alphabet, a dozen or so punctuation marks, and devices like capitals and italics. The conventions of spelling, punctuation, capitalization, and so on
(developed mostly by printers) chiefly serve to remind us of
the language we speak and hear.

With this linguistic material, we communicate with each
other in carrying on our personal and public affairs. By the
various methods of printing and writing we can communicate

with people at a distance and can even leave for later generations a record of what we have thought and felt and done.

What we are less aware of is that a great deal of our "thinking," probably all of it that is not in images of sense impressions, is done by the use of words. And since we store up so much of what we learn in the form of words, language becomes to a certain extent a means of *seeing*. We "see" more and we understand more when we have words for what we see, and sometimes we do not understand at all something that our experience in words has not prepared us for. Anyone who has played basketball, or at least has followed it closely and talked about it, sees more in a game than someone who has seen only a few games. A geologist sees more in driving through a cut in a hilltop, and an architect or a carpenter sees more in a building than most of us, in part because their language is specially developed in these fields.

Our language is such an intimate part of our lives, seemingly of our "selves," that systematically studying it seems artificial and strange. Ideally a person should not be conscious of his language, certainly not as he is using it. In a small community where everyone talked alike, he probably would not be. But in a society like ours, where several kinds of English are in use at the same time, we are often forced to choose between them and so occasionally need to be able to think and talk about the language, as well as about what it says. (Should I say—or write—*who* or *whom* here? Is *insincere* a better word than *phony* in this sentence? What is the possessive of *Jones*?) We not only need answers to such questions of usage and style, we need to have reasons for our choices. There is, unfortunately, much prejudice in the field of language, but it is now becoming easier to answer questions of usage calmly on the basis of evidence gathered by students of current English.

A professional student of language, that is, a linguist, can study all sorts of English without worrying much about which are the most useful. But in a composition course we are interested in cultivating habits and in choosing what is best for our particular purposes. We do not need all the facts or all the methods of the professional linguist, though we should not contradict his basic principles. We need to become intelligent amateur linguists, students of English. We need enough of linguistics to observe fairly accurately the language around us and to summarize and discuss the part of it that has a bearing on our own problems.

Our interests in discussing English in this book are these: first, the facts of *usage,* what people actually say and write; second, matters of *style,* for evaluating and selecting among the possible ways of saying something the way that is best for communicating what we wish to say in a particular situation; third, the terms of *grammar,* for discussing (and as a help in observing and remembering) the facts of usage and style. And back of these language matters is the *discourse* or composition, the whole that says something to someone, whose material and purpose controls the language used. It is only as we consider the nature and purpose of the whole that we can understand and judge the fitness of the small, particular facts of the language used.

1.2 Language growth in college   A student comes to college with his language habits pretty well formed. But college is a time of great language growth. This is most obvious in vocabulary, from the vocabulary of campus life (*cram, cut, double E, pledge, rushee* . . .) to words used in his various courses—most courses add several hundred words to his vocabulary, at least temporarily. Skill in listening to recitations and lectures is of increasing importance, as is skill in reading, especially of difficult material. There is more opportunity for good conversation, since social contacts are widening, and there is a need (too often slighted) for good speech in recitation, but there is special call for writing. Most courses involve impromptu writing in quizzes and examinations, as well as papers prepared outside of class. Much of this writing is academic and consequently more or less formal, but there are letters to write and, at least in a composition course, papers of more personal or more general appeal.

It is possible to look on language growth in college in a narrow way, as a tool for getting along, and certainly "Better expression, better grades" is a true saying. But college is also a time for laying the foundation for the lifelong development of effective language. In addition to the direct attention to language skills, a return to the youthful attitude toward language would help in this growth: experimenting, playing with the big new words (*schizophrenia, marginal utility, tragicomedy, thermodynamics* . . .) as well as seriously discussing the new ideas they represent, watching the language of others and imitating in both speaking and writing what seems especially effective and in line with one's own mind and temperament. It is a time to get rid of inhibitions about language and to make full use of one's language resources. In the long run, developing a feeling for language and taking an interest in it as an activity will do more to promote Good English than will memorizing facts and rules.

No one ever masters his language completely and even professional writers continue to experiment and to grow. Teachers may force attention to some of the more specific aspects of writing, like spelling or organization, but no very wide reaching growth is possible unless a student really wishes to extend his control of English and takes the lead in his own development. If he wants to extend his contacts, his influence, and his knowledge, attention to his language will help. Meeting the expectations of the college community will prepare for meeting the expectations of people in jobs and public affairs after college. But this growth is always an individual matter, the result (or by-product) of a more general development.

2 Levels of English Usage

We all know that there are a good many differences within the written language, just as there are in the spoken. Words and constructions vary a good deal in what we read, even taking no wider range than from newspapers to textbooks, and we use a little different language in writing to different people and in writing papers for different purposes. Consider these expressions:

> were it not for—if it were not for—if it was not for—if it wasn't for—if it wan't for

> I have none—I have not any—I haven't any—I haven't got any—I ain't got any—I hain't got any—I ain't got none

All these expressions are found within the English language, but they would be used under different circumstances. We would not ordinarily say or write *I have none* or *were it not for.* We would be most likely to say or write *I haven't any* and *if it wasn't for. If it were not for, if it was not for,* and *I have not any* are chiefly written forms. The other expressions are common in speech but are rarely written.

In the series of words *simulated–spurious–fraudulent–counterfeit–imitation–false–sham–bogus–pseudo–phony* the first four would be found in rather formal writing, the last four in speech or light writing. *Imitation* and *false* could go anywhere.

These examples of differences in constructions and words illustrate the range of expressions meaning nearly the same thing and show the need for approaching English on the basis of *selecting among the differences that exist the expressions that will best suit a particular occasion.* Although the names used in describing these differences vary somewhat, all realistic descriptions of current English speak of different *levels* of usage.

In this book we speak of four main levels—Formal, General, Informal, Vulgate—and some varieties that occur within them. They are summarized in the table on pp. 8-9. A level, or a variety within a level, is not a fixed compartment of the language; one shades off into another. But a particular piece of writing will ordinarily show pretty clear traits of one level: it will be clearly Formal, though it may be close to Stilted or closer to General; a passage in General English may use some words usually found in Formal English and another might be conspicuously Informal but still not Vulgate. As a rule the situation and the subject will call for one level of language, as we shall see in sections 3 and 4.

2.1 General English General English, as we are using the term, is perhaps the hardest to describe, because it is the broad range of the language that does its work without attracting special attention. It is all around us in newspapers, magazines, and books. This paragraph from a magazine discussion of the causes of disturbances between Europeans and natives in Africa is in General English:

These first settlers were also under the impression (still current) that all Africans including the Kikuyu, never own land individually but always as a group—a generalization to which the Kikuyu happen to be a notable exception. What the first settlers didn't see was the individual absentee landlords of all this rich land which seemed so empty. The newcomers wanted land for themselves and their families. They bought it from the Kikuyu and other Africans, under the strict supervision of the government, which was determined to prevent the land grabbing that had gone on in other parts of Africa. Generally speaking, fair prices were paid for the land. But according to Dr. Leakey, the Kikuyu honestly thought that they had *rented,* not sold, the land to the British because certain vital religious ceremonies for the transfer of land had not been observed.

At the same time, the settlers honestly believed that the Kikuyu were selling their land, and they had legal documents to prove it. In other words, it never occurred to the Kikuyu that the Europeans wouldn't behave like Kikuyu, or to the Europeans that the Kikuyu wouldn't behave like Europeans.—Oden and Olivia Meeker, "The Fuel That Feeds the Mau Mau Fires," *The Reporter,* June 23, 1953, p. 19

The words in this, except for the necessary *Kikuyu* and perhaps *absentee landlords,* are in general use; the sentences are about the typical length for modern writing, ranging from 9 to 37 words with an average of 24; the constructions, though more compact than those of typical speech, are close to the spoken language: *still current; what the first settlers didn't see; the land grabbing; rented, not sold; at the same time;* and the whole last sentence.

Levels of English usage

Principal levels	Typical varieties and uses
Formal English (Limited use) Speaking and writing for somewhat restricted groups in formal situations *More often written than spoken*	*Stilted* (upper extreme) Pretentious and unnecessarily heavy writing; gobbledygook *Impersonal* Academic writing: reference works, dissertations, term papers, some textbooks Scientific and technical writing: books and articles dealing with special subjects for professional groups, technical reports Some editorials and business writing *Personal* Literature of somewhat limited circulation: essays and criticism, much poetry, some fiction Addresses and lectures to special audiences
General English (Unlimited use) Speaking and writing of educated people in their private or public affairs *Both spoken and written*	Conversation of educated people Talks to general audiences Magazine articles and books on subjects of general interest Most fiction and other literature for general circulation Most news stories, features, columns Business letters, advertising

8

Levels of English usage

Principal levels	Typical varieties and uses

Informal English
(Limited use)

Speaking and writing of educated people in informal situations

Both spoken and written

Casual conversation

Writing close to popular speech, light or serious; sometimes including shoptalk or slang

Familiar   Talk and letters between intimates; diaries, personal writing; likely to include localisms

Vulgate English
(Limited use)

Not much touched by school instruction; not appropriate for public affairs or use of educated people

Chiefly spoken

Conversation of many people in their work and personal relations and representations of this in plays and stories, some radio programs and comic strips; often conspicuously local

Slovenly (lower extreme) Impoverished, thoughtless speech, often including much obscenity and profanity

The Formal, General, and Informal levels make up what is generally known as Standard English and the Vulgate level is equivalent to Nonstandard.

The levels are not to be thought of as sharply defined and mutually exclusive but as shading into each other.

Often two or more forms exist in the language in reputable use in the same level (*catalog–catalogue*). This is called *divided usage.*

Another paragraph, from a systematic introduction to the study of stars, shows that specialized information can be presented in General English:

Suppose, though, that you were to leave the north pole and go as far south as Minneapolis. This city, and all others in the same latitude, are exactly half-way between the equator and the poles. The pole star, therefore, hangs half-way down the sky instead of at the zenith where it was seen from the north geographical pole. In Minneapolis all the stars at view on any night still seem to move around the pole star, but some of them, rising out of the east and climbing above the southern horizon, will sink from view in the west and be out of sight for some time during the night. Above the northern horizon there are certain stars that continually swing around the north celestial pole and never disappear. Since they are in view for every hour of every night they are among the easiest to find and identify. They are the keystones of constellation study—the circumpolar stars. They form an easy guide to other near-by groups.— Hubert J. Bernhard and others, *New Handbook of the Heavens*, p. 20

And the emotional effects of literature can also be achieved by General English, as in this passage from a short story in which the language is simply a compressed form of what we might all use (except perhaps "the world leaps into proportion"):

The man who expected to be shot lay with his eyes open, staring at the upper left-hand corner of his cell. He was fairly well over his last beating, and they might come for him any time now. There was a yellow stain in the cell corner near the ceiling; he had liked it at first, then disliked it; now he was coming back to liking it again.

He could see it more clearly with his glasses on, but he only put on his glasses for special occasions now—the first thing in the morning, and when they brought the food in, and for interviews with the General. The lenses of the glasses had been cracked in a beating some months before, and it strained his eyes to wear them too long. Fortunately, in his present life he had very few occasions demanding clear vision. But, nevertheless, the accident to his glasses worried him, as it worries all near-sighted people. You put your glasses on the first thing in the morning and the world leaps into proportion; if it does not do so, something is wrong with the world.—Stephen Vincent Benét, "The Blood of the Martyrs," *Thirteen O'Clock*, p. 23

Most of the English that we hear and read and that we speak and write falls within the range of General English.

These examples—and the great bulk of respected writing—show that General English is the principal and most useful part of the language. Because of its effectiveness and unlimited usefulness, it is the chief goal of most speakers and writers, and the proper goal of study and practice in a composition course.

2.2 Informal English Close to and overlapping General English is the level of Informal English. Its base is the everyday language of educated people in their personal affairs, but, tidied up somewhat, it appears in print, especially in discussions of what people do and in the work of writers who assume some intimacy with their readers.

Typically in writing it shows various traits of speech: rather short sentences, contractions, spoken phrases, and words that are more characteristic of speech than of writing:

> The Junior Literary Guild, we would like you to know, is celebrating its twenty-fifth anniversary. It's doing very well thank you. We give you proof.—Harvey Breit, "In and Out of Books," *The New York Times Book Review*, June 20, 1954, p. 8

The Informal vocabulary includes words like *cop, dead pan, lambaste, whodunit, peeve.* These words are often called *colloquial,* and may be so labeled in dictionaries. This means that they suggest speech rather than writing, at least that they are not commonly found in Formal writing. But since in current style there is not the difference that there once was between speech and writing, we are not using "colloquial" as a principal label in this book but include these words and expressions in Informal English.

Informal English is likely to make some, though not very extensive, use of *slang words.* These are newly made words (*whoopee, oomph*), or old words in extended meanings (*real cool, real George, Mexican overdrive*), or phrases conspicuously overused (*way to be*). There are almost always more conventional ways of saying the same thing, but young people, some fashionable or sporty adults, and journalists or others freshening their word stock want to be a little different. So we have a continual flow of usually short-lived words for money, cheating, being clever, being drunk, for relations between the sexes, for expressing approval and disapproval. Some of them prove useful and become part of the General vocabulary. Most people do not distinguish very carefully between slang and other sorts of Informal English; in fact most words marked "slang" in dictionaries (*goo, hassle, medico*) are already in Informal usage before they are recorded.

Another type of word sometimes found in Informal English is *shoptalk*, words current within an occupation or sport, from bulldozing and baseball to medicine and atomic physics, especially words used in conversation rather than specifically technical or scientific terms. They are the common names for materials, products, tools, operations. Though they most naturally appear in accounts of the occupation itself, some slip outside to be used metaphorically in Informal English, like *bug, graveyard shift, huddle, slush fund, belting* (a song), *close-up, fade-in,* or *fade-out.*

A type of Informal English of still more limited use is Familiar English. It is what we say or write to people with whom we are intimate, when we can take for granted sympathetic attention and a considerable amount of common experience. We can be as free and easy as we like, though not careless or sloppy to the extent of being discourteous. This is characteristic of lively letters, and of writing for ourselves, like diaries.

Familiar English is likely to show a good many *localisms,* words characteristic of a particular region, seen especially in names for common things (*coal oil* for *kerosene; fried cake, cruller, fatcake* for *doughnut; sack* or *poke* for *bag*) and in special names in local occupations (*mule skinner, sheepherder, fattening* for hogs) or features of the landscape peculiar to or prominent in the region (*coulee, hogback, branch* of a stream, *bayou*). These words often reflect the language of the early settlers, as the Dutch in New York, the Germans in Pennsylvania, and the Spanish in the Southwest. Local words of course occur freely in the conversation of the people of a region, in newspapers, in fiction, and in descriptions of life that are close to the actual experience of a region. But they come most naturally in Familiar English, capitalizing on the experiences which the writer and reader have in common.

Informal English is of somewhat limited usefulness and some people are definitely prejudiced against it, but it is often appropriate to descriptions of sports, fraternity life, and other social situations, and to vigorous and perhaps breezy discussions of the various things people do, both humorous and serious.

2.3 Formal English The Formal level of usage is principally a development from General English, somewhat further from Informal or Vulgate because it is used chiefly in writing. It is more edited, more complex than General English. It is more influenced by reading and follows more closely the conventions built up by editors in the past. It usually occurs in discussions of specialized topics for people who know something about those topics and in reading addressed to rather limited audiences.

The vocabulary of Formal English naturally includes most of the General words, but not many from Informal or Familiar English. The contrast may be seen in a dictionary definition of the Informal word *arty* in Formal terms: "ostentatious in display of artistic intent." Necessarily, Formal English uses the specialized vocabulary of the subject matter being discussed; it also tends to use a good many abstract words and words that suggest literary or eloquent expression. The grammatical constructions tend to be fuller, and ordinarily the sentences are somewhat longer and more complex than in General English.

There are two principal kinds of Formal English: (1) *Impersonal* as in academic, scientific, technical, and scholarly writing; and (2) *Personal* or somewhat heightened writing (sometimes called "emotive") used in elevated literature and the expression of abstract ideas.

An example of Impersonal Formal English, requiring a little more attentive reading than the first paragraph on page 10, is this account of the mapping of Switzerland, showing the single-minded attention to the subject, the compact and orderly statement of ideas, and the use of technical terms (but no more than are needed) that characterizes good technical writing:

The heroic task of making a topographic survey and map of Switzerland fell to the lot of General Guillaume Henri Dufour (1787-1875). Under his personal supervision the work was begun in 1830 and the first sheet was published in 1842. Thirty-four years later the entire survey, on a scale of 1:100,000, was finished and the last of the 25 sheets came from the press. Soon after, the map appeared in atlas form, published at Berne. Far from being a pioneering effort that would require immediate revision, the Dufour atlas proved to be a model of accuracy and artistic delineation, not only for future map makers of Switzerland, but for cartographers at large. The sheets of the atlas were used as a basis for later surveys on different scales, and on the sheets of Switzerland's new survey references were made to the corresponding sections and subsections of the original Dufour map. The art work and conventional signs on the new map were almost identical with those on the Dufour originals. The lettering and bench marks (figures denoting heights), prominent buildings, roads, boundaries and forests were printed in black. Small slopes and passes, ravines and narrow defiles that could not be shown by equally spaced contour lines were printed in brown hachures. Black hachures were used to indicate rocky prominences and precipes, the general effect being a pictorial representation by oblique lighting. Horizontal surveys were shown in bronze and water was indicated by shades of blue.—Lloyd A. Brown, *The Story of Maps*, p. 273. Reprinted by permission of Little, Brown & Company.

A more Personal type of Formal English is shown in this conclusion of a book on ethics. Some of the words are Formal —*despite, purposiveness*—and the phrases full and rather abstract: *extraordinary capacity for survival, a majestic significance, incredibly devastating.* The construction *so colossal a massacre* in General English would be *such a colossal massacre.* But some of these phrases and others like *the good society, love adventure,* and the whole last sentence carry an unmistakable Personal emphasis.

The coming of a better world may be prevented by the hellish fury of scientific warfare, but mankind has exhibited an extraordinary capacity for survival. "It is not probable that war will ever absolutely cease," wrote W. Winwood Reade in 1872, "until science discovers some destroying force so simple in its administration, so horrible in its effects, that all art, all gallantry, will be at an end, and battles will be massacres which the feeling of mankind will be unable to endure." As a result of scientific and technological developments, such a peak of destructiveness has now been reached; and it is quite possible that the human will to survival will forever revolt against so colossal a massacre as the next World War would bring.

In every country and in the interior of every mind, the struggle is continuing between the forces of chaos and the forces which may eventually produce a far better civilization. Despite tragedy and confusion, "the hope of the great community" gives a majestic significance and purposiveness to our age. There may be an incredibly devastating war or series of wars. There may be a new Dark Age such as followed the death of St. Augustine. But the hope of the good society will live on even as then. Those who love adventure and desire a better world are not sick before the prospect that looms ahead. If they keep bright the arrows of desire, they may eventually storm and occupy the citadels of power.—Melvin Rader, *Ethics and Society*, p. 372. Reprinted by permission of Henry Holt and Company, Inc.

Educated people need to be able to read Formal English. And college students should be able to write rather Formal English when the occasion requires it. They should be able to do so with sufficient confidence to avoid a Stilted style, and they should not write Formally of matters that do not call for such a style. Formal English has a real if limited use.

2.4 Vulgate English At the opposite side of General English from Formal is Vulgate English, language that does not show much influence of school instruction or much contact with the language of public affairs. It is not a falling off from General English but a level of the language in its own right. Often its word forms (*ain't, you was, -s* in all persons of the verb), its vocabulary (especially the rougher words from *snot* up and down), and its constructions (such as the double negative—"He didn't know nothing about it") are actually older than what is now considered more acceptable by educated people.

Schools carry on their work in the language of the upper social classes, Formal or General English, which, with the Informal level, make up what is called Standard English. Students who go into the professions, into many branches of business, and into most white-collar jobs continue to use more or less consistently the standard language. Those who go into manual labor and the less well paid and less socially elevated jobs generally continue the use of Vulgate English. Naturally and necessarily, though, this speech is gradually becoming restricted because of increased schooling, the increasing number of white-collar jobs, and the greater number of contacts among people of different social position.

In the lower schools, where many pupils are in daily contact with Vulgate speech, it may form a serious problem. At the college level it is seldom a problem, though the speech of many college students is cruder than their social standing would warrant and is consequently a poor background for their writing. Some Vulgate expressions may show up in rapid writing, but since most college freshmen have had years of instruction in Standard English already, revision of a paper should remove the intrusive Vulgate signs, as well as other careless mistakes.

The objection to this level of speech should be clear. It is not that its grammar is "bad," but that Vulgate words and constructions are not appropriate to the readers for whom college students and college graduates write or to the subjects they are handling. Complex ideas and dignified subjects cannot be discussed adequately in the relatively limited vocabulary of Vulgate English. Vulgate is necessary in writing the conversation of many characters in stories, and it can be used to give a note of realism to portraits of real people. But its use must be judged by fitness. When an expression in this book is marked Vulgate, it should not be used in writing except for some very good reason.

Becoming aware of the levels of usage is the beginning of a realistic understanding of our language. And since a good many questions in our own usage depend on the appropriateness of the language, they can in large part be answered by considering the level of the particular expression that raises the question.

3 Standards for writing

Since there are so many varieties of English, you need some principles of choice among them. These principles or standards of choice are set by people with a special concern for the language and by others who have sufficient prestige to make their use of the language a guide for others.

Some standards in usage are pretty arbitrary and they may even be, like fashions in dress and manners, little more than a sort of snobbishness to give a little distinction to those who follow them. For example, close distinctions in the use of *shall* and *will*, limitations of the meaning of words like *alternative* and *alibi*, serve no particular purposes in actual speech and writing. A more reasonable standard in language is effectiveness. Using English as it has become established through successful use will best help you communicate what you need or wish to say.

3.1 Standard and Nonstandard English As it is generally used, the term Standard English refers to Formal, General and Informal English; Nonstandard refers to the Vulgate level. The selection of words, forms, and constructions for Standard English has been made over the years and now is used by writers and expected by readers as the language of business, science, education, and literature—of public affairs in general.

The important fact to remember is that Standard English is a *range* and offers considerable opportunity for choice; it is not a gathering of specific practices that you must always follow. You will avoid Vulgate words and expressions; but within the scope of Standard English you may draw upon a wide range of vocabulary, use a subjunctive or not in several constructions, produce sentences of a wide variety of patterns, punctuate heavily or with rather few marks, use many or few capital letters, select among numerous optional spellings, and so on among many equally reputable forms of usage. In these matters of divided usage you will choose the word or form that is consistent with the general characteristics of your writing. But the majority of matters are pretty definitely determined by accepted usage, and in these you will naturally aim to follow the Standard practice.

3.2 Editorial standards Because of the range within Standard English, publishers, who usually set great store by consistency and want all the articles in a magazine or a list of books to follow the same practices, select the practices that they will follow in what they print. They often print stylebooks as guides for the preparation of copy according to the usage they prefer—and admit that sometimes the choice in matters on which usage is divided is quite arbitrary. Furthermore they enforce these selections by hiring copy editors and proofreaders who see that they are followed.

Newspapers ordinarily represent a simplified usage—a minimum of capitals, open punctuation, no italics, direct constructions, relatively short sentences. The most Formal usage seems to be followed by the women's magazines and the publishers of scholarly and professional material. But publishers, especially book publishers, are now allowing writers more range, and often try only to secure consistency in a given book or article.

Books instructing people how to write usually describe the practices of publishers, and so do not represent the usage of the writers themselves but that of the editors. This is a proper basis for a standard in writing, but we should remember that it is not a single standard but again a range offered by various publishers.

3.3 Standards in a composition course In a composition course the matter of standards is more complicated, in part because students are still in the process of mastering the language. In general the aim is to help students develop their language ability so that they can use Standard English confidently and effectively. The standards of written usage in a composition course are essentially the standards that would be expected in similar published material outside.

A composition course is a practice course, basically for individual development of students. Its purpose is not to develop professional writers, and certainly not people who need as strict a command of usage as secretaries, editors, or proofreaders. It aims at progressive extension of a student's active vocabulary and expressive sentences appropriate to himself, at moving him toward a reasonable command of editorial standards found in specific types of writing.

The level of usage expected in themes will generally be defined by the instructor, in line with the practices and purposes of the course. Ordinarily the tone, as well as the method of work and the type of content, will be illustrated by readings, which can often set an example for the usage expected. Unless the nature of an assignment specifically calls for Formal style, as in a reference paper, the usual goal in a composition course is General English, because it is the most widely useful sort of English.

Your motive for meeting these expected standards is double —practical and personal. The practical motive is to make a good impression on your reader and to communicate what you wish to say. The personal motive is really a kind of pride, to make as good use of your language skill as you can and perhaps to improve over your previous expression. Outside pressures—of teachers or critics—may have some brief effect, but you will ordinarily make no permanent or genuine improvement in your use of language unless you really want to. In the long run you set your own standard, and even in a composition course you must begin to take the responsibility for the language you use.

4 The qualities of Good English

Good English is something more than writing "complete" sentences, using certain verb forms, making verbs agree with their subjects, and pronouns match their antecedents. Good English is language that is effective and appropriate for its specific purpose. It is a selection from the broad range of Standard English that will convey your facts or ideas to the readers you wish to reach. It is not so much a question of "right or wrong" as of "more or less effective." It is, therefore, a matter of selection and judgment more than of rules. It requires first some knowledge of the language as it is actually used and then a feeling for what is called for on the particular occasion.

Good English is fundamentally a matter of *appropriateness.* Specific questions are answered by considering the appropriateness of words and expressions to the immediate purpose, to the expected listeners or readers, and to the speaker or writer himself.

4.1 Appropriateness to purpose and situation In conversation we automatically adjust our language as well as our topics to the situation in which we find ourselves. Similarly, writing takes on a tone, whether it is assigned or voluntary. The tone of the language depends chiefly on the *level of usage.*

4.1a Choice of level of usage Good judgment in choice of the appropriate level of usage is one of the signs of a practiced writer. Slang may fit in a letter or in a popular newspaper column; it is ordinarily out of place in discussing a serious or elevated subject. Most talks to most audiences would be in General English, as would most fiction. Writing by and for people in the professions (teachers, doctors, lawyers, scientific and scholarly workers) is more likely to be Formal.

Obviously you need to know the styles that are typical of the sort of writing that you are to do. You shouldn't try to write for a magazine that you have never read, or try to write a technical report or reference paper without having seen one. If you are faced with the task of writing something unfamiliar to you, you should try to find what is typically done, and follow that as a general suggestion unless you have good reason for some other usage. This means that part of the preparation for a new sort of writing is attentive reading of some good examples of that writing.

The chief consequence of paying attention to appropriateness to situation is a resolve to treat most subjects simply, or, in terms of our levels of usage, to treat them in General English. Amateur writers are often not content to be themselves but assume a level that is really foreign to them, too Formal to be appropriate to them or to their subjects. A student who wanted to say that our courts are organized to give people speedy and uniform action wrote:

> The offices of justice are so arranged as to give the citizens the best of service in respect to undelayed action and uniformity of offices pertaining to the wants of the populace.

He may seriously have believed that this kind of writing was better than making a simple statement. He might even object to being told that his sentence was bad English, worse perhaps than if it had contained actual Vulgate expressions. Such errors could be quite easily corrected, but inflated and pompous language must be completely rewritten to be effective.

Teachers and students will not always agree in their judgments of particular passages, though they will in a surprising number of them. But once students understand the principle of appropriateness, they will learn to keep a Formal style for complex and elevated subjects and to write of ordinary matters in General or Informal English.

4.1b Consistency in tone   The tone of a piece of writing should be consistent unless the writer has some special reason for changing. Although the lines between the levels of usage cannot be drawn precisely, conspicuous shifts from one level to another should ordinarily be avoided, like the drop at the end of this:

> In the distant pines the rising wind whined as it played among the needles. And when the storm broke, the rain came down in buckets.

Consistency is not so important as the fundamental appropriateness to the situation, and good writing avoids monotony. Some vigorous styles show a wide range of language; the expressions are unified by the vigor and naturalness with which they are brought together. But typically, General writing should be kept General, and Formal writing should be kept Formal.

4.2 Appropriateness to listener or reader   If you are trying to reach a particular type of reader, you will adjust both your subject matter and your manner of expression more or less to his expectations. To reach him, to really get your points across, you have to be more than merely understandable, you have to meet him pretty much on his own ground. You already do this automatically in your letters, writing in somewhat different ways to different persons. Certainly in many situations you pay some attention to the language you believe is expected of you, as you do to the dress and conduct you believe are expected in meeting people you respect.

Trying to write without knowing who will read your words is discouraging. That is one reason why themes are sometimes difficult to write and why it is better for you to try to visualize some particular audience, to direct your paper to some magazine, or, more commonly, to write for the English class of which you are a member. This will help you select material that will interest and inform them, or at least that will appeal to a considerable part of the group, and it will help you judge what words and what kinds of sentences are appropriate. Remember that you are not writing for everyone (or for the mythical "general reader"), but for a specific audience. For practice work, a firm General style is best, because anyone can be reached through it.

Considering the listener or reader leads to language that is clear, correct, and interesting.

4.2a Clearness   Since your aim is to convey some fact or opinion or fancy or feeling to a person or a group, appropriateness to readers means clear expression. This means clear, exact words, and for the most part words that lie within the knowledge of the persons you are addressing. If the subject requires words that may not be familiar to them, you can throw in a tactful explanation, or in extreme instances resort to formal definition.

Clarity also calls for careful sentence construction—sentences not too long and usually with a natural, direct movement. Experienced readers can take more elaborate sentences than those who read little or who read hurriedly. But anyone will be pleased with direct, straightforward sentences.

4.2b Correctness   A large part of a beginning writer's concern for his readers should be avoiding careless errors and anything that might raise question or offend. People tend to judge us by superficial traits, in language as in other matters. Spelling, for example, bulks larger in most people's judgment of writing than it reasonably should, but this is a fact that must be recognized. Certainly many people take delight in finding what are (or what they consider are) errors in language, especially in the writing or speech of those supposed to be educated.

A writer should do his best in anything that he is submitting to another; small slips show carelessness—even discourtesy. Soiled manuscript, many interlineations, confusion of common forms like *its* and *it's*, *they're* and *their*, *affect* and *effect*, misspelling common words (*similiar* for *similar*) are ordinarily the result of carelessness or thoughtlessness. They show that the writer just isn't bothering, that he isn't doing as well as he easily could and should.

4.2c Interest   There is so much unavoidable dullness in the world that a reader will appreciate some liveliness in writing, in the expression as well as in the material. Frequently students hide behind a flat sort of language, playing safe, and so squeezing all the life out of their writing, until it sounds as though it was written by someone three times their age. The words do not need to be out of the ordinary but just those that might be used in a reasonably active conversation. The sentences should not be formless or allowed to drag but should suggest an alert interest and be varied. Reference to things people do and say, plenty of lively detail to demonstrate ideas fully and to keep up interest, all help.

Some professional writers have set themselves the rule "Don't write anything you couldn't read yourself." If you promise yourself that you will not turn in a paper that you couldn't read yourself with interest, you will be taking the responsibility for your work, doing composition of actual college grade—and permanently improving your control of expression, laying a sure foundation for continued growth in Good English.

One warning is needed: Don't aim at your reader's worst, compromising yourself and insulting him. Visualize him in his better moments and write for him as he is then.

4.3 Appropriateness to speaker or writer   In the writer-reader relationship, the speaker or writer actually dominates. As writer, you make the choices; your judgment or sense of fitness finally controls.

> The speech-usage of each one of us is constantly swinging backwards and forwards between the demands of society, and an individual expression of his momentary needs. . . . The more commonplace a person is, the more will his language bear the stamp of the community in which he lives: the more unique his nature, the more peculiarly his own will be the colouring of his language.—Otto Jespersen, *Mankind, Nation and Individual from a Linguistic Point of View*, pp. 131, 204

This quotation points up the fact that your language in the long run represents your personality, and it also suggests that you are finally responsible for the language you use. To take this responsibility successfully, you first need to make an effort to inform yourself of the possibilities of English by observing what is actually spoken and written, by using dictionaries and other reference works, by consulting people who have studied English as a language. Then you can apply this information in your own work according to your best judgment. There is nothing mysterious about the matter: it is just a natural process of learning and then applying what is learned.

An important step in the early stages of considering how to improve your language habits is to become aware of your own speech and your own writing to see what their good qualities are and what shortcomings they may have. Does your language on the whole tend to be Formal or General or Informal? Do you pronounce with confidence the words you need in conversation? Are you confident in the mechanics of writing—spelling, punctuation, sentence structure? Do you rely too much on slang or trite words? When you talk or write to someone older than yourself or when you write a paper for a college course, do you choose the best part of your natural language or do you assume an entirely different sort of English?

And finally, is the language you use consistent with the rest of your conduct? Does your language in conversation represent your better self, or do you on occasion speak beneath yourself, or on other occasions affect a more pretentious speech than is natural to you? It is also well to realize the direction in which you are moving as a person, for young people, especially in college, are changing, becoming more flexible in their ideas and manners or becoming more positive and conventional, or making some other change. Their language should be moving similarly.

In your first papers in a composition course you should write as naturally as you can, so that both you and your instructor can see the present state of your language and so that you can decide together on the direction your growth should take. It is not necessary for all students in a class to write the same, or to write as the instructor would, or like any particular professional writer.

This sincerity in usage and style is one of the conspicuous traits of the better contemporary writing. The better English that we find in print is the English the writer would use in talking to his friends, tightened up a little and freed of the irregularities that usually creep into talk, but usually well within the range of the General language. The writer does not appear at a distance or on a platform delivering an oration at us, but seems rather to be talking with us. We can come close to his mind as it actually works. In discussing "The New Way of Writing," Mr. Bonamy Dobrée, an English critic, says: "One would like to think that all of us will come to the stage of refusing to write what we would not, indeed could not, say, though that, of course, is not to limit our writing to what we actually do say."

If you approach Good English with this attitude, you should have confidence in writing. A great handicap in writing is fear—fear of pen and paper, fear of making a mistake, fear of offending the reader's (teacher's) taste. The opposite attitude, cockiness, is a nuisance and equally prevents good writing, but not so many students suffer from that as from inhibitions about their language. Psychologists can't tell us much about the mental activity involved in thinking or writing, but some of them believe that the fundamental condition for effectiveness is a positive feeling of readiness—which amounts really to a sort of faith that when we open our mouths or prepare to write, something appropriate to the occasion will come. Only with some courage and a willingness to experiment, even to gamble, can you write your best and give that extra something that places your writing above bare competence, that makes it really Good English.

Good English is not primarily a matter of rules but of judgment. You are not struggling up under a series of *don'ts* but are trying to discover among the wide resources of modern English what best suits your purpose. Good English is really simpler than it is sometimes made to seem. A desire to communicate something to another is fundamental. If you have something that you want to say, you will want to say it in a way that is best suited to your subject, to your readers, and to yourself as well.

References

The following books and articles develop further some points of sections 1 to 4:

Bloomfield, Leonard, "Literate and Illiterate Speech," *American Speech*, 1927, 2:432-439

Dobrée, Bonamy, *Modern Prose Style*, Oxford, Oxford University Press, 1934

Fries, C. C., *The Teaching of English*, Ann Arbor, Wahr, 1949

Jespersen, Otto, *Mankind, Nation and Individual from a Linguistic Point of View*, Cambridge, Cambridge University Press, 1925

Kenyon, John S., "Cultural Levels and Functional Varieties of English," *College English*, October 1948, 10:31-36

Kenyon, John S., "Levels of Speech and Colloquial English," *English Journal*, January 1948, 37:25-31

Merrill, Paul W., "The Principles of Poor Writing," *Scientific Monthly*, January 1947, 64:72-74

Potter, Simeon, *Our Language*, Harmondsworth, Penguin Books, 1950

Pyles, Thomas, *Words and Ways of American English*, New York, Random House, 1952

Whorf, Benjamin L., "The Relation of Habitual Thought and Behavior to Language," in *Language, Culture, and Personality*, ed. L. Spier, Menasha, Sapir Memorial Publication Fund, 1941, pp. 75-93

Exercises for §§1-4

1. Study the language in the following passages, describing them in terms of the levels of usage. (More than one term will often be needed for a passage.) Pick out the particular words and constructions that lead you to label the passage as you do.

1) Armies, corps, divisions and regiments do not fight battles. They direct and control and administer. The basic fighting unit on which all actions are planned is the battalion, a force of some 1000 men, divided into three rifle companies of roughly 200 men each, plus a company of heavy weapons—machine guns, mortars and recoilless rifles—and a platoon of five tanks, and perhaps a company of engineers. And these rifle companies are broken down into platoons, which again are broken down into squads of nine men each—five riflemen, a squad leader and his assistant, and an automatic rifleman and his helper. These last are the men your son will know. He will know their nicknames, and their home towns, and the way their sweethearts look in their bathing suits, and they will know all these things about him. For they are the men he lives with, and they are the only men he will see around him as, in the noise and smoke, he goes into battle for the first time.—Lt. Col. Melvin Russell Blair, "I Send Your Son into Battle," *The Saturday Evening Post,* June 23, 1951, p. 27

2) For the instinct of humanity is to be decent and to climb upward to some kind of Celestial City, to propagate the morality which will distribute the greatest good to the largest number. Most people tell the truth most of the time, even without the motive of self-interest; most people believe in fair play and justice and goodness. History, which provides a fearsome chronicle of wars, assassinations, tortures, and treacheries, which justifies a certain amount of cynicism, nevertheless affirms that through all these and a million other catastrophes the human race has gone on resolutely, arriving through the evolution of knowledge and manners at its present hopeful, if precarious, civilization. And history teaches us that one concept of the good has prevailed in

many guises, in all lands, at all times: the concept which makes human betterment, human transfiguration in some form or other, the maximum morality.—Grant C. Knight, "What Makes a Book Great," *The Saturday Review,* July 14, 1945, p. 7

3) And I reckon that's why that now I come up with an ain't once in a while, and have the Missouri teachers all stirred up. They don't like it because I say that Marty Marion or Vern Stephens slud into second base. What do they want me to say—slidded?

Me and Paul didn't have to worry about that sort of stuff when we were winning games for the old Gas House Gang. And I don't know why I should get a sweat up now.

Paul, he'd win one game and I'd win the next.

Didn't nobody come around after the game and ask whether we'd throwed or threw the ball in there to make a play.

We won 'em, no questions asked.—Dizzy Dean, United Press dispatch, *The New York Times,* July 26, 1946, p. 1

4) Ten decades have rolled around, and we meet in the first years of another century to celebrate, for the first time in the history of American colleges, the graduation of him whom most we delight to honor at Dartmouth, whose "great stone face" is carved as that of the chief orator of the new world on the walls of the academic theatre of our oldest university; and whose name was but lately selected as entitled to rank with those of Washington and Lincoln at the very top of the roll of fame of the nation, as preserved in the stately hall of learning between the Hudson and the sea.—C. F. Richardson, *Mr. Webster's College Life,* p. 22

5) The description of a language falls into three parts: grammar (including phonetics and phonemics), lexicography, and stylistic. Each of these consists essentially of an account of forms or groups of forms and of the meanings that are carried by them. The lines of division are not sharp; in actual practice lexicography treats of the words of a language as separate entities, and grammar covers the rest of the material, except style; but it is impossible to treat any part of morphology or syntax without discussing words,

and a word cannot be fully described without an account of its function in the sentence. We can more accurately describe a grammar as a set of general statements (paradigms and rules) and lists of exceptions; while a lexicon contains the material that cannot conveniently be combined into general statements. Stylistic treats of the selection among the linguistic responses possible in a given situation. It shows how one man will use certain words and syntactic constructions where another man will employ a more or less different linguistic mechanism. It also shows that different situations call for different words and phrases quite aside from the obvious requirements of meaning.—E. H. Sturtevant, *An Introduction to Linguistic Science*, p. 52

6) Down to your own Jack London: What do Jack London's stories *mean?*

They mean, as far as I can tell,—Take *To Build a Fire*, they mean, the impact between civilization and the wild. For, note, he isn't interested in the pioneer who goes native and survives fairly well, like the earlier trappers who married native wives. He means (when he is any good at all and not a pure sentimentalist) the terror and lonesomeness of the wilderness in its impact on civilized man. That, as far as I can see, is the best of him.—William Carlos Williams, *A Beginning on the Short Story*, p. 12

7) Americans in general are no great shakes at conversation, and one of the reasons for this, I think, is that we are too sympathetic. All conversation among sympathetic people tends to adjust itself to the weakest link in the chain. If one person is self-conscious, they all tend to become self-conscious. If he has a woolly mind, the conversation becomes woolly. I have seen a whole table demoralized by one poor lamb whose secret wish was merely to be somewhere else.—Van Wyck Brooks, *Opinions of Oliver Allston*, p. 82

8) Harrow No. 3 came in the shape of a negative. Despite the raves, Mr. Knott's own literary agents refused to send the play around to any more producers. As a stage play, they said stonily,

"Dial M" would flop so gruesomely that any possible film rights would be deader than the murdered fellow in the script. Smart strategy was to quit horsing around and grab off any old film deal, but quick. Soon enough Sir Alexander Korda made an offer of 1,000 pounds, or $2,800, for the screen rights. A clause in the contract specified that if the play ever *did* get into a theatre, it would fold the day the film was released. Obviously, with a lemon like "Dial M" on his hands, the agent advised Mr. Knott to brush this restrictive clause aside as pure technicality. Mr. Knott dutifully brushed.—Laura Z. Hobson, "Trade Winds," *The Saturday Review,* August 1, 1953, p. 5

9) Voices of men outside seemed inside the new house also, and the girl stood in the center of the largest room, feeling exposed and unbelonging. Around her the rooms were raw and smelled of shavings and fresh plaster. Presently she walked to a square window which faced west toward the valley. Jens had planned the big east and west windows especially for her, he kept saying: east would contain the mountain she had always seen from her old home; west would contain the town and the stretching fields around it.—Virginia Sorensen, *On This Star,* p. 3

2. Discuss the following sentences in terms of the levels of usage and suggest how they can be improved.

1) Dinner didn't taste so good because he was dead tired and after a day like that sleep is the only desire.

2) Still the youth was not rebellious and his father constantly told him, "If I had been given this splendid education, what would I have not done!"

3) Our hands were blistered, our backs and necks seemed inhabited by one great aching pain, and the sun, worst of all, burned with a seemingly diabolical fervor.

4) The church got a new paint job, a new choir and organ, and a new congregation.

5) The walk down Park Avenue was short and uneventful, save for the few "hicks" he saw staring up at the tall buildings.

31

3. Analyze the writing of a newspaper or magazine columnist: H. V. Kaltenborn, Walter Lippmann, Thomas L. Stokes, Drew Pearson, Westbrook Pegler, Hal Boyle, Walter Winchell, or any other your instructor may suggest. Characterize the level of usage, the columnist's attitude toward his readers, and the appropriateness of the language to the subjects discussed.

4. Translate the following sentences into General English:

1) The little squirt was talking to everyone and slapping them on the back.
2) We all knew he got a rake-off from the company.
3) What a rhubarb there was when the ump said he was safe.
4) Most always we do like we're told.
5) There was a hall at the top of the stairs and three apartments off of it.
6) He is one of the few who does not like to swim.
7) You oughtn't have done that.

5. Using the index, look up the following debatable or divided usages in this handbook and summarize what is said about them.

1) commas with introductory adverbial clauses
2) *due to*
3) capitalizing words like *mother, father, sister*
4) hyphening compound words
5) *like—as*
6) subjects of gerund phrases
7) shorter spelling forms
8) verbless sentences

6. Consider the influences that have affected your own use of English. Make notes of answers to the following questions, adding anything else you think important. If your instructor wishes, use your answers as a basis for a consecutive paper on your language.
   a. Where did you grow up?
   b. What places have you lived in long enough to have some im-

pression of the language used in them? Did they have any effect on your own usage?

c. Are you conscious of any specific influences on your speaking and writing—particular people, teachers, books, English courses?

d. Describe your typical speech and your typical writing in terms of regional English and in terms of levels of usage.

e. What foreign languages do you know something of, and about how much?

f. What kind of books and what writers do you read from preference? What magazines? What parts of a newspaper do you read regularly?

7. Copy from a book or magazine, giving full reference to its source, a good paragraph showing either Formal or General usage. Underline the distinctive words or constructions.

8. Keep a notebook and write down campus expressions, slang phrases, unusual pronunciations. When you have sufficient material, write a paper on student and faculty speech. Comment on differences you observe between the speech used inside the classroom and outside.

9. Why don't students, who have had work in English in almost every school year, learn and use the terms of grammar more accurately? Compare the presentation and use of grammatical terms with those of some other school subject (algebra, botany, chemistry, physics). What are some of the grammatical terms that you are sure of? What grammatical terms are you vaguely aware of or feel an occasional need for? Look up two or three in the index to this book and find out how they are used.

Composition

5 Writing a paper

While we may cheerfully concede that the great writer, like the poet, is born and not made, we need not hesitate to say that the ordinary writer is made and not born.—B. A. Hinsdale

When a paper is assigned in your composition course, the most practical way to go about writing it is to think of the assignment in terms of steps or stages, and to tackle each one separately as you come to it. In the following pages the process of writing is broken down into seven distinct steps, from the assignment of the topic to the preparation of the final copy. For brief papers, such as those written in class, you will probably be able to telescope the first four steps into one. But for more complex projects, you will find your task considerably simplified if you follow the steps in order, solving the problems of each before going on to the next.

Just as in public speaking, in swimming, or in any other skill, confidence in writing comes with practice. The regularly assigned papers in your composition course are designed to give you this practice. Your instructor's comments on your papers and his suggestions in conference are intended to help you see just what your individual problems in writing are, and how you may improve. If you consider your work from one paper to the next, your progress may at times seem disappointingly slow. But if you save a copy of the first paper you write for the course and compare it with the last, you will see that you have come much farther than you realized.

5.1 Focusing on a subject   The first step in writing is to decide what you are going to write about. This task is simplified when the topic is determined by the occasion—for instance

Stages in the Writing Process	Results of Each Stage
1. Focusing on a subject	Definition of topic, seeing problems involved and possible sources of material
2. Gathering material	Notes (in mind or on paper) from memory, observation, interview, reading, thinking
3. Selecting and evaluating the material	A tested and selected body of information to be presented in the paper
4. Planning the paper	A synopsis or outline of the paper
5. Writing the first draft	Tentative version of the paper
6. Revising the first draft	Necessary changes in material; corrections and improvements in the words, sentences, paragraphs
7. Making the final copy	The completed paper, ready to be handed in

when a businessman has to answer a letter, or a scientist reports on an experiment he has performed, or a composition student faces an assignment in which the topic is assigned. But frequently in a composition course and elsewhere the occasion will permit a choice of topics or a choice of material for a paper of a specified type, like an expository account of how something is made or done, a narrative of a personal experience, or an interpretation of an essay, story, or poem.

If you are asked to select your own subject, choose one that actually interests you—a subject that you would like to talk about and about which you feel you have something definite to say (or about which you can easily find something to say). All of us have opinions on a variety of matters—juvenile delinquency, universal military training, racial prejudice, professionalism in college sports—but on most of these matters our opinions are not formulated clearly enough to be put down on paper. It is always best to think about the subjects offered before making a final decision. Topics chosen at random or out of desperation at the last possible moment seldom make satisfactory papers.

You can also do better on an assigned topic—even one that may discourage you at first glance—if you are willing to devote some thought to it, perhaps exploring its possibilities in the light of your own background. The student who protests, "I can't possibly write on *that* topic" before he has looked at or thought about the assignment suffers from laziness rather than from inability. If for example you feel poorly qualified to write a paper characterizing the Duke in Browning's poem "My Last Duchess," remember that you are not expected to submit a scholarly analysis but rather a clear report showing your own impressions of the Duke based upon an intelligent and conscientious study of the poem.

5.1a Subjects based on personal experience   Your own experiences will provide subjects for many college themes: what you have done in school and out, the jobs you have held, your hobbies, the people you know, the places you have visited, the courses you are taking in college.

Consider this brief list of topics and see how many you could write on from your own experience:

Cures for Homesickness
A Job I Disliked
Advice to a High School
  Student About to Enter the
  University
Stretching an Allowance
Baby Sitters Earn Their Pay
How to Handle Firearms
  Safely
Sharing the Family Car

A Successful High School
  Play
The Purpose of 4-H Clubs
Why I Prefer Living in a
  Large (or Small) Town
Advantages of My Hobby
The Subject I Expect to
  Major In
What to Look Out for When
  Buying a Used Car

You need not feel that a paper based upon your personal experiences will be boring to others. Some college freshmen, particularly when writing their first themes, are afraid that their own experiences have been too limited, or that their opinions and attitudes are too commonplace to be of interest to anyone but themselves. But much published material is based upon incidents and attitudes that are in no way unique or sensational ("Making Your Hobby Pay," "Should 18-Year-Olds Vote?" "The Most Unforgettable Character I Have Met," "Diary of a City-Bred Farmer"). If a writer is interested in what he has to say, chances are his readers will be too. A fresh and lively account of the experiences of a baby sitter is more readable than a dull description of a journey up the Amazon.

5.1b Subjects for investigation Not all papers can be written entirely from personal opinion or from your own experience. Many subjects call for information that must be gathered by reading, by observation, or through personal interviews. Investigative papers offer you an opportunity to fill gaps in your general knowledge and to become better informed on matters related to general affairs or to your course work.

When the choice of subject for an investigative paper is left to you, select one that will be useful as well as interesting. Here are some typical subjects for investigation by observation or reading that may suggest others more in line with your special interests:

Civic-Supported Opera
The Movement of Glaciers
Study Habits of Students in the Library
What Foreign Students Think of American Educational Methods
How Rhodes Scholars Are Selected
Unusual Part-Time Jobs Held by Students
A Practical Application of Electronics
How American Olympic Teams Are Financed
Student Preferences in Composition Topics
What Is a Land-Grant College?
Fulbright Scholarships
College Fashions in Clothing: A Study in Conformity
Major and Minor Worries of Campus Police
The Effects of Classroom Design on Students

Gathering material from observation or from reading takes more time than calling up incidents and impressions from memory, but information is available on almost any subject you are curious about.

For an extended discussion of investigative papers, see §49, The reference paper.

5.1c Limiting the subject   There is seldom any danger that you will select a topic too small for a paper of the assigned length. It is the large subjects like "American foreign policy," "The aims of higher education," "The role of women in contemporary society," that lead to difficulty. On such ambitious subjects most writers can only repeat commonplace judgments and empty generalities, and after writing a paragraph or two, find they have said all they can think of saying.

The topic you select should be limited so that you can treat it adequately in the required number of words. Most college themes are short—even a thousand-word theme would fill only one newspaper column. Because a thousand or even ten thousand words would not be enough to cover a general subject (Justice, Crime prevention, Penicillin, Forestry), choose a specific part of the general subject you plan to write on.

Break down large general subjects into topics that you feel you can handle. "Motion pictures," for example, might suggest to you "The effect of movies on children." This is still too large a topic for the average college theme, so subdivide it once more: "The effect of Western movies on one small boy I know." This is a topic that can be discussed effectively in 500 to 1000 words.

Concentrate on a single, well-defined aspect of the subject rather than on the subject as a whole.

Too general	*Specific*
Voting as an Obligation of Citizenship	Arousing Student Interest in College Politics
Sportsmanship	How Sportsmanship Differs in Tennis and Baseball

As you gather material and think about it, your topic may change slightly. The important thing to remember is to keep the topic specific and not fall back on a general subject, saying less and less about more and more.

5.1d Subjects for writing in class Choosing the right topic from a list of those suggested for writing a paper in class is especially important because the time is limited. While you cannot explore the possibilities of the various suggestions as thoroughly as you would for a paper written outside class, you can and should select your subject with reasonable care.

First examine all the topics offered for your choice. Some you can reject at once because you do not know enough about them or are not interested in them. Your final choice will probably lie between two or, at the most, three subjects. When you have made your choice, concentrate on it and forget the other topics. In a class period, it is much better to spend the first three or four minutes deciding which subject you can best develop than it is to take one at random and later wish you had chosen something else.

5.2 Gathering material After selecting the topic you are going to write on, the next step is to decide what you are going to say about it. The material for most written work has to be collected. Even though you may know a good deal about the topic, the material that you need to expand and round out your ideas seldom comes without some effort on your part. With some topics you will have to spend a little time thinking about your subject, jogging your memory to recall everything you know about it. With others, you may have to dig up information through reading or talking with people, and sometimes both. If you have difficulty writing 1000 or even 500 words on a topic, the reason usually is that you have not taken enough time to gather material.

5.2a Material from your background For papers based upon personal experience, ask yourself as many questions as you can think of about the subject. If you are going to explain how a person should apply for a job, recall and analyze your own experiences in looking for work. How did you find out what jobs were available? How did you decide which jobs to apply for? Did you apply in person or by letter? If you were not hired, what were the probable reasons? What mistakes, if any, did you make either during an interview or in your letter of application? Would you go about getting a job in the same way again?

A similar analysis will help you gather material for papers presenting personal opinions or attitudes. If you are going to enumerate the qualities of a good teacher, think of two or three of your teachers who were outstanding and try to discover what qualities they had in common. A sound knowledge of their subject? A genuine interest in young people? A willingness to help the slower students? Fairness in grading? A sense of humor? You could extend your analysis by considering also one or two teachers who were definitely unsatisfactory, to see what qualities they lacked.

At this stage of thinking about your subject, jot down on paper every idea that occurs to you, whether you intend to use it or not. One idea often suggests another and better one. After a reasonable amount of reflection, you will usually have more than enough material to write a paper of the assigned length.

5.2b   **Material from reading**   Whenever you feel that your own information is insufficient, you can get the additional facts that you need by reading up on the subject in books, magazines, and newspapers.

Read critically, and think about what you read. Be careful to distinguish between verifiable *facts* (the number of telephones in the United States and Europe; the cost of living index in New York City in 1940 and in 1950) and *opinions* (the best motion picture produced last year; the reasons why the Republican Party won the 1952 election). On controversial subjects such as federal subsidies for farmers or for airplane companies, or the disadvantages of specialization in education, read and weigh the opinions on both sides of the questions before you arrive at an opinion of your own.

You should understand and make material from published sources your own before using it in a paper. Instead of copying an author's words, think about the ideas he is expressing. Do you agree or disagree with them? Why? Proper acknowledgment should always be made for borrowed material (in a footnote or in a statement at the end of the paper). Whatever sources you use, the material itself will become an integral part of your paper if you put it in your own words and combine it with your own ideas.

§49, The reference paper, gives details on using material from printed sources.

5.2c Material from observation and discussion You can sharpen your powers of observation by taking a real interest in your surroundings and in the ideas and attitudes of the people you meet every day. The more observant you are, the more material you will have to draw on. When everyone in class writes on the same topic (such as the difficulties of registration or the expressions of the crowd at a football game), it is the small details that a few have noticed that make their papers more interesting than the others.

Everyone is observant about the things that interest him —automobiles, women's fashions, architecture, the behavior of other students, their hobbies. Observation is trained on jobs and in college courses. A person who has sold shoes or groceries sees more in a shoe store or in a grocery store than one who hasn't had a similar experience; a person who has had a course in zoology or physics observes more about the behavior of bees or the operation of a dynamo than one who doesn't have that background. By extending the range of your interests you will be able to store up impressions useful for illustrative material in your papers. When you are reading, notice how other writers present their material and from what different activities they draw their examples.

Discussing your topic with your family or with your class-mates will often help you to increase and enrich the material for a paper. Most of us tend to see but one side of a topic. You will frequently gain fresh insight into the possibilities of a subject by discussing it with people who are perhaps better informed or who hold opinions contrary to yours.

5.3 Selecting and evaluating material Material for written work must be sorted and evaluated after it is accumulated because not all of it is of equal importance. What you have at this point is a collection of random ideas, some essential to your subject, others of minor importance, and a few per-haps that don't belong at all. For writing in class, the process of selection is simple: all you need to do is to select from your list one or two main ideas to develop, and disregard the rest.

But for longer papers, you will need to make a more thor-ough examination of your material if you intend to present it in an interesting and convincing manner. You can't put every idea that you can think of on a given subject into your paper nor can you give only generalities without supporting evidence or illustrations. The result would leave the reader either confused or unconvinced.

5.3a Determining the central idea of a paper A definite state-ment of the main point or central idea of your paper will help you to select the material you are going to use. This state-ment (sometimes called the "thesis sentence") is not the topic of your paper or the title (which is usually no more than four or five words), but a sentence that answers the question "What is the main idea that I am trying to present to the reader?"

The central or controlling idea of a paper titled "The Honor System" might read: "The honor system works only as well as the students want it to work"; or "The honor system at this college is popular with the faculty but not with the students." For the explanation of a process or activity, the central idea might be "Learning to play the violin demands patience on the part of the neighbors as well as on the part of the violinist," or "Performance is more important than appearance when you are buying a used car."

Such a statement shows you definitely what you are going to write about. Its main purpose is to help you to stick to the subject and to prevent you from wandering off into tempting but irrelevant bypaths. Any material you have gathered that is not related to your main idea should be discarded at this stage. For a paper on stamp collecting you might have jotted down these preliminary ideas:

1. My interest in stamps began in grade school
2. Learn a lot about geography from them
3. Difficult sometimes to get the ones you want
4. Stamps should be canceled
5. Most people know little about stamps
6. Historical figures and scenes on stamps have taught me much about history
7. Trading stamps is fun and profitable
8. Successful and profitable deals I have made
9. My uncle in the navy sends me stamps from all over the world
10. President Roosevelt had one of the best collections

From these random notes you could frame a central idea: "Stamp collecting is an educational and profitable hobby." Re-examining your notes, you would then be able to discard items 3, 4, 5, and 10 as irrelevant, concentrating on items 2, 6, 7, and 8 as the main ideas, and perhaps using items 1 and 9 as introductory material.

5.3b Selecting material specifically for your readers   Keep your readers in mind—the members of your class as well as your instructor—when you are selecting your material. How much do they already know about your subject? What information and explanation will they need? What kind of material are they likely to find most interesting?

If your subject is familiar to most readers—campus architecture, for example, or local traffic problems—eliminate obvious statements and develop the ideas that are most likely to arouse interest. Perhaps the majority of the class does not know that fashions in campus architecture have changed three times in the last forty years, or that the building in which the class now meets was once considered the most beautiful on the campus. If it is common knowledge that the traffic situation in your city is deplorable, concentrate on other points: plans for traffic control that have been considered and rejected; the experience of other cities with one-way streets; the method of selecting and training traffic officers; the effect of traffic congestion on drivers' nerves or on local business.

When you are writing on a subject that most people know little about (operating a switchboard, taxidermy, Aztec architecture), consider your material from the viewpoint of the general reader. What terms should be defined? What technical material should be explained or perhaps left out? What kind of illustrations and examples will help make the subject as clear to the reader as it is to you?

5.4 Planning the paper   Before you begin to write, plan the order in which you intend to present your material. For longer papers and more complex projects such as a reference paper, a formal outline is usually necessary (§6.2c, pp. 72-74). For shorter papers, notes or a scratch outline will serve the purpose. But whatever form you use, you should organize your material so that you know in advance what comes first, second, third, and so on in your paper.

With some subjects the material itself determines the order of presentation. Personal experiences, explanation of processes, and narrative usually follow the order in which the events occurred: first this happened, then something else occurred, then something else followed. In descriptive writing ("The Campus by Moonlight," "A Trip Through the Carlsbad Caverns") the normal order may be from one point to another (entering the Caverns, going down to the first level, arriving at the Big Room . . .) or from a general impression to the specific details that give rise to it, arranged more or less in the order of their strikingness.

The order of presentation is more complicated with other subjects: "Abolishing Hazing in Fraternities," "A Criticism of Olivier's *Hamlet*," "The Anatomy of the Frog Compared to That of Man." Whether you select the topic or it is assigned to you, you will find that in most instances you will have to examine your material to find the best order for your special purpose: what should come first, what last, what in the middle.

5.4a Grouping ideas together   Group related ideas together so that you can visualize the successive points of your paper. List similar ideas together, putting each group on a separate sheet of paper or using any other form that will enable you to see possibilities for development.

It often helps to try more than one order of arrangement. If you are comparing the anatomy of the frog to that of man, you might first list the aspects that are comparable:

Skeletal system
Muscular system
Respiratory system
Circulatory system
Nervous system

You could then group these systems in two categories, one in which differences were marked, and the other in which similarities were strong:

    A. Differences
        1. Skeletal and muscular systems differ greatly
        2. Man's respiratory system more complex than frog's
    B. Similarities
        1. Frog's circulatory system resembles man's
        2. Nervous system of both almost identical

If you want to emphasize the differences, you would present B first and then A; if you want to stress the similarities, you would reverse the order.

5.4b Beginning and ending The beginning of your paper should catch the reader's interest and get him into the subject. The ending should leave him with the final impression you wish to make. Remember that these should be the most forceful parts of your paper—the point at which you meet your reader and the place where you leave him.

Plan your paper so that you can get into your subject as quickly as possible. Don't begin too far back: if your topic is the assassination of Lincoln, there is no need to start with an account of Lincoln's early career or even of his presidency. The shorter the paper, the more direct your beginning should be. An important and striking fact or statement of your purpose or a rewording of your central idea is the simplest way to begin a paper. (For other openings, see §11.2, Good beginnings, p. 139.)

Make the ending definite and emphatic. The total effect of your paper will depend largely upon the way you end it. Plan the conclusion so that it won't trail off or leave your reader up in the air. If you have any doubts about the validity of the ideas you are going to present, check or verify them before you begin to write so that you won't have to end with an apology. What you put at the end of your paper is usually the most important point you have to present. It should round out your discussion in such a way that the reader will know you have said all you intended to say and that you have not stopped because you were tired of writing or because time ran out. (See §11.4, Good endings, p. 143.)

5.4c Kinds of development While you are arranging your material, consider what forms of development will best suit your subject and be clearest to your readers. These are some of the most commonly used types of order:

1. *Time:* from one event to the next, as in narrative writing (the story of a treasure hunt, for instance) or for steps in a process, such as learning to fly a plane.
2. *Space:* for expository description, such as a trip through Yellow-

stone Park, a description of a ship from bow to stern, or of a mural from one side to the other.

3. *Increasing complexity:* beginning with the simple or familiar and proceeding to the more complex or unfamiliar (for example, using a description of air escaping from a toy balloon to introduce an explanation of rockets).

4. *Comparison or contrast:* discussing all the features of one idea or situation, then all the features of another, and ending by drawing a conclusion about the two ("The Radio and Newspapers as Sources of News," "The Advantages and Disadvantages of Living in a Small Town," "Writing Papers in Class and Writing Papers at Home"). If such a plan seems to make the paper break in the middle, it is better to plan it by the separate aspects being compared—not all the points about radio and then about newspapers, but some order like this: 1. Fullness of coverage, 2. Local vs. national news, 3. Sensationalism and emphasis.

5. *Support,* or from the general to the particular: beginning with a statement of your main idea or general impression, and then supporting it with reasons, examples, details. This form of development is useful for topics such as "Universal Military Training Should (or Should Not) Be Adopted in America," "Being a Twin Has Its Complications as Well as Its Compensations," "The Importance of Reading Newspaper Editorials Critically."

6. *Climax:* beginning with a specific fact or situation and unfolding the subject until it stands completed at the end. Thus a description of the building of the Panama Canal might begin with the need for a canal, then take up the increasing difficulties that the builders encountered, go on to explain how these difficulties were overcome, and end with the final accomplishment of the task.

Often two kinds of development are used in combination; a narrative could follow both the order of time and that of climax; the method of support might be used effectively with comparison or climax. The essential thing is that you should see your material in some definite order.

5.5 Writing the first draft Papers that are composed outside the classroom should always be written out in rough draft first, then revised and copied. No matter how certain you are about your material and the order in which you are going to present it, a first draft is essential if the final paper is to represent your best work.

Up to this point you have been dealing with your ideas in abbreviated or shorthand form as notes or outline headings; now you are ready to put them down in full sentences and paragraphs, so that you can actually see the whole paper as your reader will, and make whatever changes may be necessary for continuity and effectiveness.

5.5a Getting started on a paper Begin writing your first draft as soon as you know what you are going to say and how you are going to present it. Don't wait for "inspiration" or for the proper mood. For almost everyone, writing is work, just as studying is, or changing a tire, or washing the dishes; and just as with other tasks, you must often begin writing when you would much prefer to do something else. If you wait until the last minute, your first draft may have to serve as your final paper.

The beginning of a paper is often the most difficult part to word effectively. If you can't think of a good opening sentence, begin with some other part; if the wording of a good first paragraph doesn't come to you at once, start with a part that you feel confident about. You shouldn't waste time trying to get an ideal opening; as you work, a good start will usually occur to you. Many beginnings are actually written last.

Once you have written two or three sentences, you will generally find that even though you may not be "inspired," you will at least have the feeling of being ready to write. You have to "warm up" in writing as in any other activity.

5.5b Writing without interruption As a rule, write your first draft as rapidly as you can. Your paper will have more life if you put your ideas down one after the other without pausing to worry whether each sentence is correct. This is the stage to concentrate on getting down the gist of what you have in mind. You are the only one who will see your first draft and matters of spelling, punctuation, and wording are to be taken care of in revision.

Plan your time so that you will have at least an hour for uninterrupted writing. When you are working on a paper too long to be done in one sitting (such as the reference paper), take time to read over what you have already written before you begin writing again. Don't just guess at what you have said.

Leave plenty of space in the first draft for making corrections and changes. Leave ample margins on both sides of the page, and allow space between lines for insertions and corrections.

5.5c Developing the material   Make your first draft as complete as possible. Write down more than you will probably use in your final paper; be generous with explanations, details, illustrative examples. It is much easier to cut out material when you are revising a paper than it is to look for more to satisfy the requirements of length or completeness of presentation. Papers that are heavy with material added at the last moment always seem disjointed. Those that have been pruned down from say 1400 to 1000 words are more compact and to the point.

Put in any good ideas that occur to you when you are writing the first draft, even though they may not have appeared in your original plan. An outline does not need to be followed down to the last minor subdivision in this stage. Frequently a sentence written on paper will bring to mind an aspect of your topic that you overlooked when your material was in the form of notes. If the new idea turns out to be irrelevant, it can be omitted in revision; but if it is important, you can alter your outline to include it.

5.6 Revising the first draft   If you want your paper to represent your best work, your first draft will have to be examined carefully and critically when you are revising it. The first draft is not to be copied down as it stands, after a word or two has been checked for spelling, or a comma added or deleted. The purpose of revision is to check major as well as minor matters: to tighten and improve the organization, the material, and the expression, as well as to correct the mechanics of writing.

When you have finished the first draft, put the paper aside for a while, if possible. Most people find it difficult to look at their own writing objectively while the ideas they have expressed are still fresh in their minds. For this reason, the first draft should be written as early as possible, so that you can put it aside for several hours (or better, for two or three days) before you start to revise it.

5.6a Main points to consider in revision You can save time and improve the quality of your writing if you go over your first draft in a systematic manner, knowing exactly what you are looking for. The hit-or-miss approach to revision is a waste of time, since at best only the more glaring faults will be caught.

The following four points are the bases on which papers are evaluated. Keep them in mind when you revise.

1. The material (or "content"): the ideas, facts, examples used to support the central point of your discussion
2. The organization: the order in which statements are presented, from beginning paragraph to conclusion
3. The wording: the way in which the ideas are expressed, including the choice of words, sentence structure, general effectiveness of expression
4. The conventions of writing (or "mechanics"): spelling, punctuation, division of words at the ends of lines, and so on

It is not expected that you will first examine your writing carefully for the material, then read it again for organization, then a third time for wording, and so on. The four categories overlap; often, for instance, both material and organization can be checked at the same time. The purpose of a systematic method of revision is to help you to concentrate on your individual problems.

5.6b Checking the material Read the first draft to make sure you have put in enough material to make the subject clear, convincing, and interesting to your readers. Here are five questions that may help you to judge the effectiveness of your material:

1. Are more (or better) details, examples, illustrations needed?
2. Is the information sufficiently clear so that the reader who knows little or nothing about the subject can readily understand it?
3. Are there general statements that need to be supported by the facts? If you say, for example, that Texas has the best flying weather in the United States, you should present facts and figures to support this idea.
4. Do the opinions or attitudes you have expressed represent your own convictions on the subject, or have you merely repeated what you have read or have heard other people say? It is easy for a writer to use the expression "the American way of life"; it is much more difficult for him to explain what he means by the phrase.
5. Are there any statements that do not have direct bearing on the subject you are discussing? If so, remove them before your final draft.

5.6c Checking the organization Study the first draft to see if the subject advances from one section to the next and if the emphasis falls where you want it to. As you revise the paper, ask yourself these questions:

1. Is it clear from the beginning (or near the beginning) what the paper is about? Avoid wordy and irrelevant introductions.
2. Does each paragraph advance the subject, or is there some skipping back and forth?
3. Do the important ideas stand out clearly from the minor points and details?
4. Will the ending leave your reader with the impression that you want to make?

5.6d Checking the wording Read your paper aloud (or have someone else read it to you) to see if it sounds the way you intended it to sound. Awkward repetition, clumsy constructions, and involved sentences will be easily detected this way.

1. Are there any words whose meaning you are not quite sure of? In all cases of doubt, consult your dictionary.

2. Have you used any technical term or unfamiliar expression that needs explanation?

3. Do you notice any unnecessary repetition, either of individual words or of ideas, that should be omitted?

4. Is the level of usage consistent throughout? Watch for any unintentional lapses from one level to another, as from Formal to Informal usage.

5. Are any of the sentences too involved? If you stumble over a passage while reading it, see if you can revise it for greater clarity.

5.6e Checking for accuracy Most of the common errors marked on student papers (spelling, punctuation, fragmentary sentences, omission of words, and so forth) result from carelessness or haste. You can eliminate many such mistakes from your own writing by looking carefully for the specific kinds of mistakes that have occurred most frequently in your papers.

If you aren't quite certain about the spelling of a word, don't trust to luck or rely on your roommate's opinion; find the correct spelling in your dictionary. If fragmentary or run-on sentences give you trouble, take time to analyze any statement you suspect may be incorrectly punctuated. If you have used too many commas in your previous papers or have failed to paragraph your material properly, study the sections in this handbook that deal with these matters and then apply what you have learned to your revision.

Whatever your individual problems in writing may be, the best time to correct your mistakes is during revision rather than after your instructor has returned your paper to you.

5.7 Making the final copy Make a neat and accurate copy of your revised paper to submit to your instructor. Follow the directions he gives you for the form, the size, and the kind of paper; the indention, numbering of pages, endorsement, and so on. (Typical manuscript form is described in §7.)

If you are interested in your subject and if you have developed it to the best of your ability, you will take pride in the final form of your paper. The impression your writing makes upon your readers depends not only upon your ideas and the way in which you have expressed them, but also upon the neatness of the paper itself.

5.7a Final proofreading   When you finish your final draft, put it aside for a while and then proofread it carefully before you hand it in. No matter how perfect the finished product may appear, it will pay to give it one final check. Errors somehow creep into even the most careful writing. To find them, you will have to get away from your paper for a time so that you can look at it with a fresh eye.

Look for slips of the pen or typing errors, for the omission of words and marks of punctuation. And look particularly for the kind of mistakes that have been marked on your previous papers.

5.7b Making corrections in the final copy   For minor changes —a correction in spelling, the addition of a comma, a word, or short phrase, or a new beginning of a paragraph—make your corrections neatly according to the way your instructor suggests. One method for making revisions of this kind is illustrated in §7.4, Corrections in the final copy, p. 87.

When major revisions are needed in the final copy, such as adding or deleting a paragraph, or rewording several sentences, it is best to rewrite the entire page. Manuscript with passages scratched out or with sentences scribbled in the margin is difficult to read.

5.8 Correcting the returned paper   After your instructor has read your paper, he will probably return it to you so that you can make whatever corrections are needed. He will explain the meaning of the correction symbols or numbers and will tell you how to make your corrections.

For example, a paragraph might be marked in this manner:

> Quality reproduction of music
>
> *Dir* is a much more complicated proced-
>
> ure than most people realize. To
>
> begin with, there are five basic
>
> *Sp* pieces of equiptment needed to re-
>
> *noPn* produce recorded music. These are,
>
> a record, a turntable, a pickup,
>
> an amplifier, and a speaker. The
>
> *Frag* quality of these five ranging from
>
> very poor to excellent.

You might then be asked to correct these mistakes, perhaps by using red pencil or red ink, in this manner:

> Quality reproduction of music
>
> *Dir* is a much more complicated ~~proced~~ proce-
>
> ~~ure~~ dure than most people realize. To
>
> begin with, there are five basic

sp   pieces of ~~equiptment~~ *equipment* needed to re-

no cap   produce recorded music. These are /

a record, a turntable, a pickup,

an amplifier, and a speaker. The

Frag   quality of these five ~~ranging~~ *ranges* from

very poor to excellent.

If the passage cannot be corrected neatly in the margin or between the lines, rewrite it on the back of the page, or in whatever way your instructor directs.

When you are making the corrections, study the mistakes you made so that you can avoid them in future writing. Try to see *why* you made the error, as well as what it is. If, for example, you misspelled a large number of words, what was the reason? Were these unusual or difficult words? Or (more likely) were they words you took for granted you knew how to spell? Be certain that you understand the reason for each correction. If, for example, you can't see why a semicolon should be used where you put a comma, study §33 on the semicolon.

In addition to correcting mechanics, study the comments on the more important features of your writing: content, organization, clarity, completeness. Look up the sections in this Handbook that deal with your problems, and make a note of any points on which you need further help so that you can discuss your writing problems intelligently with your instructor in conference.

The more you learn from correcting your papers at an early stage in the course, the greater confidence you will have in your future writing and the more progress you will show.

5   Writing a paper

No matter where you now are in writing, you can improve with practice.

References

Bailey, Robeson, *Techniques in Article-Writing,* New York, Appleton-Century-Crofts, 1947

Lederer, William J., *Spare Time Article Writing for Money,* New York, Norton, 1953

Munson, Gorham, *The Written Word,* New York, Creative Age, 1949

Struck, Herman R., "Some Facts on Revision," *College English,* 1954, 15:279-283

Wallas, Graham, *The Art of Thought,* New York, Watts, 1945, Ch. 4, Stages of Control

Exercises

1. Select three of the following *general subjects* and for each one write down two *specific topics* that would be suitable for a paper of 500 words, and two topics for a 1000-1200 word paper.

women's fashions
discipline in high school
rural electrification
intelligence in animals
the Girl Scouts
statehood for Alaska
soap operas
flying saucers
fire prevention
Sunday school
science fiction

music in the home
Eleanor Roosevelt
improvements in automobiles
the effects of color on food
the comics
school spirit
personality and popularity
drive-in theaters
the home workshop
water sports
R.O.T.C.

2. Make up a list of topics based upon your past experiences, of specific matters that you would like to write about and that might interest others. Make an inventory of places you have lived in or visited; people you know; jobs you have had; sports, hobbies, reading, plays, movies; subjects you like to talk or argue about. If you do this early in the course, you will have a ready supply of material for papers in which the choice of subject is left up to you.

3. Prepare a list of topics for investigation. They may range from some aspects of aeronautics to voodoo practices in the West Indies —any matter that interests you or about which you would like to know more. When your list is completed, select two subjects you think would make good papers of 500 words each, two that would make papers of 1200 words each, and one suitable for a 2500 word paper.

4. Examine the controlling idea for each of these three topics. What points listed should be eliminated? Indicate the way you would group the remaining ideas for effective development.

   a. Salmon Fishing: Salmon fishing is a thrilling and inexpensive sport.
    1) Requires skill
    2) Prizes offered for biggest fish
    3) Equipment need not be expensive
    4) Boats can be rented cheaply
    5) Salmon fight to the last breath
    6) Columbia River and Puget Sound two of the best areas
    7) Conservation efforts have paid off
    8) Baked salmon is a delectable dish
    9) How the Indians prepare salmon
   10) No thrill equals that first strike
   11) A sport for young and old

   b. Running for Office: Even though I lost the election for vice-president of the freshman class, I learned a great deal about campus politics and the voting public.

1) Candidates usually known only to students from same high school *omit*
2) Must study up on issues *omit*
3) Fraternity support helps
4) Girls not as interested as boys in politics
5) Ability to speak well is an important asset *omit*
6) Expense of my campaign—$4.25 *omit*
7) Lost six pounds during campaign *omit*
8) No party affiliations as in national elections
9) Voters get a chance to learn how voting machines work *omit*
10) Takes a lot of time from studies *omit*
11) Satisfaction of meeting so many students more important than winning office *omit*
12) Excitement of hearing election returns *omit*
13) Increased knowledge of campus issues

c. Soap Operas: Radio soap operas may not be a high form of art, but they are a comfort to many a lonely housewife.

1) Those who criticize rarely listen
2) Some programs much superior to others
3) You can always turn the radio off if you don't like the program
4) Everyone likes to hear about the troubles and joys of ordinary people
5) Listening helps to take housewife's mind off her tedious chores
6) When children are off to school, the house becomes a lonely place
7) Some programs have been running for years
8) My favorite is "Our Gal Sunday"
9) Housewife needn't take plays seriously
10) Some characters become like old friends
11) Good recipes and household hints often given after the play
12) There's almost nothing else on the air in the daytime anyway

5. Here is an example of the first page from the rough draft of a student paper. Study it carefully and then answer the questions that follow.

Why Go to College

1 ~~I think that~~ ^mMany entering freshmen who have
2 just recently graduated high school, are still a little naive
3 in their way. In high school ~~the~~ the student is constantly
4 guided by an invisible rope tied to ~~their~~ ~~wrists~~ necks.
5 by the teachers. So many times ~~the~~ student is told what
6 to do and how to do it, the teacher is always by ~~the~~
7 students side, coaxing him a little by telling ~~the~~ student that
8 if he doesn't draw any _{more} pictures of her (the teacher) on the
9 blackboard, she might give him an A instead of a B grade
10 which the student deserves. There is a lot of "teachers pets,"
11 still in high school. When the immature high school student
12 gets to college, he finds that he is going to have to make
13 a big adjustment.

14 He will at first try ~~to form personal friendships with~~
15 ~~his professors~~ to adjust the professors to his liking. This
16 is ~~not a fact and easy~~ an easy task. The next step is try-
17 ~~ing~~ for the student to adjust himself to his environment. It
18 is a gradual process but when the student completes this process,
19 he will become an independant thinker, learn to make his
20 own decisions, and be able to handle the responsibilities
21 put ~~on~~ upon him.

a. Does this paper have a controlling idea?
b. How effective are the opening lines?
c. Is there any repetition of ideas in either the first or second paragraph that needs to be omitted?

d. What changes that the writer has made are for the better? For the worse?

e. Show how you would revise this page by copying it down and making every change you think necessary—in spelling, punctuation, wording, paragraphing.

6. This is an example of careless and unsatisfactory copy. The student has made a few changes in his final draft but he has overlooked more important ones. Read it over and make a note of every proofreading change you think necessary.

Skiing as I know it

1 Hiking is something that all good skiers

2 enjoy. It is one of the best ways to build

3 up your body in a way that will help you in

4 all sorts of skiing. It may be hard work to hike

5 up the mountain, but the real thrill comes

6 when the top is reached and it is time to

7 start down. This is skiing at it's best.

8 Down through the new unbroken powder snow

9 that is hard to match in any area. When the

10 bottom of this long run is reached it is

11 usually time to go home.

12   Ski Jumping is one of the hardest and most

13   beautiful feats of skiing, it requires much

14   skill and practice. Usually the best jumpers

15   have started when they are very young and

16   have done it all their lives. The worlds

17   record jump is four hundred and fifty-six

18   feet. Approxi~~matly~~ *mately* one and one-half times

19   the length of a football field, which is a

20   long way to fly with nothing to hold you up.

21   It takes presision balance and a clear head

22   to go through a jump from start to finish.

7. The following themes were written in a class period of fifty minutes on the subject "What specific aspects of writing are most difficult for you?" The assignment was made at the end of the first quarter's work in composition.

Read the themes and be prepared to discuss them on the basis of these points:

a. Which paper most accurately describes your own difficulties in writing? If the paper does not offer a solution for your problems, what solution would you suggest?

b. Which papers sound to you most convincing and sincere? Do any of the papers sound as if they were written with more regard for what the instructor might expect than for what the student actually felt? How appropriate are the titles?

c. Which papers seem to you to get the main idea across with the minimum of repetition or backtracking? In which are the expressions most natural or original? Do any of them sound unfinished?

d. Point out any errors (spelling, punctuation, paragraphing, sentence structure) that you find. Do any of these papers unconsciously illustrate the same faults that the writer is discussing?

1)   Writing is a Difficult Operation for Me

1   While I don't especially hate writing, I find it a good deal
2   less than a joy. Class papers in particular seem to be my mental
3   nemisis. When a topic is assigned and I am given a week or so
4   to complete the assignment, I seem to have a more relaxed feel-
5   ing about the whole thing, but when a topic is assigned in class
6   and the paper has to be handed in before class is dismissed, I
7   seem to get a choked-up feeling, and don't seem to be able to
8   express myself in as clear a manner as I feel I should be able to.
9   Paragraphing is is a phase of writing that simply "gives me
10 fits." I feel that I have had a fairly good background in the
11 mechanical aspects of English, but I seem unable to distinguish
12 between a new sentence and a new paragraph.
13 This is always apparent to me and I am quite conscious of the
14 fact when I write, but even though I try my best, I am contin-
15 ually putting new paragraphs where new sentences are more
16 correct.
17 Spelling is an aspect of writing that gives me only slight
18 trouble. I don't feel that this is because I am a good speller, but
19 more because I have become accustomed to using only those
20 words of which I am certain of the correct spelling.
21 Although I feel that the subjects assigned by the instructor
22 are not those about which I am particularly well qualified to
23 write, I do feel that it alleviates me of the agonizing task of
24 making the selection myself. For that reason, I prefer to not
25 select my own topics, especially in a class paper.
26 Assignments to be done outside class, although still possess-
27 ing the same hurdles as a classroom assignment, do not effect
28 me nearly so much. I like the feeling of being able to give my

29 topic more thought and study before putting something on
30 paper. As a general rule, I take two or three days just getting
31 ideas about what to write.

32   At the end of that time I usually skim quickly through a few
33 magazines or newspapers for more material. About the fourth
34 day I write a rough draft, and then a few changes, deletions,
35 and additions. Next I write or type the final draft and put it
36 in my notebook until classtime.

37   It is at this period that I begin to get the feeling that I should
38 have added something or omitted a certain passage. But it is
39 too late to do anything about it. Good, bad or otherwise, the
40 paper is turned in "as is."

41   Although I prefer home papers to those written in class, at
42 least the suffering is of shorter duration in the latter type. In
43 either case, however, it is a difficult operation for me. But I
44 do feel a little less tense and a little more at ease with a pen
45 in my hand than I did eleven weeks ago.

2)   Two of the Barriers Involved in Writing a Composition

1   The two most difficult aspects of writing that I encounter
2 involve the opening and closing paragraphs. The former being
3 the most difficult of the two.

4   Perhaps my trouble lies in the approach to composition writ-
5 ing. I do not like to work from an outline and I therefore begin
6 my work without a great deal of preparation. Once I have pre-
7 pared an opening sentence and paragraph, and feel that it is
8 satisfactory, the rest of the composition is comparatively easy.
9 After constructing my opening paragraph, I feel that I have a
10 sound foundation on which I can construct a satisfactory
11 composition. Of course my papers are not for the most part all
12 that I would like them to be, but I am definitely of the opinion
13 that with a clear, concise opening paragraph, the paragraphs
14 that follow are much easier to construct.

15   Once I have actually settled down to writing and have over-
16 come this first barrier, my writing flows along quite rapidly
17 until I meet with my second obstruction, the closing paragraph.

18   This paragraph, along with the first, is probably the most

19 difficult to compose. Not only does it have to be clear, concise,
20 and to the point, but it also has to unite the entire composition
21 so that the reader will be left with a lasting and convincing
22 impression. More times than not I will rewrite an ending para-
23 graph three or four times until I feel that I have attained the
24 forcefulness it should have and the impression I want to create.
25 Here, my difficulty is trying more or less to put into one para-
26 graph the meaning that I have been trying to convey through-
27 out the entire composition. Not only is it difficult to condense
28 an entire composition in this manner, but I also find it extreme-
29 ly difficult to find an appropriate sentence for the closing that
30 will, as I said before, give the reader the desired lasting
31 impression.

32   As is fairly evident, judging from the preceeding paragraphs,
33 composition writing would be much easier medicine to take if I
34 could eliminate two barriers, the first and last paragraphs.
35 However, with these eliminated, a composition would not be a
36 composition, so I will therefore reconcile myself to the fact that
37 this is one barrier that I will have to overcome in one way or
38 another.

3)   A Frustrated Writer

1   I find several aspects of writing difficult. Spelling, grammar,
2 punctuation, and wording all give me trouble when I am
3 preparing a paper. There is one particular aspect however, that
4 stands out as a real trouble spot for me. I never seem to say
5 what I really think.

6   When a subject is given by the instructor, ideas usually come
7 quite freely and so I begin to write. I will write a rough draft
8 by pouring my soul out on paper and then go back and delete
9 and change, until there is, or what seems to be, an organized
10 essay. When this is done, I read the paper to my roommate.
11 Often he has some very good suggestions for revision so I fre-
12 quently make a few more changes.

13   The final step is copying the scribblings into the finished
14 product. It is at this point that my difficulties become apparent.
15 I have finished writing a paper and yet I feel dissatisfied with

16 it. Many new ideas now pop into my head that I think should
17 have been included in the paper. Possibly a whole new ap-
18 proach to the subject seems advisable, but by this time its too
19 late to think of writing another paper or even adding fresh
20 thoughts to the original.

21   The result of this inability to put my thoughts just as I would
22 like them to be on paper is a feeling of frustration. I have failed
23 time after time to make my ideas on a given subject clear
24 enough or full enough to be valuable to anyone else. Or to
25 myself.

26   This is the part of writing that bothers me the most. I believe
27 that much of my trouble could be cured by using better out-
28 lines, and by thinking my subject through before I begin to
29 write. Practise will also help. Possibly as I write more papers I
30 will find my weak spots and be able to express myself more
31 fully. That is, if inspiration doesn't continue to come to me just
32 when I'm ready to turn my paper in.

6 Outlining

Words and sentences are subjects of revision; paragraphs and whole
compositions are subjects of prevision.—Barrett Wendell

The main purpose of an outline is to make writing easier
and more effective. The time to make an outline is during the
planning step of the writing process described in the preceding section. After you gather and think about the material,
and before you write the first draft, you need a plan of attack: In what order are you going to present your ideas?
Which are the main ideas and which are the less important
ones? How are you going to show the relationship between
them? These questions are best answered by making an outline to represent the plan of your paper.
  The form and completeness of the outline will depend on
the writing assignment, and will range from random scratch

notes for a brief class paper to a detailed, carefully worked out sentence outline for more complex assignments. The values of outlining are summarized in the following sentence outline:

Central idea: A good outline leads to an effective paper.

   I. An outline is a systematic and workmanlike approach to the job of writing.
      A. It indicates that you know what you want to say before you begin writing.
      B. It saves time and minimizes rewriting.
  II. It helps to make a paper unified.
      A. Irrelevant ideas can be detected and removed in the outline stage.
      B. The relationship between your ideas can be more easily seen in outline form.
 III. It enables you to put the emphasis where you want it.
      A. You can distinguish fully developed ideas from vague, half-formed ones.
      B. You can find out which ideas are major and which are minor.
      C. You can visualize the amount of space you are giving to each topic.
      D. You can arrange the topics in an order that represents your judgment of their importance.

One of the best ways to fix in your mind the subject matter of your texts or lecture notes or outside reading is to outline the material so that you can concentrate on the main points. Similarly, you can test your own writing by outlining the finished paper to see whether the organization and the emphasis are as effective as you wanted them to be.

6.1 Making an outline An outline begins to take shape as soon as you have some material to work with and a fairly definite idea of the main point you want to make. It grows out of the material you actually have to present. For extemporaneous writing and for examination papers, the topic or the question itself usually takes care of the subject matter and the viewpoint. All you need to do is to jot down the ideas you want to cover so that they won't slip your mind while you are writing.

But for work to be done outside class, you will find it helpful to build up your outline by definite stages, as follows:

6.1a Arranging ideas The first thing to do is to get all your ideas down on paper. On the subject "The Army as a Career," your preliminary thinking might produce this rough, unsorted list of ideas:

Security
Promotion slow but steady
Many different branches appeal to different men
Pay not very high
Depression won't bother you
Can't be fired
Cost of uniforms
Discipline often annoying
Frequent moves hard on soldier's family
See interesting places and people
Social life restricted to small circle
Good retirement benefits
Annual vacation with pay
Many military men successful in politics and
    business after retirement

A quick glance reveals that some of these points stress the advantages of an army career; others, the disadvantages. The next step then is to divide the notes into two columns:

Advantages	*Disadvantages*
Security	Pay not very high
Promotion slow but steady	Cost of uniforms
Many different branches appeal to different men	Discipline often annoying
Depression won't bother you	Frequent moves hard on soldier's family
Can't be fired	Social life restricted to small circle
See interesting places and people	
Good retirement benefits	
Annual vacation with pay	
Many military men successful in politics and business after retirement	

You will notice that in this form the relationship between the various ideas is not shown (What is the relationship between "promotion slow but steady" and "many different branches appeal to different men"?) and that there is no clear balance between the two columns (Is "security" supposed to balance "pay not very high"?).

Looking at the columns above you can see that there are two main ideas in each—the financial aspect of an army career and the living conditions. You might try balancing the notes in this way:

I. Financial aspect
  A. Disadvantages
    1. Pay not very high
    2. Cost of uniforms
  B. Advantages
    1. Security
    2. Slow but steady promotion
    3. Depression won't bother you
    4. Can't be fired
    5. Good retirement benefits
    6. Annual vacation with pay
    7. Many military men successful in politics and business after retirement
II. Social aspect
  A. Disadvantages
    1. Discipline often annoying
    2. Frequent moves hard on soldier's family
    3. Social life restricted to small circle
  B. Advantages
    1. Many different branches appeal to different men
    2. See interesting people and places

6.1b Getting a central idea When you have arranged your notes according to some system, decide what is the main point you want to make in your paper. "The Army as a Career" doesn't tell what you are going to *say* about the subject; it is a title, not a central idea.

From your outline at this stage you can see that you have more and stronger material on the financial advantages of a military career than on its disadvantages. On the other hand, the disadvantages of living conditions seem to outweigh the advantages. But assuming that you want to treat the subject fully and in a favorable light, you could frame a tentative statement of your purpose: "Although there are definite disadvantages to an army career, the advantages outweigh them."

This statement will now govern the reworking of the outline. At this stage your outline is still tentative, and can be changed to suit your purpose as it becomes clearer in your mind.

6.1c Revising the outline   With the central idea as your guide, arrange your outline so that every part of it contributes directly to the purpose of the paper. Examine each heading separately to see if it needs to be strengthened or elaborated upon, if it repeats or overlaps another heading, or if it is unrelated to the central idea.

In the first part of the outline "Cost of uniforms" seems to be a weak point. Aren't officers given allowances for their uniforms? Probably "Expense of frequent entertaining" is a stronger point, so substitute it for "Cost of uniforms."

The financial advantages of an army career seem to stand out, but if you look at these entries closely, you will see that some overlap or are actually minor parts of other points. The heading "Security" obviously covers "Slow but steady promotion" and "Can't be fired." The third heading, "Depression won't bother you," is probably superfluous, since it really is part of "Can't be fired." Closer examination reveals that "Annual vacation with pay" is an aspect of living conditions rather than of finances; it should therefore be shifted to the second main heading.

Under "Advantages" in the second main heading, the first entry "Many different branches appeal to different men" seems out of place or else incorrectly phrased. Perhaps the point is that military men can find the job they like or are best fitted for.

As the plan now stands, the first part seems to be the

stronger. To make the argument more convincing, it would be a good idea to reverse the present order: begin with "Living conditions," and then end the paper on an emphatic note—the training that the army affords for success in other fields.

After these changes have been made, and after some headings have been reworded to make them parallel in form, the final outline would be as follows:

Central idea: From the standpoint of finances and living conditions, there are some disadvantages to an army career, but the advantages outweigh them.

I. Living conditions
   A. Disadvantages
      1. Discipline often annoying
      2. Frequent moves hard on soldier's family
      3. Social life restricted to a small circle
   B. Advantages
      1. Opportunity to find the job one is best fitted for
      2. Annual leaves with pay
      3. Chance to travel, to see new places and meet new people
II. Financial aspect of an army career
   A. Disadvantages
      1. Pay not very high
      2. Expense of frequent entertaining
   B. Advantages
      1. Security
         a. Slow but steady promotion
         b. Permanent employment
         c. Good retirement benefits
      2. Preparation for success in business or politics after retirement

The outline now can be the basis for an orderly paper that will make a definite point.

6.2 Types of outlines Three kinds of outlines are in general use: the scratch outline, the topic outline, and the sentence outline. Your instructor will tell you which form he wants for outlines that are submitted with your papers. For your own use, select the form that best suits your purpose and your methods of work. Try experimenting with different kinds to find the one you prefer.

6.2a Scratch outline   A scratch outline is a series of notes—single words or phrases—jotted down to jog your memory as you write, like those in §6.1a. The following is a sample scratch outline on the subject of clerking in a large department store:

Learning the ropes
5-day training period
Store's policies
Methods of selling
Customers—good and bad
What I learned

An outline of this sort is useful when time is limited—when you are writing examinations, for example, or brief papers in class. The exact form of the outline is not particularly important, since ordinarily you will be the only one who sees it. If the list is longer than four or five items, you will need to arrange the entries in order (or number them) before beginning to write.

6.2b Topic outline   The topic outline is the most frequently used kind of formal outline. It consists of brief phrases or single words (not sentences) which are numbered or lettered to show the order and relative importance of the ideas. The central idea, which stands at the head of the outline, is in sentence form.

Central idea: Through training and actual experience as a clerk, I learned a good deal about the operation of a large department store and about human nature as well.

I. Getting preliminary training
   A. Necessity for training
      1. To learn to meet the public
      2. To learn store policies
      3. To learn stock

    B. Kind of training
       1. Lectures and demonstrations
       2. Tours through store
II. Waiting on customers
    A. Disagreeable
       1. Want to be waited on first
       2. Want to handle goods
       3. Can't make up their minds
    B. Pleasant
       1. Consider clerk's problems
       2. Know in advance what they want
       3. Ask for help when they need it
       4. Treat clerks as equals
III. Learning through experience
    A. About operation of a large store
       1. Overhead costs
       2. Profit margin
    B. About shopping wisely
       1. Avoiding "come-on" specials
       2. Looking for quality as well as price
       3. Taking advice of conscientious clerks
    C. About human nature
       1. Through waiting on all kinds of people
       2. By observing different types of clerks
          a. Indifferent
          b. Overeager
          c. Conscientious

The headings in a topic outline should be sufficiently complete so that they will mean something to you if you have to put the outline aside for a day or two before writing the paper.

6.2c Sentence outline Each heading in a sentence outline is a complete sentence, usually having just one main clause.

Central idea: The training and experience I received as a clerk in Moore's Department Store gave me first-hand information about retailing methods and taught me something about human nature.

  I. Every new clerk, experienced or not, was required to attend a five-day training school.
    A. A school is necessary because Moore's policies are different from those of other stores.
       1. Moore's specializes in quality merchandise.

2. Most of the customers have charge accounts.
3. Many of them expect to be greeted by name.
   B. The training period was thorough and interesting.
1. The instructors were efficient and cooperative.
2. They explained the operation of the entire store, department by department.
3. They acted out actual selling situations.
4. They told us what to do in emergencies.

II. My customers included all kinds of people.
   A. Some were disagreeable and annoying.
1. A few always wanted to be waited on first.
2. Some women thought the clerk had as much time to waste as they did.
   a. These included the people who could never make up their minds.
   b. Two of my customers came frequently to chat but never to buy.
3. The most disagreeable were those who treated the clerks contemptuously.
   B. But the majority were thoughtful and pleasant to wait on.
1. Most people realized that the clerk was often rushed for time.
   a. Some would wait patiently until I had finished with another customer.
   b. Others would make up their minds what they wanted before I waited on them.
2. My customers generally treated me with respect.
   a. The men in particular were willing to take my advice.
   b. They didn't blame me for the high prices.
3. Most customers treated the clerks as equals, not as inferiors.

III. I gained considerably more from this experience than the salary I earned.
   A. I gained first-hand information about good business methods.
1. The management of Moore's actually practiced many of the retailing principles I had studied in economics.
2. I learned the importance of controlling overhead and incidental expenses.
   B. I learned how to shop wisely and efficiently.
1. It pays to study the ads before visiting a store.
2. Bargains are often misleading.
   C. Most important was the knowledge I picked up working with and for other people.
1. I learned how to meet the public.
2. I learned that tact, patience, and cooperation are needed to get along with others.

Each heading is a complete sentence, and only one sentence—not two or three. Each sentence is also in the form of a statement, not a question.

The chief advantage of a sentence outline is that the ideas will have to be clear and fully thought out before they can be stated in complete sentences. For that reason it is sometimes assigned for training in writing long formal reports such as the reference paper. But in current practice, the sentence outline is not widely used.

6.3 Outline form Numbering, indention, punctuation, and other physical aspects of outlines follow certain conventions, particularly when the outlines are to be read by someone other than the writer. When you are required to turn in an outline with your paper, put it in the form that has been assigned.

Make the outline neat as well as accurate. If your instructor asks you to turn in an outline, it is certain that he intends to read it.

6.3a Numbering and indention Make the numbering of your headings consistent throughout. This is the typical method for numbering and indenting a topic or sentence outline:

Central idea: _____
_____. (Sentence statement)

I. _____ (Roman numeral for main head)
  A. _____ (Capital letter for subhead)
    1. _____ (Arabic numeral for second subhead)
    2. _____
      a. _____ (Lower case letter for third subhead)
      b. _____
        1) _____ (Arabic numeral with parenthesis for fourth subhead)
        2) _____
  B. _____
II. _____

The main heads (I, II, III . . .) are set flush with the left-hand margin. The subheads are indented four or five spaces in typed copy and about three-quarters of an inch in longhand, or they may be indented so that they are directly under the first word of the preceding heading, as shown in this book.

When a heading runs over one line, the second line is indented as far as the first word of the preceding line:

I. The photoelectric cell, known as the "electric eye," has been put to a variety of practical uses.
   A. It is used in elevator floors to enable the elevator to stop at exactly the right level.

When you make an outline, avoid overelaborate and confusing systems. There is rarely any need to go farther than the third subhead (a, b, c . . .). Two levels are often enough for a short paper; longer papers may need three or more.

6.3b Headings Each heading in your outline should be specific and meaningful.

Vague and useless

The Profession I Want to Follow

  I. Introduction
 II. Why I prefer this work
III. What the opportunities would be
IV. The chances for success
 V. Conclusion

Specific

The Profession I Want to Follow

  I. Lifelong interest in veterinarian's work
    A. Grew up with animals on a farm
    B. Saw importance of veterinarian's work
    C. Worked with a veterinarian last two summers
 II. Many opportunities in veterinary work today
    A. In rural areas
    B. In cities
III. Worthwhile and well-paid profession

Headings like "Introduction," "Body," and "Conclusion" aren't useful unless you indicate what material you are going to put into these sections. Instead of using general labels such as "Causes" and "Results," indicate exactly what the causes or results are; it will save time when you write your paper.

Putting headings in the form of questions or in statements that will have to be filled in later is not an efficient practice. The necessary information will have to be supplied when you write, so you might as well supply it in the planning stage.

Indefinite	*Definite*
I. The Wars of the Roses	I. The Wars of the Roses
A. When they began	A. Started 1455
B. Why?	B. Caused by rivalry between Houses of Lancaster and York

6.3c **Punctuation and capitalization**   In a topic outline, capitalize the first letter of the word beginning the heading (and all proper nouns), but do not put any punctuation at the end of the entry, because these headings are not complete statements.

I. Present need for nurses
  A. In the Army
  B. In public health

Punctuate every heading in a sentence outline just as you would punctuate the sentences in your paper: begin with a capital letter and end with a period or other end stop. Except for proper nouns, other words in the heading are not capitalized (a heading is not a title).

I. The advantages of specialization in college are numerous.
  A. The student is able to set a goal for himself.

6.3d **Dividing the material**   If a heading is to be divided at all, it should be divided into more than one part. This practice is based upon the principle that nothing can be divided into fewer than two parts. For every heading marked *I*, there should be at least a *II*, for every *A*, there should be a *B*, and so on.

Inaccurate division	*Accurate division*

The Three Branches of the Federal Government

I. The executive branch
  A. President and Cabinet

II. The legislative branch
  A. The House of
    Representatives
  B. The Senate
    1. Functions

III. The judicial branch
  A. The Supreme Court

The Three Branches of the Federal Government

I. The executive branch
  A. President
  B. Cabinet

II. The legislative branch
  A. The House of
    Representatives
  B. The Senate
    1. Special functions
    2. Special privileges

III. The judicial branch
  A. The Supreme Court
  B. Lower courts

When there is only one heading under a topic, it usually repeats what is in the topic, and should therefore be included with it.

Unnecessary division	*Accurate division*

The Smithsonian Institution

I. Established by an Englishman
  A. James Smithson
    1. In 1846

The Smithsonian Institution

I. Established by James Smithson, an Englishman, in 1846
not necessary

The main heads of your outline should represent equally important divisions of the subject as a whole.

Unequal headings	*Equal headings*

Books I Have Enjoyed

  I. Adventure stories
  II. Historical novels
  III. *Treasure Island*
  IV. Autobiographies
  V. What I like most

Books I Have Enjoyed

  I. Adventure stories
  II. Historical novels
  III. Character studies
  IV. Autobiographies
  V. Science fiction

Similarly the subdivisions should designate equally important divisions of one phase of the main divisions.

Unequal subheads

I. Purpose of slogans on car
   license plates
   A. To attract tourists
   B. California plates used to
      have a poppy as decoration
   C. To advertise state's leading
      industry
   D. Bucking bronco on
      Wyoming's

Equal subheads

I. Purpose of slogans on car
   license plates
   A. To attract tourists
   B. To advertise state's
      leading industry

Headings of equal rank should not overlap: what is in *II* should exclude what is covered in *I; B* should be clearly distinct from *A,* and so on.

Overlapping

Services of the Weather Bureau

   I. General Public Service
  II. Reports of newspapers
 III. Aviation Service
 IV. Flight Advisory Service
   V. Crop Weather Service
 VI. Bulletins to farmers

Accurate

Services of the Weather Bureau

   I. General Public Service
  II. Aviation Weather Service
 III. Crop Weather Service
 IV. River and Flood Service
   V. Climatological Service

6.3e **Making headings parallel in wording** Headings in the same series are put in the same grammatical form. In a topic outline, if *I* is a noun, *II* and *III* are also nouns; if *I* is a prepositional phrase, so are *II* and *III.* The same principle applies to subdivisions: when *A* under *I* is an adjective, *B* and *C* are also adjectives. Under *II,* however, *A, B,* and *C* would not have to be adjectives, but could be nouns or any other parallel forms. A sentence outline should use complete sentences throughout and not lapse into topic headings. The following examples show how headings can be made parallel in form:

Headings not parallel

The Art of Putting

   I. The stance is fundamental
  II. The grip

Parallel headings

The Art of Putting

   I. The stance
  II. The grip

III. Importance of the backswing
IV. Stroking the ball
  V. Follow through with care

III. The backswing
IV. The contact with the ball
  V. The follow-through

The Selective Service System

II. Four reasons for deferment
  A. Because of occupation
  B. Dependents
  C. Some are physically unfit
  D. Because of age

The Selective Service System

II. Four reasons for deferment
  A. Occupation
  B. Dependents
  C. Physical disability
  D. Age

For extended examples of parallel form, see the outlines in §6.2b and §6.2c.

6.4 The outline in relation to the paper When you are asked to submit an outline with your paper, it should represent the plan of the paper as it actually has been written, and not as it might have been written. In other words, your outline serves as the table of contents. If you have found it necessary in writing the paper to depart from the original outline, make the corresponding changes in the outline before handing it in. The order and relative importance of the ideas should be the same in both.

6.4a Length of the outline An outline should be long enough to suit your purpose, and no longer. It should be no more complex than the material demands. An outline that is nearly as long as the finished paper may be a tribute of sorts to the writer's industry, but it also represents misdirected effort that might better have been spent on the paper itself.

The number of main headings for most papers ranges from three to five. A larger number of main heads for a 1000 word paper suggests that the division is haphazard or that the organization is faulty. The same principle applies to subheadings. Outlines that run from *A* through *M* or *S* need revision, for no single topic needs such minute subdivision. And except with very complex material, there is seldom any need to go beyond the third subhead.

6.4b Writing the paper from the outline An outline will be as useful to you as the material you put into it. No matter how correct the form—in numbering, punctuation, and parallel structure—if the outline doesn't help you in writing your paper, its main purpose has been defeated.

A good outline is a useful guide for better paragraphing. You can estimate both the number and the relative length of the paragraphs in your paper from the main divisions in the outline. You can construct topic sentences for these paragraphs by rephrasing or expanding the statements in the outline headings. And the divisions will show where transitions are needed—within and between paragraphs—as well as the kind of expression: contrast, comparison, additional illustration, summary, and so forth.

Practice in constructing and using outlines for relatively simple subjects is good training for organizing papers on more complex topics that you will probably have to discuss in other courses.

Exercises

1. To see how professional writers plan their material, make an outline of an article in a magazine or volume of readings, or of a chapter from one of your textbooks. Your instructor may designate the form of the outline as well as select the article. When you have finished, check the outline carefully for proper form, and then answer these questions:

a. Has the author stated specifically the central idea of his article? If not, can you frame a statement of the central idea?

b. Does the plan of the article show through in the writing? In other words, were you conscious of the framework as you read the article?

c. Can you suggest any alternative plan of development that might have been equally satisfactory, or perhaps better?

2. Write a scratch outline on any one of the following topics that appeals to you. When you have jotted down all your notes, frame a central idea and put the notes in the form of a topic outline. Use the proper form and accurate subdivisions.

Learning to dance	Managing a rummage sale
Why writing is difficult	Speaking in public
Why people watch excavations	The process of rushing
Radiant heating	Hot rods
Secrets of good cooking	Unusual place names
Should physical education be required in college?	Forecasting the results of football games
Income is not the primary goal of education	I prefer Bach
	Our local parking problem

3. Tell what is wrong with the form of the following outlines and show how you would revise them.

1) The Four Freedoms

I. Outlined in January 1941
   A. Freedom of speech
   B. Everyone should be able to worship God as he sees fit.
   C. Economic
   D. Freedom from fear.

2) Why everyone should be able to swim.

I. Everyone should learn to swim.
   A. As early as possible.
      1. Children have been taught as young as three years
II. The Ability to swim may save your life.
   1. never swim alone
   2. don't show off in the water
3. Many schools require students to pass swimming tests.
   a. my experiences
   b. Red Cross lifesaving test.

3) A special agent for the FBI must have an excellent character, perfect health, and superior mental ability.

I. There are three main qualifications for the job
   A. Physical
   B. Mental
   C. Character
II. The candidate must pass a formal interview and a written examination.
   A. Oral Questions
      1. Purpose
   B. Written Exams
   C. If he passes both of these, his name is put on a waiting list.
III. Special training for successful candidates
   A. Classroom
   B. In the gym
   C. Intensive practice on the target range
      1. With the pistol
      2. Submachine gun practice

4. Study the following outlines from the standpoint of effective and useful planning. Then state specifically what you consider to be the unsatisfactory aspects of each one either in form or content.

1) Central idea: The mailman hasn't an easy job and he has many things to complain about.

I. The weather
II. Mailboxes
III. The recipients of the mail
IV. People who have savage dogs
V. Other things

2) Quality Reproduction of Recorded Music

I. Five basic pieces of equipment
   A. Turntable

    B. Pickup
    C. Amplifier
    D. Speaker
    E. Records
       1. 78 rpm
       2. 45 rpm
       3. 33⅓ rpm
 II. Qualities to look for in a turntable
    A. Good changer
    B. Made by reputable manufacturer
    C. Others
III. Qualities to look for in pickup
    A. Most important part of equipment
    B. Consists of three parts
       1. Needle
       2. Cartridge
       3. Pickup arm
    C. Sapphire tipped needle best for 78 rpm records
    D. The cartridge
       1. Low output variable reluctance type best
         (a) But requires pre-amplifier
 IV. Amplifier
    A. From five to ten tubes. Needs ten watt output
  V. Speakers
    A. Twelve to fifteen inches in diameter. A good speaker
       should be able to produce notes from 30 to 20,000 cycles
       per second.
       1. The case or cabinet
       2. Height from floor
 VI. Records: good and bad
VII. Conclusions

5. Some of the headings in the following outlines have been left blank. After you have examined the outline, indicate by number which heading from those at the right you would put in each blank space. Give reasons for your choice.

1) United States Passport Regulations

I. Where passports are needed
   A. In Western Hemisphere
   B. In western Europe
   C. _____

II. Who may get a passport
   A. Native-born citizens
   B. _____

III. _____
   A. Photographs
   B. Witnesses
   C. Health certificates

1. In Mexico
2. What a passport is
3. In the Orient
4. Not needed in Canada
5. Not issued for China

1. Children
2. People of good character
3. Students
4. Naturalized citizens
5. Soldiers use military permits

1. How to apply
2. Miscellaneous
3. What the cost is
4. What a passport is
5. What you must furnish

2) The Organization of a Newspaper

I. Business department
   A. _____
   B. Collects money
   C. Pays bills
   D. Sells advertising space

II. Editorial department
   A. Gathers the news
   B. Writes the news
   C. Edits the news
   D. _____

III. Printing department
   A. Sets type
   B. Composes the page

1. Is very important
2. Comes first
3. Keeps accounts
4. Run by business manager

1. Run by the editor
2. Writing editorials is hard work
3. Reports the news as it sees fit
4. Determines and expresses the newspaper's policies

1. Involves many complicated processes
2. Corrects proof

C. _____
D. Prints the paper

IV. _____
  A. Distributes paper to
    newsstands
  B. Distributes papers by
    delivery boys

3. Uses expensive printing
  presses
4. Selects size of type
5. Linotype operators are
  highly skilled
1. Getting the paper to you
2. The final step
3. The circulation manager
4. The role of the delivery boy
5. The circulation department

7 Manuscript form

All writing that someone else is going to read—personal correspondence, business letters, papers for a college course, or copy that is to go to a printer—should be neat, easy to read, and in good form. The very first impression a reader will get from your writing will depend on its appearance.

7.1 General instructions If you have a typewriter and know how to use it, it is good practice to type all papers written outside class. Typed manuscript is easier to read than most handwriting and it is generally preferable for written work in all college courses. But if you cannot type, you need not worry that your work will suffer, for typed papers do not automatically receive better grades. Typographical errors are more common than slips of the pen, and mistakes of all sorts stand out more prominently in typed copy. With reasonable care, handwritten papers can be made just as acceptable as those that are well typed.

7.1a Handwritten papers Use lined white paper 8½ by 11 inches, with the lines about one-half inch apart. Themes written on closely lined paper are hard to read and difficult to correct. Do not use paper torn from spiral bound notebooks, because their rough edges stick together. Use black or dark blue ink; green or violet ink is in dubious taste and annoying to many readers.

Handwritten papers should be easy to read. If a word looks misspelled or is difficult to decipher, it will probably be marked as an error. Handwriting that is too small puts an unnecessary strain on the eyes of the reader; handwriting that is excessively large is no less difficult to read. Try to strike a happy medium in the size of your handwriting. If you have developed what you consider to be an individual style of penmanship, make certain that it will be as legible to others as it is to you.

7.1b Typed papers For typed papers, use unlined white paper 8½ by 11 inches of good quality bond. It is discourteous to a reader to use onion skin paper or other transparent sheets which let the type show through. Never use colored paper.

All typed papers should be double spaced. The only exception is for long quotations, which should be indented and single spaced.

Follow standard conventions in typing. For the figure 1 use lower case l (not capital I). For a dash, use two hyphens without a space between the words:

```
The book--a first edition--was missing.
```

Use black ribbon and change it before it gets pale. Keep the type bars clean by frequent brushing.

Before you hand your paper in, check it carefully for typographical errors. Uncorrected typing mistakes are counted as errors in composition courses.

7.2 Spacing Leave ample margins on each side of the page. An inch and a half on the left and an inch on the right are the customary margins in handwritten and typed papers. Leave at least an inch and a half at the top and an inch at the bottom of every page.

Indent paragraphs uniformly. Five spaces from the left-hand margin is the customary indention for typed papers, and about an inch for those written in longhand. Don't indent any line that is not the beginning of a paragraph. (Especially don't indent the first line on a page unless it begins a new paragraph.) The last line on a page should not be left partly blank unless it is the end of a paragraph.

Don't crowd your writing at the bottom of a page. Start a new page, even if it will contain only a line or two.

7.3 Division of words

Div **Division of words. Correction: Divide a word at the end of a line according to the syllabication given in a reliable dictionary.**

If you leave plenty of room at the right-hand side of your page, you will not have to divide many words at the ends of the lines. It is a good idea to divide words only if writing them out or putting them on the next line would make the lines conspicuously uneven.

Words of one syllable should not be divided at all: *through, played, bright.*

Avoid breaking a word if a single letter will be left at the beginning or end of a line. There is no point in dividing a word like *a-lone* because the single letter at the end of the line is less attractive than leaving space and carrying the whole word over to the next line.

Words spelled with a hyphen (*mother-in-law, well-behaved*) should be divided only at the hyphen to avoid adding another.

7.4 Corrections in the final copy

Changes and corrections should be kept to a minimum, particularly on important papers. When you have to make major changes in the final copy (rewording sentences, revising paragraphs), do the page over. For minor changes (spelling, punctuation, adding or striking out a word), make the corrections as neatly as possible and according to standard practices.

To add a word, use a caret (^) and write the missing word directly above it:

Manuscript should＾*be* easy to read.

To strike out a word, draw a straight line through it (don't use parentheses or brackets):

Final copy should be ~~as~~ as accurate as possible

To indicate the beginning of a new paragraph where you have failed to indent, write the symbol ¶ immediately before the first word of the new paragraph:

So ended my first day away from home. ¶ The second day . . . .

To show that an indented sentence should not be the beginning of a new paragraph, write No ¶ in the margin.

To correct a misspelled word, draw a line through it and write the correct form directly above:

quantity
~~quanity~~

This makes a neater and more legible correction than an erasure.

To indicate in typed copy that two letters should be reversed in order (transposed), use a curved line:

b e w t e e n   r e c i e v e

7.5 Titles of papers   Word your title so that it gives a definite and accurate idea of the subject matter in your paper in as few words as possible. A title need not mystify or startle the reader, although it may perhaps arouse his curiosity or appeal to his sense of humor. Interesting titles are always appreciated, but any one that is brief, simple, and exact will serve the purpose. Just name the subject accurately and let it go at that.

7.5a Framing a title   A title should not suggest more than the paper actually covers. If you are discussing your tastes in music, avoid such sweeping titles as "Modern Jazz" or "Music of Today"; use instead "Music I Like" or "Why I Prefer New Orleans Jazz." A report on the experiences of a baby sitter scarcely deserves the title "Child Psychology" or "The Care of Infants"; "Experiences of a Baby Sitter" will be good enough if you cannot think of a better title.

Unnecessarily long titles are not satisfactory, especially those that merely repeat the assignment: "An Experience in Childhood That Left a Lasting Impression on Me." The central idea (or thesis sentence) of your paper is not intended to serve as a title. Instead of writing "Reading Taught by Sound Should Replace Sight Reading," name the subject: "Reading by Sound."

If a title doesn't occur to you in the early stages of writing the paper, forget about it and go on. It is usually easier to think of an appropriate title when you have finished than before you have started to write.

7.5b Position and capitalization of the title   The title appears on the first page of your paper. On unlined paper, place it in the center and about two inches from the top of the page; on lined paper, write the title on the top line. Leave a blank line between the title and the first line of the text in handwritten papers, and at least three lines of space in typed papers.

Capitalize the first and last words in your title and all other words except short words like *and, the, a, an,* and prepositions less than five letters long.

Breaking and Training a Horse	How Not to Become Overweight
The Art of Making Friends	Victory Through Airpower
To Europe on a Cattleboat	

7.5c Punctuation of the title   No period is needed after a title. If the title is a question or an exclamation, use the proper end punctuation.

A Cure for Homesickness   Man Overboard!
Why Not UMTC?

Titles are not inclosed in quotation marks. Even when familiar quotations are used as titles, no marks are needed:

Blood, Sweat, and Tears   Music Hath Charms . . .

7.5d Reference to the title   The title is not part of the paper,
and it should not be referred to by a pronoun in the first sentence. If you want to mention the title in your opening, re-
phrase it slightly.

Unsatisfactory   *Satisfactory*

Becoming a Citizen   Becoming a Citizen

   This is not a difficult process   It is not difficult for an immi-
in the United States. . . .   grant to become a citizen of our
                            country. . . .

7.6 Numbering pages   The first page is not numbered. Begin
with the second page, using Arabic numerals (2, 3, 4 . . .) for
paging. Numbers are customarily put at the top of the page in
the right-hand corner or in the center.

Make certain that the pages of your paper are in the right
order before you turn the paper in. Even though numbered,
pages are frequently not in the proper sequence when the
paper is submitted.

It is not correct to write "more" at the bottom of each page
or "30," "Finis," or "The End" at the conclusion.

Long tables, diagrams, charts, and other material supplementary to the words of the text are usually put on separate
pages, placed near the part that refers to them, and numbered
consecutively with the other pages.

7.7 Endorsing the paper   Endorse your papers as your instructor directs. Include all the information he asks for, and put
it in the right order. Clear and uniform endorsement is a real
convenience to the teacher who must handle the papers.

Most papers in college courses are folded lengthwise, with the outer fold endorsed in this way:

Peter D. Avery	[Student's name]
English 101--B	[Course and section]
Oct. 14, 1954	[Date submitted]
No. 2	[Number of paper]
Mr. St. Clair	[Instructor's name]

If the pages are not folded, the endorsement should be on the back of the last sheet or on a special title page. Sheets should be held together by paper clips that can be slipped off, not by fasteners or staples that pierce the paper, or by pins, bobby pins, or string. Use binders only for longer papers.

7.8 Submitting manuscript for publication   Manuscript that is to be submitted for publication, in a campus magazine or elsewhere, should be typed and follow the directions in §7.1b.

The writer's name and full address should be typed in the upper left-hand corner of the first page. A stamped, self-addressed envelope should be inclosed for the possible return of the manuscript. It is not necessary to write a letter to a publisher when submitting a manuscript unless there are facts to be given about the sources of material used, its accuracy, or possibilities for illustration.

See §49, The reference paper, for special instructions on the form of reference papers.

Exercises

1. On the basis of this section, make a checklist of points to look for when you are making a final check on the form and appearance of your paper.

2. Study your last theme in the light of the directions given in this section. Does it conform to all of them that apply?

3. Count the number of words on a page of a book or magazine and on a typical page of one of your themes to see how much space your copy would take in print.

Exercise 6, p. 60, also involves matters of manuscript form.

8 Letters

Letters should be easy and natural, and convey to the persons to whom we send them, just what we should say to the persons if we were with them.—The Earl of Chesterfield, *Letters to His Son*

What you say in your letters and the way that you say it will depend upon your purpose, the person you are writing to, and above all, upon the way you customarily express yourself. You should, however, be familiar with the conventions that are followed in current business and social correspondence, so that the form and the appearance of your letters will make the impression you wish.

8.1 General letter form   In letter writing, just as in writing papers for class, form and appearance are important. All letters follow a pretty well standardized form, and their appearance will make an immediate impression—favorable or unfavorable—upon whoever receives it.

8.1a Stationery   Select stationery of appropriate size and of good quality, with envelope to match. Good stationery costs little more than an inferior grade, and the favorable impression it will make upon your readers is well worth the slight difference.

For business letters the standard size sheet (typing paper) is 8½ by 11 inches. With long envelopes, paper this size is folded twice horizontally; with shorter envelopes (about 3½ by 6½), the sheets are folded once across the middle and twice vertically, like this:

Folded twice for long envelopes

Folded three times for standard envelopes

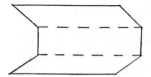

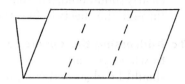

For personal correspondence and informal notes, either club paper or note paper is appropriate. Club paper, probably the more popular, consists of single sheets (from 6 by 10 inches to 7½ by 11 inches) which are folded twice when placed in an envelope of standard size. Note paper, a four-page sheet, is folded once across the page before being placed in an envelope.

Whether you should type a letter or write it in longhand depends upon the kind of letter you are writing and the person to whom you are writing. Typed letters are standard in business correspondence, and they are becoming increasingly more popular for personal correspondence between friends and relatives. If your handwriting is not easy to read, your friends will probably appreciate typed letters. In the earlier stages of a friendship, handwriting is perhaps preferable. It is always better for invitations and replies and for letters that convey sentiment or sympathy.

8.1b Spacing and general appearance　The pages of a letter should appeal to the reader's eye. Leave good margins and center the body of the letter so that the page will be well balanced.

Space paragraphs distinctly, using either block or indented form. Block paragraphs—more common in typed than in handwritten letters—are set flush with the left margin of the letter. When the lines are single spaced, two spaces are left between paragraphs. For indented paragraphs, begin five or six spaces from the left-hand margin. Be consistent throughout the letter in the form that you use for paragraphs.

Both sides of the page may be used in handwritten letters but only one side in typewritten. Take care that the pages are clearly numbered, so that your reader won't have to sort through the sheets to find the right sequence.

8.1c Addressing the envelope   Both the address of the person to whom you are writing and your own (or return) address should be clear and complete on the envelope. A block style —with the left-hand margin even—is the standard form for both addresses.

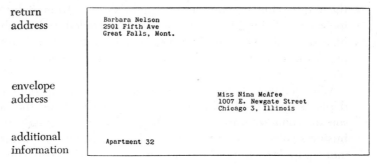

return
address

> Barbara Nelson
> 2901 Fifth Ave
> Great Falls, Mont.

envelope
address

> Miss Nina McAfee
> 1007 E. Newgate Street
> Chicago 3, Illinois

additional
information

> Apartment 32

No punctuation is used at the end of the lines in this form. A comma is used between the name of the city (or the postal zone) and the state if they are put on the same line: Chicago 3, Illinois.

When you abbreviate street designations, use the standard forms (*St.* for *Street*, *Ave.* for *Avenue*, *Blvd.* for *Boulevard*). For names of states, use only those abbreviations given in your dictionary (*Penn.*, *Okla.*); avoid misleading abbreviations, such as those for states with short names: write *Maine*, not *Me.*

8.2 Personal correspondence   Familiar correspondence is like conversation between friends: the tone is cordial and relaxed, the form less rigid than in other types of correspondence. This does not mean, however, that letters written to friends and relatives should be sloppy or careless, or sound as if the writing was a disagreeable chore to be gotten over with as quickly as possible.

Familiar correspondence should be neat and easy to read as well as interesting. Taking a little pains with the appearance of the letter and with such matters as spelling and punctuation is a courtesy that you owe your reader. It also helps to revise an occasional personal letter, a practice that will perhaps raise the level of all of your correspondence.

8.2a The form of personal letters The form of personal correspondence varies with the degree of intimacy between writer and reader. No heading except the date is needed between regular correspondents. But it never hurts to include your address in the heading, particularly when you are writing someone at infrequent intervals. The envelope with your return address is often discarded long before your letter is answered.

The greeting between friends is usually *Dear Bob* or *Dear Ruth.* If you are writing to an older person, someone you do not call by first name, either of these forms will serve (the colon is more Formal):

Dear Miss Breckenridge,

Dear Professor Brown:

The complimentary close ranges in warmth from "Love," for the appropriate persons, through "Yours," and "Sincerely," to "Yours very truly," for persons whom you know only slightly.

8.2b Social notes Many invitations are now given and answered by telephone. When a note is called for, it should be brief but adequate in details, written in longhand on note paper. Here are two notes between a teacher and a student:

Dear Helen,

I am having a little supper party for my voice students next Sunday evening, and I hope that you will be able to come. We shall eat at six o'clock and later listen to recordings of fine voices. The program won't be long, so if you have an engagement later in the evening this should not interfere.

Cordially yours,

Marian Hall

Dear Miss Hall,

Thank you for your invitation for Sunday evening. But our sorority is giving a pledge banquet that same evening that I have to attend. Consequently I am afraid that I cannot be at your home then. I am sorry to have to miss the party, because home cooking is a treat and I would like very much to hear the recordings.

Sincerely yours,

Helen James

In notes of this kind, a cordial tone, complete information, and promptness in answering are more important than mechanical form.

8.3 Formal social correspondence Formal social correspondence—such as wedding announcements, invitations to formal functions, and the answers to these invitations—is impersonal and standardized. Both form and wording should conform to established patterns.

Delta Kappa Epsilon

requests the pleasure of your company

at a reception

in honor of

John Hughes Hunter

on Friday, the twenty-sixth of May

at eight o'clock in the evening

The favor of a reply
is requested

Names are given in full, dates and other numbers are written out in words, and no punctuation is used at the end of the lines. An engraver or printer will help with the style of notes for different occasions.

If the note is written in longhand, the same form is followed:

Mrs. Henry Jackson
requests the pleasure of
Miss Jeanette Loy's
company at a luncheon on
Monday, June sixth, at one o'clock
at the Kingston Club

Usually a reply is requested, either by *R.S.V.P.* (*répondez, s'il vous plaît*) or by *The favor of a reply is requested.* Since invitations of this kind are important to the person who sends them, it is a mark of good manners to reply as promptly as possible.

Answers to formal invitations are written in longhand on good quality note paper, either in the form of the invitation or in a block paragraph. Use the third person and, as nearly as possible, follow the exact wording of the invitation. Names, dates, and place are repeated, as in this reply accepting the invitation in the preceding example:

Miss Jeanette Loy
accepts with pleasure
the kind invitation of
Mrs. Henry Jackson
to a luncheon at the Kingston Club
on Monday, June sixth, at one o'clock

If you are unable to accept the invitation, your reply might read:

Miss Jeanette Loy regrets that
because of a previous engagement she
will be unable to accept Mrs. Henry
Jackson's kind invitation for the
sixth of June at the Kingston Club

8.4 Business letters   Neatness, clarity, and directness should be the chief virtues in business letters. Letters written by an individual to a firm follow the same form as those from a business house to an individual. Whenever possible, they should be typed, and on one side of the page only.

All relevant information should be given (dates, prices, description of merchandise, a person's qualifications for a job) and in as brief a fashion as is consistent with clearness. The tone should be courteous, even though the writer may be complaining about an error in his bill.

The best way to become informed on business letters is to study the practices of reputable companies, perhaps keeping a small file of good business letters you receive. Below is an example of a typical business letter:

6482 East 72nd Street
Seattle 5, Washington
December 11, 1953

Brown, Stewart Company
382 Fifth Street
Milwaukee, Wisconsin

Gentlemen:

The Clear-Vu Projector, Model 3-B, that I ordered from you (Invoice No. 4823) came yesterday.

The slide magazine was bent so that it cannot be used. I am returning it by mail with this letter and hope that you will replace it.

Can you tell me about when you expect the strip film attachment for this model will be ready?

Yours very truly,

Adrian C. Hopwood

Adrian C. Hopwood

8.4a Headings   The heading in the upper right-hand corner gives the writer's complete address and the date. The standard form is the block pattern.

Block   *Indented* (less common)

2435 Bancroft Way   2435 Bancroft Way
Berkeley 4, California   Berkeley 4, California
October 18, 1953   October 18, 1953

The heading is placed at least an inch and a half from the top of the page (and lower, if the letter is short), and the lines do not extend beyond the right-hand margin of the letter. No punctuation is used at the ends of the lines. The name of the city, the state, and the month are generally written out in full.

8.4b Inside address and greeting   The inside address of a business letter gives the full name of the company to whom you are writing and its address. It appears flush with the left-hand margin and about three spaces lower than the last line of the heading. The greeting or salutation appears two spaces below the address.

Consumers Union
38 East First
New York 3, New York

Gentlemen:

To address a particular person in a business firm, this is an accepted form:

Mr. Stephen Lange
Graham, Sutton and Company
411 W. Monroe Street
Chicago 8, Illinois

Dear Mr. Lange:

If you wish to mention the person's title, or his position in the firm, put the designation immediately below his name, either indented slightly or flush with the margin as in this example:

Mr. Leonard T. Hosie
Personnel Manager
Allen, Swift and Company
4836 Commercial Street
Allentown, Ohio

Dear Sir: (or Dear Mr. Hosie:)

No punctuation is used at the end of the lines in the inside address. After the greeting, a colon is the standard form of punctuation. Other forms of greeting include:

Dear Sirs: (addressing the company as a unit)
Gentlemen:
Dear Madam:

The forms *Messrs.* and *Mesdames* are old-fashioned; use instead *Gentlemen* or *Ladies.*

8.4c Centering and spacing   Business letters are centered so that they present a balanced appearance on the page. Margins of about one and one-half inches are customary on both sides, and as much whitespace is left at the bottom of the page as at the top. A letter will not have an attractive appearance if it begins at the very top of the page or continues to the bottom edge. Using an extra page will prevent such crowding. If the letter is quite short, it is a good idea to double space it and use narrower margins than usual.

8.4d Close and signature   A conventional expression called the close is used at the end of the letter. *Yours truly* and *Sincerely yours* are the most common. The general tone of the letter will suggest whether an impersonal or a less formal close is more appropriate.

Impersonal	*Less formal*
Yours very truly,	Cordially yours,
Respectfully yours,	Cordially,
Yours truly,	Faithfully yours,
Very respectfully yours,	Sincerely,
Very truly yours,	

Only the first word of the close is capitalized. A comma customarily follows the phrase.

The signature is always written out in longhand below the close. For clarity, the writer usually types his name below his signature:

Sincerely yours,

Thomas R. Nelson

Thomas R. Nelson

In business letters a woman may indicate in parentheses whether she is *Mrs.* or *Miss* by any of these formulas:

(Mrs.) Lucille S. Stowe
(Miss) Lucille S. Stowe

Lucille S. Stowe
(Mrs. Ralph G. Stowe)

8.5 Letters of application   Among the more important—and possibly the most difficult—kinds of letters that you may have occasion to write are letters of application. When you apply by letter for a job, or perhaps for admission to a school, you are in effect trying to "sell yourself" through your writing. In such situations you may be torn between undue modesty and an understandable desire to present yourself in the most favorable light. The best thing to do is to express yourself simply and with sincerity, to give all the information asked for, and to put your letter in the most attractive form you can.

8.5a Form of an application letter   The form of most letters of application—the heading, spacing, close, and so on—follows that of typical business letters. You will of course want the appearance of your letter to create a favorable impression. Use good quality stationery and type the letter, unless legible handwriting is a requisite for the job. Use one side of the paper only and leave generous margins. To get the proper arrangement on the page, type an experimental draft of your letter.

Before you mail the letter, be particularly careful to check for mechanical errors. Your prospective employer will not be favorably impressed if you misspell his name or any common words.

8.5b Contents of the application letter Give all the information asked for (age, previous experience, education, salary expected), and any details that you believe might be useful to the person who reads your letter: why you want the job, what special qualifications you possess, and so on. Be careful, however, that you do not include irrelevant material. A letter that is brief and to the point will receive more favorable attention than one that is long-winded.

Notice in the sample letter on p. 103 how the writer says right at the beginning that he wants a job and tells what job he is applying for. The body of the letter then lists useful personal data, the writer's previous experience, and his references. In closing he suggests an interview or invites the employer to inquire further.

When you include the names of friends, employers, teachers, as references, always ask permission of these people before you use their names. Give their complete addresses in your letter, and indicate their correct titles (Professor, Dr., Mrs.)

Make certain also that you have given your complete address, both inside the letter and on the envelope. Include your phone number if you wish to be called for an interview.

If you are asked to include documents (such as a photograph, transcripts of academic records, or photostats), use an envelope or a folder large enough so that the documents won't be crushed. If you want the inclosures returned to you, include a self-addressed, stamped envelope.

It won't hurt to keep a carbon copy of your letter. If you don't get the job, you can study the letter and try to improve on it next time. If you do get the job, the letter may serve as a model for future applications.

8.5c Application forms Many business firms, particularly large ones, have printed application forms for the job applicant to fill out. A letter of application is sometimes included with these forms, but when the questionnaires are long and detailed, no letter is usually necessary.

Answers to the questions asked on these forms should be accurate, legible, and complete. Some forms can be filled in with one- or two-word answers, or by checking the proper blanks. But with others, you may be asked to make 25 to 50 word statements about your qualifications and background. These statements should be as clear and as compressed as you can make them; cut out any deadwood or irrelevancies, and avoid any statements that sound overly ambitious, apologetic, or ambiguous.

546 Rollins Avenue
Cincinnati 22, Ohio
June 5, 1953

Box 288
The Metropolitan Herald
Cincinnati 8, Ohio

Gentlemen:

I would like to apply for the position of part-time stock clerk listed in your advertisement in today's Herald.

I am nineteen years old, single, and in good health. Because of a knee injury I received in a high school football game two years ago, I have been deferred by the draft board.

At Emerson High School, from which I graduated in June 1952, I took courses in typing, shorthand, filing, and bookkeeping. I have just completed my first year at Midwestern College, where I am majoring in business administration.

During the last three summer vacations I have worked in the parts department of the Hackbarth Chevrolet Company, first as clerk and later as assistant to the stock control manager. I also worked three weeks last Christmas vacation in the shipping department of Kilworth's Department Store, in East Bloomington, Ohio.

The following persons have consented to furnish letters of reference:

Mr. Milton Hoehn, Principal, Emerson High School, Cincinnati 3

Mr. Gordon Arter, Stock Control Manager, Hackbarth Chevrolet Company, Cincinnati 8

Mrs. Bea Blair, Assistant Manager, Kilworth's Department Store, East Bloomington, Ohio

If my qualifications are satisfactory, I would appreciate an interview at your convenience. My telephone number is Fireside 6-8401.

Very truly yours,

Frank H. Remus

Frank H. Remus

References

Cooper, Charles W. and Edris B., *The Letter Writer, A Manual with Models for Your Personal Correspondence*, Stanford, Stanford University Press, 1954

Gaum, Carl G., and others, *Report Writing*, 3rd ed., New York, Prentice-Hall, 1950, Ch. 2, The Report in Letter Form

Post, Emily, *Etiquette*, New York, Funk and Wagnalls, 1945, Chs. 41, 43

Smart, Walter K., and L. W. McKelvey, *Business Letters,* 3rd ed., New York, Harper, 1950

Vanderbilt, Amy, *Complete Book of Etiquette,* New York, Doubleday, 1952, Chs. 44, 45

Exercises

1. Study the following letter and make detailed comment on its form and content. Point out specific instances of faulty or inconsistent spacing, indention, and punctuation. Indicate any wording that you consider unsatisfactory, and tell how you would revise it.

GOSS AND KIMBELL IRON FOUNDRY

Harold T. Ogden,　　　　　　　　　　　　Syracuse N.Y.
　2027 Wedgewood Drv.　　　　　　　　　8/18/53.
City.

Dear sir

Your remittance of the 15th inst. just received. This pays your account in full to date, as you suggested in your accompanying letter.

We would like to take this opportunity to thank you for the prompt manner in which you have taken care of this transaction. It's been a real pleasure, believe me, to handle an acct. like yours. We hope to do business with you in the near future and if we can be of any further service, please do not hesitate to let us know, either by dropping down to our Foundry or by calling us on the phone (Mutual 3516).

Hoping to hear from you again shortly, we beg to remain,

Yours,

Ted Davidson　　Credit Mangr.
　　Ted Davidson

P.S.: Now that you've established your credit, remember that you can take advantage of our time-payment plan. There's always a chance prices will go up, and it's a good idea to buy now at the present market prices. —T.D.

2. Collect three or four typical business letters—from magazines asking you to renew subscriptions, from civic or charitable organizations soliciting contributions, or from any business firm offering goods or services for sale. Be prepared to discuss these letters on the basis of the following questions:

a. Which one appeals most to the eye, and why?

b. Which letter or letters would you be most likely to read through from beginning to end? Which would you discard after a quick glance at the contents?

c. What words or phrases do you consider stereotyped or old fashioned (such as "May we have the pleasure of an early reply?" or "Thanking you in advance, we beg to remain . . .")?

d. Are any of the letters conspicuously wordy, that is, do they say too little in too many words? Are there any that seem to be labored in style, perhaps striving too obviously for novelty or freshness?

e. From your collection, select the letter you consider the most effective, both in appearance and content, and give the reasons for your choice.

3. Find an editorial in your college newspaper or in a local paper on a subject that interests you. After you have read the editorial carefully, prepare a letter of not more than 200 words explaining why you agree or disagree with the viewpoint expressed in the editorial.

4. Write a letter of from 150 to 200 words to the lost and found department of the railroad or bus terminal in your city, inquiring about some object you believe you left on the bus or train. Give all the information you think necessary: a description of the object, the number or other designation of the train or bus you traveled on, your time of arrival, and so on.

5. Write a letter to one of your teachers or to a former employer, asking permission to use his name as a reference for a job you are seeking.

6. On the basis of the kind of work you intend to follow when you finish college, compose the most effective answers you can to the following questions. Limit each answer to 25 to 40 words:

a. What are your reasons for wishing to follow this line of work?

b. What training have you had (in school or out) that would qualify you for this occupation?

c. What special qualifications or personality traits do you possess that you think would be useful in this work?

9 Writing paragraphs

No, paragraphs are not made by spacing or pausing. The spacing or pausing merely indicates where they are after they are made. . . . A paragraph is planned, therefore, before it is written. It is not yet a group of sentences; it is a group of ideas or facts in the writer's mind. It is going to be one of the little compositions which he will build up into his single whole composition. He does not yet know in what words he will express it; but he knows exactly what ground it will cover.—Charles Sears Baldwin

A paragraph indention may be considered a mark of punctuation indicating a unit of the subject larger than a sentence and smaller than the whole paper. The paragraph itself is actually a unit of thought. It includes the statements that the writer thinks together and wishes the reader to see together, and the paragraph break shows that a somewhat different part of the subject comes next.

9.1 Writing by paragraphs Try to write at least a complete paragraph at a time without pausing. The paragraph will more accurately reflect the flow of your thought if you have the material for each stage clearly in mind and get it down on paper without pausing for any appreciable time. If you stop for a few minutes before you have finished a paragraph, you are apt to begin thinking ahead to the next one, or perhaps to the end of the paper, or even about something else. When you do have to pause, try to pause between paragraphs or larger stages of the paper.

9.2   Working from an outline   If you have a good outline, paragraphing should be easy because the actual paragraphs will have a definite relation to its headings. For example, if you were writing a paper of about 600 words from the outline on the advantages of army life given in §6.1c, p. 70, the paragraphs might go like this:

I.   Living conditions
    1.   A. Disadvantages
            1. Discipline often annoying
            2. Frequent moves hard on soldier's family
            3. Social life restricted to a small circle
    2.   B. Advantages
            1. Opportunity to find the job one is best fitted for
            2. Annual leaves with pay
            3. Chance to travel, to see new places and meet new people
II.   Financial aspect of an army career
    3.   A. Disadvantages
            1. Pay not very high
            2. Expenses of frequent entertaining
    4.   B. Advantages
            1. Security
               a. Slow but steady promotion
               b. Permanent employment
               c. Good retirement benefits
    5.   2. Preparation for success in business or politics after retirement

The five paragraphs would average 120 words, but some would probably be longer than others, perhaps numbers 2 and 4. Topic II.B would make two because that is the main point of the paper and presumably you have a good deal of information about its subheads. There could be brief intro-ductory and concluding paragraphs, but in a short paper like this these are usually unnecessary. It would be better to lead directly into the first topic by some such remark as "Most men, especially those who have been in service, know the undesirable living conditions that a military career often in-volves," and to end the paper with II.B.2, which is the most extensive of your ideas and which will enable you to end the paper with a firm, positive concluding statement.

Paragraphs, then, follow the order of the outline heads and correspond to the heads, though not in a one-to-one relation. A subhead developed to its fullest extent may take a whole paragraph, or even more than one in a long paper, but might be only part of a paragraph in a short treatment of the same topic.

9.3 Developing ideas fully   Since you are trying to "tell someone something" quite definite, you will consider your readers: what they will be interested in, what they already know, what they should know (from your point of view)— what you must tell them so that they will understand and believe you. Give them credit for common sense and a fair amount of general information, but don't take too much for granted.

Some ideas need but a few statements to make the mean-ing clear; others may require from 100 to 200 words or more of explanation or illustration. The following paragraph, for example, is too short to convey adequately the ideas in the writer's mind:

> Man has been faced lately with many different ideas and systems of government. Each has tried to win the majority to its side, frequently if not by force, by unscrupulous propaganda. Each man thinks of him-self as being representative of the majority.

The paragraph could be improved by listing some specific examples after the second sentence (Russia? China? Argen-tina?), and by using a separate paragraph to explain the third sentence.

What underdeveloped paragraphs may lead to is shown in the following student narration of a trip:

> Two years ago I took my first trip to Alaska. On this particular voyage there were only forty-five passengers. I learned from the steward that the usual number of weekly passengers ranged from seventy-five to two hundred.
>
> The fruit basket in each cabin was filled daily with apples, oranges, and other kinds of fruit. Since meals were included in the price of the ticket, we could choose anything we wanted from the menu without worrying about the price.
>
> We arrived at our first port, Sitka, on a rainy day. We were told that the ship would be there for about four hours unloading cargo and that we could go ashore if we so desired. After taking a good look at the town, I decided that I would very much prefer to be on board ship.

These paragraphs are unsatisfactory because they raise questions which the writer fails to answer: Why were there so few passengers on this trip? (This should be explained in the first paragraph or else not mentioned.) What is the point of the second paragraph, which jumps so abruptly from the introductory statements? The abundance of food? How cheap it was? How much the writer enjoyed it? Some statement is needed at the beginning of this paragraph to link it with the preceding one, and to express the main idea ("Because there were so few passengers, we were offered more food than we could eat...."). The third paragraph leaves the reader wondering what Sitka looked like, what unpleasant things the writer saw that made him prefer to stay on his ship. Three or four explanatory sentences would have cleared up this point and would have made the paragraph more interesting reading.

Put your material down fully in the first writing. If there is too much or if something gets in that doesn't belong, it is easily crossed out. It is usually easier to cut out sentences than to open up a paragraph to add the specific details it needs.

9.4 Using both details and general statements The bits of thought that we have in mind and that we build our paragraphs out of differ in various ways, but especially in their specificness, in their closeness to what can be seen, heard, definitely sensed. For convenience we will divide them into two sorts of statements:

1. *Details,* particular observations and facts (He is eleven years old; This lily is a Henryi; In two years the town's population increased by 1,460), and summaries of facts (All day the planes had been running late).

2. *General statements,* ranging from attitudes and opinions (This is the better plan; You are wrong) to large generalizations (Everyone needs some form of artistic expression; There is no such thing as a universal truth).

By taking care, we can be pretty sure of the accuracy of our details; opinions obviously vary and are soundest when they are kept closest to the facts to which they apply, and generalizations are the most complex and the hardest to be sure about. A general statement usually needs to be supported by details, and in fact most writing is made up of details with occasional general statements that hold them together and show their meaning. (Compare §21.2, Specific and general words, p. 257.)

The details and the general statements in the following paragraph are labeled in the margin:

It should be clear that scientific polling studies justify prediction, not	General statement
forecasts. That is, they do not say that 61.2 per cent of the vote next	Specific detail
week will be for Smith; they say that *under specified conditions* the Smith vote will be 61.2 per cent.	Detail
It is assumed that future conditions will probably remain the same as conditions when the sample groups were interviewed, but it is also assumed that a last-minute development may	Summary of details
shift the election. A sudden snow storm may keep farmers away from	Detail
the polls. This may cut down the Smith vote if he is more popular	Detail

among farmers than among city dwellers. Actually an elaborate set of predictions might be made in every specific election: "If the weather is clear, Smith will probably poll 61.2 per cent of the vote; if the weather is very bad he will probably get 10 per cent less." "If the President endorses Smith in the last week of the campaign, the vote among middle class women will probably increase 5 per cent as shown by the popularity of the President with these women." Forecasts say flatly that such an event *will* occur in the future.—Harold D. Lasswell, "Effects of Communication," in Bruce L. Smith and others, *Propaganda, Communication, and Public Opinion,* pp. 106-107

General statement

Detail

Detail

General statement

Sometimes conscientious students feel that developing an idea fully, building out a statement with details, is "just padding." There are two chief reasons why a general statement by itself is insufficient: First, it does not really represent the consecutiveness or fullness of the writer's thought and often gives such a small sample that he does not seem to know his subject or at least does not seem to be thinking about it at the time of writing. Second, it cannot convey to a reader, who may know almost nothing about the matter, enough to let him see the subject as the writer sees it. To make an impression on the reader, it is necessary to control his mind for a brief time; it is necessary not just to mention the subject but to present it, develop it, lead him to think about it and to see it as the writer sees it.

Actually developing paragraphs by full use of details also removes a frequent worry of student writers, "getting the required length." Most writing is planned for a fairly definite length so that specified length for compositions is natural. "About 600 words" means that the student is to take a subject and select from his thinking about it what can be conveyed in about that number of words. The bulk of the actual space in most papers should be taken up with specific details, with occasional general statements to point up their meaning. A final test question for a paper is "Have I put in enough of what I know and believe about this subject to lead a reader to see it as I do?"

9.5 Continuity of statements in a paragraph A paragraph represents a chain of thought, statements that are associated in your mind and that you want the reader to see in the same relationship. In the following paragraph the relationships between successive statements are shown in the margin:

Have you got termites? In your house, I mean. It is the newest and most fashionable house disease. It	Three sentences presenting the subject
used to be called "ants" and no one was interested. Also sinus used to	Contrast
be called catarrh. But "sinus" made	Comparison
the old disease under another name	Comparison continued
popular. Last summer in the fashionable country places the talk was all	Repetition of third sentence
of termites. How so and so suddenly stepped on her floor and went right	Example of the "talk"
through. And, my dear, they had to	Example continued
call an exterminator and it cost hundreds and hundreds of dollars to get rid of the things; the whole house was almost torn apart and they had to treat the floors with	
the most awful smelling stuff! If you	Repetition of "most fashionable"
hadn't termites, you just weren't in Society.—Roy Chapman Andrews, *This Amazing Planet*, p. 101	

It is not so important to be able to name the relationships as it is to make sure that they will be clear to your reader. He may need more guidance than you do, because you are already familiar with the chain of thought.

The commonest ways of showing the continuity between

the statements are these: repetition of an important word from a previous sentence; a synonym, a different word of much the same meaning as one already used; a pronoun referring to a word or idea in the preceding sentence; and a connecting word, an adverb or a conjunction that points out the thought relationship. These signs of the relationship between the statements are labeled in brackets in the following paragraph:

An instructive example of the failure of a people to take advantage of available materials is afforded by the Onas of South America. In this respect [synonym for: failure to take advantage of available materials] they [pronoun: the Onas] may be contrasted with the Eskimos. Here [adverb: connecting with preceding two sentences] are two peoples [synonym: the Onas and the Eskimos] living in cold environments, the one to the north, the other to the south. The Eskimos [repetition] have made a most satisfactory adjustment to their environment. They [pronoun: the Eskimos] have good houses and a complete wardrobe. Indeed [adverb: connects and emphasizes], the latter [pronoun: a complete wardrobe] surpasses that of most civilized peoples of the past. The Onas [repetition] on the other hand [connective: shows contrast with preceding statements], go practically naked, and lacking adequate shelter, seek unsuccessfully to keep warm before an open fire. Yet [connective: contrast] the Onas [repetition] hunt the guanaco, the skin of which is suitable for clothing. In trying to account for the backwardness of these people [synonym: the Onas], then [connective: result], geographic conditions are not to be emphasized.— William F. Ogburn and Meyer F. Nimkoff, *Sociology,* p. 96

The thought of the paragraph is a unit, and each statement follows the other clearly. You couldn't start to read it after the first sentence without realizing that something had gone before. (The sentence "The Eskimos have made a most satisfactory adjustment to their environment" could start a paragraph, but if it did, the paragraph would be about Eskimos, not about Onas.)

We are inclined to overlook the absence of guides to the reader in our own writing, but we notice immediately when other writers forget to use them. Consider how the following unconnected paragraph is improved by showing the relationship between the statements:

Unconnected version

While working in a five and ten cent store last summer, I learned several things that will help me in the future. I learned to be tolerant toward other people. Most people don't realize all that a clerk has to do while waiting on her customers. I didn't realize this when I started clerking. When I am waited upon by some other clerk, I am not so impatient, for I know what a clerk goes through. It works the other way, I found out also. A clerk learns to be considerate of her customers and as helpful as possible.

Relationships shown

While working in a five and ten cent store last summer, I learned several things that will help me in the future. *First of all,* I learned to be more tolerant toward other people. Most people don't realize all that a clerk has to do while waiting on her customers. *At least* I didn't when I started clerking. *But now* when I am waited on by some other clerk, I am not so impatient, for I know what a clerk goes through. *Of course* it works the other way, too. A clerk learns to be considerate of her customers and as helpful as possible.

9.6 Paragraph length The length of paragraphs is determined primarily by the kind of ideas you are discussing and the way you are developing them. The more complex the subject, the longer the paragraphs are likely to be. If you are writing a factual account of the reasons why more women attend college today than fifty years ago, your paragraphs might run from 65 to 200 words (or from seven to twenty lines in typewritten copy), and perhaps average 100 words (ten to twelve typed lines). But in an informal discussion of your own reasons for attending college, the paragraphs might vary from 35 to 150 words, and average about 75 words.

9.6a Paragraphs in published material To get an idea of the way your paragraphs look, compare the length of those you have written with paragraphs in books and magazines.

The following table shows the lengths of consecutive paragraphs from various kinds of published material. As you examine this table, keep in mind that a handwritten page of theme-paper size seldom contains over 175 words, and that a typed page averages from 240 to 290 words.

Number of words of the paragraphs in order	Range in number of words:		
	Longest	Shortest	Average
A book for children (*Heidi* by Johanna Spyri) 22, 26, 36, 40, 51, 14, 6	51	6	28
An article in the *Ladies' Home Journal* 80, 96, 52, 128, 34, 39	128	34	71
An article in *Time* 103, 24, 49, 138, 76, 115, 108	138	24	88
An article in *The Atlantic Monthly* 66, 96, 153, 65, 85, 101, 83, 112, 100	153	65	96
A college textbook (*Sociology* by Ogburn and Nimkoff) 119, 133, 139, 217, 84, 162, 103, 118	217	84	134

9.6b Length of student paragraphs   In the table below are listed the lengths of paragraphs in typical papers written by college freshmen at different periods in a composition course. (These figures are intended as bases for comparison, not as standards.)

Total number of words in paper		Number of paragraphs	Number of words in paragraphs		
			Longest	Shortest	Average
Papers written in a 45-minute class period at the beginning of the course:					
Student A	255	5	75	38	51
Student B	385	6	115	28	64
Student C	302	4	123	51	75
Papers written outside of class in the middle of the first quarter:					
Student A	539	8	96	30	67
Student B	671	7	153	53	96
Student C	525	5	201	54	105
Research papers written at the end of the second quarter of freshman composition:					
Student A	1862	22	187	64	85
Student B	1529	15	248	37	102
Student C	1468	13	220	42	113

Notice that though the three students do not write paragraphs of the same length, each has somewhat lengthened his paragraphs while taking the composition course and brought them closer in length to those in published books.

9.6c Testing the length of your paragraphs This discussion of length is to help you visualize your paragraphs in comparison with those of other writers. The questions to ask yourself are not "Do they contain enough words?" but rather "Are they adequately developed?" and "Should any one of the paragraphs be written as two paragraphs, for clarity or for emphasis?" or "Are two conspicuously short paragraphs so closely related that they should be combined?"

Examine closely any of your pages that contain more than two paragraphs or that have only one, to see whether you have put too little or too much into each unit. You will soon know—if you do not already—whether you tend to write paragraphs that are too short or too long, or whether they fall in the typical range of paragraph length.

References

Fries, C. C., *The Structure of English*, New York, Harcourt, Brace, 1952, pp. 287-290

Johnson, Wendell, *People in Quandaries*, New York, Prentice-Hall, 1946, especially Chs. 11 and 12

Lewis, E. H., *The History of the English Paragraph*, Chicago, University of Chicago Press, 1894

Read, Herbert, *English Prose Style*, rev. ed., New York, Pantheon Books, 1952, Ch. 5

Summey, Ch. 2

Thomas, Joseph M., Frederick A. Manchester, and Franklin W. Scott, *Composition for College Students*, 5th ed., New York, Macmillan, 1948, Ch. 3

Williams, George G., *Creative Writing*, New York, Harper, 1935, Ch. 9

Exercises

1. Examine the following opening of a paper to see how effective you think it is. Rewrite it as a single paragraph, noticing what changes you make to build the ideas together and in what respects the new version is better.

After working for three years for the Union Pacific, I am convinced that there are many advantages to this work. I shall point out what seem to me to be the chief advantages.

First, there is little of the cut-throat competition for jobs in railroading that there is in most other work.

Second, you have security through seniority rights and the Railroad Retirement Act.

Third, the employee who has performed his work properly is left pretty much on his own, with a minimum of supervision from his superiors.

Next, the people with whom you work are generally agreeable and cooperative.

Lastly, you have ample opportunity to learn about freight and passenger rate structures and thus qualify for a better position.

2. The following passage from a magazine article was written in five paragraphs. After reading it through, indicate by number which sentences you believe should begin new paragraphs. Be prepared to give reasons for the divisions you have made.

(1) This little essay could as easily be entitled "Frankly Partisan" for it concerns juvenile literature and on that subject I hold strong if unsupported opinions. (2) Under stress of Christmas they grow firmer still. (3) This is the time of year when the flood of children's books rises highest, engulfing the book review sections of Sunday newspapers, washing over the bookshop counters so that even the historical novels are dampened down, lapping at the solid embankments of the comics. (4) Like the ubiquitous wreath, like the needle-shedding tree, this interest in stories for children is a symbol of the season. (5) And like the tree and the holly spray, the good stories will be sentimental. (6)

The good ones have always been sentimental. (7) I say this with full knowledge that it is a kind of heresy frowned on by child psychologists, progressive educators, many a librarian. (8) It was only last spring that I realized how the dogma of realism had closed in around our young. (9) Somewhat to my surprise, I found myself one member of a jury gathered to hand out awards to juveniles published daringly in the spring instead of the customary fall. (10) My fellow judges and I had agreed on two books quite readily but on the third there was discussion which terminated abruptly when a strong-minded jurist said flatly, "I will not vote for it. (11) It's sentimental." (12) She gave no other reason for its damnation. (13) It was an engaging book—well written, peopled amusingly with sprightly characters, and it concerned itself with flesh and blood people instead of the more usual elephants or rabbits or chipmunks. (14) Simply, it was sentimental. (15) And I found myself marshalling arguments all the way home on the commuting train that evening—arguments I had been too flabbergasted to invent at the time of trial. (16) What on earth is wrong with sentiment? I asked myself. (17) "How now, Madam," I kept saying to the lady in my imagination, "Hoity-toity and pray tell! (18) On what meat must these, our children feed, that they should grow so dry?"—Phyllis McGinley, "Frankly Sentimental," *Harper's Magazine,* December 1950, p. 112. Reprinted by permission of *Harper's Magazine.*

3. Study the paragraphs in one of your recent papers. About how many words do you get on a typical page of manuscript? How long are the longest and the shortest paragraphs and what do they average? Compare these figures with those in §9.6b.

Consider your paragraphs in the light of points made in this section. How do they correspond with your outline? Do you now think your outline might be revised to advantage? Are your paragraphs developed with enough details to make the points you wished to? Is the relation between all the statements clear?

4. Study the following paragraphs for:
   a. Their use of details and general statements (§9.4)
   b. The signs of continuity between sentences (§9.5)

1) Two cats are actually less care than one, as they are more self-sufficient; they can be left alone for longer periods without fear of their being lonely. As a rule they use the same bed, the same sanitary tray, and the same scratching post. The cost of feeding two is very little more, but it is necessary to take the precaution of feeding them separately (if you have no cage, they can be fed in separate rooms). Obviously, two cats should not be able to steal each other's food, nor should they eat too fast in order to get the other's food or to prevent their own from being taken. It is no trouble to feed cats separately, as each cat will go to his regular place of eating as the dishes are put down.—Doris Bryant, *The Care and Handling of Cats*, p. 13

2) In one of her bad periods, "Orphan Annie," whose ups and downs used to be of the most innocuous character, was sent to live with a villainous old woman who was a kind of Murder Incorporated. Annie found out about the murders, hid the bloody coat, knew the woman was lying in wait for her, and finally had to run for her life, the woman pursuing her with a hatchet. Although the wretch fell down a well, her punishment was decidedly inadequate, since Annie was brought to trial for having pushed her into the well. The ensuing trial was such a broad lampoon on our courts that lawyers and judges were moved to protest. Although crime did not prevail in this series, neither did virtue. Annie led a much rougher life than the villainous old woman and her vicious son. If children are to be introduced to the crime world as soon as they can follow pictures (which the complacent makers of the comics seem to regard as desirable), then at least the comics should demonstrate that crime really does not pay, and that villains are adequately punished.—May Hill Arbuthnot, *Children and Books*, p. 543

3) Furthermore, the automobile weakened the roots which held the family to one spot. Always a mobile people by comparison with the peoples of Europe, now Americans followed the economic tides more readily than ever before, moving by automobile—and before long by trailer—wherever there might be a call for con-

struction workers, or fruit pickers, or airplane mechanics. Sober intellectuals were wont to deplore the growing American restlessness and to praise the man who was rooted to the land where he and his forefathers had been born and bred; but the automobile suited the American genius. For that genius was not static but venturesome; Americans felt that a rolling stone gathers experience, adventure, sophistication, and—with luck—new and possibly fruitful opportunities.—Frederick Lewis Allen, *The Big Change*, p. 152

4) The young dislike their elders for having fixed minds. But they dislike them even more for being insincere. They themselves are simple, single-minded, straightforward, almost painfully naive. A hypocritical boy or girl is rare, and is always a monster or a spiritual cripple. They know grownups are clever, they know grownups hold the power. What they cannot bear is that grownups should also be deceitful. Thousands of boys have admired and imitated bandits and gunmen because they felt these were at least brave and resolute characters, who had simply chosen to be spades instead of diamonds; but few boys have ever admired a forger or a poisoner. So they will tolerate a parent or a teacher who is energetic and violent, and sometimes even learn a good deal from him; but they loathe and despise a hypocrite. Gilbert Highet, *The Art of Teaching*, p. 21. Reprinted by permission of Alfred A. Knopf, Inc. and Methuen & Co., Ltd., British publishers.

10 Kinds of paragraphs

Remove a good sentence from a good paragraph and you leave behind, not a gap with clean-cut edges, but an ugly rent with broken threads at both ends.—P. B. Ballard

Paragraphs may be classified according to their purpose: to inform and explain—*expository;* to tell the story of an event—*narrative;* to give a picture—*descriptive.* Whole compositions can be classified in this way also, but in this section we are talking about the individual paragraphs, which may be of different kinds within the same paper. For instance, a paper that is dominantly narrative may have some paragraphs that are descriptive or expository in it, and one that is in general expository may have some paragraphs that are descriptive or narrative.

10.1 Expository paragraphs The purpose of exposition is to enlighten a reader, to carry his knowledge of something beyond its present point, to make him understand a situation, to show him how something is made, to help him understand an idea or a belief. It ranges from the explanation of small personal matters to erudite scientific treatises. The bulk of writing is expository, in magazine articles and books giving information and discussing opinions and general ideas. In fact, exposition can be defined negatively as writing that does not give a picture or a narrative of events. In college, practically all reading except in literature courses and all writing except in advanced composition courses in writing fiction is expository. Consequently increasing your skill in expository writing is the chief aim of beginning composition courses, and practice in expository writing is of great use to you for all college work.

An expository paragraph, then, is a unit of facts (details) and ideas (general statements) to inform, explain, convince a reader. Here, for example, is the way a doctor begins an explanation of coronary thrombosis, a term most of his readers would not be familiar with:

The diagnosis of "heart disease" is feared by all of us, and not without reason. As long as the heart beats there is hope, but we all realize that if the heart stops beating we will die.

The ability of the heart to function depends primarily on the state of the heart muscle or myocardium, as it is technically known. Our existence, therefore, depends largely on the state of the blood vessels that bring nourishment to the myocardium—the coronary arteries. The heart can, of course, be damaged by other disease processes. For instance, the heart may fail because it is irreparably damaged by an infection as in rheumatic heart disease, or by poisons, or toxins, as in diphtheria.—William A. R. Thomson, M. D., "Coronary Thrombosis," *Today's Health,* September 1952, p. 30

This opens by making contact with the reader's common knowledge and concern, and then begins the actual exposition, explaining the meaning of the technical word *myocardium* and rapidly adding other facts, which with those that follow will finally enlighten the reader on coronary thrombosis.

10.1a General qualities of expository paragraphs The general qualities that are desirable in expository paragraphs are those that have been presented in §9:

1. Full development (§9.3), that is, complete enough to lead the reader to see the point you are making

2. The use of both details and general statements (§9.4) to make your point convincing and interesting

3. A clear relationship between the statements (§9.5) so that the reader will grasp your point easily

Another example will re-emphasize these points. The following two paragraphs are from a discussion of the impression of immigrants that students might get from their textbooks. The first begins with a general statement and develops it by other general statements and summarized details. The second begins with a series of details that lead to general statements at the end.

Many texts give the impression that the "old" immigrants were always enthusiastically welcomed and well treated. This, of course, is untrue. Struggles on the parts of immigrants for place, prestige, and acceptance are as old as the Indian's exclamation, "Ugh! Foreigner!" when he saw the Pilgrims. Opposition to immigrants lay behind the Alien and Sedition Act of 1798 and the Know-Nothing movement of the 1850's. To look, speak, or behave like a foreigner has always been a handicap in America. It has been as if one's Americanism were proved by condemning someone with different ways of living.

Irish-Americans were at one time victims of prejudice and persecution at the hands of the older English groups. Later, however, many of the Irish-Americans came to look down on the Scandinavian-Americans. Many of the Scandinavian-Americans, in turn, looked down on Poles and Italians, and many of them, in turn, snubbed Spanish-speaking Americans. The groups that came earliest have tended to rise highest in the social scale despite the fact that they were themselves scorned when they first arrived. Only if he understands the changes that are constantly taking place in group prestige and position, can the student be expected to arrive at an understanding of the problems of the "new" immigrants—M. S. Stewart, "Prejudice in Textbooks," Public Affairs Pamphlet No. 160, pp. 11-12. Reprinted by permission of the Public Affairs Committee.

10.1b Topic sentences   Both the clearness and completeness of an expository paragraph will often be helped by stating its main idea in what is called a topic sentence: a key sentence to which the other statements in the paragraph are related. It may be the first sentence, as in this paragraph:

> *The first inducement to good composition is to allow students to write on things in which they are interested.* This frequently means romance and, oddly enough, often means religion. But there is no reason to act as if romance and religion are taboo. The first, at least, is the topic most often discussed in bull sessions, and the instructor might as well get the benefit of the enthusiasm thus engendered. Sports and fashions are other favorite subjects. Although I have a positive distaste for sports in any form, I would rather read a good paper on basketball than an anemic or laborious one on "The Difficulties of Setting a Good Example," "How to Press a Suit," or "The Case for Vertical Unions." These are three of the charming topics to be found in a text widely used this year. Now I ask you, could *you* lose yourself in a discussion of "The Case for Vertical Unions"? The student who has written on football or flying or designing clothes or why he believes in early marriages is more willing to spend time on that onerous task, the correction and even rewriting of his faulty paper, than one who has sweated over a topic about which he knows nothing and the importance of which he cannot see.—Ruth Davies, "A Defense of Freshmen," *College English*, May 1951, p. 443. Reprinted by permission of *College English.*

Another method is to work toward the topic sentence, using it as a summary or a conclusion for the details in the paragraph:

> These students average eighteen years of age, come from the middle-class range of families, and most of them live in towns under 10,000. Data from the American Council of Education Psychological Examina-

tion and the English and Reading tests show that these students are about average in academic aptitude, when compared to students of today from the smaller liberal-arts colleges. Like most American adolescents, these students, when free from the compulsions of classroom assignments, read little. Their selection of newspapers is confined to the local or nearby metropolitan newspapers. The magazines which they read on national or world affairs are generally limited to *Life, Reader's Digest, Time,* and the like. In their summer vacation reading, they average little more than one book a student. *They are, then, fairly typical of college freshmen.*—Leo J. Alilunas, "Personal Setting as an Influence in the Study of the Attitudes of College Freshmen Toward Capitalism," *School and Society,* April 16, 1949, 69:284

The purpose of a topic sentence is twofold: (1) to help the writer focus his ideas on one central thought so that every statement in that paragraph is directly related to that thought, and (2) to make it easier for the reader to see what the paragraph is about, to show him, by a specific statement, what the other statements in the paragraph add up to.

10.2 Narrative paragraphs In narrative paragraphs events are written down in the order in which they occurred:

On June 30, 1863, some of Lee's units began withdrawing from their positions along the Rappahannock to move west to Culpepper. Troop movements continued for several days until the lines facing the Union Army across the river were drawn very thin. On July ninth, Confederate plans were suddenly upset when Federal cavalry swiftly crossed the river and drove toward Brandy Station, where they caught Stuart by surprise and gave his proud horsemen some bad moments. Lee was forced to change his plans for moving part of his troops east of the mountains and to concentrate on the Shenandoah Valley.—Philip Van Doren Stern, "Gettysburg," *Holiday,* June 1952, p. 63

10.2a Narrative movement When you are relating an experience, describing an incident, or summarizing the plot of a story or play, keep the action moving in one direction, and avoid unnecessary interruptions. Sentences 4 and 5 in the following paragraph halt the narrative:

(1) It was the seventh of August, 1952. (2) My friend and I were hitchhiking from a small town in the northern part of the state. (3) Unlike most adventurers I did not notice the sky nor did I feel the

impending danger. (4) I guess I don't make a very good hero. (5) Now I must get back to my story. (6) After waiting by the side of the road for some time, we were picked up by two men in an old Chevvie.

The events following this paragraph should show whether or not the writer is "a very good hero." This unnecessary remark not only slows down the story, but also suggests the outcome of the incident before it is unfolded.

The connection between statements in a narrative paragraph is usually simple: time controls. One detail appears after another as they happened in time or as they are imagined to have happened. The verbs usually carry this movement, and the continuity is made stronger by the continuation of the same grammatical subject from one sentence to another. The time may be emphasized and made more obvious by adverbs—*then, after this, before, soon, when, in a few days* —or by adverbial phrases or clauses: *When he got to the corner. . ., After the last dance. . . .*

Italicizing the verb forms and adverbs of time in this opening paragraph of a short story shows how large a part action and time play in narrative:

Elizabeth Montgomery *woke up in the morning wondering* whether or not she *was engaged.* She *had been out* with Bob McEwen *the night before* and *at the end* there *had been* some spontaneous and apparently serious love-making. That is, she *knew* she *must have felt* pretty serious about it because *this morning* she *couldn't remember* where she *had put* her gloves. And *now* he *had left* for Chicago *for a few days* and he *had promised to write.*—Sally Benson, *People Are Fascinating,* p. 27

10.2b Consistent tenses   Keep the tense of verbs consistent in narrative paragraphs. If you start with one tense—the past or the present—don't shift without reason to another. This paragraph illustrates unnecessary and confusing tense shifts:

As I *hop* [present tense] on the city transit that will take me to the University, I notice that as always the bus is filled past capacity. As I *turned* [past] around, I saw a blind man sitting directly behind me with a dog lying at his feet. I *watch* [present] the dog, sitting there perfectly still, looking through the glass doors. Suddenly the dog *got up* [past], nudged his master, who pulled the cord above his head and with no difficulty got off the bus and proceeded up the street. I *wondered* [past] how a dog could be trained to know when to get off the bus, when to cross the street, and when to wait for a signal. Dogs seem to have more sense than some humans.

Either the present tense should have been kept throughout or the present tenses changed to past.

In most narrative writing, the past tense is the customary form, but the present (or "historical present") is sometimes used to create a sense of events actually happening, as in this paragraph:

Our ship is hooting for all she's worth. An important last-minuter comes surging up. The rope hawsers are being wound clankily in. Seagulls—there are never very many in the Mediterranean—seagulls whirl like a few flakes of snow in the upper chill air. Clouds spin. And without knowing it we are evaporating away from the shore, from our mooring, between the great *City of Trieste* and another big black steamer that lies like a wall. . . .—D. H. Lawrence, *Sea and Sardinia,* p. 41

For most narratives, the past tense is the easier to use, but whichever tense you begin with, stick to it throughout.

10.2c **Adequate details** Include enough details to make the narrative interesting and understandable. A remark may seem perfectly clear to the writer and yet be confusing to someone less familiar with the subject. Avoid any statement that might leave the reader wondering "What?" or "Why?" or "When?" or "Who?"

In this paragraph the writer fails to tell *why* the arrival of the old couple was "quite interesting":

Just about two years ago a family moved into the house next door to us, a family consisting of just two middle-aged women. They had no servants in their employ and thus did all the housework by themselves. Both of these women lived quite happily together and then one day late in summer an old couple, a man and his wife, came along and moved in with them. *The cause of the arrival of this old couple is quite interesting.* The man was about seventy years of age, while the woman was just under sixty-five, and after the arrival of this old couple, all the work was shifted to their shoulders while the two women who owned the house lived a life of comparative ease. It turned out that one woman and the man's wife were sisters.

This does not mean that narrative paragraphs should be loaded down with minute and unimportant details. You can make your point and still keep the action moving by selecting two or three lively incidents, as in this example:

> Grandmother didn't need reasons for fussing at Grandpa. She told everyone that he wouldn't chop wood or carry water for her. If he did bring wood to her, she would throw it out the window, stick by stick, not caring where it landed. If he brought her water, carrying it from the spring, several hundred feet away, she would pour it out—over him, if possible. Then she would take the empty pail and her cane, and trudge painfully down the long slope to the spring and back again, though it might take her half the morning, the time depending upon her mood and strength. "If I want fresh water, I have to carry it myself, because George is walkin' to Marionville or sittin' on his behind somewhere," she would say to anyone she chanced to see. "And if I want wood, I have to get my boy Jake to come over and chop it for me."—Bertie Johnson, "The Never-Ending Time," *The New Yorker*, October 4, 1952, pp. 86-87

10.2d Direct action. When you are reporting an action, try to focus attention directly on what went on. In this passage the reader's attention becomes fixed less upon the action that is being unfolded than upon the person who is telling the incident:

> I was riding with a friend late one night, returning from a long weekend trip. I was extremely tired, and I am sure he was too, and as a result we weren't very observant about traffic lights. I did notice in the distance one very red blinker light, though. I also saw a car directly in front of ours, like a slow moving ship in a submarine's sights. I knew immediately that we were going too fast to stop, so my natural reaction was to brace myself for a crash. It seemed to me that I could hear the tires squealing for minutes before anything happened. I was surprised to find during those actually few short seconds that I was seeing a variety of vivid colors that I hadn't even noticed before. I was aware of the yellow dividing strip of the highway, and still off in the distance, the brilliant red flashes of the traffic signal. There were also the browns and grays and whites of the surrounding buildings, that I hadn't seen a few moments before, but now were things of sharp beauty.

This narrative could be tightened up, and the *I*'s made less conspicuous, by revising some of the sentences:

Late one night I was riding with a friend. We were both extremely tired after a long weekend trip, and not very watchful of the traffic lights. But I was dimly aware of one very red blinker light in the distance. Suddenly in front of us a car loomed up, like a slow moving ship seen through a submarine's sights. We were going too fast to stop, and instinctively I braced myself for the crash. Our tires squealed for what seemed minutes. Actually only a second or two passed, but in that brief instant, all the color of the scene jumped into view—the bright yellow dividing strip of the highway, the brilliant red flashes of the traffic light, the browns, grays, and whites of the nearby buildings. For one sharp moment everything took on a strange and fearful beauty.

Instead of talking about what went on, show the action itself. A reader will realize your experience more clearly if you concentrate on the events as they happened instead of on your feelings about them.

Paragraphing conversation, often a part of narrative, is discussed in §37.1, Quotation marks to inclose conversation, p. 420.

10.3 Descriptive paragraphs In descriptive writing, selected details are used to give the reader a picture of a place, a person, or a scene that the writer has himself experienced or imagined:

He had that most miserable of Navy watches, the twenty-four-hour stretch as duty officer on a cold ship in drydock. The *Caine* was a corpse of iron. Heat, light, power were gone. Boilers and main engines lay disemboweled. The fuel oil was all pumped out, and the purr of the ventilators, the vessel's breathing noise, was stilled. A thousand rattles, bangs, screeches, scrapes, and grinding shocks replaced it. Yard workmen were executing yet another rejuvenation by plastic surgery on the scarred old ship. The foggy San Francisco air drifted stagnantly through the passage ways, rancid with the smell of mildew, and the staterooms and crew's quarters were a chaos of scattered books and magazines and dirty linen.—Herman Wouk, *The Caine Mutiny*, p. 197

Good descriptive writing requires an eye for significant details and a knack for phrasing sensations of sight, smell, sound, and so on. No two persons look at a scene in exactly the same manner. What makes one writer's description more vivid than another's is the kind of details he selects and the way he arranges them for the reader.

10.3a Focusing details The details of a descriptive paragraph should give your reader a clear, unified impression. Descriptive writing is more than enumeration. You need to choose the most effective details and arrange them so that the more important ones stand out. The following paragraph illustrates a lack of selection and focus. Too much attention is given to minor details, and as a result no single impression emerges:

> We entered the Roundup Room through a curtained entrance just past the check room on a right turn. The Roundup Room was a long ell-shaped affair with the end of the ell angling off to the left. It was about 200 feet long and probably forty-five to fifty feet in width. Along the wall on the left ran a long bar. Behind the bar five bartenders were busily filling orders and giving them to a dozen or so waitresses who were just as rushed. Above the bar mirror on the wall were paintings of western scenes and cartoons, like those I described on the outside of the building. Down the aisle in front of us there seemed to be a bee-hive of activity, with couples going and coming from the small dance floor. I say "small" because it couldn't have been more than twenty-five feet square. On our right were small tables, all filled with customers, and on the right wall, farther down, were a number of small booths. We threaded our way through the smoky haze to an empty table.

If the writer intended to emphasize the overcrowding and confusion in this room, he should have concentrated on those features, and omitted or briefly summarized such unnecessary details as the shape and dimensions of the room, the paintings above the mirror, and so on.

Descriptive writing does not have to be drawn out and minutely detailed. A few well-selected details give a sharper picture than a large number of ill-assorted ones:

> The next morning Peter arose early and made his way directly to the Veterans Administration office, where he had explained his problem to the Vocational Counselor. The office was enormous. It was a nearly bare loft in which several dozen young men milled about, smoking, swearing, arguing, or merely reading the morning papers listlessly and

sleepily, as though they were still resentful at their mothers for having routed them out of bed at such an hour. The floor was littered with hundreds of ground-out cigarette butts, and the walls were placarded every few feet with large red and white NO SMOKING signs.— Harvey Swados, "The Dancer," *New World Writing 1952*, p. 235

If you are writing a character sketch, remember that what a person does or says may be more revealing than his physical appearance. This brief paragraph tells the reader more about what kind of person Mrs. Matson is than would a good many lines of purely personal detail:

A blind Negress, a tray of pencils hung about her neck, a cane monotonously tapping the pavement before her, came down the street. Mrs. Matson swerved sharply to the curb to avoid her, wasting a withering glance upon her. It was Mrs. Matson's immediate opinion that the woman could see as well as she could. She never gave to the poor on the streets, and was distressed if she saw others do so. She frequently remarked that these beggars all had big bank accounts.— Dorothy Parker, "Little Curtis," *Laments for the Living*, p. 128

Before you begin any kind of description, get clearly in mind the main impression you want to achieve, then arrange your material so that all the statements contribute to this impression.

10.3b Vague description If in describing a person you write "I first noticed this lady because she was wearing a funny hat," your description won't mean much to the reader because there are many kinds of funny hats. State in specific terms what the hat looked like: perhaps it was a black velvet beret covered with sea shells or perhaps it was a miniature merry-go-round.

Notice how lifeless the description is in this paraphrase, from which all the specific expressions have been removed:

After Lincoln became a lawyer, he started to pay more attention to his appearance. But even though he wore his hair in the accepted fashion of the time, he still wasn't well-dressed. As a result, he acquired the reputation of being one of the most careless dressers in town, along with another local man, who was a judge, and who was equally careless about the way he looked.

By way of contrast, compare the description as it was actually written:

> And though Lincoln had begun wearing broadcloth and white shirts with a white collar and black silk cravat, and suggestions of sideburns coming down three-fourths the length of his ears, he was still known as one of the carelessly dressed men of Springfield, along with Stephen Logan, who wore unbleached cotton shirts and had sat two years as a circuit court judge wearing an unbleached cotton shirt with no cravat or stock.—Carl Sandburg, *Abraham Lincoln: The Prairie Years*, 1:302-303

Being specific in descriptive writing doesn't mean that you should overload your sentences with adjectives and adverbs. While such words are used to "describe" or qualify other words, too many of them can be disastrous to any piece of descriptive writing. To refer to the Grand Canyon as "*absolutely* the *most marvelous* sight I have *ever* seen in my *entire* life" may give the reader some hint about your emotions, but it won't tell him much about the Canyon or help him re-create your feelings for himself.

Good descriptive writing demands restraint and discrimination. It also takes practice to get the exact effect that you want. One way to get additional practice is to analyze, in magazine articles and in books, examples of descriptive writing that appeal to you, to see what kind of details the writers use and how they present them.

Exercise

1. Study the following paragraphs in the light of the ideas on kinds of paragraphs presented in this section.

a. What kind is it—expository, narrative, descriptive? In which paragraphs do you find more than one kind?

b. In the expository paragraphs, try to find the topic sentence. Where is it placed? Do any of the descriptive or narrative paragraphs have topic statements?

c. What ideas do these suggest to you for improving the development of your own paragraphs? Answer this question in a single expository paragraph.

1) It was one evening in December 1915 that I saw, and spoke to, a ghost. We had marched up at an hour's notice into the front line, to replace a Scottish regiment which had been so badly and unexpectedly mauled that the Staff had been compelled to withdraw it. It must be borne in mind that as a result we had been deprived of the usual few days' rest between spells of duty. It was, of course, dusk when I took over my portion of the trench, and after I had ordered the posting of the men, I entered my dugout. On leaving it, a few minutes later, the evening had become already much blacker. In the corner of the bay opposite, I saw a private soldier, with his hands in his pockets, and noticed that his rifle was by his side, although it had long been an order that all the men should stand to, with their rifles on the parapet at dawn and at dusk. I could not see his face very distinctly owing to the growing darkness: but I swore at him for his carelessness, asking him what he meant by it. As I finished, with the words "I'm tired of having to tell you . . ." he was, suddenly, no longer there in front of me, and I was talking to nothingness. . . . I took up the abandoned rifle, and carried it with me to the dugout. It belonged to the regiment we had just relieved.—Sir Osbert Sitwell, *Laughter in the Next Room*, pp. 115-116. Reprinted by permission of Little, Brown & Company and Macmillan & Co., British publishers, copyright 1948.

2) It has been said by many, and in various ways, that the problems of knowing and understanding center around the relation of language to reality, of symbol to fact. These ink marks over which your eyes are racing, these ink marks that we agree to call words, and these words that we agree to accept as "legal tender" for the exchange of information, by what magic, or by what humdrum rules, do they serve their strange functions? If you stare at a word long enough, it does indeed become, for you, mere ink marks, a peculiar pattern of lines. At first it looks as

though it were spelled correctly, then you cannot be sure, and
finally you are overcome with the feeling that to consider its spelling at all is to enter into the most entangled mazes of humanity.—
Wendell Johnson, *People in Quandaries*, p. 91. Reprinted by permission of Harper & Brothers

3) A storm came up that morning—a wretched, all-day rain that
greased the ground and later soaked it, so that the rearward
wagons floundered half-stuck in the mire. The rain was cold,
slanted by a chilly breeze. The drivers climbed up in the wagons
to escape it and got colder yet for want of exercise and climbed
back down and stumped along, their feet heavy and misshapen
with the clinging mud. But they went on. That was the point.
Women driving, children driving, they went on.—A. B. Guthrie,
Jr., *The Way West*, p. 112

4) The third of the indirect values in the relations between
anatomy and personality is the effects of one's physical appearance
upon others. Mere size and strength may do a great deal to
bludgeon a boy's way into social acceptance, or keep a girl lonely
because the boys feel inferior to her. And though handsome is as
handsome does, a harelip or a facial blemish, or even flapping ears
or knock-knees, may ruin a boy's, and especially a girl's existence.
If these malevolent pranks of nature can make life lonely, it is
likely that many lesser handicaps do a great deal to fray the cord
by which social contact is maintained. To be good-looking, on the
other hand, is half the game for girls in our society and in many
others. (Standards differ; but the fact that she would be a belle
in the Straits Settlements is no great comfort to the Hoosier wall-
flower.) One's own personality is partly a response to the habitual
judgments and attitudes of others. There is, moreover, a tendency
to stereotype the possessor of rotundity as good-natured, the possessor of a long jaw as firm-willed, etc.; it is hard not to act as one
is expected to act. There is probably no intimate relation between
facial structure and character; but if society reacts as if there were,
a secondary relation may develop.—Gardner Murphy, *Personality*,
pp. 151–152. Reprinted by permission of Harper & Brothers.

5) Until a decade or two ago the phenomenon of turbulence in a fluid stream was of interest only to engineers; it seemed to have very little significance in what is usually called "pure" science. Turbulence is that extremely irregular internal motion which can be observed in fast-flowing liquids and gases. When a smooth-flowing stream breaks up into a chaotic mixture of whirlpools or eddies of all different sizes, we say it has become turbulent. You can see this happen in the flow of water from the kitchen faucet. When you open the faucet a little bit, the water streams out smoothly in what is known as laminar (or streamlined) flow. Increase the speed of the stream by opening the faucet all the way, and the motion becomes turbulent.—George Gamow, "Turbulence in Space," *Scientific American*, June 1952, p. 26

6) More men than women came down the gang-plank, many of them wearing trousers with ill-fitting overcoats buttoned around them. In the harsh neon light they appeared to have a curious kin-ship. They all looked as though something had been chilled inside of them and then hollowed out. Although some were shouting like the men and women on the pier, although some were hysterical like the men and women crowding around the plank, although some were dazed, there was a difference between them and the persons who awaited them. Some cheerful, recognizable human quality had been subtracted from them. They were the second group of survivors from the *Matrix*, the pleasure ship that had gone to the bottom before it had even reached Caribbean waters. —Leane Zugsmith, *Home Is Where You Hang Your Childhood*, p. 65

7) The offices of Barstow, Barstow and Bryce, the firm that had employed Bob Tasmin after his graduation from law school, occu-pied a major part of the fourteenth floor of a building off lower Broadway. The elevator took you up to a large waiting room with comfortable leather chairs, from which anxious clients could get a glimpse of the library when the door was open. Then came a broad passageway flanked by the partners' offices. First was the corner office of the former senior partner, Mr. Barstow, now deceased,

currently occupied by Mr. Bryce, the sole surviving partner of the original firm. Bob Tasmin often thought that Mr. Bryce rattled slightly in the mid-Victorian furniture of the late Mr. Barstow. Then came the room of Mr. Harris, the trial lawyer, from which you got a fine view of the Battery. Next came the office of Mr. Willoughby who handled divorces and family disputes, a gayer, more modernistic room than the others, reflecting Mr. Willoughby's bland disposition. The junior partners' offices farther down the passage each grew smaller depending on seniority, and the partners' row reached an end at the partners' toilet with its private key.

Beyond this line the offices of Barstow, Barstow and Bryce degenerated into a grim series of stuffy rooms, furnished with golden oak and green filing cabinets, and occupied by the secretaries and clerks. Finally came the rooms where those bright boys worked who had been selected according to their grades from the leading law schools.—John P. Marquand, *B. F.'s Daughter*, p. 184. Reprinted by permission of Little, Brown & Company and The Society of Authors, copyright 1946.

11 Paragraphs in sequence

The first thing to remember is that the division [into paragraphs] is for the benefit of the reader or hearer. It is a device for making the whole clear to someone else. This does not in the least make the process less valuable to the writer: it merely forces upon him the right point of view. A division is good in proportion as it helps a hearer or reader to follow.——Charles Sears Baldwin

11.1 Continuity between paragraphs   Just as the statements within a paragraph should represent a continuous flow of thought, the individual paragraphs should represent a progressive development of the subject. If there is too wide a gap in ideas between the end of one paragraph and the beginning of the next, the reader may not be able to follow the line of thought.

11.1a Showing the relation with the preceding paragraph
Link paragraphs together by connecting the topic of a new paragraph with the topic of the preceding one. The easiest way to do this is to phrase the opening statement of a paragraph so that it grows out of what you have just said. This method of continuity is illustrated in the following sentences from the first five paragraphs of an essay comparing the chances of marriage of girls who go to women's colleges with those of girls who go to coeducational institutions:

. . . Yet surely a woman has as much—or as little—natural right to spurn matrimony as a man has.	End of first paragraph
Nevertheless not many of us today care to sing the praises of celibacy . . . . Today we as a people set more store on marriage than ever before in our history.	Beginning of second paragraph End of second paragraph
This growing sense of the value of matrimony has boosted the prestige of coeducation among us. . . .	Beginning of third paragraph
By contrast it is suspected that separate colleges for women . . . by supposedly cloistering the girls and reducing their contacts with men to social events, cut down chances of marriage.	End of third paragraph
In defense, the advocates of women's colleges have been a bit sniffy and condescending about the "matrimonial bureaus" which they say are operated on coeducational campuses.	Beginning of fourth paragraph
At times they have even implied that . . . only college girls of relatively feeble intellect will let themselves lapse into domesticity.	End of fourth paragraph
The American public has enough common sense to see that most of this is an elaborate whistling in the dark.	Beginning of fifth paragraph

—Lynn White, Jr., "Do Women's Colleges Turn Out Spinsters?" *Harper's Magazine,* October 1952, p. 44

Even with the supporting statements omitted from these paragraphs, you can see how showing the thought connection between paragraphs makes it easy to follow the development.

The preceding example also shows that paragraphs are connected by the same methods used to link sentences within a paragraph (see §9.5): by repetition of an important word (paragraph 4: *women's colleges*), by a pronoun or synonym (paragraph 5: *this*; paragraph 3: *this growing sense of the value of matrimony*), or by a connective word (paragraph 2: *Nevertheless*).

11.1b   **Showing the relation to the topic of the paper**   When the material and development permit, show the relation between the paragraph and the topic or central idea of the paper. This is a good way to keep your paragraphs going in the same direction. As an example, in this discussion of the games played by primitive peoples, the author begins each paragraph with a different kind of sport:

Wrestling is probably universal. . . .	First paragraph (four sentences follow)
Races are far more common. . . .	Second paragraph (three sentences follow)
Ball games are also widespread, but vary greatly in type. . . .	Third paragraph (six sentences follow)
Frequently the ball games are played in a more elaborate way. . . .	Fourth paragraph (fourteen sentences follow)
In the Plains and Southwest of our country the "hoop and pole" game enjoyed great popularity. . . .	Fifth paragraph (six sentences follow)
Compared with such sports rope-skipping seems simple, but the Australian Euahlayi make an art of it. . . .	Sixth paragraph (two sentences follow)
Polynesians lead in aquatic sports. . . .	Seventh paragraph (four sentences follow)
Maori stilt-walkers raced one another across streams and also tried to upset one another's balance. . . .	Eighth paragraph (two sentences follow)

—Robert H. Lowie, *An Introduction to Cultural Anthropology*, pp. 164-166

11.1c Transition paragraphs Occasionally for major transitions in material, such as from one main section of a long paper to another, a brief, self-contained paragraph will prepare the reader for what is coming next. This is a typical transition paragraph:

> No such startling change in the habits of a people could have taken place without far-reaching social effects. Let us glance at a few of them.—Frederick Lewis Allen, *The Big Change*, p. 125

Ordinarily the relation of the subject matter of paragraphs is so close that transition paragraphs are not needed, and in short papers they are usually out of place.

11.2 Good beginnings The first paragraph of a paper has two functions: to get the subject started and to attract the reader's interest. A good beginning will fulfill both these functions, but for the purposes of a composition course, getting the paper started is perhaps more important than making an original or unusual opening. The less you think about an "introduction," the more immediately you are likely to get your topic going.

If you find it difficult to construct a satisfactory opening when you are writing your first draft, don't waste time, but go on to the next paragraph. You can go back later and write the opening sentences. Or if you have written what is obviously a weak beginning in your first draft, see if the second or third sentence, or even the second paragraph, wouldn't serve better as the starting point. You may find, as many writers do, that the first few lines of writing represent nothing more than a warming-up process, and that the paper actually begins after a few sentences.

11.2a An important fact One of the quickest and clearest ways to open a paper is with the statement of an important fact that will lead to the general topic. This is a natural opening for a narrative or presentation of a situation, but it is also good for a discussion of general ideas, as these from articles discussing important problems in education show:

Defense Secretary Charles E. Wilson recently ordered that all post schools—public schools located on military reservations—will be operated on a non-segregated basis beginning September 1, 1955.—L. R. Davis, "Federal Operation of Post Schools," *School and Society*, May 29, 1954, 79:165

Graduates of the Class of 1950 at Newark College of Engineering were asked to complete a questionnaire which evaluated their extracurricular program from 1946 to 1950. The College is about five minutes distant from the downtown section of Newark, a city of about a half-million people. All commuters, the students come to college from Newark and from suburbs within an hour's travel Their heavy schedule of technical subjects and the difficulties of commuting demand so much of their time in many cases as to make participation in the extracurricular program difficult.—Herman A. Estrin, "Engineering Graduates Evaluate Their College's Extracurricular Program," *Journal of Higher Education*, June 1954, 25:328

11.2b A statement of your purpose or point of view This need not be an obvious statement of purpose ("In this paper I am going to give you my reasons for majoring in business administration") or a flat rewording of the assignment, but a natural leading into the topic:

When I decided to enter the university, like most freshmen I had only the vaguest notion of what subject I intended to major in. But now after two quarters of haphazardly chosen course work, and after a good deal of self-analysis, I have decided that *there are at least four good reasons why I should major in business administration.* . . .

11.2c A definition that applies directly to your topic Instead of starting with a dull and stereotyped statement like "According to Webster, a hobby is 'an engrossing topic, occupation, or plan, etc., to which one habitually returns,'" make a definition that fits *your* approach to the subject:

A hobby, as I see it, is an activity that takes up most of your spare time and all of your spare money. At least that has been my experience since I started building model airplanes. . . .

11.2d A reference to your experience with the subject For example, in an article discussing the question of segregation in college fraternities, the author starts off in this way:

During the year just past I have found myself deeply concerned with the affairs of a group of fine youngsters who, acting from high motives, were unexpectedly embroiled in a major social problem. Under vicious attack, for a time they were dismayed and confused; but they came through and, I think, won their final trial.—Alfred S. Romer, "The Color Line in Fraternities," *The Atlantic Monthly,* June 1949, p. 27

11.2e **The aspects of the subject you are going to discuss** This beginning clearly indicates that the writer is not going to talk about Yellowstone Park, but about vandalism in the Park:

Yellowstone Park is the most spectacular wonderland of its kind in the world. Its geysers and hot springs are unrivalled anywhere. Princes, kings, and savants travel from all parts of the earth to marvel at them. Our Federal Government has spent millions of dollars for roads and other facilities to enable the great American public to behold these matchless hydrothermal wonders. *Yet, the great American public is ruining them—choking them simply because some people can't resist the temptation of throwing tons of assorted trash into the funnels of geysers and springs.*—George D. Marler, "Who Is Choking Yellowstone's Geysers?" *Natural History,* June 1952, p. 276

11.2f **Details likely to catch the reader's interest** One of the best ways to get the reader to go beyond the first sentence is to arouse his curiosity—perhaps with an anecdote or an apt quotation or an allusion to some current topic. Such "human interest" material should of course be tied in with the subject of the paper, as it is in this beginning of an article on the Korean war:

Arthur Dailey, in his "Sports of the Times" column, tells how Frank Leahy, the football coach at Notre Dame, began a lecture to his squad on its disregard of fundamentals by picking up a football and saying, "This, gentlemen, is a football." He was interrupted by Ziggy Czarobski, one of the tackles. "Just a minute, coach," said Ziggy, "please don't give it to us so fast."

Right now, we could use Ziggy, or someone like Ziggy, to monitor what we are hearing about the gloomy fundamentals of the tragic problem in Korea, its evils and their cure. It is all coming at us so fast that the spectators can no longer see the game through the fog that has settled over the field. . . .—S. L. A. Marshall, "Korean Stalemate—The War of 'Where Do We Go From Here,'" *The Reporter,* November 11, 1952, p. 17

11.3 **Beginnings to avoid**   The opening paragraph should mark the actual beginning of the paper and be clearly related to the subject. If it does not get the subject under way, or if it does not create interest in the subject, it probably does not belong in the paper.

When you are working on the opening of a paper, be careful to avoid these common mistakes, all of which make poor beginnings:

11.3a **Beginning too far back**   If you are discussing the organization of the United Nations, there is no need to begin with the reasons for the failure of the League of Nations, nor is there any reason to begin a paper on Eisenhower as President with an account of his military career. The shorter your paper, the more direct should be your beginning: a statement of your purpose or a rewording of your central idea is the simplest way to begin a paper written in class.

11.3b **An apology or a complaint**   A statement such as this is discouraging to most readers: "Being a lowly freshman, I'm afraid that what I have to say on this topic won't be of much value. . . ." Complaints are also better left unwritten: "Before I started to write this theme, I thought I could find some interesting material on it in the library, but there wasn't any. . . ." Remember that readers are only interested in the ideas that you present, not in the difficulties or disappointments you may have had while writing the paper.

11.3c **Too broad a generalization**   "Science in the last fifty years has made more progress than any other branch of knowledge" is a generalization far too sweeping to explain or prove in a 500 or a 5000 word paper. Statements such as this are likely to be more impressive to the writer than they are to the reader. Wherever possible, begin with a specific statement: "Though smaller than your thumb, a new electronic device called the transistor is likely to have a tremendous effect on radio and television sets of the future."

11.3d A self-evident statement Avoid starting a paper with a remark so obvious that it need not be mentioned: "America has a great number of resorts situated in her many scenic localities." And resist the temptation to open your topic with some commonplace observation that gives no hint of your subject: "It has been said that the only thing constant in life is change." If you have started your paper with a self-evident remark, see if the sentence immediately following doesn't mark the actual beginning of the subject.

11.4 Good endings The purpose of a conclusion is to round out the subject and to give final emphasis to the paper. The last paragraph should sound like an ending, so that the person who reads it will know you have finished your paper and have not merely abandoned it. This doesn't mean that you should mechanically summarize what you have said or draw your discussion to a close with some such stilted expression as "Thus we have seen . . ." or "In conclusion I would like to say . . . ." The reader will know he has come to the end if the final paragraph ties together the ideas you have been developing and emphasizes the main point of the paper, or, in a narrative, sounds like the conclusion of the action.

Following are some suggestions for good concluding paragraphs:

11.4a Rounding out the idea Make your final paragraph the culmination of the ideas you have been developing, or save the most important idea for the last. The concluding paragraph thus becomes the climax of the paper. A student paper of about 1000 words, which has described in detail the operation of a large used-car lot, brings all the details to a focus in this conclusion:

> This used-car lot was sponsored by an organization which sells over a million cars a year, so it was by no means a fly-by-night affair. Although no sloppy repairs were done, and no highly crooked deals were tolerated, there was just a slight suspicion that the company was getting the best of every customer on every deal. This company, however good or bad, is representative of many similar organizations in the United States.

11.4b Tying the ending in with the beginning The final paragraph may repeat, in different wording, the central idea stated in the beginning. This method is particularly useful for longer papers, both to remind the reader what the main idea is and to give it final emphasis. For example, an article in defense of radio begins and ends in this manner:

> Radio is accused of a multitude of sins, by a multitude of persons. Senators, cranks, and congressmen attack it. Lawyers, psychiatrists, doctors, educators, editors, and clergymen all take swipes at it. Many of these people are important and their views are often given wide publicity. Many, alas, are neither informed nor fair. . . .

> No man in American radio has ever said that everything in radio is right, and no radio man ever will. But they will tell you this: if you make radio a public issue, radio will bring it to the public. Broadcasters have never flinched from a public issue and as long as democracy exists they never will.
> Public trust is radio's only security, public response its mold.—Max Wylie, "Washboard Weepers: a Small Case for Radio," *Harper's Magazine*, November 1942, pp. 633-638

11.4c Giving suggestions for action If you have been criticizing some situation (parking on the campus, the price of textbooks, daylight saving time), end your paper with a positive suggestion for action. "Something should be done about this" is too weak to serve as a conclusion. Make the statement definite, as in this ending of an article about international cooperation:

> There is only one way out. We have to learn the lesson that nations, asserting their petty ideas of sovereignty, prestige, national self-interest, must combine to act together for the common good of humanity—which is the meaning of acting morally. There is still time to learn this lesson. *But the time is short.*—W. T. Stace, "Have Nations Any Morals?" *The Atlantic Monthly*, November 1945, p. 87

11.4d Summarizing the main points in the paper Longer and more formal papers are sometimes concluded by restating the main points of the discussion. This final paragraph, for example, sums up the reasons which the author has discussed in detail for preferring Rugby to American football:

The general mood which most distinguishes the Rugby scene from American football is that of temperance; and this temperate mood is made possible to a considerable extent by the simplicity of the game. The intemperance which is associated with American football may have a number of causes, but frustration is a prominent one. The American game will not allow many ablebodied and interested people even to join a team; it will not allow many of the members of a team to play a full game; and of those actually playing, only a few can engage in the full range of activity. These are serious weaknesses in the American game, and anyone interested in getting rid of them ought to observe how Rugby football is played in England.—Allen Jackson, "Rugby Is a Better Game," *The Atlantic Monthly,* November 1952, p. 72

But for most papers written in composition courses, it is seldom necessary or advisable to summarize what has been said. Perhaps the most unemphatic and trite way to end a 500 or 800 word paper is with a mechanical summary such as this: "Therefore, as I have shown, the benefits of intramural athletics are twofold—physical and mental."

11.5 Endings to avoid Avoid unemphatic, inconclusive, or contradictory endings. These are some typical pitfalls to watch out for in your closing paragraphs:

11.5a An apology Ending a paper with an apology for its shortcomings only serves to emphasize them:

I am sorry this paper is so short, but I always have a difficult time putting a paper like this together.

11.5b A qualifying remark If the last sentence of a paper is an exception or qualifying remark, it weakens everything that has been said before:

Although I haven't answered why some people refuse to face facts, I have come to the conclusion that not facing facts may be a natural part of human nature. Of course this can be carried to extremes.

There are two sides to every subject, but when the purpose or scope of your paper is limited to the arguments for one side only, don't suddenly shift to the other side in your conclusion. If for example you have been presenting every argument you can think of in favor of universal military training, don't end like this: "Of course, there is much to be said for the other side also." If you feel such a qualifying statement is necessary, put it earlier in the paper.

11.5c Minor details or afterthoughts A paper describing the role of the pitcher in baseball shouldn't end with a remark about other aspects of the game:

> Baseball is one of America's favorite sports, and to spend an afternoon at the Yankee Stadium or Polo Grounds, watching two great pitchers battling for a victory, attracts thousands of fans. What I have said about pitching gives you an idea as to what a pitcher must keep in his mind while out there on the mound, or as a substitute on the bench. *There are eight other players on the team besides the pitcher and the same can be written about each individual player and his position.*

It would be better to save an idea like that in the last sentence for the topic of another paper.

11.5d Unfinished ideas Some concluding statements make a reader wonder whether the writer actually finished his paper or was called away in the middle of an idea:

> I could go on and on for pages and pages describing the other interesting people I met on the ship, but the length of this paper doesn't permit it.

Instead of putting a sentence such as this at the end of your paper, round out the description fully, or if the topic is already developed sufficiently, see if the next to the last sentence wouldn't make a respectable conclusion.

Final paragraphs are important because they create the impression that the reader will carry away with him. A good conclusion, like a good beginning, is an asset to any paper, but it is not advisable to waste valuable time trying to think of a punch line or a dramatic close. When you have said all that you have to say, stop.

Exercises

1. Study an article in a magazine or in a volume of readings for the ways in which the individual paragraphs are tied together. Make a list of phrases or statements relating separate paragraphs to the subject of the article and those linking each paragraph to the preceding one.

2. The following paragraphs are the beginnings of student papers of from 500 to 800 words in length. Which openings seem most effective to you, and why? What specific faults do you find in the unsatisfactory beginnings?

1) After reading the assigned essay five times and trying to ferret out something that interested me to comment upon, I realized that I did and did not wholly agree with some of the author's observations. Then the thought came to me that that was my subject. I have concentrated on the first part of this essay. I have wondered if some of the observations in it were meant to be provocative. I have asked myself: who am I to disagree with someone like that? However, to use a cliché, I have put myself out on a limb, so here goes.

2) The medical word for baldness is "alopecia," derived from the Greek word meaning a disease of foxes. There has been baldness among men and women for thousands of years. Scientists have been working on a cure for it for a long time, but it is still incurable. In the past years doctors have found out what causes baldness. Like most other diseases, baldness is not free from false advertising. There are many ways that a person can prevent baldness.
The hairs on the human head grow from a papilla about a quarter of an inch below the surafce of the skin. . . .

3) The footlights are turned up, the curtain rises, and the play begins. Last year the University's Touring Theater did this two hundred times on an itinerary of one hundred seventy cities and whistle stops. The tour was so well received that this year the troupe will play at least two hundred fifty shows in two hundred

theaters. This is the first show to tour the entire state in many years, and it is one of the very few student organizations of this type in the country.

4) Marriage, in its true meaning, is a word greatly misused and misunderstood. The problem lies in its interpretation. The word itself is comprehended very easily, and yet, as is the case with a great many words and phrases, the depth and hidden meanings are greatly misunderstood. When a young couple is united in matrimony, exactly what do they hope to find in their life together?

To begin with, marriage should not mean the reconstructing of one's own ideas and habits to suit those of another. . . .

5) How does that song go? "Me and my shadow . . . follows me wherever I go . . ." or words to that effect. "Me and my ulcer" would be more appropriate for me.

About two years ago, following a huge meal, I suffered a constant pain in my stomach for over three days. . . .

3. Study the beginnings and endings of at least three informational articles in one issue of a magazine or in a volume of readings. What is the relation of each to the subject and the purpose of the article as a whole, what does it *do?* How effective are they?

4. Study and evaluate the beginnings and endings of the papers in exercise 2, pp. 153-163.

12 Revising paragraphs

Anyone who can write a good paragraph can write a good paper.
—Old saying

Par **Paragraph correction: This paragraph is unsatisfactory. Check it by**
or ¶ **the following questions and revise or rewrite it to make it more**
effective.

This section reviews the points made in sections 9 through 11 by asking questions that may lead to improving ineffective paragraphs. You can use the questions in revising your papers before handing them in, or if one or more of your paragraphs have been marked by your instructor, you can find here the reasons why they were marked and suggestions for improving them. If you need more information you can refer to the section whose number is given in parentheses.

12.1 Does the paragraph develop a clear cut stage of the topic? If more than one or two paragraphs fail to develop a clear cut stage of the topic, your difficulty is due either to a faulty outline, which will have to be thought about and revised (§6), or to not following the outline you have (§9.2). In either case some rewriting of the paper will be necessary.

If the paragraphs represent the right order of topics but are too brief, they may merely represent too many indentions, as in this example:

> The day of the game finally arrives and the first thing you do is look out the window to check on the weather.
> As the paper predicted, it is a beautiful sunny morning with very little wind—real football weather. You try to pass the morning by reading about the game, while you are counting the hours and the minutes until the game starts.
> Finally you start for the game, only to find the nearest parking lot over a mile from the stadium. You begin the long walk across the campus, joining the thousands of people all as eager as you are, all hurrying in the same direction.
> As you pass the impressive Gothic buildings, memories of your college days come back to you, and you wish for a moment at least that you were back in school again.

The first two "paragraphs" concern the morning of the game and hence should be written as one; the last two "paragraphs" also deal with one topic—the trip to the stadium—and should not be separated either.

A paragraph that attempts to cover more than one stage of the topic should be divided:

> About three years ago when I started my junior year in high school, a neighbor who was the captain of the local National Guard unit paid me a visit. He started talking about the wonderful possibilities the

Guard had to offer—training in radio, electronics, and other technical subjects. Evidently he must have been a good recruiting officer, for after he talked for an hour, I fell for his argument and joined, thinking I might learn something. I did. [*Next sentence starts a new stage of the topic.*] After attending a few drills, I was able to draw some conclusions about this outfit and my place in it. All the fancy talk I had heard was just propaganda, for as soon as I got my uniform, they hustled me down to the anti-aircraft installation. From then on, for two and a half years, I spent most of my weekly drills wiping the guns while the NCO's stood around talking baseball and women to each other. Occasionally they would look busy when they saw an officer coming, but most of the time they loafed while I worked.

Since the discussion of recruiting clearly stops with "I did," the next sentence should begin a new paragraph.

Paragraphs that are conspicuously short or conspicuously long should be examined carefully to see whether they are developed properly (§9.6, Paragraph length).

12.2 Is the relation of the paragraph to the topic of the paper clear?   A reader should see the relationship of the statements of a particular paragraph to the topic of the paper. The relationship can be tested in your outline by tracing it from the subhead through any intervening head to the central idea (§9.2). The beginning and ending of a paper need to be watched especially for irrelevant matter and for direct relation to the topic (§§11.2, 11.3, on beginning paragraphs; §§11.4, 11.5, on concluding paragraphs). If you have conspicuous trouble in keeping the subject before the reader, see that the first sentence of each paragraph contains the key word of the topic or a pronoun or a synonym referring to it, or a clearly indicated subdivision of the topic (§11.1b).

12.3 Is the relation between the thought of a paragraph and that of the preceding one clear?   Your paper should have unbroken continuity so that a reader who may be unfamiliar with the subject can move easily from one paragraph to the next. The continuity of the subject helps in this, but you may need to use pronouns or connecting phrases or some repetition of important words to make the relation absolutely clear (§11.1a). Occasionally a short transition paragraph may be needed between the stages of a paper (§11.1c).

12.4 Is the paragraph fully developed? The most common defect in paragraph development is not putting down enough material, especially specific details, to convey your meaning to your reader. The point is not just bulk but sufficient information to make your reader see your point as you see it. Lack of detail usually means rewriting a paragraph on a larger scale (§9.3, Developing ideas fully; §10, which discusses characteristic material of expository, narrative, and descriptive paragraphs). One way to test the development of a paragraph is to see that the topic sentence (§10.1b) is actually supported by enough detail to make it convincing.

12.5 Is the relation between the statements of the paragraph clear? In revising paragraphs for continuity, try to put yourself in the reader's place and ask yourself such questions as these:

Does any sentence sound as if it marks the beginning of a new paragraph?
Does each statement seem to be in its proper place within the paragraph?
Is it easy to get from one sentence to the next, or are there any noticeable gaps in thought?

If it is difficult to get from one statement to the next, perhaps a slight revision—repeating a word, using a pronoun or a connective—will show the continuity (§9.5).

Exercises

1. In the following paragraphs, the sentences have been shifted from their original order. Read each selection first to get its mean-

ing, and then indicate by number what you think would be the best order of the sentences to make a unified and emphatic paragraph. If you think that more than one arrangement would be effective, be prepared to discuss alternative possibilities.

a.   1) Boards with knots, cracks, and other imperfections are not discarded or used only in concealed locations.

2) There is no loss of strength or safety, but the finish of the house reflects the builder's economy approach.

3) Naturally enough, the mass builder of the low cost houses must save in some ways that would be unacceptable to many individuals.

4) Warped boards often go up in full view.

5) Often he uses rough framing lumber throughout the house, and uses it pretty much as it comes from the mill.

—"More Living Space," *Sunset Magazine,* November 1952, p. 45

b.   1) Pretending to have more money than one actually has is an acutely uncomfortable business, and usually no one is deceived by the pretension.

2) While a certain amount of Dutch treating goes on, especially in group entertainment, a boy usually does pay for the entertainment of his special date.

3) And boys should learn to be unembarrassedly frank with girls about what entertainment they can afford to offer.

4) Dating, for boys, does bring with it increased financial responsibilities.

5) If his allowance is not adequate for his participation in the social activities of his high school group and if his parents cannot comfortably increase it, then after-school jobs must provide the difference.

—*Amy Vanderbilt's Complete Book of Etiquette,* p. 539. Copyright 1952, 1954 by Amy Vanderbilt, reprinted by permission of Doubleday & Company, Inc.

c.   1) In later years they went bowling and played tennis together and it had done Mr. Beech much good physically.

2) He wanted Addison to grow up to be his pal, not only his son.

3) Excepting of course, any good-looking female teenager of fifteen, sixteen, or seventeen.

4) So, in the pre-adolescent days, much to the amazement and resentment of the less doting, more sedate fathers in the park, Mr. Beech could have been seen playing marbles, shooting down the slides, skating, swinging, seesawing and bicycling with his son.

5) When his son was young Mr. Beech had laid the groundwork for future love and companionship by devoting the best part of his Sundays to the boy's amusement.

6) But Addison was always a restless one and there could be no hearth sitting with him.

7) Now, as Addison approached the twilight of his teens, it was a source of satisfaction and reward to Mr. Beech to realize that his company was yet as stimulating and gratifying to Addison as anyone's.

—Harry Dubin, *Hail, Alma Pater*, pp. 263–264

2. *A Set of Themes.* The following themes, written near the end of the first quarter of freshman composition, are typical papers of varying quality. Read each one through first, and then answer the following questions:

a. *Organization:* Which papers are most effectively organized? (Try making an outline of any papers you may be doubtful about.) Are there any passages in which the writer wanders from his subject or repeats himself? Which papers contain a sentence that definitely states the central idea? In the other papers, what sentence or sentences come nearest to expressing the central idea?

b. *Development:* What is the dominant kind of development— expository, narrative, or descriptive—in each paper? Can you suggest any other methods by which each of these subjects might have been developed?

c. *Paragraphing:* Point out any paragraphs that seem to you over- or underdeveloped. Which paper has the most effective opening paragraph? The strongest closing?

d. *Interest:* Indicate which paper you consider the most interesting reading and explain why (on the basis of subject matter, choice of details, liveliness, wording, the clarity of the explanation, and so on). In what order would you rank or grade these papers?

1)   The SCA

The Students' Cooperative Association, better known as the SCA, was organized in the early 1930's. The main reason given for the organization at that time was that a group of students could reduce their living costs through cooperation. Since then, the activities that the SCA has engaged in have offered its members a number of other advantages.

How is the SCA able to offer board and room rates that its members could not get anywhere else?

The answer to this is that the members do the housework, such as serving meals, washing dishes, sweeping floors and washing windows. At the beginning of each quarter the student is assigned a specific task which requires that he give about three hours of his time each week to perform. It is surprising the amount of work that can be done when all the individuals in a group do their job.

In recent years the co-op has added other services designed to ease the burden on the student's pocketbook. One of these is the arrangement with a cleaning establishment which gives the student good cleaning service with pickups and deliveries at less than cash and carry rates. Other arrangements have been made with other cooperatives and wholesale houses which give the members the right to purchase at reduced rates a wide variety of items such as jewelry and clothing. The most recent additional service is an arrangement with the Group Health Cooperative, which gives the students health insurance covering a wide variety of conditions not covered by many nation-wide health programs. This service is obtainable at a very small fee.

For the student who needs part time work to earn his living the co-op offers a number of jobs, such as working in the kitchen, and a limited number of office jobs, doing routine office work and helping with the bookkeeping.

If jobs are not available at the co-op, it is often possible to get a part time job with a former co-op member.

The student who is interested in obtaining practical experience in running a business has a couple of alternatives. The best of these is to get a job on the Board of Directors. If the individual is unsuccessful in his attempt to be a part of the governing body, there are always committees which can use the services of other members.

Another advantage is to meet and live with students from a number of countries. The relationship established in such a group gives both the foreigners and the natives an unparalleled opportunity to become better acquainted with the other's customs, history, and a number of other things. It would be hard to find a better way to give students an understanding of the reasons for the ways in which things are done elsewhere.

The group's activities can be broken down into three kinds: educational, social, and athletic. The educational program offers a number of speakers, educational movies, and fireside discussions. The social program offers a variety of activities including dances, parties, and several others. We also have an annual picnic, the all-co-op banquet, a formal dance and a theater party every quarter.

Athletics offer the student a chance to compete on a team in the University intramural program or with the co-op's inter-house program. In some sports we compete with other organized houses.

I have attempted to show you that this organization offers the student attending school on a limited budget many advantages which might not be available with some other group. While it has been impossible to cover all the advantages in the time at my disposal, I feel the more important ones have been covered.

2)   Observations at a Carnival

"Step up, folks, and take your places for your favorite game of 'Bingo.' You may be a winner, so hurry, hurry, folks." So blares out a voice throughout the long gymnasium, temporarily converted into a place of amusement with numerous concession and food stalls. The salty, buttery aroma of popcorn, the tangy smell of mustard and the tantalizing savor of hamburgers permeate the air. Behind the food stalls decorated in a splash of colors, the girls wearing crisp white aprons dart back and forth to serve their impatient customers. Tiny tots tug at their mothers' dresses and beg for a chocolate bar or double decker ice-cream cone. Either to satisfy their childrens' hunger or to quiet them, the mothers finally give in to their whimperings.

The crowd becomes thicker by the hour, the voices become louder by the minute. People forget the common courtesies and elbow their way from one concession to another, oblivious of the other person's feelings. Little boys drawn by curiosity, crane their necks to get a glimpse of the fish bowls into which their brothers or sisters are striving to throw small balls. One youth's face lights up with pleasure as he performs this feat and is rewarded with the bowl and the goldfish. The "Penny-Pitch" is surrounded with youngsters between the ages of 8 to 12, doubled over the railings which separate them from the checkered board on the floor. With each throw of the coin, they bend farther and farther until their bodies are at a rakish angle with their heads practically touching the board and their feet up in the air. At this point, they lose their balance.

In this Carnival atmosphere of noise, people, food and games, by far the greatest drawing card appears to be the "Bingo" stand. It is appropriately situated in the center of all the other stands, and seems to attract the crowd as wool attracts moths. Here stands the best barker with the loudest, most persuasive voice. The powerful voice becomes more powerful as it booms forth from the microphone. The owner of the voice is small but wiry, myopic and mustached, and possesses a remarkable vocabulary that beckons men, women and children of all ages to his booth. Within the booth are rows and rows of prizes: the oriental table lamp with an imitation jade base, the set of gleaming silverware, a Motorola bedside radio and numerous toy ducks and pandas. The mahogany Admiral table model television set is certainly a temptation. To the call of the barker, the chairs encircling the booth quickly fill with people and the game is begun.

"3-2 under G, 6-7 under O, 1-3 under B." For a while that is all that can be heard from this booth, with the numbers being called out with purposeful distinctness. It is as though the players had suddenly been cast in a spell and save for the voice of the caller, the area around the booth is deathly still. The majority of the participants hover over their cards, guarding it as if it were money. They listen intently to the numbers called and nervously finger their markers. A youth sits in the East corner, clutching an orange popsicle in one hand, a marker in the other, and shakes his head in disgust as the numbers are called. Two teen-age girls, under the impression that quantity may prove to be the winner, share three cards instead of one and become more confused as the calling progresses. They giggle and call out in an audible whisper, "Give us 48 under N." Sandwiched between two elderly ladies is a spry looking man of 60 odd years, his halo of wispy grey hair being the only indication of his advancing age. His far-sighted eyes make it difficult for him to distinguish the letters and numbers of the card and the lady on his right points the exact square for him. The two ladies check and recheck their cards and the three of them enjoy the game immensely as evidenced by their nods and smiles. Immediately opposite this threesome, sits a player wearing an expression of utter boredom, hardly hearing what is being said but with his face turned toward the center figure from whose hand the decisive marker is released. In sharp contrast to this, another player two chairs to the left of him sits in deep concentration, staring at his card without batting an eye, as though he were solving a mathematical problem. Then in the South corner is a little boy, half out of his chair, hardly able to contain himself as his card shows that he has only one more square to be completed.

The silence is suddenly broken by a jubilant voice from another corner which sings out "Bingo!" abruptly bringing the game to an end. A low groan in unison is heard from the other players. Some dejectedly leave the booth, others tell their neighbors of their short-lived luck, and still others, the "die-hards," fumble for a quarter, change their cards and anxiously wait for the next game to commence. Just one individual walks away with triumph written all over his face, grinning from ear to ear, with a prized possession carefully tucked under his arm.

3) Pen Pals

Ever since I was a little girl I have always had a desire to travel. Then, I wanted to see China and Alaska. Now, it is Sweden, Switzerland, India, Africa, and all the warm, tropical countries. Since I couldn't travel, I have seen much of the world through the medium of letters.

I vividly remember the first letter I received from my first pen-pal who lives in Japan. I had waited with eager anticipation for her reply to my letter. Days and days went by. The days turned into weeks. Then, in exactly two months, the big day arrived. Through the mail slot came a large envelope with strange stamps. My heart beat quickened and I beamed with excitement and wonderment as I picked up the letter. The ragged condition of the envelope told me it had had a rough passage across the Pacific. Inside was the warmth of a new friendship: a friend in a land newly conquered, adjusting her ways to a new life with an eager desire to make friends with her conquerors.

That was the way it started. But I was not satisfied with just one pen pal for very long. I thought it would be more exciting to have letters coming from all parts of the world. So I wrote to the International Friendship League, at different intervals, and received names and addresses of boys and girls in the following countries: Egypt, Holland, Sweden, North Ireland, Hawaii, South Australia, Colombia, England, and India. It was then up to me. I had the task of writing the first letter, and it was quite difficult to write to a person I had never seen, and of whom I knew nothing. This I found out when I wrote to the girl in Japan for the first time. So I wrote to my new prospective friends in much the same manner, telling them about myself, my hobbies, school, and our city and state.

Letters soon came and I was amazed at the writers' keen

interest in America, and to find out the things they enjoyed most about our state. The boys and girls in Australia, Egypt, and India were thrilled with what they had read of our lakes, waterfalls, mountains, and parks. I was surprised to find that a boy and girl in Egypt had never seen snow.

Nylon hose is a luxury, if it comes from the U.S., to my friend in North Ireland. Their nylon hose is of poor quality, low in quantity, and very expensive. My pen pal in Australia recently wrote about seeing a sea-plane land and take off for the first time. This is an unusual sight because there aren't any lakes large enough to accomodate sea-planes and the ocean is usually too rough. Novelties of plastic (coin purses, letter openers, etc.) are never seen.

In some of these countries, England and Ireland in particular, the people are easily influenced by American films. This is their way of finding out what life is like in our country. My pen-pal in North Ireland wrote to me of some of these "queer" ideas the people had, quote: "America is a kind of paradise where all of the people have plenty of money, good health, and consequently an abundance of happiness. The people are physically fit, have lovely curly hair and sparkling white teeth. The food is very good and plentiful. People wear lovely clothes that are apparently not expensive. But on the other hand, American people are liable to be shot in the back any minute by gangsters and such like. There is a lot of crime, and policemen drive huge streamlined cars with sirens screaming." Unquote. She told me not to take these ideas too seriously, as they are for the most part, the result of American films, and the films sent to North Ireland are of poor quality to express our life in America. A good percentage of them are gangster movies, or westerns, and as she wrote, "rather hopeless."

Although these boys and girls are from far away lands with strange customs, they all seem to act and think very much like typical American teenagers. The boy in Egypt is the best example of this. I wrote to him some time ago of the freezing weather and spring thaws we had just had and he replied, quote: "We are eager to see rain falling heavily and water pipes bursting for that will give us just cause for being absent from school!" unquote.

I have spent many enjoyable hours reading and writing letters, exchanging ideas and comparing ways of life with people of my own age in countries around the world. Through the medium of letter writing, I have learned to understand and accept the ways other people live.

4)   Aircraft Rescue

It's a warm, sunny afternoon and the water of the wide bay laps quietly against the shore that fringes the airport. Airplanes of all types have been landing and taking off; the air traffic is abundant today.

Another speck on the horizon enlarges into an airplane as it approaches the airfield from out over the water. It is still too far to hear its engine as it descends on its approach. Its altitude seems abnormally low compared to the other planes and it continues to glide toward the water. Suddenly it splashes noiselessly into the bay in a cloud of spray. Many minutes seem to pass as the other planes begin to circle aimlessly around the airport. Then a larger plane appears and circles over the downed craft, whose tail is now the only portion visible above the surface of the water. There's a yellow flash in the sunlight indicating that the pilot has inflated his emergency life raft. Slowly the tail of the plane sinks from view as the big plane continues to circle above the scene of the crash, marking the location of the pilot.

Suddenly, activity bursts forth from all quarters of the airfield! First, a huge fire engine with its siren screaming lurches across the ditch at the airport boundary and stops at the water's edge. Another fire truck creates great excitement as it crashes through a fence and enters the airport from another direction. It stops beside the first as its crew hurl yards of hose along the shoreline. An ambulance moans to a stop followed by a jeep, some cargo tugs, a pickup truck, and an assortment of autos and tractors. Each vehicle seems to be packed to capacity and people cling to any available perch as they make the dash across the field. Soon kids on bicycles arrive, followed by others stumbling and running breathlessly to the water's edge. The bay seems to create an insurmountable barrier for all of the costly equipment and the firemen stand frustrated with hoses dripping fire fighting foam. One smoke eater stands impatiently digging the sand with a huge fire axe as he gazes toward the downed aviator. Another grotesque figure wearing one rubber boot and an asbestos helmet wades in front of the trucks. The doctor and his driver stand in the doorway of the ambulance and look aimlessly out across the bay. Two youngsters carrying air rifles seem more preoccupied with the fire trucks than with the cause of the excitement. The noise increases as more autos arrive and the same questions arise. "What happened?" seems to be the chief concern. New arrivals have difficulty seeing, as others take great pains to point out the yellow raft far out on the bay. Tension continues to mount and one can feel the sense of helplessness of the rescuers in spite of all of their massive equipment. Members of the crowd wade further out into the water in a futile attempt to find a solution.

Two of the would-be rescuers suddenly shout as though a great discovery has been made. They race toward a small yellow pickup truck and extract a large rubber life raft. Carbon dioxide soon inflates the raft and after hurling aside their shoes, the two awkwardly embark on their mission. Apparently no oars or paddles are available and they begin madly paddling with their hands. This activity brings great cheers from the onlookers and the two proceed slowly out into the water. By this time, the firemen have taken off their heavy asbestos suits and recoiled much of the fire hose. The doctor now sits on the front bumper of the ambulance quietly smoking a cigar. People are sitting on auto tops and standing on the roofs of trucks and other heavy equipment. In fact, the vantage points are swollen to capacity and now and then someone falls from his perch on an overcrowded car top. The rescue raft still has many hundreds of yards to go. People stand with their hands in their pockets or talking in small groups; just looking.

Soon a speck from the other side of the bay increases into the recognizable form of an amphibian plane which lands and picks up the unfortunate flyer. Following this rescue, the amphibian takes off, extends its landing gear and heads straight for the airport. This action seems to be the signal for great activity as the autos and heavy equipment roar into action racing the crowd to the aircraft parking area to meet the rescue plane. In shorter time than it had taken to gather, the entire crowd departs from the shoreline. Silence again prevails and the view is peaceful, interrupted only by the ill-fated rescue mission whose members are still paddling their rescue raft listlessly shoreward.

5)   Nursing Is My Ambition

Nursing as a career offers expanding opportunities as to types of work. No longer is nursing just taking care of the sick. Nurses today hold positions involving administrative responsibilities. They are also concerned with education. For the well qualified girl, there is no need to ever be without work once she has secured a license to practice.

There are many types of nursing open to the registered nurse, but there are four major fields. These are institutional nursing, public health nursing, nursing education, and private duty nursing. Institutional or hospital nurses perform a variety of services. They must work in the ward, in the operating room, and in the dispensary. Starting with general ward duty, nurses in this field can advance to staff positions. The public health nurse meets people and their health problems. Her goal is to prevent disease and demonstrate good nursing care, and bring health teaching to the home. Nursing education consists chiefly of teaching in nursing schools. Private duty nurses work under the direction of a physician in the care of the sick, in the patient's home. Either at home or in the hospital, the nurse meets the challenge of a variety of cases in a variety of conditions.

The educational requirements for entering a nursing school vary. The minimum requirements for most is graduation from high school. Some nursing schools require one or more years of college work. The work includes general courses intended for the broader development of the individual's education. While in the nursing school, the student learns nursing procedures, principles, and practices of nursing care. Studies begin with general medical and surgical nursing and advance to more specialized nursing care procedures. The number of years one must spend in the nursing school ranges from three to four years.

Besides these educational requirements there are personal qualifications a nurse should possess. A few of these are good health, good judgment, a liking for people, imagination, humor, and sympathy.

I have tried to bring out in these past few paragraphs the main fields open in a nursing career which it is my ambition to be a part of. Also I have pointed out in general the requirements to become a nurse. I do not know exactly why I have chosen nursing as my ambition, but as far back as I can remember, I've always wanted to be a nurse. The nursing field is expanding rapidly and with this expansion, new opportunities are offered. Also there is a deep satisfaction in knowing that by the work you do, you will be helping someone. This is one reason I have chosen nursing as my ambition.

Sentences and words

13 Grammar of sentences

> Sentences, not words, are the essence of speech, just as equations and functions, and not bare numbers, are the real meat of mathematics. . . . As we shall see, the patterns of sentence structure that guide words are more important than the words.—Benjamin Lee Whorf

A written sentence is one or more words punctuated as an independent statement, that is, with a period, question mark, or exclamation point after the last word:

> It looks like rain tomorrow.
> Why not?
> How happy we were!

Some knowledge of grammatical terms is obviously necessary for meaningful discussion of sentence structure so that a writer may understand why a modifier is misplaced or "dangling," or why a verb does not agree with its subject, or why a pronoun should be in the objective case.

This section reviews the grammatical terms that are needed in analyzing and describing sentences, and in discussing the relations between the words that make them. Most of these terms are probably familiar ones, but you will find it helpful to go over them so that you will better understand the matters of usage in the following sections.

13.1 Main sentence elements   Most English sentences are made with a subject and verb, a pattern known as the "favorite" or "major" type of sentence.

13.1a The subject   The subject (S) of a sentence is a noun or a noun equivalent (pronoun, noun clause, gerund, infinitive) that is the starting point of the statement:

The British *submarine* (S) sank the cruiser.
He (S) went for a walk.
What they don't know (S) won't hurt them.

The *simple subject* is a single word, like *submarine* in the first sentence above. The *complete subject* is the simple subject and any words modifying it: *The British submarine.*

13.1b **The verb** The verb (V) of a sentence indicates an action, condition, or process of whatever the subject names. It may consist of one or more words:

The British submarine (S) *sank* (V) the cruiser.
He (S) *looked* it *up* (*looked up* is the verb) in a dictionary.
The baby (S) *has been sleeping* (V) since one o'clock.
Perhaps the plaintiff (S) *should be given* (V) the benefit of the doubt.

The *predicate* is the verb and whatever words are related to it, such as objects, complements, and modifiers:

The doorbell *rang*. [The verb is the complete predicate.]
The submarine *sank* (V) *the cruiser.*
Dressed entirely in black, Estelle *was* (V) *certainly not the most colorful person at the reception.*

13.1c **The object** The *direct object* (O) of a verb is a word or group of words, usually following the verb, that completes the statement, often naming what the action of the verb is directed toward.

The submarine (S) sank (V) the *cruiser* (O).
Mr. Sherwood (S) sells (V) *real estate* (O).
The government (S) decreed (V) *that candy rationing would end Monday* (O).

The *indirect object* (IO) used with verbs of telling, asking, giving, receiving, and so on, names the receiver of the message, gift, etc., and comes before the direct object, except when it is a prepositional phrase:

He (S) gave (V) the *church* (IO) a memorial window (O).
He (S) gave (V) a memorial window (O) *to the church* (IO).

13.1d The complement   A complement (C) is a noun or an adjective in the predicate. It is related directly to the subject rather than to the verb, in contrast to an object of a verb. A noun used as a complement is called a *predicate noun;* an adjective used as a complement is called a *predicate adjective:*

> Florence (S) was (V) his eldest *sister* (C). [predicate noun]
> The radiator (S) felt (V) *warm* (C). [predicate adjective]

The *linking verb* (LV) sometimes called a *copula,* connects the subject with a noun or adjective complement in the predicate: In the sentences above, *was* and *felt* are linking verbs.

The most common linking verb is *be* in its various forms: *was, were, is, had been, might be,* etc. Other linking verbs include *seem* and *appear,* and in some contexts, *feel, grow, act, look, smell, taste.*

13.2 Word order   In English, word order is an important way of indicating relationships between sentence elements. Though the form of the words is the same, it makes a great deal of difference whether you say "the ball hit the boy" or "the boy hit the ball."

13.2a Typical word order   The typical order of the main elements is subject-verb-object (or subject-verb-complement). This is the order in which we make most statements and the means by which we understand them.

In "The class congratulated Rachel" we know through experience that *class* is the subject of *congratulated* because it precedes the verb, and that *Rachel* is the object because it follows the verb. When the verb is in the *passive voice,* the subject is represented as the recipient of the action, but the order of the elements remains the same:

>   s   v
> Rachel | was congratulated by the class.

So familiar is this order that we recognize it even though the statement itself may be gibberish, or "jabberwocky," as in these lines from *Alice in Wonderland:*

> . . . the slithy toves
> Did gyre and gimble in the wabe.

Whatever the meaning, most people would agree that because of the order of the words, the subject is *toves* and the verbs are *did gyre* and *gimble.*

13.2b Inverted order The typical subject-verb-object order is varied for questions, for emphasis, or for other purposes:

```
             V      S        O
Question: Have | you | a minute to spare?
                C              S        LV
Exclamation: How sour | these grapes | taste!
                     O        S      V
Emphatic object: A better job | I | never had.
```

When the usual order of elements is reversed, you can find the subject of the sentence by locating the verb and then seeing what word belongs with it. Thus in the expression "A lot he knows about it!" *knows* is the verb, and since *he* is obviously the one who *knows, he* is the subject, and not *lot.*

13.3 Subordinate sentence elements In addition to the main sentence elements (subject-verb-object or subject-linking verb-complement), most sentences also contain subordinate or secondary elements. These are related either to the sentence as a whole or to certain words in it by one of three ways:

13.3a Single word modifiers Single words used as modifiers are usually related by means of word order. Adjectives typically stand before the nouns they modify (a *steep* climb), though they may come immediately after (a climb *steep* and *dangerous*). Adverbs are more varied in position, but when they definitely modify a verb, they usually stand close to it (They *particularly* wanted to go; He ran *fast* but *wildly*). Nouns in apposition (appositives) ordinarily follow the nouns that they identify or explain (Mr. Jenkins, *the lawyer*).

13.3b Phrases Phrases are groups of related words connected to a sentence or one of the elements in it by means of a preposition or a verbal. They have neither subject nor verb and function very much like single word modifiers.

A *prepositional phrase* connects a noun (and any modifiers it may have) to the rest of the sentence by means of a preposition (*at, by, in, of, under,* and so on):

> In the late twenties, numerous accounts were published *about the extensive damage* caused *by field mice in California.*

Other phrases are linked by a participle, gerund, or infinitive, none of which has full verb function. These are called *verbid phrases:*

> *Finding the motels filled* [participle phrase], the Johnsons drove on to the next town.
> *Opening the heavy gate* [gerund phrase] took longer than he thought.
> The most profitable way *to understand grammatical constructions* is *to analyze your own sentences* [infinitive phrases].

13.3c Clauses Subordinate (or dependent) clauses are connected to sentences by relative pronouns (*who, which, that*), or by subordinating conjunctions (*because, although, since, after, while,* etc.), and function as *part* of the sentence—as subject, object, or modifier. Main (or independent) clauses express the principal statement of the sentence. Both kinds of clauses contain a subject and a predicate and are thus easily distinguishable from phrases, which do not have a subject or a predicate:

> *Because he* (S) *found* (V) *my wallet* [subordinate clause, modifying the main clause, which follows] I gave him a reward.
> He (S) confessed (V) *that he* (S) *had stolen* (V) *my wallet* [subordinate clause, object of the verb *confessed*].
> Cellophane (S) is made (V) by a process [main clause] *which* (S) *differs* (V) *very little from the production of rayon* [subordinate clause, modifying *process*].

Subordinate clauses are used either as nouns (as subjects, objects, or complements), as adjectives (modifying nouns or pronouns), or as adverbs (expressing relationships of time, cause, result, degree, contrast, and so forth).

Noun clause (subject): *What interested me most about my new roommate* was his accent.

Adjective clause (modifying *criminals*): Many of the criminals *whose cases crowded the docket each year* were third- or fourth-time offenders.

Adverb clause (of time): *When the ship approached the pier,* the band began to play.

Adverb clause (of cause): They were discouraged *because they had tried to do their best.*

13.4 Subordinate elements as modifiers In most statements the subject, verb, and object are not sufficient to convey the writer's meaning and they are therefore further expanded or qualified by means of word, phrase, or clause *modifiers* (M).

13.4a Typical modifiers Modifiers are typically used to describe, limit, or make meaning more exact. The parts of the statement "The orchestra played a selection" may be modified in various ways as the following examples show:

$$\overset{\text{s}}{\text{The orchestra}} \mid \overset{\text{v}}{\text{played}} \mid \overset{\text{o}}{\text{a selection.}}$$

Subject modifiers

By a word: The $\overset{\text{M}}{local}$ $\overset{\text{s}}{\text{orchestra}}$ played a selection.

By a phrase: The $\overset{\text{s}}{\text{orchestra}}$, $\overset{\text{M}}{consisting\ largely\ of\ amateurs}$, played a selection.

By a clause: The $\overset{\text{s}}{\text{orchestra}}$, $\overset{\text{M}}{which\ had\ practiced\ hard\ for\ several}$ *weeks*, played a selection.

Verb modifiers

By a word: The orchestra $\overset{\text{v}}{\text{played}}$ the selection $\overset{\text{M}}{brilliantly}$.

By a phrase:

V   M
The orchestra played the selection *with more enthu-siasm than technique.*

By a clause:

V   M
The orchestra played the selection *as if they had never rehearsed together before.*

Object modifiers

By a word:

M   O
The orchestra played a *difficult* selection.

By a phrase:

O   M
The orchestra played a selection *of old folk tunes.*

By a clause:

O   M
The orchestra played a selection *which no one in the audience had ever heard before.*

Sentence modifiers

By a word:

M
Then the orchestra played the selection.

By a phrase:

M
Considering their lack of experience, the orchestra played the selection fairly well.

By a clause:

M
Since there were no other requests, the orchestra played the selection.

When they are used to modify other sentence elements, phrases and clauses function like single-word modifiers; in other words, they are equivalent to adjectives when they modify nouns or pronouns, and to adverbs when they modify verbs, adjectives, adverbs, or the sentence as a whole.

13.4b Appositives   An appositive (A) is a word or group of words following another expression, and modifying it by amplifying its meaning or making its meaning more specific:

A
The word *apposition* means "putting beside."

A
Kling, *a retired furniture manufacturer,* began studying insect life when he was past fifty.

13.4c Modifiers of modifiers Words, phrases, and clauses that modify main sentence elements may themselves be modified. These expressions are modifiers of modifiers (MM).

> MM   M   S   V   M   M   O
> The *local* high school orchestra played several difficult selections
> MM   M
> *very* well.

13.5 Minor sentence types While the great majority of written sentences contain both subjects and verbs, some statements do not. In speech, we may express ourselves by a single word ("Yes." "Oh?"), a phrase ("In a minute."), or a clause ("If you say so."). Likewise we find in published material single words, phrases, and subordinate clauses as sentences:

> And so on to Bangkok. Spit and hiss of water, the gramaphone quiet. The lights out along the deck, nobody about.—Graham Greene, *The Shipwrecked*, p. 17

We do not have to supply any "missing" words to get the author's meaning (such as "And so *the ship sailed* on to Bangkok."). Such statements are meaningful and complete as they stand. But they are minor types, exceptions to the typical English sentence with subject and predicate. When they appear in print, they are used deliberately and for a special purpose (for dialog, for emphasis, or to avoid colorless or repetitious verbs).

13.5a Subjectless sentences Imperative sentences (commands and requests) generally do not have subjects:

> Don't let me hear you say that again.
> Please try.

The subject is sometimes omitted in Informal or Familiar writing when it is easily carried over from the context:

> They took no interest in civilized ways. Hadn't heard of them, probably.—Clarence Day, *Life with Father*, p. 30

Hear Alabama and Mississippi walk out of convention. Hear Governor Donnelly nominate me. Both on the train radio. Hard to hear. My daughter and my staff try to keep me from listening. Think maybe I will be upset. I won't be.—President Truman's diary for July 14, 1948, in William Hillman, *Mr. President*, p. 137

It would be inappropriate and ineffective, however, to begin a factual discussion in this manner:

Am writing on this subject because I have been interested in chemistry since childhood.

13.5b Verbless sentences   Several types of sentences without a main verb are used in all levels of speaking and writing. The verbs are not left out; they are not thought, spoken, or written. The statements are complete and independent without them.

1) Exclamations: *Ouch!, Oh!,* and other single words; *What a pity!, For goodness' sake!,* and similar phrases.

2) Answers to questions: *Yes; No; Not if I know it.* These may include answers to questions raised by the writer:

What is a hero? *The exceptional individual.* How is he recognized, whether in life or in books? *By the degree of interest he arouses in the spectator or the reader.*—W. H. Auden, *The Enchafèd Flood*, p. 93

3) Descriptive details are sometimes set off for emphasis or to avoid colorless verbs like *is, are, has:*

I made him open and show me his book. It was chockfull. *All kinds of names of all kinds of people from all over everywhere. New pages clean, and old pages scratched out. In purple indelible pencil.*—Eudora Welty, "Kin," *The New Yorker*, November 15, 1952, p. 47

There was one in particular of Mother looking very roguish and chic in her voluminous dress, sitting way up on top of a tall and insolent camel, with two big black men in white turbans standing off at one side. *No other member of the party around. Not a soul in sight but the black men and Mother.* Father looked at that photograph often and groaned about it at night, and kept shouting things to himself about "the ends of the earth."—Clarence Day, *Life with Father*, p. 116

Often in passages portraying a character's thought there are no verbs, increasing the speed and naturalness of movement:

If he had any common sense at all, he would stop seeing her. *Now. Before it was too late.*—Florence J. Soman, "Dangerous Engagement," *Woman's Home Companion*, July 1952, p. 93

4) Appositional sentence: A phrase that stresses the meaning of the preceding statement or looks forward to the next one is sometimes written as a complete sentence:

An understatement, this.—S. E. Morison, *Harvard College in the Seventeenth Century*, p. 320

He never appeared on Sundays for the usual midday dinners. *No sight or sound of him.*—Isabel Bolton, *Many Mansions*, p. 111

Appositional sentences frequently serve as transitions:

So much for the contemplative aspect of man's place in a scientific cosmos. I come now to the practical aspect.—Bertrand Russell, *The Impact of Science on Society*, p. 14

13.6 Grammatical classification of sentences　Sentences may be classified according to the kind and number of clauses they contain, as *simple, compound, complex,* or *compound-complex.*

13.6a Simple sentences　A simple sentence contains one main clause (a grammatically independent statement) and no subordinate clauses (dependent statements):

The man went across the street.

Simple sentences need not be of the one-small-idea-to-the-sentence type; they may contain any number of modifiers. The following has one main clause (*Mr. Bates paused briefly in New York*) and six phrase modifiers:

Two years later, with the reflection safely bound between the covers of his twelfth published novel, Mr. Bates paused briefly in New York, in transit between England and the Bahamas.—Lewis Nichols, "Talk with H. E. Bates," *The New York Times Book Review*, February 15, 1953, p. 14

Either the subject or the predicate, or both, may be compound:

S   S
Teachers and students will not always agree on some matters in

English.

S   S   S   V
Students, youths and workers, led by Communists, attacked Indian
                    V   V   V
government property, cut telegraph wires, damaged railroads, burned
              V   V   V
rail cars and stoned fire engines, looted railroad restaurants, hoisted

black flags of mourning over government buildings.—*Time*, December

29, 1952, p. 22

13.6b Compound sentences   Compound sentences contain two or
more main clauses:

> [First main clause:] Mexico has had some loyal and patriotic leader-
> ship, but not for any long periods of time, [second main clause:] and
> few leaders have been of great stature.—Herbert Cerwin, *These Are the
> Mexicans*, p. 318

Each statement in a compound sentence is a main clause
and is *coordinate* (of equal importance) with the other statements. There are no subordinate clauses in compound sentences

Clauses in a compound sentence are separated or joined in
one of three ways:

1) By coordinating conjunctions: *and, but, or, for,* or the
correlatives *either . . . or, neither . . . nor:*

> The game was nip and tuck all the way *but* we finally managed to win.
> *Either* you learned these simple things in high school *or* you will have
> to learn them in college.

2) Without connectives: Independent clauses not joined
by coordinating conjunctions are conventionally separated by
semicolons:

> They are generous-minded; they hate shams and enjoy being indig-
> nant about them; they are valuable social reformers; they have no

notion of confining books to a library shelf.—E. M. Forster, *Aspects of the Novel*, p. 33

3) By conjunctive adverbs: These include such words as *accordingly, also, consequently, however, nevertheless, therefore, then.* Main clauses joined by these adverbs are conventionally separated by a semicolon:

The state police had proved themselves expert in publicizing their solution of crimes; *consequently,* some local police gave them only grudging support.

13.6c Complex sentences A complex sentence consists of one main clause and one or more subordinate clauses. The main clause expresses the principal statement, the subordinate clause the secondary statement:

As far as I could determine [subordinate clause], Paris hadn't changed at all [main clause] *since I last visited it ten years before* [subordinate clause].

Nearly half of all sentences in current writing are complex sentences. They offer more variety than simple sentences and are generally more exact than compound sentences, because the subordinating conjunctions are more numerous and more precise in meaning than coordinating conjunctions.

13.6d Compound-complex sentences A compound-complex sentence contains two or more main clauses and one or more subordinate clauses:

When two men fight a duel [first subordinate clause], the matter is trivial [first main clause], but *when 200 million people fight 200 million other people* [second subordinate clause] the matter is serious [second main clause].—Bertrand Russell, *The Impact of Science on Society*, p. 38

13.7 Sentences classified by purpose According to meaning or purpose, sentences are conventionally classified as:

1) *Declarative:* those that make statements or affirmations:

Sue smiled.
Considerably more than nine-tenths of the sentences that we speak and write are declarative.

2) *Interrogative:* those that ask questions:

At what temperature does water boil?

3) *Imperative (or directive):* those that make requests, commands, or give instructions:

Come!
Please try to be more prompt.
When the liquid boils, remove it from the heat.

4) *Exclamatory:* those that express feelings, facts, or opinions emphatically:

How lucky you are!

References

Burnet, MacCurdy, "Structural Syntax on the Blackboard," *College English,* October 1954, 16:38-43

Curme, *Syntax*

Jespersen, Ch. 10

Roberts, Ch. 13

Exercises

1. Copy the sentences from this paragraph and indicate the main and subordinate sentence elements (see the example below). Then classify the sentences as simple, compound, complex, or compound-complex. Use the letters in §13.1 and §13.4 or whatever other terms your instructor specifies. This example illustrates one method of analysis:

```
 S      V           M        O                    M
 I | remember | the Easter | services | in the Roman Catholic
                    M
 Church | in Moscow. (Simple sentence)
```

1) It was gloomy, and a fine, cold rain—half rain and half sleet —was falling.

2) Even the enclosure around the church was jammed with crowds of Russians, so that we could not drive to the entrance, but had to push our way through on foot.

3) Two or three rows in front had been reserved, and we finally made our way there.

4) One little old lady was on her knees in front, leaning patiently against the wall near the altar as if tired, covered with a great open-knitted white shawl tied around her throat.

5) Every bit of space was packed with people.
—Leslie C. Stevens, "The Russian People," *The Atlantic Monthly,* May 1952, p. 29

2. Analyze this passage, following the directions for exercise 1.

1) Some people talk a great deal; others speak hardly at all.

2) This is one of the most obvious ways in which people differ so far as language behavior is concerned.

3) The amount of speaking done by an individual varies greatly, of course, with the circumstances in which he finds himself. . . .

4) But if one gives attention to the matter in the course of everyday observations, a fair sense of the normal range of verbal output can be acquired.

5) One soon becomes sensitive to those persons, at least, who talk much more and those who talk much less than the general run of people, and these extreme individuals are of considerable interest.—Wendell Johnson, *People in Quandaries,* p. 244. Reprinted by permission of Harper & Brothers.

3. Make a similar analysis of the sentences in one of your recent papers. Do you tend to use one type of sentence pattern more than another? Are the relationships between different parts of your sentences clear and reasonably exact, or do some of the statements seem merely to be tacked on? On the basis of your analysis, what particular points in sentence structure should you bear in mind when revising future papers?

14 Basic sentence faults

The two most serious and conspicuous errors in sentence construction are fragmentary sentences and comma faults. The first error occurs when a subordinate part of a sentence— a phrase or a dependent clause—is carelessly punctuated as a complete sentence, as in this fragment: *Since her health was poor at that time.* The second error occurs when two sentences that are distinctly separate have been spliced together with a comma (*Iodine helps prevent simple goiter, this ailment affects young and old alike*), or have been fused with no separating punctuation at all (*Iodine helps prevent simple goiter this ailment affects young and old alike*).

These constructions are considered serious errors because they suggest that the writer is either extremely careless about his punctuation or, when they appear again and again in the same paper, that he may not know what a complete sentence is. Comma faults confuse the writer's meaning and force the reader to supply the proper punctuation; fragmentary sentences that are unintentional and ineffective cannot be justified as examples of minor sentence types (§13.5, p. 171).

14.1 Fragmentary sentences

Frag The construction marked is not a complete sentence. Revise it by joining it to another sentence, by making it a complete sentence, or by rewriting it.

More often than not, a fragmentary sentence is the result of careless writing rather than ignorance of sentence structure. If you can readily see why the construction marked on your paper is a fragment, correct the mistake by the most effective of the following methods. But if you do not know why the construction is faulty, study the discussion of sentences in §13 before you read this section.

14.1a Joining a fragment to another sentence A fragmentary sentence usually is a part of the preceding sentence. If you read the passage aloud, you will notice that you pause slightly less and do not drop your voice as noticeably before the fragment as you do at the end of complete sentences. This means that the fragment should be joined to the preceding sentence, usually with a comma, and perhaps rephrased.

Sentence fragment	Revised
The next afternoon we made our way through the wreck-strewn harbor of Okinawa. *That island which had made history less than seven years before.*	The next afternoon we made our way through the wreck-strewn harbor of Okinawa, the island which had made history less than seven years before.

1) Phrases are subordinate sentence elements and should not be carelessly punctuated as complete sentences:

Sentence fragment	Revised
I cite these examples to show how interesting accounting can be. *And to give you an idea of the kind of problems an accountant has to solve.* [infinitive phrase]	I cite these examples to show how interesting accounting can be, and to give you an idea of the kind of problems an accountant has to solve.
For the past five years I have been contributing a small amount annually to the March of Dimes. *Without ever suspecting that one day a member of my own family might benefit from this foundation.* [prepositional phrase]	For the past five years I have been contributing a small amount annually to the March of Dimes, without ever suspecting that one day a member of my own family might benefit from this foundation.
Professor Brown suddenly glanced up from his notes. *His eyes twinkling with suppressed laughter.* [*Twinkling* is a participle, not a full verb.]	Professor Brown suddenly glanced up from his notes, his eyes twinkling with suppressed laughter.

2) Explanatory phrases beginning with *such as, for example*, and similar expressions belong in the same sentence as the statement they explain:

Sentence fragment	Revised
After the cards have been run through, the firm knows what	After the cards have been run through, the firm knows what

volume of business has been done during the week in each of the departments. *Such as tobaccos, candies, canned fruits, fresh produce.*	volume of business has been done during the week in each of the departments, such as tobaccos, candies, canned fruits, and fresh produce.

3) Subordinate clauses are only parts of sentences and should not stand alone without definite reason:

Sentence fragment	*Revised*
At the time, my old rowboat with its three horsepower motor seemed a high speed job to me. *Although it only attained a speed of about twelve miles an hour.* [adverb clause, beginning with *Although*]	At the time, my old rowboat with its three horsepower motor seemed a high speed job to me, although it only attained a speed of about twelve miles an hour.
Green Mansions is an unusual story. *The main part of which is taken up with a description of the South American jungles.* [adjective clause, introduced by *which*]	*Green Mansions* is an unusual story, the main part of which is taken up with a description of the South American jungles.

In sentences like these a relative pronoun (*who, which, that*) or a subordinating conjunction (such as *although, because, if, when, while*) indicates that what follows is a subordinate clause and that it should be combined with a main clause.

14.1b Making a fragment into a complete sentence   If the fragment is a phrase that deserves special emphasis, it can be made into a complete and separate sentence by inserting a subject and a predicate:

Sentence fragment	*Revised*
He talked for fifty minutes without taking his eyes off his notes. *Apparently not noticing that half the class was asleep.* [*Noticing* is a participle, not a verb.]	He talked for fifty minutes without taking his eyes off his notes. Apparently he did not notice that half the class was asleep. [The subject is *he*; the predicate is the verb *did notice* plus the words related to it.]

National elections and student elections may be compared as closely as an object and its photograph. *The only difference being in size.* [*Being* is a verbal, not a verb.]	National elections and student elections may be compared as closely as an object and its photograph. The only difference is in size. [*Is* is the verb, and *difference* is the subject.]

14.1c Rewriting a fragment   Sometimes sentence fragments that are involved or hopelessly snarled up will have to be completely revised and reworded. This long "sentence" has three phrases that seem to be subjects, but there is no verb:

Sentence fragment	*Revision*
The people who only said "Oh, too bad," on seeing the lifeless puppy, *the small boy* who removed the dead puppy from the gutter, and the *middle-aged man* who kept saying over and over that the people were making a greater fuss about this incident than had been made over his own accident at this same corner a year ago, when he was almost run over by a taxi.	When the small boy removed the dead puppy from the gutter, some people only said "Oh, too bad." But the middle-aged man kept saying over and over that the people were making a greater fuss about this incident than they had made over his own accident at this same corner a year ago, when he was almost run over by a taxi.

See §13.5, Minor sentence types, p.171, for the occasional effective use of subjectless and verbless sentences.

14.2 Comma faults

CF Revise the sentence marked by changing the comma to a semicolon or period, or by inserting an appropriate conjunction, or by rephrasing.

A comma fault (sometimes called a "comma splice" or "run-on sentence") is two or more complete statements (main clauses), each with a subject and a predicate, written with a comma but no conjunction (*and, but, or*) between them. The result is that one statement is simply backed up against the other, as in this comma fault:

The card catalog is the key to the books in the library, many large libraries have separate catalogs for certain collections of books.

One way to detect comma faults in revision is to read your paper aloud. If your voice drops or if you pause noticeably at a comma, check the sentence to see if it is actually two separate statements. For example, try reading this sentence aloud to see how much more marked the pause is at the comma following *past* (a comma fault) than at the comma following *six-thirty:*

The long days of Front and Market streets were a thing of the past, the store now opened for business at ten in the morning and closed at six-thirty, including Saturdays.

The marked pause indicates that there are two statements here; a new sentence should begin after *past*.

14.2a Revising by making two sentences   A comma fault may be removed by using a period instead of the comma, making two full sentences:

Comma fault	*Revised*
He took a couple of steps, stopped, reached out, and turned a valve, as he did so, he told us the valves had to be checked daily.	He took a couple of steps, stopped, reached out, and turned a valve. As he did so, he told us the valves had to be checked daily.

This is usually the best solution when the ideas are clearly distinct or when commas are numerous in either or both statements. But correcting a comma fault by putting a period between two very short, closely connected statements may result only in two weak sentences.

14.2b Revising by using a semicolon   Comma faults may sometimes be corrected by substituting a semicolon for the comma.

Comma fault	*Revised*
Charley then crossed the room and threw a switch which started the motor, returning, he wiped the sweat from his forehead with the back of his hand.	Charley then crossed the room and threw a switch which started the motor; returning, he wiped the sweat from his forehead with the back of his hand.

A semicolon is the conventional punctuation between two main clauses connected by a conjunctive adverb (such as *accordingly, consequently, however, therefore*).

Comma fault

The person with a college education has training far beyond that which he obtained solely from books, *therefore* his chances for success are much greater than are those of a person without this education.

Repunctuated

The person with a college education has training far beyond that which he obtained solely from books; therefore his chances for success are much greater than are those of a person without this education.

A large number of comma faults in student papers occur with conjunctive adverbs. Since most conjunctive adverbs are more appropriate to Formal usage than to student writing, a good way to avoid such errors is to use other kinds of connectives. A better revision of the comma fault just given might read:

Because a person with a college education has training far beyond that which he obtained solely from books, his chances for success are much greater than are those of a person without this education.

14.2c Revising by using an appropriate connective Usually the best way to remove a comma fault is to revise the sentence, using a connective that will show the relation between the statements. This may be a coordinating conjunction (such as *and* or *but*), a subordinating conjunction (*although, because, if, since, when . . .*), or a relative pronoun (*who, which, that . . .*) referring to a noun in the first statement:

Comma fault

It is a personal matter, everyone has to cope with it sooner or later.

Revised with connective

It is a personal matter, *and* everyone has to cope with it sooner or later. Or: It is a personal matter *that* everyone has to cope with sooner or later.

I bloom in the midst of a party, particularly if I feel some responsibility for its success, con-

I bloom in the midst of a party, particularly if I feel some responsibility for its success, *because*

| versation is a stimulant more powerful than drugs. | conversation is a stimulant more powerful than drugs. |

| They still produce aluminum tips for broken skis, these are very successful as a device for temporary repair. | They still produce aluminum tips for broken skis *(which* are very successful as a device for temporary repair.*))* |

14.3 **Fused sentences**   A fused sentence is the same kind of error as a comma fault, except that no punctuation at all appears between the main clauses. It represents plain carelessness and should be corrected in the same way as a comma fault:

Fused sentence: Two volumes of his great work are now completed the first will be published next year.

Possible revisions: Two volumes of his great work are now completed, the first of which will be published next year.

Two volumes of his great work are now completed, and the first will be published next year.

Exercises

1. Point out which of the following statements are fragmentary sentences and which contain comma faults. Then show how the wording or punctuation could be changed to put these sentences into acceptable form. Label correct those sentences that you think need no revision.

1) My little sister often begged to play on the sand bank, knowing the danger involved, we would never let her go unless someone went with her.

2) What a strange feeling it was to arrive in New York as a total stranger in the early morning hours of a bleak December day!

3) Statistics are not yet available to show the actual decrease in accidents, Since this program is still in the process of being completed and traffic has doubled in the past few months.

4) If all of the people in this country considered their education completed when they finished high school, things would be very different, for one thing, there would be no atomic age such as we are now going through.

5) The market thrives on competition since the same kind of shops are all grouped together. An example of this being the four bakeries, which are in the same area.

6) Dad always complained when we asked him for money to buy firecrackers, then he would go out and bring home a lot of them himself.

7) We do not know all the answers, therefore much must be carried on by love and understanding in this world.

8) The tendency in recent years has been toward urban living, chiefly because there is a great variety of employment in the larger metropolitan areas, Such as New York, Chicago, and Los Angeles.

9) When a boy lives at home, he is dependent on others, they help him out of his difficulties and provide at least for his necessities.

10) Looking carefully through his water glass he finds a liner deep in the quicksand, lying on her side. The nearest porthole being twelve feet down. He dives down to the porthole and tries to break it.

11) Near the grill was a freshly painted picnic table, its bright green surface glittering in the sunlight.

12) Parents should realize that a child will grow up satisfactorily if he is left alone, if suggestion is substituted for nagging, he will be a happy, well-adjusted person.

13) Then at the other end of town is the opposite extreme. The people who live in large homes with two Cadillacs parked in their double garages.

14) The one weakness most widely cultivated by the advertisers, however, is our susceptibility to flattery.

15) I have spent many enjoyable hours reading and writing letters, Exchanging ideas and comparing ways of life with people my own age in countries around the world.

2. In the passages below are some sentences without subjects or without verbs. First read each passage to see what effect the writer is trying to achieve. Then indicate by number which sentences lack either subjects or verbs or both. How would you justify (or criticize) their use in each instance? Would "complete" sentences be just as effective, or would they slow down the movement or weaken emphasis? (See §13.5, Minor sentence types, p. 171.)

a.   (1) Down Barrow to Greenwich Street. (2) He looked up at the houses. (3) Patsy told him they were so cute. (4) Little red houses, dormer windows. (5) Cute enough. (6) Why shouldn't he cash that check? (7) After all, whose fault was it that he was down and out? (8) He'd paid the bills when he'd first gone to live with Patsy. (9) He stopped and took the check out of his pocket. (10) Made out to Patricia Smith, signed by Philip Ropes the third and countersigned by Patsy. (11) Quite a story in it, a little story à la Tchekhov called "The Check." (12) Should he cash it, should he tear it into ten thousand bits?—Isabel Bolton, *Many Mansions,* pp. 33-34

b.   (1) He held out his papers in fingers like thick half-smoked cigars. (2) Welsh took them and, opening the worn *Soldbuch,* discovered the man in front of him as a smooth-faced smiling boy in the identification picture. (3) He checked the necessary entries. (4) War service 1914-18. (5) Wounded. (6) Recalled to the Landstrum in 1938. (7) Exempted from military service because of age and infirmity.—Robie Macauley, "The Thin Voice," *The Kenyon Review,* Winter 1951, p. 54

c.   (1) What's a poet good for? (2) To give us words for the music in ourselves. (3) To give us words to live by; great swinging words for our dreams to march to. (4) For just as it takes a child to remind us of the joy in simple things, so it takes a poet to show us the wonder of what is before our eyes.—Louis Redmon, "Boyhood: Made in America," in *The Wonderful World of Books,* edited by Alfred Stefferud, p. 97

15 Subordinate clauses

About half the sentences in most kinds of writing contain one or more subordinate clauses. A subordinate clause has a subject and a predicate, but is shown to be a subordinate or secondary part of the sentence by a special kind of connective that relates it to the main clause. In the following sentence, *when* is the connective: *When* the hunting season started [subordinate clause], there were at least five eager hunters in each field [main clause]. The principal gain from using subordinate clauses is that the relationship between statements is indicated more exactly than in a series of simple or compound sentences.

15.1 **Adjective clauses**   A clause that modifies a noun or pronoun is an adjective clause. The relative pronouns *who, which,* and *that* are the words most frequently used to introduce adjective clauses and may serve as subjects or objects within the clause:

Those *who criticize Mr. Sill for being harsh* don't really understand the background of the situation. [*Who* is the subject of the clause which modifies *those.*]

The speaker wore a long black coat, *which was obviously in need of cleaning.* [*Which* is the subject of the clause which modifies *coat.*]

Fingerprinting newborn babies is a practice *that is being adopted in more and more hospitals.* [*That* is the subject of the clause which modifies *practice.*]

The poem *from which most of these quotations were taken* is Gray's "Elegy Written in a Country Churchyard." [*Which* is the object of the preposition *from.* The clause modifies *poem.*]

The caller turned out to be Betsy, a distant cousin *whom I had not seen for ten years.* [*Whom* is the object of the verb *had seen;* the clause modifies *cousin.*]

Adjective clauses may also be introduced by the relative adverbs *when, where,* and *why:*

There comes a time *when you have to decide.*

I'll show you the place *where I was born.*

Another reason *why many people prefer oil heat* is that there are no ashes.

15.1a ***Who, which, and that*** *Who* refers to persons, *which* generally refers to things, and *that* refers to persons or things.

Students *who* [or *that*] plan to enter the university in the fall quarter should forward transcripts of their records to the registrar.

The number of men *that* [or *who*] fell within the age limits of the draft was 3,500,000.

In five minutes he solved a problem *that* [or *which*] I had struggled with for nearly five hours.

This is a matter about *which* more information is needed.

15.1b Clauses without relative words With many adjective clauses we have a choice of using the relative word or not using it (the relative in such cases is always the object, not the subject):

The steaks [that] we get in restaurants today seem much smaller than those [that] we used to get five years ago.

Getting on the plane was a person [whom] I hadn't seen for at least ten years.

The shorter constructions (they are still subordinate clauses) have long been used in English and are acceptable at all levels of writing.

15.1c ***And which*** *And* is sometimes carelessly and unnecessarily used to join an adjective clause to the rest of a sentence. The relative pronouns *which* or *who* are the connectives; the use of *and* or *but* is superfluous:

Inaccurate	*Revised*
Her gown was of heavy green brocade, and which was most becoming to her.	Her gown was of heavy green brocade, which was most becoming to her.

15.2 Adverb clauses A clause that modifies a verb, adjective, or adverb is an adverb clause (Come *when you can;* You are thinner *than you were a year ago;* He danced as smoothly *as she did*). While they may modify single words (*Come, thinner, smoothly*) adverb clauses often modify main clauses by expressing relationships of time, place, direction, cause, effect, condition, manner, concession. For example, in "The game was continued *although light rain kept falling,*" the clause does not modify the verb *was continued,* but qualifies the whole main statement.

15.2a Conjunctions for adverb clauses We have a good many connectives in English for expressing adverb relations. Some of the most common are the following:

after	because	provided	till
although	before	since	unless
as	if	so	when
as if	in order that	so that	where
as long as	like	though	while

In speaking we tend to rely on only a few of these words (especially *as, so, like*), but in writing, greater exactness is expected.

15.2b As The conjunction *as* may introduce various kinds of adverb clauses.

Degree or manner: I went as fast *as I could go.*
Time: Our guests arrived *as the clock struck nine.*
Cause: *As it was getting dark,* we made for home.
Comparison: Lettuce is not as fattening *as avocados are.*
Attendant circumstance: *As the fire raged,* the sky grew lighter.

The variety of its meanings makes *as* a word to be watched in writing. In some instances it is the proper and only connective to use—to express comparisons, for example (We went as far *as the others did*), or in clauses of manner (*As Maine goes,* so goes the nation). But in many other constructions, *while, when, since,* or *because* would be more exact and emphatic.

While we were walking, he told us stories.
The street lights came on *when* [or *just as*] the snow started to fall.

As is weak in the sense of *because*. To introduce clauses of reason, purpose, or result, *since* or *because* is better in most writing and certainly in Formal English.

> He refused to join in the square dancing *because* [not *as*] he was afraid of making a fool of himself.

15.2c So   *So*, like *as*, is an overworked and inexact connective. In most writing it should be replaced by a more definite word.

Spoken	*Written*
She works afternoons *and so* she couldn't go to the tea.	*Since* she works afternoons, she couldn't go to the tea.
He reads faster, *so* he finished before I did.	*Because* he reads faster, he finished before I did.

In clauses of purpose, *so that* is usually preferable to *so:*

> I got up *so that* [not *so*] the lady could have my seat.

15.3 Noun clauses   Subordinate clauses used as subjects, objects, and appositives are called noun clauses. Most of them are introduced by *that*, but *whatever, whoever, who, what, why, when, where,* and *whether* are also used.

15.3a As subjects   Subject clauses introduced by *that* or *whether* are more characteristic of Formal writing than of General usage, particularly when the clauses are relatively long:

> *That he could raise his grade by studying harder* had never occurred to him.
> *Whether or not they should have a vice-president* was the principal topic of debate.

In most kinds of writing—and certainly in conversation—constructions of this kind would ordinarily appear after the verb:

> It had never occurred to him *that he could raise his grade by studying harder.*
> The principal topic of debate was *whether or not they should have a vice-president.*

Other kinds of subject clauses are common in all levels of writing:

Whatever is worth doing at all is worth doing well.
Why so many people insist on munching popcorn at movies is something I'll never understand.

15.3b As objects   The most common use of noun clauses is as objects:

Object of a verb: He said *that it was quite impossible*. He asked *why it had to be that way*. Everyone knows *that Columbus discovered America*.

Object of a preposition: She is always sure of *what she believes*. There is a prize for *whoever gets there first*.

In the second sentence, *whoever* is the correct form rather than *whomever;* the pronoun is the subject of the clause.

15.3c Reason is because   Formal English uses a *that*-clause after "reason is"; General and especially Informal English more often have a noun clause introduced by *because*:

Formal	*General*
The reason for my poor work in French was that I disliked the subject intensely.	The reason I did poor work in French was because I didn't like the subject.

15.4 Subordinate clauses for exact statement

Sub Make the relation between clauses exact by subordinating those of lesser importance.

Ideas that deserve equal emphasis should of course be grammatically coordinate (as in *I came, I saw, I conquered*). But those that describe or explain another statement, or tell how, when, where, why something happened should be expressed in subordinate constructions whenever the relationship is not immediately clear from context.

For example, there is no reason why three separate sentences should be made of these obviously related ideas:

Mozart made his first trip to Italy in 1769. He was thirteen years old. His father went with him.

If the first statement is the important one, the others could be subordinated in this way:

In 1769 *when he was thirteen years old* [adverb clause], Mozart made his first trip to Italy [main clause], *accompanied by his father* [phrase].

Or if Mozart's youth is to be stressed, the other ideas could be subordinated thus:

Mozart was only thirteen in 1769 [main clause] *when he made his first trip to Italy with his father* [adverb clause].

15.4a Using exact connectives   Subordinate clauses are exact because their connectives show a specific relationship to the main clause. Coordinating conjunctions, especially *and,* are much less definite in meaning than adverb connectives like *because, since, when, while,* or the adjective connectives *who, which, that:*

Coordinate statements	*One statement subordinated*
Sandra was waiting for the bus and she saw a purse on the sidewalk.	*While she was waiting for the bus,* Sandra saw a purse on the sidewalk.
My favorite earrings looked like spirals of silver, and John had given them to me for my birthday.	My favorite earrings, *which John had given to me for my birthday,* looked like spirals of silver.

15.4b Showing relative importance of statements   A subordinate clause also shows that the statement subordinated is less important than the main statement. That is, it is less important for the subject being discussed. To judge the rightness of subordination it is usually necessary to know what the emphasis of the passage is.

For instance, in joining the two statements "The lightning struck the barn" and "Mother was setting the table for supper," the first would be the main statement in a general account of the event: The lightning struck the barn (main clause) just as mother was setting the table for supper (subordinate clause). But if the point was what mother did, the sentence would probably be: When the lightning struck the barn (subordinate clause), mother was setting the table for supper (main clause). The paragraph would probably go on to tell what mother did in the crisis.

In revising sentences, then, it is important to see that the parts are related according to their importance to the subject.

See §18, Sentence economy, p. 216, and §19, Sentence variety and emphasis, p. 228, for other effects of subordinate clauses.

15.5 Unsuccessful subordination Faulty subordination is as ineffective as excessive coordination in sentence structure. It usually results from a careless stringing together of ideas as they happen to pop into the writer's mind. When you go over your papers, revise any subordinate elements that weaken sentences or obscure their meaning.

15.5a Haphazard subordination Haphazard use of dependent constructions or too much subordination may be worse than no subordination at all:

> Because her mother died when Barbara was five years old, and since her father lived a solitary life, Barbara had a very unhappy childhood, having no family to confide in.

To gain some semblance of proportion from a statement as cluttered as this, a rearrangement of the elements is necessary:

> Barbara had a very unhappy childhood. She was five years old when her mother died, and since her father led a solitary life, she had no family to confide in.

See also §17.4, Stringy sentences, p. 213.

15.5b Tandem subordination Avoid statements in which a series of dependent clauses are tacked on to one another. Too many clauses beginning with similar connectives (*who, which, that; when, since, because,* etc.), each built upon the preceding one, are called *tandem subordination,* or "house-that-Jack-built" constructions:

Tandem subordination	*Revised*
He had carefully selected teachers *who* taught classes *that* had a slant *that* was specifically directed towards students *who* intended to go into business.	He had carefully selected teachers who had specifically slanted their courses toward students intending to go into business.
All of the remains *which* are left of civilization seem weird, dangerous, and fantastic to the new generation *of which* John is a member, *which* is struggling to rebuild itself.	All of the remains of the past civilization seem weird, dangerous, and fantastic to John and to his generation, a generation struggling to rebuild itself.

Sentences that begin and end with the same kind of subordinate clauses are frequently awkward because of their see-saw effect: "When he came home at night, Dad would always complain when the children weren't in bed." Such constructions can be improved by changing one of the connectives: "When he came home at night, Dad would always complain *if* the children weren't in bed."

15.5c Inverted subordination   Putting the main idea of a sentence in a subordinate clause or phrase may result in an awkward or incongruous statement ("inverting" the proper relationship between statements):

Inverted	*More accurate*
She was eighteen when her hands were severely burned, which meant that she had to give up her lifelong dream of becoming a concert pianist.	When she was eighteen, *her hands were severely burned* [main clause]. As a result, *she had to give up her lifelong dream of becoming a concert pianist* [main clause].

Inverted or "upside-down" subordination frequently occurs in sentences that trail off into weak participle phrases:

The road was blocked, *causing us to make a twenty-mile de-tour.* Such sentences can be improved by putting the less important statement in an adverb clause: We had to make a twenty-mile detour *because the road was blocked.*

Exercises

1. Some clauses in the statements below should be put into subordinate constructions to make better sentences. In others, the subordination is not successful because of faulty relationship between ideas or because of inexact connectives. Read these examples through first, and then write out your revision of them.

1) John is really a fine boy and he is a sophomore at the local high school.

2) He sprinted the first twenty yards; he began to fall into his stride rounding the first turn.

3) The course I was taking was algebra and it came to me quite easily and I enjoyed it very much.

4) There are various forms of eczema. In infancy this disorder occurs on foreheads. Or often in the folds of the elbows or knees. A deficiency of food protein causes this.

5) People who buy houses that have been built in times in which conspicuous traits of architecture prevailed that have now been abandoned often have to remodel their houses completely.

6) As an enormous mountain slide blocked the road, we had to turn the car around and drive back four miles to a detour.

7) If a fellow has been fortunate enough to attend prep school and been made to study, college studying comes much more easily to him if he wants an education, but there are many things much more interesting to him than studying but now there is no one going to tell him that he had better get his homework in.

8) Not long ago a new means of testing wool was adopted by the government. It was a mechanical-chemical-photographic method.

9) Upon arrival at the army base, I was slogging through a sea of mud, thus getting a premonition of things to come.

10) I strolled through the Student Union Building, thoroughly inspecting everything, especially the billboards displaying the efforts of the art students, and pausing long enough to assure myself that I preferred more conventional art, and then walking toward the end of a long hall, where busily preparing food and thoroughly enjoying his work was a student cook.   ʃ

2. List the subordinate clauses in the following paragraph and tell how each is used in the sentence (whether a noun clause is a subject or object, what word or words an adjective or adverb clause modifies):

(1) There is an ancient saying that no man knows what he is and what he values until he has been tested in loneliness. (2) It was certainly true of me as far as Africa was concerned. (3) I had no idea how much Africa meant to me until one day in the recent war. (4) I was lying alone in a Japanese prison cell, in great pain and shivering with a malarial ague. (5) A sentry had just left me with the announcement that my head was to be cut off in the morning. (6) I was so exhausted and in such pain that I recall feeling little else than relief at having come to some finality, and I fell quickly into a trance of fatigue. (7) But hardly had I done so when a flash of lightning flared at the small window, followed by a sustained, solemn and majestic roll of thunder; and then down came the rain. (8) It fell so fast and thick that it muffled the glare of the lightning and released instead into the darkness of my cell a soft but imperative purple; while on the 12,000-foot volcano at whose base my prison stood, roll after roll of thunder crashed like the drum of a great orchestra performing a symphony of defied and defeated fate.—Laurens van der Post, "Africa," *Holiday*, March 1954, p. 35. Reprinted by permission of *Holiday* magazine.

Further exercises involving subordinate clauses may be found at the end of § 16, p. 205.

16 Infinitives, participles, and gerunds

Infinitives, participles, and gerunds are parts of verbs that are much used in subordinate constructions. A gerund is used as a noun, a participle is used as an adjective, and an infinitive may be used as a noun, an adjective, or an adverb, as shown by the examples in the table on page 199. Since they cannot be used to make a sentence of the typical subject-verb pattern, they are called *verbals* rather than verbs.

Although verbals usually function as nouns or adjectives or adverbs, they still show some characteristics of verbs. They may have subjects and objects and may be modified by adverbs (gerunds and infinitives may also be modified by adjectives):

Bob's hitting won the game [*Bob's* is the subject of the gerund *hitting*].

Opening the *door*, he took a final look [*door* is the object of the participle *Opening*].

He wanted to leave *quietly* [*quietly* is an adverb modifying the infinitive *to leave*].

They knew that their uniforms needed a *good* brushing [*good* is an adjective modifying the gerund *brushing*].

16.1 Infinitive phrases   Most infinitives are closely related to a single word in a sentence: He tried *to go* by bus (object of *tried*); The sergeant gave the signal *to resume* the march (modifies *signal*); Her friends were happy *to hear* that she was feeling better (modifies *happy*). But some infinitives are "absolute" and modify the whole statement: *To be exact,* there were only eight clams.

16.1a Infinitive phrases as close modifiers   When the infinitive phrase is closely related to the main clause, its subject should be the same as that of the main clause. This means usually that the subject of the main clause should be the "doer," not the "recipient" of the action; in other words, the verb in the main clause should be active rather than passive.

Faulty relation (passive verb)	*Close relation* (active verb)
To get into my car, the window had to be broken.	*To get into my car, I* had to break the window.
In an effort *to arrive at an understanding, a number of conferences* were held.	In an effort *to arrive at an understanding, officials* held a number of conferences.

16.1b Infinitive phrases modifying the whole statement
Infinitive phrases that modify the main statement are said to be used "absolutely." Though they are equivalent to subordinate clauses, the subject is usually not expressed.

> *To do the job better and faster,* the railroad had invested several million dollars in new equipment.
> *To tell the truth,* none of these books is worth reading.
> England has produced a number of famous scientists—Bacon, Newton, Priestley, *to mention only a few.*

16.1c Infinitive clauses   An infinitive construction with an expressed subject is known as an "infinitive clause": He wanted *the whole group* [subject of the infinitive] *to go that afternoon.* If the subject of the infinitive is a pronoun, it is in the object form: They asked *her* [subject of the infinitive] *to make a cake.*

16.1d Complement with *to be*   In Formal English, a pronoun used as a complement after the infinitive *to be* is in the objective case:

> They had thought *me to be him* [*him* is the complement of the infinitive *to be*].

This construction is unlikely to occur anywhere except in the most rigidly Formal English; certainly it would be conspicuous in General English, where a regular clause would be used: "They had thought that I was he"; or in Informal English, "They had thought that I was him."

16.2 Participle phrases   Present participles (ending in *-ing*) and past participles (ending in *-ed* or changing the vowel,

Forms and uses of infinitives, participles, and gerunds

Infinitive   An infinitive is (1) the basic form of the verb, with or without *to*; (2) any verb phrase that may be used with *to*.

Forms: Active   Passive

Present   (to) ask, (to) be asking   (to) be asked
Perfect   (to) have asked, (to) have been asking   (to) have been
                                                                     asked

Uses:

Subject: *To be asked to that party* makes any girl proud.
Object: He does not like *to express his opinion.*
Adjective: I have plenty of work *to do.*
Adverb modifier (to show purpose, cause, etc.):   The students came
   to learn.
"Absolute" phrase: *To make a long story short,* we didn't go.
"Infinitive clause" (here as the object of a verb):   They all wanted
   us to come.

Participle   A participle is a verb form used as an adjective.

Forms: Active   Passive

Present   asking   being asked
Past   having asked   asked, having been asked

Uses:

Simple modifier: a *smiling* candidate; a *clogged* drain
Participle phrase: The candidate *getting two-thirds of the votes* will
   be nominated.
"Absolute" phrase (modifying the whole statement):   *Taking everything into consideration,* a portable typewriter seems the most practical gift.

Gerund   A gerund is a verb form used as a noun.

Forms: Active   Passive

Present   asking   being asked
Past   having asked   having been asked

Uses:

Subject: *Taking anthropology* opened a whole new field for him.
Object: She taught *dancing.*
Complement: Seeing is *believing.*
Noun modifier: the *dining* room; a *fishing* boat; the *melting* pot

as in *sung*) are used as adjectives. As a simple modifier, a participle is closely related to the noun or pronoun it modifies:

> The town hall, completely *renovated* four years ago, creates a favorable impression on visitors. (*Renovated* is a past participle modifying *town hall*.)
>
> I first noticed him *sitting* alone in a corner. (*Sitting* is a present participle modifying *him*.)

16.2a Participle phrases modifying specific words   When a participle phrase modifies a single word in the main clause, the reference should be clear and accurate. This means usually that the phrase should be placed near the word it modifies and that if the phrase precedes the main clause the participle should modify the subject of the clause.

Inaccurate	*Accurate*
Trying to write a theme in class or at home, my thoughts sometimes get jumbled up. (The phrase seems to modify *thoughts*.)	*Trying to write a theme in class or at home,* I find that my thoughts sometimes get jumbled up. (The phrase clearly modifies *I*, subject of the main clause.)

When a participle of this sort is not clearly related to its noun or pronoun, it is said to be *misrelated*.

See §16.4, Misrelated modifiers, p. 202.

16.2b Participle phrases used "absolutely"   Participle phrases may be used "absolutely," modifying the main statement. (These are sometimes called nominative absolutes.) The typical absolute phrase has a subject and a participle: Just then the tow truck came around the corner, *its chains* [subject] *clanking* [participle] *noisily*. These constructions are frequently used in descriptive and narrative prose for adding details or parenthetical material:

> He stalked like the specter of a soldier, *his eyes burning with the power of a stare into the unknown.*—Stephen Crane, *The Red Badge of Courage*

On March 7 Napoleon entered Grenoble at the head of his army. With his snuffbox he rapped on the city gates, *torchlight playing on his face.*—C. W. Ceram, *Gods, Graves, and Scholars*, p. 99

The Portuguese listened with his head cocked to one side, *his dark eyes ringed with ash-gray circles*, and now and then he wiped his damp veined dead-white hands on his stained apron.—Carson McCullers, *Member of the Wedding*, p. 71

16.3 Gerund phrases   Gerunds and gerund phrases may be used as nouns—as the subject or the object of a verb, as predicate complements, or as appositives with other nouns. In addition, gerund phrases are also used as modifiers, either of individual words (the disagreeable task *of cleaning the furnace*), or of main statements (Sue went to the movies *after finishing her work*). When used to express relationships of time, cause, manner, result, these phrases function like adverb clauses:

Gerund phrase: *Immediately on arriving in New York*, he telephoned his lawyers.

Adverb clause: *As soon as he arrived in New York*, he telephoned his lawyers.

Gerund phrases used as modifiers can be distinguished from participle phrases by the preposition that links the gerund phrase to the rest of the sentence:

Gerund phrase: *On reaching the summit of the mountain*, we paused to enjoy the view.

Participle phrase: *Reaching the summit of the mountain*, we paused to enjoy the view.

16.3a Subjects of gerund phrases   In many gerund phrases a noun or a pronoun serves as the "subject" of the gerund.

Everyone was bored *by his* [subject] *incessant talking* [gerund].
There is little possibility *of radio and television* [subject] *providing* [gerund] all of our entertainment in the future.

When the subject of a gerund is a personal pronoun or proper noun, the possessive form is generally used:

The less said about *his* singing, the better.
We looked forward to *Bob's* coming.

With other noun forms, usage is divided. Formal English usually prefers the possessive form, but the common form of the noun is used in General English.

The neighbors finally complained about the *dog* [Formal: dog's] howling at night.
It was a case of *imagination* getting the upper hand.

In some constructions the possessive form would be unnatural and unidiomatic, as when the subject of the gerund phrase is modified by other words:

There was something peculiar about the *daughter* of the former principal winning two scholarships.
At the outbreak of the Civil War no one in Washington foresaw the possibility of *Grant,* who had failed in so many undertakings, leading the Union forces.
In spite of the *plan* of the committee being voted down, nobody could offer a better one.

References: Marckwardt and Walcott, pp. 94-95; Curme, *Syntax,* pp. 485-491

16.3b *The* **and** *of* **in gerund phrases**   Gerunds are more direct when they are not preceded by *the* and when a direct object is used instead of an *of* phrase.

Awkward	*Direct*
In *the* revising *of* the first draft, the writer can check his spelling.	In revising the first draft, the writer can check his spelling.

16.4 Misrelated modifiers

Mis **Misrelated modifier. Correction: Revise the sentence marked so that the modifier is clearly related to the word required by the meaning.**

A construction that from its position seems to modify a word in the sentence that it should not or cannot sensibly modify is a misrelated (or "dangling") modifier: I borrowed a radio from a friend *with a short-wave attachment*. These constructions may be momentarily confusing to the reader (or unintentionally humorous), and consequently should be avoided. In revision, verbal phrases used as modifiers need to be checked especially closely for faulty reference because they are loosely tied to the other parts of a sentence; but prepositional phrases (such as the one in the example above) and subordinate clauses may also be misrelated if their reference isn't as clear to the reader as it was to the writer.

16.4a Inaccurate reference   When a modifier seems to refer to the wrong word in a sentence, the sentence should be revised to make the reference accurate. Sometimes the correction can be made by putting the modifier immediately before or after the word to which it should refer:

Inaccurate	*Accurate*
On the other side of the valley, *grazing peacefully like cattle,* we saw a herd of buffalo [the participle phrase seems to refer to *we*].	On the other side of the valley we saw a herd of buffalo, *grazing peacefully like cattle* [the phrase clearly refers to *buffalo*].

But merely shifting a modifying phrase will not always result in a clear sentence. If the sentence is rather involved, it is better to rewrite it completely:

Inaccurate	*Accurate*
One early-day western senator is said to have passed out campaign cards to the voters *with five-dollar bills pinned to them.* [At first glance, the phrase seems to refer to *voters*.]	One early-day western senator is said to have pinned five-dollar bills to the campaign cards he passed out to voters.

16.4b Modifier without a reference word   Modifiers are incorrectly used when they should refer to a word that is implied rather than actually stated in the sentence:

Inaccurate	*Accurate*
In *painting four of these pictures,* his wife was used as his model. [Obviously his wife did not paint the pictures. Who did?]	In painting four of these pictures, *he* used his wife as his model.

Faulty constructions of this kind occur chiefly with verbal phrases. The easiest—but not always the most satisfactory—way to correct them is to name the agent or the "doer" of the action immediately after the phrase:

Inaccurate	*Accurate*
After *reading a dozen books,* the subject is still as puzzling as ever. [Who did the reading?]	After reading a dozen books, *I* find the subject as puzzling as ever.

Generally it is better to revise the sentence entirely, making the relationships more accurate by using other constructions:

Inaccurate	*Accurate*
Having been delayed by a train accident, the leading role was played by a local girl. [Who was delayed?]	Because the leading lady was delayed by a train accident, her role was played by a local girl.

A writer should distinguish clearly between obviously misrelated modifiers such as these and absolute modifiers—phrases that refer to the statement as a whole and that need no specific agent or "doer" of the action in the main clause:

Absolute phrase: *Considering that they are handmade,* the price is reasonable enough.

16.4c   **Ambiguous reference**   Modifiers are occasionally placed so that they seem to refer to either of two elements in the sentence. (Yesterday I started my research *on cannibalism* in the library.) These constructions (sometimes called "squinting" modifiers) can be avoided by changing the position of the modifier or by otherwise revising the sentence.

Ambiguous	Clear
Doctors have found out what causes baldness *in recent years*.	In recent years, doctors have found out what causes baldness.

Sometimes the ambiguity can be cleared up by using appropriate punctuation:

Ambiguous	Clear
In addition to being fond of lobsters, *like you,* she is a connoisseur of oysters.	In addition to being fond of lobsters, like you she is a connoisseur of oysters.

References

Curme, index references

Pooley, pp. 107-118

Roberts, Ch. 17

Exercises

These exercises involve principles discussed in §15 and §16.

1. First copy down the number of each of the italicized groups of words and write the word or statement that each one modifies, or, if it does not modify, write its use in the sentence. Then identify the word groups as adjective or adverb clauses, or participle, gerund, or infinitive phrases.

The original aim of public education in America, (1) *prepar-ing the young for citizenship in a democratic community,* has been replaced in many instances by the nondemocratic concept (2) *of training the human unit solely for a specific job in the economic machine.* The full development of the individual personality, (3) *accepted by the eighteenth-century political theorists as the goal of a democratic society,* has been reshuffled into the narrower channels of material usefulness (4) *so that the development of mechanical skills rather than the whole personality has become the order of the day.* This constitutes a narrowing not only of the educational focus but also of the democratic view and is a blow against the total culture which a democracy, in the largest sense, can be expected (5) *to produce.* The full life must necessarily include the acquisition of economic skills; but it has many other resources as well, and (6) *to neglect them* is (7) *to distort the powers and potentialities* of the *individual* man.—Leo Gurko, *Heroes, Highbrows and the Popular Mind,* p. 86

2. Follow the directions given for the preceding exercise.

. . . Brodie was rowed to the nearby New Pier, *where,* (1) *at the sight of Bridge Officer Lally waiting for him,* (2) *he jumped back into the water.* (3) *Pulled out again,* he was hustled off to the Oak Street station house, (4) *where he was provided with a towel and charged with "endangering his life."* He complained of a sharp pain in his side, but the resident surgeon of the nearby Chambers Street Hospital, (5) *who was called in,* could find nothing but two modest bruises; he said Brodie was shamming. Brodie was sent to the Tombs for the night, and on his arrival there seemed (6) *to have become suddenly drunk.* (7) *When a reporter from the Times showed up,* Brodie again appeared (8) *to be in terrible pain*—so terrible that he was barely able to gasp out that he had leaped (9) *to win a two-hundred dollar bet,* that it had been a "darling jump," and that he had protected himself (10) *by wearing an electric belt.*—Stanley Edgar Hyman, "This Alluring Roadway," *The New Yorker,* May 17, 1952, p. 59

3. Some of these sentences contain misrelated clauses and phrases; others contain absolute constructions which need no correction. List those modifiers that are ambiguous or misrelated and rewrite the sentence as you think it should be written.

1) Near the end of the last century the Dukhobors decided to emigrate to Canada, but not having enough money for the trip, Count Leo Tolstoy gave them $17,000.

2) Subjected to the scrutiny of scholars as well as to the less

critical reading of the general public, it nevertheless appears that the real meaning of these poems has escaped almost everyone.

3) The miniature camera is not very useful to people with poor eyesight with the exception of the reflex type.

4) The author states that most love affairs are blind when in the process of courting.

5) In looking for a better way to make the paper more flexible, a softening treatment using a white crystalline solid was tried.

6) Mr. Graham comes of an old pioneer family, born in Astoria, Oregon, in 1909.

7) To get the best results from your new pen, first flush it with cold water before filling it with ink.

8) The big steam shovels would fill a flatcar in an hour which would hold 400 cubic yards of gravel.

9) A citizen entering the smoke-filled room found Ed propped up on one elbow and at gun point had the situation well under control.

10) Believing in fair play as most Americans do, it is surprising to see how many of us faithfully read the most biased columnists.

4. What constructions in these sentences do you think would be inappropriate in Formal English? Which ones would be clumsy or inexact in General writing? Make the changes you think should be made for more effective wording.

1) To spear flounder underwater, it takes a quick eye and a steady hand.

2) Ultra-violet blood irradiation was reported successful on 23 patients, all of which were children between 3 and 13 acutely ill with inflamed heart muscles.

3) After changing to my work clothes, I passed the foreman's shack to see how much steel would be coming over that night, and this being done, I headed toward the scarfing skids.

4) The subject that I am writing on is one that plenty of material can be found in the library to help me.

5) Hers was the kind of childhood which is thought to breed insecurity and that leads to troubles in later life.

6) Many small business firms have been taken over by large business, which is true in every form of business, from farming to running a drug store.

7) The early years are most important, for that which a child learns then, he is likely to retain throughout life.

8) Working quickly and thoroughly, I was able to finish three ingots before forced to stop.

9) After the war the United States replaced Amsterdam, who before had had a monopoly on the diamond cutting industry for centuries.

10) The society in which we live demands someone must do the dirty work.

17 Sentence length

[A sentence] is as much of my full purpose as I care to reveal at the very moment—as much of my meaning as I wish to deliver in one handful.—P. B. Ballard

Good sentences are varied in length and kind. Sometimes they are leisurely, unfolding slowly, and gradually rounding out the idea; sometimes they are direct and emphatic. In other words, they have qualities of style that make them readable and sensible.

These qualities are matters of choice rather than of rule; they are "better or worse" rather than "right or wrong." Attentive reading of first draft sentences and revising them for effectiveness is well worthwhile, for after a while the first drafts will need less revision.

17.1 Sentences as units of meaning The first matter to consider is the length of sentences, not so much in terms of the actual number of words but as a portion—large or small—of the total meaning of a paragraph.

17.1a Each sentence should contribute its share of meaning

Self-evident or extremely obvious statements contribute nothing to writing:

> Our scientific theories came into being only after definite steps had been taken.

Of course definite steps were taken. This statement is so general that one could substitute for "scientific theories" almost anything that comes to mind—Brooklyn Bridge, the United Nations, a college dance, or a term paper.

Some sentences say too little because a simple idea has been broken up unnecessarily into two or more statements:

> I took my first course in math at Riverdale High School. This was first year or elementary algebra.

A reader will not feel that he is getting his money's worth from these individual sentences. They might better be combined:

> I took my first course in math, elementary algebra, at Riverdale High School.

In writing in class you can avoid empty statements by thinking your sentences to yourself before you put them down on paper. In writing done outside the classroom you can also examine your sentences during revision for their meaning as well as for their form.

17.1b The relation of ideas in a sentence should be clear

Avoid combining unrelated ideas in the same statement. If there is a relationship between the ideas, so that they can be reasonably combined, it should be clearly shown and not left to the reader to puzzle out:

> As Byron is the poet of youth, it is appropriate that the new and completely reset edition of his poems should be published on March 1.

What is the relation between *youth* and the date of publication?

He was blond and handsome, with the sweetest smile she had ever seen, and they were married the following June.

No doubt there was some kind of relationship between the man's appearance and the marriage, but whatever it was, it should have been stated.

Sometimes sentences that seem haphazard, or even those that contain contradictory statements, can be revised to be meaningful by showing actual relationships between ideas.

Haphazard	*Revised*
Her marriage to another writer may have some influence upon her style; however, there is no evidence to support this.	Although her marriage to another writer might have some influence on her style, there is no evidence to support this.
Anyone who doesn't read *The Old Man and the Sea* is missing one of the great literary masterpieces of our time, although of course there are a great many people who don't like Hemingway's novels.	I think that anyone who doesn't read *The Old Man and the Sea*, including those who haven't liked Hemingway's other novels, will be missing one of the great literary masterpieces of our time.

17.2 Sentence length in current writing   Written sentences vary in length according to the writer's purpose, the way in which he typically expresses his ideas, and the type of material he is presenting. Longer sentences generally occur in discussions of ideas, as in textbooks, and in Formal writing; shorter ones in rapid narrative and other General writing.

Sentence length varies somewhat according to the fashion of the times. Early nineteenth-century writers built their ideas into sentences that averaged 30 to 40 words. Current writing uses somewhat shorter sentences, averaging between 20 and 30 words. Since these figures are averages, they usually mean that sentences today range from 5 or 6 words to 70, with the majority not far from 20.

As young people grow up, their development in writing is conspicuously shown by the increasing variety and fullness of their sentences. In the early grades, pupils' sentences average

11 or 12 words; in high school, 17 to 19; in college, usually in the low 20's. If your sentences in an expository paper average less than 18 or 20 words or more than 30, you should look at them to make sure, if the figure is low, that you are grouping your details sensibly, or, if the figure is high, that the sentences are clear and appropriate to the material. There is no special virtue in long or short sentences, but the length may be a symptom of other qualities.

Sentence length is also a distinguishing trait between Standard and Nonstandard writing. Professor Fries' comparison of letters by educated and uneducated writers shows that the latter use more very short sentences and also more long, formless ones. Although the two groups averaged the same, their range of length and type of sentence varied conspicuously:

Length in words	1-9	10-19	20-29	30-39	40-49	50-59	60-69	70-79	80-89	90-100	100+	Average
Standard writers	84	369	373	165	105	29	19	5	0	2	2	23.46
Vulgate writers	205	338	156	84	42	27	20	17	8	3	14	23.16

—From *The Structure of English* by Charles Carpenter Fries, p. 291, copyright 1952, by Harcourt, Brace and Company, Inc. Used by permission of the publishers.

Longer sentences are of course not "better" than shorter ones. More important than the number of words in the individual statements is the total effect of a passage in which the sentences are conspicuously long or short. In this paragraph by a well-known scholar and teacher, the sentences are considerably shorter than the average given for professional writers (usually in the low 20's). Yet the form is appropriate because the statements—many of them directives or suggestions for action—are intended to be emphatic. (The one long sentence near the middle varies from the pattern, but it is itself a series of brief statements):

Concentration must be learnt. It should be learnt in school. A good teacher can teach it to his pupils. It should not be imagined as nothing but an effort of the will. Concentration is also an intellectual process. It is choice. Take the same boy who reads his book slowly, grudgingly, five lines at a time, and increase the urgency of his study—somehow, anyhow—make the choice clearer to him, and the importance of his study paramount—put him to work on the prize essay—and then watch. "Turn that radio off!" he shouts. He clears the table, except for one photograph. He sits fixed in one position till he is cramped. Sometimes, when he is really intent, he will miss meals and forget about sleep. All this because he has chosen one aim and discarded others. And that, after all, is what we learn to do throughout life.—Gilbert Highet, *The Art of Teaching*, pp. 68-69. Reprinted by permission of Alfred A. Knopf, Inc. and Methuen & Co., Ltd., British publishers.

But in another work, Mr. Highet uses a longer, more complex and leisurely sentence pattern, appropriate both to the subject matter and to the kind of audience he is addressing:

Are these shadows on so many of our horizons the outriders of another long night, like that which was closing in upon Sidonius? We cannot yet tell. But modern scholars must regret that they have to work during a time when instead of that general supranational comradeship which helped to build the learning and culture of the sixteenth and nineteenth centuries, it is becoming more and more difficult to exchange opinions across the world, to bring from distant countries books where new and vital points of view are freely expressed, to carry on many-sided correspondences with far-off scholars and encounter no difficulties other than those involved in the common search for truth, and to feel oneself part of a world-wide structure of art and learning, greater than all the things that divide mankind: nationalities and creeds, fear and hate.—Gilbert Highet, *The Classical Tradition*, p. 472

The problem of length in most student sentences is seldom a matter of the average number of words per statement. More often it is variety and appropriateness: the ability to use the form, long or short, that best suits the writer's purpose and his material, and that will give variety and liveliness to his writing.

17.3 Choppy (too short) sentences   Too many short sentences interrupt the flow of thought, making the reader stop and start again too often for comfortable reading. More than that, such sentences do not show how the separate ideas are related to each other:

We left Japan the next morning. I remember watching three boys sailing. They were in a cat boat. It was so tiny! I felt sure they were going to tip over half a dozen times. A cat boat was new to me. I hadn't seen one before.

The choppy movement of this passage gives an effect the writer did not intend. The passage could be made smoother by combining statements:

When we left Japan the next morning, I remember watching three boys sailing in a cat boat, a kind of boat I had never seen before. It was so tiny that I felt sure they were going to tip over half a dozen times.

Short sentences are useful in various writing situations— for dialog, for emphasis, for creating a feeling of rapid action or of tension—but some judgment must be exercised if they are to be used successfully. In the following passage, for example, the writer's intention was probably to convey her own feeling of excitement, but the breathless style defeats this purpose because it is continued too long, with no break in sentence pattern:

It was my senior year in high school. Our basketball team had won the trophy the year before. This year the team was considered even stronger. Nearly every member of the pep club was seated. It was the final game. We had come all the way through the tournament without a defeat. This game would determine which team would be the champion. I looked toward the end of the gym. The referees were talking. They, too, were excited. Would that starting gun never go off! My hands were clammy. My cheeks burned.

It is a good idea to examine closely any passage in your writing that contains a conspicuous number of sentences under 18 words. Try reading the passage aloud to see whether it conveys the effect that you intended or whether it is careless or hasty writing.

17.4 Stringy sentences Avoid stringing together (with "and," "but," "so," "and then") statements that should be written as separate sentences or as subordinate elements. Sentences carelessly tacked together in this manner are not only monotonous to read but lose all their emphasis because every idea seems to be of equal importance:

> About fifty feet away I saw a buck deer running for safety *and so* I kneeled on my right knee *and then* I brought the rifle to my right shoulder. He was still running, *so* I fired one shot at him, *but* I missed, *but* he stopped and looked at me, *and then* I had a much better target to shoot at. *So.* . . .

Reading such flabby sentences aloud should reveal their weaknesses and help you to revise them for better organization:

> About fifty feet away I saw a buck deer running for safety. Kneeling on my right knee and bringing the rifle to my shoulder, I fired once, but missed. He stopped to look at me, providing a much better target. . . .

Stringy sentences result either from linking too many main clauses together (*Most people know that our productive system is the world's best* and *they have grown to expect great things from this system,* and *they should*), or from excessive repetition of the same sentence pattern. The cure lies in cutting down the number of coordinating conjunctions (*and, but, so*) and in subordinating ideas of lesser importance.

See §15, Subordinate clauses, p. 187.

Exercises

1. Study the length of twenty consecutive sentences in one of your recent papers, recording the shortest, the longest, and the average number of words. How do these figures compare with those given in this section? What specific advice would you give yourself on the basis of what you found?

2. Study the following statements and be prepared to discuss them from the standpoint of meaning and effectiveness of com-

munication. Which ones would you consider contradictory? Ambiguous? Unnecessarily involved? Is it the wording or the complexity of the thought that makes the statement confusing?

1) There is a great deal of work to be done before this program is completed; however, there is not so much as a person might think.

2) By being in the fresh air most of the time as a hunter is, it tends to keep a person healthy and to develop his body meanwhile.

3) The slums seem to be centered in one section of the city, which has acquired the reputation of being such an area.

4) This book is the most important contribution to the literature of church history in the last twenty years. Were the author's style pedestrian (which it is not), were his interpretations of people and events unrealistic and inaccurate (they are quite otherwise), even if (the shade of Gibbon forbid!) his book lacked balance, good temper, and seasoned judgment (all of which it has in abundance), the statement above would still be true.

5) Though still in its fifties, the twentieth century is turning, turning meats and fowls on electric rotisserie spits.

6) Mailing a letter which contains misspelled words and which is poorly organized is certainly not a compliment to the one who receives it.

7) The harm done to Resistance morale by this lack of supplies was, perhaps, greater than that not done to the Germans.

8) Billy Buck, the central character in the story, directs our minds to the extreme sadness felt by the death of the pony.

9) One reason that prefabricated houses are less satisfactory than architect designed homes is that they lack the personal touch, generally.

10) It cannot and should not be denied that I have no great sympathy for this author, despite my admiration for his style.

3. Revise the passage describing the basketball game in §17.3, p. 213, making the sentences more exactly meaningful and smoother to read.

18 Sentence economy

Literature maintains an endless quarrel with idle sentences.—Robert Lynd

Sentence economy means wording statements so that their meaning can be grasped by the reader without unnecessary effort. No one likes to listen to a speaker who talks too much and says too little; and no reader likes to cut his way through a tangle of words or repetitious ideas to get at a relatively simple statement.

Sentence economy doesn't mean that you should strip your sentences down to the bare essentials, as you might in composing a telegram or writing a classified ad. The shortest words and simplest constructions are not always the most economical, for they may fail to convey your exact or complete meaning. Economy of expression requires rather that you should try to find the most exact words possible, and that the constructions you use—whether brief or expanded—convey your meaning directly and accurately.

Wordy Correction: Revise the sentence or passage marked by using more direct expressions (§18.1), by cutting out deadwood (§§18.2, 18.3), or by changing a clause to a phrase or a single word (§18.4).

18.1 Using direct expressions Try to eliminate roundabout phrases and indirect expressions from your sentences. Phrases, clauses, or other constructions that use too many words to say what should be said in a word or two are called *circumlocutions*. Below are some circumlocutions with suggested revisions for more economical wording:

Roundabout	*Direct*
The way psychologists measure ability is by tests.	Psychologists measure ability by tests.
I believe that most parents have the desire to help their children.	I believe that most parents want to help their children.

The reason that prices rose was that the demand was increasing at the same time that production was decreasing.	Prices rose because the demand increased while production decreased.
During the time that she was in Los Angeles, she had at least six different jobs.	While she was in Los Angeles she had at least six different jobs.

Wordiness is more conspicuous (and annoying) in writing than it is in speech. For that reason a writer should avoid the wordy formulas that serve as fillers in casual conversation:

come in contact with	means	*meet* or *know*
in this day and age	means	*today*
due to the fact that	means	*because* or *since*
in the year of 1954	means	*in 1954*

Such expressions occur in first drafts because a writer usually puts down the first thing that comes to mind. But they should be replaced in revision by terms that say the same thing more exactly and directly:

the money that you have to pay to get into the theater
    means *the admission price*
that shiny stuff that they coat automobile bumpers with
    means *chromium*

18.2 Removing deadwood   "Deadwood" is a term for lazy words and phrases that clutter up a statement without adding anything to its meaning:

Anyone acquainted with violin construction knows that the longer the wood is seasoned, the better *the result will be as far as* the tone of the instrument *is concerned.*

Empty expressions, like those in italics above, find their way into written sentences because they are so common in speech, but spoken or written, they are excess baggage and do nothing to further communication.

Eliminating deadwood won't change the meaning in the least. It will make the statement neater and more direct, as in these examples (deadwood in brackets):

Every thinking person these days seems to agree [with the conception] that the world has gone mad.

At the end of an hour and a half we arrived at [the spot where] the red flag [was situated].

To my surprise the damage was not as bad as I had expected [it to be].

The following statistics [serve to] give a good idea of the effects of tobacco.

18.3 Words to watch   Certain words, because they are repeatedly overused, account for much of the deadwood found in student writing. This list, while not exhaustive, illustrates phrases built upon the most common of these words:

Word	As deadwood	Deadwood eliminated
case	In many cases students profit from the research paper.	Many students profit from the research paper.
character	His paintings are of a vigorous and intense character.	His paintings are vigorous and intense.
exist	The crime conditions that existed in Chicago became intolerable.	The crime conditions in Chicago became intolerable.
fact	We must realize the fact that the producer's hand is felt at every stage.	We must realize that the producer's hand is felt at every stage.
field	I have been interested in the fields of literature and music for several years.	I have been interested in literature and music for several years.
instance	Forest rangers prefer to work outdoors in most instances.	Most forest rangers prefer to work outdoors.
line	He always thought he would be successful along agricultural lines.	He always thought he would be successful in agriculture.
nature	She seldom talks on any subject of a controversial nature.	She seldom talks on any controversial subject.
seem	It seems that two years ago Howard lost a leg in an automobile accident.	Two years ago Howard lost a leg in an automobile accident.

tendency	Following a severe emotional shock, a person *has a tendency* to want to be alone.	Following a severe emotional shock, a person wants to be alone.
type	Some students take business courses because they want an executive *type* position.	Some students take business courses because they want an executive position.

These words have of course definite meanings in other expressions (a *case* of measles, a minor *character* in the play, a *field* of clover, and so forth). But as deadwood, they are meaningless and unnecessary.

If your papers are frequently marked for wordiness, it may help you to keep this list of words in mind when you are revising your work. You needn't examine every word you have written to see whether it adds something to the meaning or not, but you do owe it to your reader to strike out from your sentences the more obvious and annoying examples of deadwood.

18.4 Using words and phrases instead of clauses Eliminate unnecessary words by reducing full clauses to shorter constructions wherever possible. A complete predication (a sentence or a clause) can often be effectively reduced to a short phrase or a single word:

Sentence: *The snow lay like a blanket.* It covered the countryside. [two predications]

Clause: The snow, *which lay like a blanket,* covered the countryside. [two predications]

Phrase: The snow covered the countryside *like a blanket.* [one predication]

Word: The snow *blanketed* the countryside. [one predication]

Either the phrase or the single word would be preferable here, because both say just as much as the longer constructions, and say it more economically.

Since each clause you use increases the number of predications, one way to tighten sentence form is to see what verbs

their modifiers can be eliminated without loss of effec-
ess.

Two predicates	*Reduced*
We taxied back and forth in front of the starting line, waiting impatiently for the sound of the gun *which would mean that the race was started.*	We taxied back and forth in front of the starting line, waiting impatiently for the sound of the *starting* gun.

The two verbs that can most frequently be eliminated without any loss of meaning are *be* in its various forms, and *have:*

Excessive predication	*More economical*
I am a native of Florida and am very glad to write on this subject.	*As a native of Florida,* I am very glad to write on this subject.
A few of the fellows *who were less serious* would go into a bar *where they would have* a steak dinner and a few glasses of beer.	A few of the *less serious* fellows would go into a bar *for* a steak dinner and a few glasses of beer.
There is only one excuse *that is acceptable,* and *that is* "I have a class this hour."	*Only one excuse is acceptable:* "I have a class this hour."

If a large number of your sentences begin with *There,* see if some of them couldn't just as well start with another word later in the sentence:

Wordy	*More direct*
There were two plays in our anthology and I like them both very much.	I like both plays in our anthology very much.
There is a suggestion box in almost all big business houses where employees may put ideas for the management to consider.	Most big business houses provide suggestion boxes for their employees.

While a writer's style and the general movement of his sentences determine to a large degree whether short or longer constructions are more appropriate, the careless habit of consistently using two or more statements where one would be just as effective should be avoided in all styles of writing.

18.5 Avoiding careless repetition

Rep Repetition. Correction: Eliminate the ineffective repetition of words, meaning, or sound.

Unless repeated for a definite reason, a word or a phrase should not be made conspicuous by too frequent use in the same passage:

> The landscape is *beautiful*. There are myriads of *beautiful,* stately trees, which contribute greatly to the *beauty* of the place in every season of the year. There are also many *beautiful* wild flowers and other kinds of plants. The climate makes it easy to cultivate *beautiful* lawns, with flowers and shrubs.

18.5a Useful repetition Some kinds of words must of course be used over and over again: articles (*a, an, the*), conjunctions (*and, but, or*), prepositions (*of, in, at*), and pronouns (*it, that, my, which*). Because their purpose is strictly functional, these words are usually not noticed.

Useful repetition may be of two kinds:

1) *Essential,* for meaning or for sentence structure:

> I believe that the greatest frontier of our ignorance lies in the relationship of *man* to *man*. *I* do not discount the marvelous *development* in the world of things, nor do *I* devaluate the contributions of those who have made these *developments* possible.—General Lewis B. Hershey, "We Just Can't Play with Spools," in *This I Believe,* edited by Edward R. Murrow, p. 67

2) *Intentional,* for emphasis:

> Thus, our conventional habits of language have to be reversed when we come to deal with poetry. For here it is the *tail* that wags the dog. Better still, here it is the *tail* of the *kite*—the *tail* that makes the *kite* fly—the *tail* that renders the *kite* more than a frame of paper blown crazily down the wind.—Cleanth Brooks, "Irony as a Principle of Structure," in *Literary Opinion in America,* edited by Morton D. Zabel, p. 729

18.5b Useless repetition Unintentional, unnecessary, and ineffective repetition is shown in these sentences:

When I was in high school, I would take a book home once or twice a week and maybe read it two or three hours at a *time*. *Most of the time* I would read *most* of my homework just in *time* to have it ready before class began. It was very easy *most of the time* to read the assignment and have it prepared when my *time* came to be called upon for recitation.

Repetition of this kind is obviously undesirable. It diverts the reader's attention from the ideas to the words themselves, adds unnecessary words to the statement, and suggests either careless writing or an inability to revise.

1) Repetition of words. Repeat words in a passage only when you have good reason for doing so. Key words (such as the subject) may sometimes be repeated for clarity or emphasis, but less important terms should not be used more often than necessary.

Careless repetition	*Revised*
The *many* psychology and sociology classes give *many* people the opportunity to understand *many* of the family and community problems better.	The many psychology and sociology courses give people the opportunity to understand family and community problems better.
The *problem* of feeding her ever-increasing population is one of India's most acute *problems*.	Feeding her ever-increasing population is one of India's most acute problems.
Many people think *that* if an article is endorsed by a prominent person *that* it is a good product to buy.	Many people think that if an article is endorsed by a prominent person it is a good product to buy.

Especially to be watched is repetition of the same word in two different meanings:

My *marks* showed a *marked* improvement.	My *grades* showed a marked improvement. Or: My marks showed a *decided* improvement.
Astrology is so popular in Hollywood that many movie *stars* won't sign a contract unless the *stars* are favorable.	Astrology is so popular in Hollywood that many of the movie stars won't sign a contract unless their *horoscopes* are favorable.

It is not always possible to correct careless repetition by striking out a word or substituting another of similar meaning. When a passage becomes badly cluttered like this one, complete revision is the only way to clear it up:

There has been a *theory* advanced that the Vikings were here long before Columbus. As time goes on, more evidence is found to substantiate this *theory*. After reading several *articles* about *this*, I ran across some *articles* on the first discovery of America by people other than the Vikings. *This* interested me greatly, and I decided to investigate *this* as my topic for the research paper.

The passage could be made both neater and clearer by rewording it in this way:

I began looking for a topic by reading several articles on the discovery of America by the Vikings, a theory that is being substantiated by increasing evidence as time goes on. Then more or less by accident, I found that even the Vikings may not have been the first people to visit America. This idea interested me greatly, and I decided to make it the topic of my research paper.

2) Repetition of meaning. Adding a word or a phrase that repeats the meaning of another expression (a form of repetition called *tautology*) is one of the most common forms of unprofitable repetition.

The italicized expressions in these sentences should be omitted because they merely repeat ideas that are sufficiently expressed in other words in the sentences:

The modern college student *of today* must choose between specialization and a broad general education.

It is believed that the age of the earth is about two billion years *old*.

She decided to trim the kitchen in bright red, but the *resultant* effect was not what she had anticipated.

Some writers, apparently more interested in the sound of words than in the sense, like to use them in pairs, even though the words overlap in meaning. This can become an annoying mannerism in writing:

First we should consider what *equipment* and *paraphernalia* are necessary.

The elderly woman's feet were encased in a pair of *obsolcte* and *almost antiquated* high-button boots.

An elementary kind of useless repetition occurs sometimes with words like *color, size, shape:*

Unsatisfactory	*Revised*
His hair was brick-red *in color.*	His hair was brick-red.
The length of the locks is about two-thirds of a mile long.	The locks are about two-thirds of a mile long.
Behind the house was an enclosed court which was rectangular *in shape.*	Behind the house was an enclosed rectangular court.
The odor of the water that the flowers had been in was offensive *to smell.*	The odor of the water that the flowers had been in was offensive.

3) Repetition of sound. A sound should not be made conspicuous by careless repetition in the same passage. The cumulative effect of certain suffixes like *-ly, -ment,* and *-tion* may be unfortunate when a number of similar ones occur close together:

The concept of such sanctuary immunity unquestionably predominantly influenced the enemy to enter into the conflict.

Written permission of the administration is required for re-registration of those students who are on probation.

Alliteration—the repetition of the same sound at the beginning of words in a series—is out of place in expository writing when it attracts attention to the words at the expense of the ideas:

He then made himself comfortable in a rather rickety rattan rocker.

The most dangerous intersection is Fifth and Alder, where three streets come together to make a terrific tangle of traffic.

Even though your papers are not written to be read aloud, you should try to avoid sound patterns that may be momentarily distracting to a reader with a sensitive ear: The Yakima Indians have never forsaken certain sacred rites.

Exercises

1. The following sentences from student papers contain many words and phrases that add nothing to the meaning: unnecessary predications, roundabout phrases, and other fuzzy constructions. First point out in each sentence what words or phrases should be omitted or tightened up, and then indicate how you would revise the sentence for more direct wording.

1) In each stove there is a coil of pipe which is enclosed in a cast iron container and which is known as the waterfront.

2) Generally one would suppose of such a person that he had a lack of education.

3) When the stain is dried, the entire surface of the desk is steel-wooled in order to take off any excess stain that may be present.

4) Our instructor made a statement to the effect that if the city officials and the county officials combined some of their duties together, the expense in terms of taxes would be much less.

5) He attacked the statement of Harold Stassen which was to the effect that the Mutual Security Program needed more monetary assistance.

6) This area has some of the best ski trails in the country and as far as the other cold weather sports are concerned, it has them too, along with one of the most fashionable hotels in the country.

7) My friend seldom seems to care to discuss any subject that is of a controversial nature.

8) Many people have the belief that ignorance is an inborn trait, but in this they are quite wrong, for if they investigate the facts pertaining to this situation, they will be quite surprised by what they find concerning the actual facts of the case.

9) To prevent hair from falling out, brushing of the hair each day should be practiced.

10) Another factor entering this adustment of the flow of water in the ditches is the reduction of the amount of soil erosion which takes place.

2. Follow the instructions given above for removing the deadwood from these sentences. If eliminating a word or phrase doesn't result in a satisfactory sentence, revise the entire statement.

1) The book is divided into various sections, all of them dealing with the matter of unemployment.

2) The hours that a dental hygienist has correspond quite closely to the schedule of the dentist by whom she is employed.

3) Education should be continued beyond the grades of high school.

4) There are some individuals who think that the modern college student of today who has received four years of a liberal arts education is no wiser after this period than a person who has had only the twelve years of formal education in the elementary and high schools.

5) The Hindu boys diving in the water to retrieve the coins didn't seem to mind the water, but to us it seemed to have a very filthy and contaminated appearance.

6) This column can be enjoyed for its content of humor.

7) The kind of papers I like to write best are on the topics of the experiences I have had personally.

8) There are two reasons for my preference in wanting to write on a subject that is related to a course which will be part of my major: the first reason is influenced by the fact that I have a large amount of material on hand to write about; and in the second place, the time limit for writing this theme makes it important that one have a good grasp of his subject matter so that he won't have to waste time on organization.

9) There used to be a habit I once had that sometimes caused me much embarrassment.

10) In many cases a corporation may wish to carry on only one type of business and in such a case it is necessary for a charter to be obtained in a state where this particular line of work is to be carried on.

3. Revise the following sentences to eliminate careless or unnecessary repetition of words or of meaning:

1) The business that definitely makes this port what it is, is the business carried on by shipping.

2) I hoped to get an A grade instead of a B grade in physics.

3) One thing that the author used throughout the article and that made it easy to read was his use of examples familiar to every reader.

4) The Indian culture was so different from the white man's culture that he had done very well to change as much as he had in such a short period of time.

5) Almost everyone of the industries or companies which produce or manufacture this country's necessities of daily living is controlled by stockholders.

6) Our home, being built in 1946, was built without a garage because such a building would have been an improper use of critical materials, according to the building code then in force at that time.

7) The many heart diseases that attack people today are numerous.

8) Attitudes or viewpoints are laws or rules that regulate your behavior, and you are the only person who can change or regulate these laws.

9) At eight-thirty in the morning you punch the clock for the start of another day.

10) The thrill of riding a galloping horse over the hills was only one of the many thrills I experienced during the summer months I spent on a ranch in the summer of 1955.

4. Revise any sentence in this group that contains careless or ineffective repetition. But if the repetition in any statement seems to you intentional and effective, explain what purpose it serves, and why it should be allowed to stand.

1) The aim of this plan is to create a good infant-mother relationship between the mother and her baby.

2) The biography was an amazingly complete and objective account of an amazingly rich and complex career.

3) When I first took the reading ability test, my average num-

ber of words per minute was 215 words per minute, which was comparatively low.

4) Each day during that long, long winter I had to trudge three miles each morning through drifted snow to school, and then three miles back home again at the end of the day.

5) The advantages and disadvantages of daylight saving time arc many and varied to different people.

6) Our eating club is as much a fraternity as any house along the row, and our feelings of unity and fraternity have brought us real satisfaction.

7) I believe that colleges should offer scholarships but they should not offer athletic scholarships alone.

8) I wrote the paper and rewrote it, and then rewrote the re-written paper, but it all came out in the same unsatisfactory way.

9) The plain fact of the matter is that our planes are inferior in some respects to those of the enemy.

10) In addition to the regular switchboard operators, the tele-phone company trains girls for special tasks, such as Alaskan operator, overseas operator, conference operator, and mobile unit operator.

19 Sentence variety and emphasis

Imagine for a moment that all the sentences you have uttered during the course of the last two weeks are somewhere accurately recorded and that you can now scrutinize them at leisure. You will probably find them to be surprisingly varied: long and short; simple, double, multiple, and complex; statements, commands, wishes, questions, and exclama-tions; balanced, periodic, and loose. The words have been largely of your own choosing, but the sentences have seldom been of your own making. You have inherited them from the immediate, the distant, the long-distant past.—Simeon Potter

Variety in sentence form is desirable because it makes read-ing easier and more enjoyable and conveys your meaning more effectively. A lecturer who utters each statement in the same tone, with no effort at emphasis, risks losing the attention of his audience. Similarly, a writer who uses again and again sentences of the same length and stress risks losing his reader's interest.

We are seldom aware, when reading good writing, of the flexibility of sentence pattern; it is only when the pattern remains rigid, either in length or arrangement, that we become critical of the writer's expression:

> I get about the country a lot but I never meet any American folk. I have lived most of my life in New England, where "natives" are plentiful. These natives speak with intonations that are traditionally Yankee, especially those who live in the northern part. But they aren't the Yankees of tradition because they don't dress, act, or think in accordance with the accepted cliché. The cliché Yankee remains a stock voice on radio programs. He may occasionally stroll into a movie with a scythe over his shoulder and a blade of grass between his teeth. But he has vanished from American society and so have his counterparts in rural America at large.

This passage is monotonous not only because the sentences are of similar length (ranging from 14 to 20 words), but more particularly because they all follow the same pattern—beginning with the subject and ending with modifiers. Compare it with the passage as it was actually written:

> I get about the country a lot but I never meet any American folk. Take New England, where I have lived most of my life. Plenty of "natives," especially in the northern part, speak with intonations that are traditionally Yankee but they are by no means the Yankees of the tradition; they do not look, dress, act, or think in accordance with the accepted cliché. The Yankee of that cliché remains a stock voice on radio programs and occasionally he strolls into a movie with a scythe over his shoulder and a blade of grass between his teeth, but he has vanished from American society. So have his counterparts in rural America at large.—Bernard DeVoto, "The Easy Chair," *Harper's Magazine*, December 1952, p. 54

The sentences in the second passage vary much more in length (from 9 to 40 words) than they do in the paraphrase. But what makes the ideas easier to grasp in Mr. DeVoto's version is the movement of the statements—a movement casual and natural, and yet with considerable variety in sentence structure.

It is not advisable to try too hard for sentence variety: the result will probably be artificial and strained. Style reflects the writer's mood as well as his personality, and a good deal of monotonous writing is merely the result of weariness or a lack of interest in the subject. When you find that each statement you are writing is almost identical in form to the one preceding, put the paper aside for a while before continuing it. A fresh view of a subject often helps make the sentence structure as well as the material more lively and varied.

19.1 Varying sentence beginnings   A typical and effective way of varying the basic subject-verb-object pattern is to begin with a modifier—a word, phrase, or clause:

> Phrase: *In my career* I've been hit by rotten eggs, firecrackers, tomatoes, seat cushions, umbrellas, compacts, beer cans, and leftover liverwurst sandwiches.—Bill Stewart, "Loneliest Man in Town!" *The American Magazine,* October 1952, p. 26

> Clause: *If I could collect all the pop bottles that have been thrown at me* I could start my own soft-drink company.—*Ibid.*

> Word: *Maybe* some of them felt sorry about that later on, but they didn't apologize, because who ever apologizes to an umpire?—*Ibid.*

Because the subject is usually a conspicuous and emphatic word, a series of sentences beginning with unmodified subjects may become monotonous. Note the flexibility of this passage, in which only two sentences begin with the subject:

> Possibly the most censored man in radio is Fred Allen. Allen gets his ideas from current news. His jokes are invariably pointed, and pointed jokes usually sting somebody. As a result, Allen's fourteen years in radio have been an almost continuous battle with censors and he has lost many an engagement. After fourteen years of this, Allen is a little bitter toward radio censorship. Recently he left for a vacation in Maine and in his suitcase was a collection of notes which, he refers to as his "white paper" and which he plans to turn into a "Saturday Evening Post" article during his vacation.—John Crosby, *Out of the Blue,* p. 272

Of course the effect will be no less monotonous if sentence after sentence starts with the same kind of modifier, such as an adverbial clause. Deliberately inserting or shifting modifiers to gain variety is a makeshift and usually ineffective practice. The emphasis you wish to make and the general movement of the passage should determine the way you begin your sentences.

19.2 Varying S-V-O order A less common means of varying sentence patterns is *inversion*, or changing the usual order of subject-verb-object in declarative statements:

       M   V   S

To this period | belongs | one of those many items of literary advice which Chekhov was apt to give throughout his life.—V. S. Pritchett, "Books in General," *The New Statesman and Nation,* November 15, 1952, p. 577

Except in questions and requests, inversion is ordinarily not used unless the words put first really deserve special emphasis. It is more appropriate to Formal than to General writing, and should not be used solely for the purpose of variety. Unhappy inversion may have painful results, as in this reversal of subject and complement:

A garden city, with one of the most delightful climates in the world, is Victoria.

19.3 Varying kinds of statement An occasional question or a statement in the form of a directive will help vary sentence patterns:

Only by resurrecting our own memories can we realize how incredibly distorted is the child's vision of the world. *Consider this, for example. How would Crossgates appear to me now, if I could go back, at my present age, and see it as it was in 1915? What should I think of Bingo and Sim, those terrible, all-powerful monsters?* I should see them as a couple of silly, shallow ineffectual people, eagerly clambering up a social ladder which any thinking person could see to be on the point of collapse. I would be no more frightened of them than I would be frightened of a dormouse.—George Orwell, *Such, Such, Were the Joys,* p. 61

Both questions and commands should be used when the occasion warrants. But they should not be used solely as a device to change sentence pattern, or perhaps to startle the reader. It is unnecessary and in rather bad taste to conclude a paper with some such blunt question as this: "What do *you* think?"

Unless the answer is self-evident ("Who would trade freedom for tyranny?"), a writer should not ordinarily raise a question without answering it.

19.4 Parallelism

Paral **Parallel structure. Correction: Make the elements of the construction marked on your paper parallel in form.**

Ideas of equal value in a statement should be made *parallel* —that is, they should be expressed in the same grammatical form. If the first is a noun, the rest should be nouns; or if the first is a prepositional phrase, the others should be prepositional phrases; and so on.

The purpose of putting coordinate ideas in parallel constructions is chiefly for clarity, to help the reader see in which direction the statement is going. But the same principle may also make for smoother writing, since it helps prevent unnecessary shifts in person and number, and in the tense and mood of verbs.

19.4a **Elements in series**   Words, phrases, and clauses in series are best stated in parallel form. These subjects are parallel because each is a noun phrase:

In the dressing rooms were whole *boxes* of white gloves and *yards* of all colors of ribbons and *maids* to aid in fitting them on pretty little girls.—Bess Furman, *White House Profile*, p. 116

The compound predicates in this sentence are also parallel:

His dramatic attempt to take over the conduct of his own case *alienated* him from his counsel, almost *broke up* the trial, and probably *helped* to cost him his life.—Joseph Kinsey Howard, *Strange Empire*, p. 516

When this pattern is not followed, the statement may be awkward or at best untidy:

Not parallel

We were told to write in ink, that we should use but one side of the paper, and we should endorse our papers in the proper manner. [an infinitive phrase and two clauses]

Parallel

We were told *to write in ink, to use but one side of the paper,* and *to endorse our papers in the proper manner.* [three infinitive phrases]

19.4b Parallelism clarified by connectives When it is necessary for clearness, a preposition or a conjunction should be repeated between the items of a series:

Preposition lacking

These problems are currently of great concern to the school system, teachers, and many parents.

Clearer

These problems are currently of great concern *to* the school system, *to* teachers, and *to* many parents.

Conjunction lacking

The opposing citizens argued that the increased rates were exorbitant and the commissioners should find some other way to raise the money.

Clearer

The opposing citizens argued that the increased rates were exorbitant and *that* the commissioners should find some other way to raise the money.

19.4c Parallelism with correlative conjunctions Elements that are compared or contrasted through the use of pairs of conjunctions such as *either ... or, neither ... nor, not only ... but* (or *but also*) are usually clearer and more emphatic when they are stated in parallel constructions:

It is not always easy to select, at your bookshop or library, the particular book which will best serve your purpose, but if, before deciding, you give a little attention to certain points, you are less likely *either to buy one* which will not give you full return *or to take home* from the library one which will cause you disappointment, delay or inconvenience.— Lionel McColvin, "How to Use Books," *The Wonderful World of Books,* p. 180

This is the life of a musician in which are recorded *not only the events* of his life, *but also details* of all his works, which are analyzed and described fully.—*Ibid.*, p. 176

Since a reader expects similar constructions to follow pairs of conjunctions, he may be momentarily confused or side-tracked if the pattern is shifted:

Shifted	*Parallel*
You may go to the ski jump either *by special train* or *a chartered bus may be taken.*	You may go to the ski jump either by special train or by chartered bus.
He objected to fraternities not *because they were snobbish,* but *that many students couldn't afford to belong.*	He objected to fraternities not because they were snobbish, but because many students couldn't afford to belong.

Making related ideas parallel is one of the jobs of revision. Similar forms for similar ideas help hold a sentence together, and make for clear and easy understanding.

19.4d Balanced sentences   When parallel constructions, especially clauses, are noticeably equal in length and similar in movement, the sentence is called *balanced.* Balance is useful for emphatic statements, for comparing and contrasting ideas:

Either we live by accident and die by accident, or we live by plan and die by plan.—Thornton Wilder, *The Bridge of San Luis Rey*

The best model of the grand style simple is Homer; perhaps the best model of the grand style severe is Milton.—Matthew Arnold, *On Translating Homer*

Elaborately balanced sentences are more characteristic of Formal than of General writing, but the same principles of sentence structure can be used to highlight important statements.

19.5 Loose and periodic sentences   Sentence patterns may be varied by using loose and periodic sentences. Loose sentences follow the pattern of most conversational statements. The main statement comes first, followed by subordinate elements that give explanatory or amplifying details:

[*The Seven Storey Mountain*] was an extraordinary book in which the author told how he had come by crooked, dirty ways, from worldliness and sin and disbelief, to a saving faith in the dogmas of the Roman Catholic Church, and had thereafter pursued his spiritual pilgrimage until it carried him through the gates of Gethsemani, a monastery of the Cistercians of the More Strict Observance—commonly called Trappists—situated not far from Louisville, in the Kentucky hills.—Ben Ray Redman, "In the Belly of a Paradox," *The Saturday Review,* February 21, 1953, p. 45

A *periodic sentence* is one in which the main statement is not completed until the end or near the end of the sentence:

Most men in his position—burdened with business drudgery, harassed by domestic worries, and hampered by narrow means and a lack of college education—*would have found sufficient excuses for stagnating intellectually.* Not so Charles Lamb; despite all his disadvantages, *he achieved* in the course of time *a rare degree of culture and a mastery of style.*—Ernest Bernbaum, *Guide Through the Romantic Movement,* p. 114

Because they require more careful planning, periodic sentences are much less common than loose sentences and are usually more typical of a Formal than of a General style. When using this pattern, a writer should be careful to see that the suspension is not awkward or unnatural, as it is in this example:

The reader will probably agree after reading this essay *that Pearl Buck's example* of the woman who, after being married for a number of years and raising a family, gradually loses interest in most of her former outside activities, *is true.*

19.6 Sentence emphasis

Emph **Emphasis. Correction: Revise the passage marked so that the position and expression of the ideas will show their relative importance.**

The purpose of emphasis is to help your reader see your ideas in the same relative importance as you regard them—to see the most important as most important, the less important as less important, the incidental as incidental. Emphasis does not necessarily mean force, but rather the accurate conveying of your view of the subject. While emphasis depends in large part upon the way that the whole paper is put together, from the beginning to the final paragraph, individual sentences can weaken or strengthen this effect.

The sentences in this paragraph, for example, are unemphatic because they are haphazardly constructed: they are wordy, the beginnings are weak, and each ends in a similar flabby construction:

> There are some valuable points about child guidance that were brought out in this article by Lincoln Steffens. There are many parents of today who would gain much by reading this article and by following the advice that Mr. Steffens brought out. In understanding the fundamental needs of children, one must realize what is to be expected of these children, as was illustrated in Mr. Steffen's article.

To make the statements more forceful, and the passage more readable, the writer might have revised the sentence structure, perhaps in this way:

> In his essay, "The Influence of My Father on My Son," Lincoln Steffens brought out some points about child guidance that are still valuable to parents today. He pointed out, for example, that before a parent understands what his child needs, he must first realize what is expected of the child.

19.6a Emphasis by position in the sentence   Important ideas can be stressed by putting them in emphatic positions in the sentence. In longer statements, the most emphatic position is usually at the end, and the next most emphatic at the beginning:

> If it was the workings of our democracy that were inadequate in the past, *let us say so*. Whoever thinks the future is going to be easier than the past *is certainly mad*. And the system under which we are going to have to conduct foreign policy is, I hope and pray, *the system of democracy*.—George F. Kennan, *American Diplomacy, 1900-1950,* p. 73

Sentences—particularly those that introduce or sum up the main points of a topic—should end strongly. Statements that are qualified by a phrase or a word at the end are usually weak:

Unemphatic	Improved
The work at the mill was hard and often dangerous, but the mill hands didn't complain, *or at least very seldom.*	The work at the mill was hard and often dangerous, but the mill hands very seldom complained.
This is nobody's fault but their own, *with few exceptions.*	With few exceptions, this is nobody's fault but their own.

Because the main statement is not completed until the end, periodic sentences are frequently more emphatic than loose sentences (See §19.5 for definitions of loose and periodic sentences):

Loose	Periodic
Sociology 101 should interest every thoughtful student with its discussion of the theoretical as well as the practical aspects of human behavior.	Sociology 101, with its discussion of the theoretical as well as the practical aspects of human behavior, should interest every thoughtful student.

Sentences that begin with *There is* or *There are* tend to be unemphatic, and frequent use of these constructions will make your writing seem flat and uninteresting. See §18.4, p. 220, for examples of this particular kind of beginning.

19.6b **Emphasis by separating statements**   Ideas can be emphasized by setting them off from other parts in the sentence with strong internal punctuation—semicolons, colons, or dashes:

It is one thing to read *Time*; it is another to pronounce the words correctly.—E. B. White, *Quo Vadimus?* p. 94

He needed the support of the Princeton seniors and graduates, of Dean West of Princeton, of Harvey the political manager, of Colonel House, of the people of Europe, of the people of America—and he got it.—Edward Ryerson, "The Leadership of Woodrow Wilson," *The American Scholar,* Summer 1952, p. 305

The most emphatic separation is into individual sentences:

Adolescence is a kind of emotional seasickness. Both are funny, but only in retrospect.—Arthur Koestler, *Arrow in the Blue*, p. 82

19.6c Emphasis by repeating key words Statements can be made emphatic by repeating important words or phrases:

In the light of eternity, the question whether a girl should wear a short or a long dress is trivial. It is not trivial if you are the girl and you are going to a party.—George C. Homans, *The Human Group*, p. 20

Now for a fighter, for a worker in ideas, it is dangerous, it may prove fatal to one's effectiveness, to betray that one's feelings have been hurt.—Edmund Wilson, *Classics and Commercials*, p. 60

Effective (and intentional) repetition should be distinguished from careless repetition; see §18.5b, p. 221.

19.6d Emphasis by mechanical devices The least effective way to emphasize ideas is by underlining or capitalizing words, setting them off in quotation marks, or by using emphatic punctuation marks (!!!). Certain kinds of advertising rely heavily on such devices:

"Oh, of course," you may reply, "it's just a matter of calories." But IS it? Suppose you had to choose between a large glass of orange juice and a half a sirloin steak? You would probably reach for the orange juice. Actually, *the steak would give you 15 times as many ENERGY-stimulating calories. Yet the total number* of calories in each is roughly the same! So, you see, it ISN'T "just a matter of calories." It's the KIND of calories that makes the big difference.

In college writing, mechanical devices for emphasis should be avoided; the wording of the statement or its position in the sentence should give it the emphasis it deserves.

References

Brooks, Cleanth, and Robert Penn Warren, *Modern Rhetoric,* New York, Harcourt, Brace, 1949, Chs. 9–13

Cox, Sidney, *Indirections for Those Who Want to Write,* New York, Knopf, 1947, Ch. 16

Dobrée, Bonamy, *Modern Prose Style,* Oxford, Clarendon Press, 1934, Part IV

Earnest, Ernest P., *Foreword to Literature,* New York, Appleton 1945, Ch. 5

Graves, Robert, and Alan Hodge, *The Reader over Your Shoulder,* New York, Macmillan, 1943, Part I, Ch. 13

Wellek, René, and Austin Warren, *Theory of Literature,* New York, Harcourt, Brace, 1949, Ch. 14

Exercises

1. Recast the following sentences, putting shifted constructions and related elements in parallel form:

1) This book seems interesting and an informative piece of work.

2) Associating with these fellows and how to adapt myself to live with them will be helpful throughout my college career.

3) My landlady was one of those women who spend most of their time gossiping with the neighbors, puttering around the garden, or else she fusses over a hot stove.

4) People living in the city must pay relatively high prices for dairy products, whereas if you live in a rural community, you can get the same products for much less.

5) I heard complaints about the plot being weak, and that the setting was played up too much.

6) Other questions asked in the census concerned incomes, type of work, how many days people had been sick, did they own their own homes, and many other items.

7) Making a preliminary outline has improved my speaking ability, but my problems in writing haven't been solved by the same practice.

8) It is a coincidence that with the Republicans back in office, the country should find men going in for such correct attire rather than the casualness reflected under the New Deal.

9) At home I was always overshadowed by an older brother, who could lick me in a fight, pitch a baseball much better, was able to pass or kick a football farther, and had the ability to find his way in and out of more trouble than I ever dreamed of.

10) I believe that the important thing I learned in Writing Laboratory was not that anyone can write or that everyone has something to say, but it is how we say it and if we are sincere or not that makes a composition good or bad.

11) Along these walks are the cottages, many of which have stood since the founding and others more recent.

12) Dad gave us our choice either of earning the money by doing odd chores around the house, or we could borrow against our future allowance.

13) The most important factors are time and temperature, careful control at every point, and the mechanical equipment must be in perfect operating condition at all times.

14) Anyone who has persistence or who is desperate enough can get a job on a ship.

15) How many times have you seen a fisherman trying to get to his favorite fishing spot without scaring all the fish away but instead he sends out messages with his rhythmic squeak-splash, squeak-splash?

2. Make a close study of at least twenty consecutive sentences in one or more of your recent papers. Take notes on the following points:

a. The length of the sentences in words: the shortest, the longest, and the average number of words per sentence. Compare your figures with those in the table, page 211.

b. The kind of sentences you have used: simple, complex, compound, complex-compound; statements, questions, exclamations; loose, periodic, and balanced.

c. The pattern of your sentence structure. Compare the number of sentences that follow the typical subject-verb-object order with the number of sentences in which you have varied this order.

d. The economy of the statements in your sentences. Put brackets around each word, phrase, or clause that adds nothing to the meaning or clarity of any statement and around any sentence that does not actually advance the thought. Estimate the amount of material that you might have omitted without changing either the meaning or the effectiveness of your paper.

3. On the basis of the analysis in the preceding exercise, write a report telling what you have discovered about your sentences. Discuss them with reference to any of the points brought up in this section or the preceding section that may be helpful in solving your problems. Mention the good features of your sentences as well as those that need improving.

4. In your reading of books, textbooks, magazines, or newspapers, look for examples of (a) the dullest and flattest sentences you can find, and (b) the best sentences of several different types. Be prepared to comment on the reasons for the effectiveness or the ineffectiveness of your examples.

5. Read the following passages carefully, so that you can compare and contrast the methods used to gain emphasis. Notice the length and movement of the sentences, the choice of words, use of repetition, and various devices of punctuation. Considering the material and the kind of audience the writer had in mind, which seem to you most successful, and why?

a. An advertisement in a woman's magazine:

Good housekeeping is a "breeze" to me . . . for I've found a way to make things sparkle, make 'em shine . . . get them cleaner in half the time! How? By using SCRUB-O Sponges on every clean-up task . . . and thanks to their *exclusive* new "Free-Breathing Action," they make every drop of water and every bit of suds work *harder!* SCRUB-O Sponges save you money, too . . . because they use less soaps and cleansers while cleaning *better*. And they're tough . . . but oh-so gentle! You can trust them for everything. . . . Come in sizes to fit every chore, colors to match every room . . . seafoam green, ocean blue, shell pink and natural. So if I were you, I'd get a complete assortment. . . . Remember to ask for SCRUB-O, though . . . they're the genuine cellulose sponges I recommend.

b. One of several crucial moments in a detective story:

I edged back to the wall and felt around for a light switch. There's always a light switch. Everybody has light switches. Usually on the right side as you go in. You go into a dark room and you want light. Okay, you have a light switch in a natural place at a natural height. This room hadn't. This was a different kind of house. They had odd ways of handling doors and lights. The gadget this time might be something fancy like having to sing A above high C, or stepping on a flat button under the carpet, or maybe you just spoke and said: "Let there be light," and a mike picked it up and turned the voice vibrator into a low-power electrical impulse and a transformer built that up to enough voltage to throw a silent mercury switch.—Raymond Chandler, *The Little Sister*, p. 190

c. "The Four Freedoms," an address by President Roosevelt to Congress, January 6, 1941:

In the future days, which we seek to make secure, we look forward to a world founded upon four essential freedoms.

The first is freedom of speech and expression—everywhere in the world.

The second is freedom of every person to worship God in his own way—everywhere in the world.

The third is freedom from want—which, translated into world terms, means economic understandings which will secure to every nation a healthy, peaceful life for its inhabitants—everywhere in the world.

The fourth is freedom from fear—which, translated into world terms, means a worldwide reduction of armaments to such a point and in such a thorough fashion that no nation will be in a position to commit an act of aggression against any neighbor—anywhere in the world.

d. The leader of the French Himalayan Expedition of 1950 describes his emotions on reaching the summit of one of the highest mountains climbed by man:

The summit was a corniced crest of ice, and the precipices on the far side which plunged vertically down beneath us, were terrifying, unfathomable. There could be few other mountains in the world like this. Clouds floated halfway down, concealing the gentle, fertile valley of Pokhara, 23,000 feet below. Above us there was nothing!

Our mission was accomplished. But at the same time we had accomplished something infinitely greater. How wonderful life would now become! What an inconceivable experience it is to attain one's ideal, and, at the very same moment, to fulfill oneself. I was stirred to the depths of my being. Never had I felt happiness like this—so intense, and yet so pure. That brown rock, the highest of them all, that ridge of ice—were these the goals of a lifetime? Or were they, rather, the limits of man's pride?—Maurice Herzog, *Annapurna*, pp. 208–209

6. Examine these sentences for clarity, form, and general effectiveness. Is the meaning in any statement difficult to grasp because of sentence length, amount or kind of detail, or the position of the main elements? Do any strike you as unintentionally or intentionally humorous?

1) Mrs. Maude Porter, who has devoted many years of her life rearing her sons, the elder of whom, Richard, is now married and engaged in business in Baltimore, and the younger, Harold, who is at present in the United States Navy, stationed in San Diego, and rearing her nephews, Thomas McIntosh, who will in three weeks be graduated from the State University, and will then be inducted into the army, and Stewart McIntosh, Jr., who will be married, as has been reported in *The Times*, to Miss Sue Anne Hines, of Tampa, Florida, has decided to move out of the house at 711 East Spruce, where she has lived for twenty-five years, and will move into an apartment.

2) No degree will be conferred upon the applicant unless he shall have sustained a good moral character, given evidence of academic ability, and returned all books to the library.

3) However, the fact that we have to date not been able to prepare and hold in the schools any substantial body of teachers who know enough about the present-day world so as to be able to lead children and youth into a comprehensive understanding of general concepts and relationships concerning that world, but only teachers who can develop no more than a limited understanding shackled to the few specific items of content which the teacher is able to muster in trying to explain these concepts, does not mean that the process of teaching a person how to think must necessarily include teaching him what to think.—H. H. Punke, "Teaching How to Think Without Teaching What to Think," *School and Society*, September 2, 1952, p. 67

4) So this is the Gateway, where up on the hill the people who hold the strings that control the puppets who make up the peasant populace, live.

5) I often say that college is a microcosm, a tiny world in which is foreshadowed the turbulence of actual life. That is what I often say.

6) It may at first sight seem unlikely that the pull of gravity will depress the centre of a light cord, held horizontally at a high lateral tension; and yet no force, however great, can stretch a cord, however fine, into a horizontal line that shall be absolutely straight. [from a late Victorian work on mathematics]

7) It was then that I realized how little I actually knew my father—what he thought about the family, what plans and ambitions he had for us children, or even what size shirt he wore.

8) Yes indeed, as one slowly glides away on the *Princess Pat* or on the *Princess Margaret,* when once the boat has passed the

uninviting façades of the Peerless Paint Company and
Weather Roofing Company, on looking back across the harb.
over Beacon Hill to the massive stone Cathedral, one gets the
ing that one has just left a garden city of Old England.

20 The meaning of words

> . . . "meaning" is a property of the mutually relevant people, things,
> events, in the situation. Some of the events are noises made by the
> speaker. But it is important to realize that "meaning" is just as much
> a property of the people, their "sets," their specific behaviour, the
> things and events of the situation as of the noises made.—J. R. Firth

We ordinarily take our words for granted, except perhaps
when we are faced with a question in what we are writing:
the meaning of *turbo-prop*, the difference between *concave*
and *convex*, the appropriateness of *job* or *position*, of *lousy*
or *unsatisfactory*. But we know that our words are tremen-
dously important for the accuracy of what we say and for its
effectiveness, the impression it makes on others.

To make our writing more effective, we need to continue
to grow in our understanding of words, to take an active interest in them as words: what gives them meaning, the various
sorts of meaning, the various ways in which they are used, the
impressions they make. These are some of the topics of *semantics*, the study of the meaning of words.

20.1 Denotation: the core of a word's meaning Words are
arrangements of sounds or letters that we use to bring various
notions to another person's attention. These notions may be
objects or "things" (*typewriter, Golden Gate Bridge*), qualities (*excellent, hard*), relationships (*without, hers*), actions
or conditions (*running, homesickness*), or ideas (*democracy,
beauty*).

When we think first about the meaning of words, we think of what is known as their *denotation,* what they have come to point to or to represent as a result of the ways they have been used. This is the meaning that dictionaries record and try to describe for us. The thing that a word refers to or suggests is called its *referent* (ref' er ent).

Some kinds of words have more definite denotations than others because their referents are more limited or more exact. These three classes of words show how definiteness may vary:

1) Concrete words: words that name specific people, places, or objects are the most exact in meaning: *Walt Whitman, Lake Erie, my bicycle, the library, reindeer, a Boy Scout knife.*

2) Relative words: words that name qualities are less definite than concrete words, and frequently depend for their meaning on the situation or the writer's past experience with the term: *hot, pretty, honest, angry, silly, impossible.* In New York City, a *tall* building might mean any structure over twenty stories, while in a city with no skyscrapers, *tall* might refer to any building higher than five stories.

3) Abstract words: words that refer to general concepts— acts, situations, relationships, conditions—are the least definite: *reasoning, citizenship, education, intelligence, culture, objectives, art.* Since these words have a range of reference (Think of all the activities that may be included in *education,* for example) rather than a specific referent, they are more difficult to use exactly than concrete words. But we need all kinds of words in our writing and we can learn to use all of them in responsible communication.

20.2 Connotation: the suggestion of words   Most words have been used by so many different people, in such different circumstances, and for such different purposes that they have acquired associations and suggestions that go beyond their denotation. These qualities of suggestion are called *connotation. Coffee,* for instance, has a clear denotation, or group of related denotations (the plant, the grocery product, the drink), but it may also carry connotations of the labor of growing or processing, of the price, of the taste, or the aroma, or of the coffee break as a time of relaxation.

Very often the chief difference between words of closely related denotation is in their connotation: both *inexpensive* and *cheap* refer to low price, but *cheap* may suggest also poor quality; *average* and *mediocre* refer to the middle of a range, but *mediocre* suggests dispraise; *belief, faith, creed, dogma* all refer to ideas held but they differ widely in suggesting how the ideas are held. Most dictionaries offer a choice of synonyms with some distinctions between such shades of meaning. But the best way to find the exact connotations of words is to observe them as they are actually used in talks, conversation, and reading.

Both denotation and connotation are parts of the meaning of words and both must be considered for effective speaking and writing. In writing that calls for great objectivity—scientific reports, legal documents, dictionaries, directions for making or using things—words are chiefly used for their denotative meanings. In more personal or in persuasive writing—poetry or fiction or argumentative discussions condemning, praising, or calling for action—the connotation of the words may be as important as their core of meaning. Only in special situations, like a discussion of scientific facts or mathematical certainties, are words used strictly for their denotation.

In almost all everyday affairs, as well as in poetry, attitudes and feelings are present and are part of what our words suggest. There has been a good deal of discussion of "emotive" words. But the emotion is not in the words, any more than the denotative meaning is: the emotions are in the people who speak or write them and in those who hear or read them. We are in the habit of using words more intensely than the situation demands, and many people respond to words with more intensity than seems reasonable to someone who does not have the same attitude. The speaker or writer, as a user of words, does not need to suppress the suggestions of attitude and feeling that belong to the situation, but he does have a responsibility to see that they represent his more complete and "better" self, to see that they are justified in the situation.

We are especially likely to use words loosely in discussing ideas and ideals. In this excerpt from a radio discussion of education, the words are so general that they convey chiefly a vague notion of approval without helping us understand much about the actual process of education:

> What do you mean by "education for freedom," or "education for the citizen"?
>
> The way in which I like to think of it involves the phrase "the liberal arts" or "a liberal education," the word "liberal" there being the word that means freedom. Over the long history of Western civilization the liberal arts have been those that have made men free.

Since most writing done in composition courses is neither wholly objective nor entirely personal, both kinds of meaning should be considered when choosing a word for a specific spot.

20.3 Words in context and situation   So far we have been talking about separate words, but strictly speaking, words by themselves or in a list do not have "meaning," but only typical or possible meaning. They do not actually "mean" something unless they are *used* in speaking or writing. Consequently they always have a *context*, other words around them, and they are always in a *situation* that involves the attitudes and purposes of either a speaker and listener or a writer and reader. The context and situation are both factors in meaning.

It is easy to see how the meaning of a word that has several denotations is made definite by the context it is in. By itself a word like *deck*, *run*, *fly*, or *battery* might have several senses, but usually in a particular sentence it could have only one:

> Fill the tank with gas and put water in the *battery*.
>
> *Batteries* for the game were Grim and Berra for the Yankees, Lemon and Hegan for the Indians.
>
> A *battery* of cameras was turned on the President as he walked to the plane.
>
> When I joined the National Guard, I was assigned to *A Battery*.

Not only the context of the word but the situation in which it is used helps clarify meaning. The word *bill* in "The bill is too large" would mean one thing in identifying a bird and another in discussing family finances. The situation includes the people who are actually using the words, writer and reader. In so far as their experience is similar, they can communicate easily. If their experiences are different, the writer has to take more pains in using words to lead the reader to an understanding of his matter.

20.4 Increasing your vocabulary We learn and keep in memory words not as words but as representing meanings—we probably store them away as they are used in contexts. We have a good stock of words in the fields that interest us. Consider the vocabulary of a baseball fan, the color words of a painter or a girl who is a clothes fancier, the radio and electronic words of a ham operator, the biological and chemical vocabulary of a premedical student.

Our vocabulary is of two sorts, a *recognition* vocabulary of words we understand when we hear or read them, and an *active* vocabulary that we use ourselves in speaking and writing. Professor Seashore estimates that the average college student's recognition vocabulary is about 62,000 main words with 96,000 more derivative from them.

A person probably uses only about a third as many words as he recognizes. Consequently the obvious way to "enlarge one's vocabulary"—since by "I have such a small vocabulary" he usually means that he feels he does not use enough different words—is by talking and writing more, especially about subjects that he lets lie unused in his mind. Even using words in fun helps to fix them in mind. The most natural way to acquire new words is by learning something new—from observation, from doing something, from conversation, or from reading. Occasionally you hear or find a new word in reading (*diploma mill, electroencephalogram, pecking order, spelunker* . . .) and learn its meaning from the context or from a dictionary.

The meaning of some words can be figured out by knowing their parts, especially the "compounding elements" from Greek or Latin that are used in forming many scientific words:

mono- (one)	*-graph* (writing, written)	*hemo-* (blood)
bi- (two)	*bio-* (life)	*poly-* (many)
tele- (at a distance)	*photo-* (light)	

Since the sum of the meanings of the parts only approximates the meaning of the whole word, it is safer and easier to learn the whole words.

Groups of words are learned when you learn something new, because you can't take facts or ideas away with you unless they are in verbal form. A newly acquired interest in fishing, in television, in music, in T. S. Eliot's poems, or in biology or sociology will add many new words, some of them of general usefulness. The typical college course adds several hundred new words and old words in new senses to a student's vocabulary.

New words that you are going to need to use should be accurately learned the first time they are met—their pronunciation and spelling as well as their usual meaning. A good deal of students' trouble in courses comes from only partly understanding the specialized words when they are first met. Once they are understood, they should be used. Many of them you will need in recitation or examinations or term papers, but using them in conversation when they are appropriate or in talking over the course work with someone else will fix them in your mind and make them come more easily when you need them.

References

Fries, C. C., *The Teaching of English*, Ann Arbor, George Wahr, 1949, Ch. 4, Standards of Acceptable English: Vocabulary

Hayakawa, S. I., *Language in Thought and Action*, New York, Harcourt, Brace, 1949. This book and Johnson's *People in Quandaries* are introductions to the system of "general semantics" developed by Alfred Korzybski.

Hixson, Jerome C., and I. Colodny, *Word Ways,* New York, American Book Company, 1946, Part 3, English Word Building

Johnson, Wendell, *People in Quandaries,* New York, Holt, 1946

Kennedy, Arthur G., *Current English,* Boston, Ginn, 1935, Ch. 10, The Modern English Vocabulary

Nelson, L. G., "In Defense of Ezra," *English Journal,* 1938, 27: 513–517. On the increase of vocabulary needed for current reading

Nida, Eugene, *Morphology,* Ann Arbor, University of Michigan Press, 1949, especially Ch. 6. A treatment of meaning from a linguist's point of view

Oxford English Dictionary, prefaces to volumes 1 and 10

Ramsay, Robert L., "Taking the Census of English Words," *American Speech,* 1933, 8:36–41

Russell, I. Willis, "Among the New Words," in most issues of *American Speech*

Seashore, R. H., "The Importance of Vocabulary in Learning Language Skills," *Elementary English,* 1948, 25:137–152

Seashore, R. H., "How Large Are Children's Vocabularies?" *Elementary English,* 1949, 26:181–194; discussed in 26:407–413

Walpole, Hugh R., *Semantics,* New York, Norton, 1941. An introduction to the doctrine of I. A. Richards

Exercises

1. Classify by number the words in the following list as (1) words you now use in speaking or in writing; (2) words that you understand but do not generally use; (3) words that you believe you have seen before and might understand in context; (4) words totally unfamiliar to you. Look up the words that you number 3 or 4 in a dictionary. Which might be useful to you?

actuary	featherbedding	lurid	scherzo
bauble	fugue	magneto	semantics
beige	ganglion	martial	snide
bibliography	gasket	megacycle	sonar
braise	gerund	myopia	statism
candor	gossamer	nadir	suave
cartel	hedonist	pabulum	synthesis
claustrophobia	histrionic	paradox	tête-à-tête
cliché	ides	parallelism	thesaurus
combine (noun)	innuendo	pleistocene	toxic
context	intelligentsia	proboscis	tycoon
decalcomania	intransigent	psychosomatic	tyro
deciduous	jabot	quixotic	unilateral
entrepreneur	laissez faire	quotient	vignette
essential oil	libretto	riffraff	virtuoso
euthanasia	lobotomy	satiate	zealous

2. In two or three paragraphs, discuss a word or expression whose connotation has changed conspicuously for you from your childhood to the present time (or in the last year or two, or since you entered college). Describe as accurately as possible the associations the word originally had for you, the way in which you first used it, what its associations are for you today, and why. The words in this list are offered as suggestions; they may remind you of others:

psychology	mice	success
Santa Claus	taxes	spelling
poetry	New York	dancing
war	professor	philosophy
sorority	science	vacation

3. Rearrange the following lists so that the word with the most favorable connotation is at the top, the one with the next most favorable second, and so on. Check the word that seems to you to represent the "core of meaning" of the group. What is suggested by the other terms, and in what circumstances might they be

appropriately used? In which words does their level of usage (§2) influence the connotation?

1)	in want	2)	limousine
	broke		car
	penniless		jalopy
	indigent		means of transportation
	poor		Chevie
	impecunious		automobile
	hard up		wreck
	flat		horseless carriage
			machine

3)	kids	4)	weary
	progeny		pooped
	young 'uns		exhausted
	juveniles		fatigued
	children		dog tired
	the innocents		used up
	little ones		tired
	brats		spent

5)	demented	6)	blurted
	crazy		said
	lunatic		opined
	psychopathic		uttered
	mad		mouthed
	insane		cried
	bughouse		stated
	mentally ill		spake
	nutty		

4. If letter grades were not used to evaluate your papers, which of these comments, by itself, would most nearly approximate your idea of "C"? Which would suggest that your work was nearer "B" or "D," and why?

1) Adequate
2) Satisfactory
3) Acceptable
4) Passing
5) Satisfies the assignment
6) Not outstanding, but apparently conscientious work
7) Average
8) Competent
9) Not too badly done
10) Fair
11) Good idea, but inadequately developed
12) Your writing is potentially good

5. In a sentence describe the differences in the attitudes reflected in the following pairs of words:

intoxicated—drunk
public information—propaganda
nonunion worker—scab
discriminating—finicky

a hearty eater—a glutton
saliva—spit
antique—antiquated
isn't—ain't

6. Make a list of a dozen or more words of different kinds that you have added to your vocabulary in recent weeks. To refresh your memory, consult some of your recent papers, check the indexes of textbooks, and consider the various new activities you have engaged in. Prepare a brief statement about the circumstances in which you acquired these words and the way you learned their meaning.

7. The following groups of words are made up of compounding elements from Greek and Latin. Break each word into its parts and, reasoning from those that you know, try to discover the meaning of the first word in each group. When you have a probable meaning for the first word, look in a dictionary to see how close you have come to the definition given there.

1) antiseptic
   antifreeze
   antitoxin
   septic sore throat
   septic tank

2) audiometer
   audible
   audition
   speedometer
   thermometer

3) circumlocution
circumference
circumnavigate
elocution
interlocutor

4) genocide
homicide
suicide
genetics
genus

5) megacephalic
megacycle
megaphone
cephalopod
cephalic index

6) pneumectomy
pneumonia
pneumatic
appendectomy
tonsillectomy

7) quadruped
quadrangle
quadrilateral
centipede
pedal

8) supersonic
superior
superman
dissonant
sonorous

9) transfluent
transatlantic
transition
fluid
confluent

10) unilateral
uniform
unify
bilateral
lateral pass

21 Accurate words

I think we shall have to say that a word is used accurately (1) when its literal meaning does in fact embrace the objects to which the word is applied, and (2) when its emotional character corresponds to the feelings which those same objects, viewed without prejudice, would generally excite.—Barrows Dunham

WW Wrong word or Diction. Correction: Replace the word marked by
or one that is more correct (§21.1), more specific (§21.2), or more fair
D (§21.3).

Words should be meaningful—they should represent your intended meaning, so that they can lead your reader to an understanding of that meaning. Where exact words are necessary or desirable, as in most factual writing and most writing in college, they should be used in their established forms and senses. This we do most of the time, but sometimes—when we are writing on a subject that is new to us, or when we are not sure of our attitude toward it, or when we are nervous, or perhaps just in a hurry—we either find the choice of words a problem or actually make mistakes in using them. This and the next two sections take up some common problems in words and make suggestions for getting full value out of the stock of words that we have.

21.1   **The right word**   A writer should be careful to check and to correct in revision any words that are not a part of his usual vocabulary, or that he has reason to suspect may be incorrectly used. In particular he should watch words that are easily confused.

21.1a   **Words of similar sound or spelling**   *Moral* and *morale* mean two quite different things; so do *personal* and *personnel, historic* and *histrionic,* and a large number of other words that resemble each other in form but not in meaning.

Words that are pronounced exactly alike are called *homonyms (meat, meet, mete; bear, bare; sweet, suite).* When one form is substituted for another in writing, the mistake may be marked as a spelling error, especially if the words are common and their sounds are very close or identical *(their, there).* But the error is more likely to be labeled WW (wrong word) if there is a suspicion in the reader's mind that the exact meaning is not clear to the writer:

> It turned out to be just a *fragment* of my imagination. [for *figment*]
> A person who is sincerely attempting to attain a *harmonic* and satisfying life will not use this philosophy as an excuse for falling into a state of mental or physical laziness. [for *harmonious*]

Usually accurate proofreading will catch such errors. If you have a question, look the word up in a dictionary.

21.1b **Words of opposite meanings** Distinguish between words that have contrasting or wholly opposite meanings but that are very commonly confused. Some words that seem to resemble each other in sound or in association are actually *antonyms* (words that mean the opposite of other words) or near-antonyms: *convex—concave; condemn—condone; physiological—psychological; temerity—timidity.*

Other pairs of words, while not antonyms, have equally distinct meanings and should not be carelessly substituted for one another: *astrology—astronomy; notorious—famous; ingenuous—ingenious; conscientious—conscious; respectively—respectfully.*

Half knowing a word may be more dangerous than not knowing it at all.

21.2 **Specific and general words** When you are writing a paper, you should discuss the topic in as specific terms as possible. General words and vague expressions will not impress a reader any more than they will impress you when a month or so later you reread what you have written. Even if an assignment is so worded that it seems difficult to discuss in specific terms ("The Importance of Education," "What Good Citizenship Means"), you can make your report reasonably factual, concrete, and convincing by treating it in words that represent your own experiences and beliefs. (See §9.4, p. 110 for using both details and general statements.)

Words can be classified according to the nature of their referents as *general* or *specific.* General, or abstract, words refer to ideas, qualities, acts, or relationships. Specific, or concrete, words refer to definite persons, places, objects, and acts. (See §20.1.) This list indicates the differences between the two kinds of words:

General (abstract)	*Specific* (concrete)
corporation	Standard Oil Company
labor	running a lathe
youth organization	Boy Scouts of America
height	five feet, ten inches

food	lamb chops
an educator	our biology teacher
crime	car theft
entertainment	the Junior Prom

Often a word cannot be labeled as general or specific until we see it in context:

General	*Specific*
War never solved any problems. [Abstract, a generalization about *all* wars]	When the *war* ended in 1902, the Boer Republics lost their independence. [Specific, a reference to the Boer War]

21.2a   Use of general and specific words   Specific, concrete words are appropriate—and essential—in discussions of situations, incidents, processes that are based upon personal experience or direct observation: impressions of people or places, plans for the future, explanations of the writer's attitudes or interests.

As a rule, general, abstract words are most necessary in discussing general ideas (such as "The Intangible Values of Education"), for summarizing facts or stating opinions, or for theoretical problems ("Is Specialization in Education Dangerous?"). They are more characteristic of Formal than of General or Informal English and of writers with a good deal of experience in handling ideas. In this paragraph, for example, a philosopher used but three concrete words (*me, you,* and *the drama*), yet his meaning is clear to anyone familiar with the kind of ideas he is discussing:

Let me remind you that the essence of dramatic tragedy is not unhappiness. It resides in the solemnity of the remorseless workings of things. This inevitableness of destiny can only be illustrated in terms of human life by incidents which in fact involve unhappiness. For it is only by them that the futility of escape can be made evident in the drama. This remorseless inevitableness is what pervades scientific thought. The laws of physics are the laws of fate.—Alfred North Whitehead, *Science and the Modern World,* p. 11

But ideas can be discussed in words that are specific, and usually they are, especially when written in General English for a fairly large audience. This discussion of "the American way of life," an extremely abstract notion, begins in language that is conspicuously specific:

> But what is the American way of life?
>
> This morning, my mail included a notice of a Rotary meeting, an appeal for funds from World Federalists, an announcement of a meeting of the state trustees of Vermont Forums, Inc., some pamphlets published by the Friends, a letter from the Institute of International Education, an invitation to join a sociological association, and a program announcement from an organization new to me—the National Cooperative School for Group Organization and Recreation. During the morning, my wife (who is active in twice as many community services as I am) was out campaigning for the Red Cross. A phone call invited me to speak at a church club, and we were notified of a square dance.— Bradford Smith, "We're Selling America Short," *The American Scholar,* Summer 1952, p. 310

Words of all kinds are essential for mature, intelligent communication, but no one kind should be used to the exclusion of the others. If a person relied wholly on extremely specific, concrete words (as children do when they are learning to talk), his ideas would not range very widely. And conversely, if he insisted on using nothing but very general, abstract words, he would soon lack an audience, for few traits of style are more fatiguing or boring.

21.2b   Inappropriate use of abstract words   The most common fault in the wording of many freshman papers is a fondness for abstract terms where specific words would be more meaningful and certainly more interesting. The reason may be that some students believe the more general the word, the more convincing and impressive it is.

It is perfectly proper to use general words when you are certain that your material calls for them, and when you are confident that you can use them with accuracy and clarity. But no matter what your subject is, your writing will be improved if most of your words are specific: it is much easier, and usually more convincing, to generalize at the beginning or end of your paper, on the basis of a number of specific facts, than it is to build generality on generality throughout the paper.

A general or indefinite expression, where one would ordinarily expect a concrete term, is annoying to readers:

> I think that this quarter's work has helped me to form *new physical actions* and broadened my *mental ability*.

If the writer means that he has learned *to swim,* or *to play baseball,* or *to dance,* he should say so; and he might also indicate just how the quarter's work has broadened his "mental ability": helped him to concentrate? taught him better study habits? enabled him to solve chemical equations?

The use of abstract words, where concrete words would be more exact and vivid, can become an unfortunate habit in writing. Some students never take *physics, history, economics,* or *French;* instead, they *encounter various interesting courses of study;* instead of going to a specific college or university, they attend *an institution of higher learning;* they do not play *golf, bridge,* or *tennis,* but *participate in various recreational activities.* Their lives, at least on paper, are so abstract that one wonders whether they are in the class as actual persons or as disembodied spirits.

21.2c Catchall expressions   Certain general words and phrases are commonly misused as "cover-up" or "catchall" expressions. "I have long been interested in psychology and *things like that*" may mean something to the writer, but for the general reader, the meaning ends with the word *psychology.*

> When I was a boy of fourteen, I was mainly concerned with swimming, *etc.*

Some boys of fourteen are concerned with swimming, fishing, hunting, sailing, and other outdoor sports. Others are concerned with swimming, turning in false fire alarms, learning to dance, stealing milk bottles, and other commendable or not so commendable activities. It is better to give three or four sample specific items than to rely on catchall expressions.

21.2d Weak intensives   Don't rely too heavily on intensive adjectives and adverbs to emphasize your meaning. Some expressions that are frequently used to stress statements in conversation have become too general to be effective in writing:

> very: a *very* dull lecture
> so: *so* happy to see him looking *so* well
> quite: *quite* an unusual experience
> lots: and *lots* of other reasons
> most: the *most* essential part
> really: an experience that was *really* unbelievable
> such: We had *such* a charming evening.
> too: I'm not *too* interested in geography.

These words do of course serve a purpose and should not be eliminated entirely in writing. But when they are overworked they do not emphasize the meaning, and may actually weaken a statement.

Certain descriptive words have also become weakened through overuse, and should be used with caution in most kinds of writing:

| interesting | lovely | fine | nice |
| fascinating | wonderful | awful (awfully) | terrific |

When these words appear frequently in your writing, try omitting some of them to see if your statements don't gain rather than lose in forcefulness.

21.3 Fair words   Statements in serious discussions should be in words that suggest a fair and reasonable attitude toward the subject. Since people are not by nature exact and since they often "go by their feelings," they frequently use words loosely and with connotations that show these feelings. Words that conspicuously suggest attitudes and feelings are called *slanted.*

21.3a Unfair slanting   Too intense words should be avoided in factual statements, and so should exaggerations that will interfere with a reader's belief:

The great forest fire of August 7, 1949, will be remembered by millions of forest rangers, because it could have ruined smoke jumping forever. [How many forest rangers are there, anyway?]

All movies are produced solely for morons.

This last statement is fair neither to the movies nor to the reader's intelligence. Considered charitably, it suggests that the writer is familiar only with mediocre movies, or that he has perhaps confused *morons* with some less extreme word; but probably the statement was just careless. Often an *all* or a *most* should be *many,* or a superlative should be reduced to a less extreme word, or an *only* or *nothing but* should be changed to allow for other possibilities.

Much unfair slanting occurs in statements of opinion. There is nothing slanted in a simple statement of one's likes or dislikes: "I can't stand turnips in any form." But if the same opinion is stated as a general fact in slanted wording ("Turnips are fit only for animals and not for human beings"), it implies that the writer expects his readers to share his opinion without thinking about it.

The most serious instances of slanting come in writing on social situations, especially when the words reflect prejudice ("a judgment or opinion held in disregard of facts that contradict it; unreasonable bias"). Such slanted words can be objected to on at least four grounds: they are inaccurate in representing the situation being discussed; they give an impression of a writer at the very least careless of what he says and more probably willing to distort for his purpose; they are against the social interest because they prevent understanding and intelligent dealing with situations often of considerable public importance; and they are likely to antagonize a reader, unless he is similarly prejudiced, and so prevent clear communication.

Conspicuous slanting is out of place in the writing of responsible people, including college writing. Information must be presented in more accurate words, and even opinions can be presented convincingly in words that are more scrupulously chosen.

21.3b **Legitimate slanting**   But it is not possible to lead our lives, nor to write, in completely neutral, objective language. Interest, liveliness, effectiveness in factual writing as well as in the imaginative writing of literature depend in large part on the connotation of words. When the slanting is not inconsistent with the facts and when it represents attitudes and feelings that fall within a reasonable, defensible range, it is legitimate. The harmless exaggerations of conversation ("Jim's the best freethrow shot in the history of basketball") usually are toned down in writing ("Jim's the best freethrow shot I've ever seen"), but certainly we have a right to our enthusiasms.

Well-based opinions are usually more readable and more effective when expressed with a degree of slanting. The following paragraph on one aspect of television programs is obviously rather one-sided, but it is emphatic and convincing in part because of the connotation of many of the words (*phoniness, huckster mind, sniggers, molasses, cream puff*). The style warns the reader that it is slanted and is to be taken as opinion and evaluated on the basis of the evidence given and the reader's own experience.

In a medium where actuality and naturalness are obviously the most effective instruments, there is a vast deal of manufactured falsity. Part of this is a holdover from radio's basic drive toward phoniness, especially vocal phoniness; part of it is the huckster mind, which like a diseased pancreas converts everything to sugar. Apart from some wan sniggers by comedians, the only awareness of sex I encountered . . . was in a commercial. While the screen showed a pair of hands, the announcer made love to Ivory Soap Flakes—so soft, so wonderful, how delicate they are, the secret of mildness is in them. He could say "delicacy" with a lewdness and lubricity that would have got him jailed if he had spoken the word from a Boston stage. Amourousness about soap is combined with stereotypes about nearly everything, and most of them afloat on a sea of molasses. . . . The woman who operates a cooking school makes salad and stew and biscuits but her manner is all cream puff and her voice marshmallow. The one who is angling for the preschool child says "ooh" and "yes" and "fun" with grace notes and cadenzas encrusted with sugar (and a simper); her guest, the director of a zoo, is probably offhand about his job when offstage but she talks baby talk to him so horribly that he catches the infection and talks baby talk to a monkey he has brought with him.—Bernard DeVoto, "The Easy Chair," *Harper's Magazine,* March 1953, p. 53. Reprinted by permission of *Harper's Magazine.*

21.3c The responsible use of words If a person wishes to deceive, language offers him the means; by intentional misuse of words or by an irresponsible manipulation of the emotional suggestion in words a "propagandist" (or anyone else) can distort facts and make error prevail, at least for a time.

But in spite of some selfish and even evil intentions, an honest attempt at communication can be made to succeed. The difficulty is not so much in the words as in the intent of the person using them or the lack of a responsible purpose. Honest failure in communication is possible because of careless or unhappy choice of words, and sometimes we fail to make full use of the language we have. But a sincere effort to convey to others material with which we are really familiar can be made to succeed.

21.4 Synonyms A synonym is a word of nearly the same meaning as another:

sick—ill
multitude—throng—crowd—mob
tremble—shiver—quake—shake
misrepresentation—untruth—falsehood—fib—lie

A few words have precisely the same meaning and are therefore interchangeable (*flammable, inflammable; ravel, unravel; toward, towards*). But most synonyms, while they refer to the same idea or object, differ in connotation, and cannot be substituted for each other without affecting in some degree the tone of the statement. Thus, while *my father, daddy, pa, the old man* all refer to the same person, they reflect different attitudes on the part of the speaker or the writer toward his parent.

Since synonyms have the same general core of meaning, it is important for a writer to know in what way they differ. One term may be more Formal than another (*coiffure—hair-do*); more concrete (*soldiers—army personnel*); more exact (*charitable—kind*); or more personal (*dad—father*).

21.4a Synonyms for more accurate denotation Usually it is not the more subtle distinctions between closely related words that cause trouble (*necessary, indispensable; intrinsic, inherent*), but the failure to distinguish between common words in different contexts:

> The mysteries of the unknown arouse curiosity that must be *fulfilled.* [for *satisfied*]
>
> A hobby would have satisfied his *want* for something to do in his spare time. [*desire*]

21.4b Synonyms for more accurate connotation The connotation of synonyms should be appropriate to the context and to the general tone of the writing. Notice how unexpected the last word in this statement is:

> In the 1870's, Dodge City was a lawless gathering place for gun-toting cowboys, professional bad men and killers, and other scamps.

Scamps might be quite appropriate in referring to mischievous children, but the term is conspicuously out of place in this company of desperadoes.

Some synonyms are too heavy or too strained for the context:

> I sat down to study with my *tomes of learning* stacked around me. [*textbooks*]

Others may be too Informal (or even flippant) for use in serious discussions:

> I enjoyed studying Plato, because among other things, I *got the lowdown* on what is meant by a Platonic friendship. [I *learned* what is meant . . .]

Even though the accurate word may seem a little commonplace or flat, it is better to use it than to risk offending or startling the reader by an inappropriate synonym.

21.4c Unnecessary synonyms   Do not use different names for the same thing just for the sake of variety. If you are writing a paper on the care and feeding of cats, don't refer to them variously as *felines, furry beasts, tabbies, nine-lived creatures,* or by other fanciful synonyms. The actual name of these animals is *cats* and that is what your reader will expect you to call them.

Writers sometimes worry that using the same expression for an idea or object will lead to awkward repetition. But we expect key words to be repeated to keep our attention focused on the subject. Pronouns can of course be used freely to refer to the key words (cats . . . *they*), or some factual synonym (*these animals*); such terms are unobtrusive and will seldom be noticed no matter how many times they are repeated.

A studied avoidance of calling the same thing by the same name twice ("elegant variation," to use H. G. Fowler's term) is more noticeable—and annoying—than necessary repetition.

It was suggested that if *the children* try to print at home, parents should show *their offspring* [better: them] the small as well as the capital letters. Suggestions like this help people to understand the methods used to educate *their young ones* [better: their children].

Women are as human as men, and if six hours is proper for men, it is proper for *females* [better: women], too. Many *members of the fair sex* [better: women] work and manage a home at the same time; can their husbands say as much?

21.4d Sources of synonyms   Your desk dictionary groups words of similar meaning and indicates the distinctions among them. Books of synonyms, obtainable in most libraries, are also useful:

Fernald's *Standard Handbook of Synonyms, Antonyms, and Prepositions,* New York, 1947
   Roget's International Thesaurus, New York, rev. ed., 1946
   Soule's *A Dictionary of English Synonyms,* Boston, 1938
   Webster's Dictionary of Synonyms, Springfield, Massachusetts, 1942

The *Thesaurus* (also available in abridged pocketbook form) is the most used book of synonyms, offering a wide range from slang to formal expressions and even obsolete terms. But since it does not define words nor indicate their level of usage, the *Thesaurus* should be used with an up-to-date dictionary. Its most practical use is to jog a writer's memory, to supply him with a word that he knows but that has momentarily slipped his mind.

References

Chase, Stuart, *Power of Words*, New York, Harcourt, Brace, 1954

Estrich, Robert M., and Hans Sperber, *Three Keys to Language*, New York, Rinehart, 1952; examples chiefly from American political discussion

Fowler, articles titled "Elegant variation," "Homonym," "Synonyms"

Gowers, Sir Ernest, *Plain Words*, London, Her Majesty's Stationery Office, 1948, Ch. 8, Choosing the Concrete Word

Walpole, Hugh, *Semantics*, New York, Norton, 1941, Ch. 2, Emotive Language

Exercises

1. For each of the following words, write two sentences to illustrate (1) what you consider a reasonably exact use of the word, and (2) the way the word might be carelessly or inexactly or unfairly used in speech or writing:

alibi	moron	deal (noun)	real	mean (adjective)
dumb	smooth	mad	hopeless	neat
funny	bird	divine	vicious	politician

2. Each of the following sentences from student papers contains one or more mistakes in the meaning of words. Point out what word or words are incorrectly used and state what the correct

word should be. If the mistake seems to you to be one of spelling rather than choice of word, indicate how the word should be correctly spelled:

1) Two years of this kind of treatment gave John a marked inferior complex.

2) Education in Mexico is optional, and the parents there do not stress their children to go to school.

3) Nearsightedness is one disease that is increasing each year in number.

4) Because he had always made good grades with little effort, Chuck had a contemptible attitude toward those who spent hours over their books.

5) It is doubtfully thought that Lodowyk van Berghen was the first person to advise a method for cutting diamond facets.

6) I believe that a brief summary of the primitive years of algebra would be of great help to any student at the beginning of his first college math course.

7) The city had five broadcasting stations, but WKLX was the only twenty-four-hour radio-active station.

8) Although it lacks the extreme compactness of miniature cameras, this medium size camera is able to get around quite well.

9) I was disparaged to find that my name was misspelled in the society columns of both newspapers.

10) The less the top of a convertible car is put up and down, the more it will last.

3. Follow the same instructions as for the preceding exercise:

1) Through the tenacious efforts of the father and his three sons, the family was at last able to meet all monetary obligations auspiciously.

2) Because all mental patients need some nursing care during the day, other than that which the untrained workers can give, the present small nursing staffs are trying to do an almost inhuman task.

3) Why do housewives listen to soap operas? The inferred reasons are obvious.

4) Most men who commit serious crimes are either economically or psychologically ill.

5) Statistics showed that Americans spent over 900 million dollars for dental care in 1949, an average of 36 million dollars over the preceding year.

6) Physical labor shouldn't bear any blame on anyone.

7) A good many martial difficulties that end in divorce could be prevented by mutual understanding and cooperation.

8) The remarks I overheard at intermission indicated the usual reactions of an unprepared and therefore miscomprehending audience reaction.

9) The book was difficult to understand because the author was always eluding to something I didn't understand.

10) I imagine that to most young men entering the service and spending a few years away from home, their impressions of the service aren't too likable.

4. To illustrate what abstract wording may lead to, George Orwell translated this selection from Ecclesiastes into "modern English of the worst sort," in the passage following. Read both versions carefully and be prepared to discuss why the commonplace, "everyday" words of the original are more effective than the vague, inflated words of the revision. Does the translation affect chiefly the sound, or the meaning, or both equally? Note that while the translation contains fewer words than the original (38 as against 49), it contains a great many more syllables (90 as against 60):

I returned and saw under the sun, that the race is not to the swift, nor the battle to the strong, neither yet bread to the wise, nor yet riches to men of understanding, nor yet favour to men of skill; but time and chance happeneth to them all.—Ecclesiastes, 9:11

Objective considerations of contemporary phenomena compel the conclusion that success or failure in competitive activities exhibits no tendency to be commensurate with innate capacity, but that a considerable element of the unpredictable must invariably be taken into account.—George Orwell, "Politics and the English Language," *Shooting an Elephant*, pp. 84-85

5. This student paper is an extreme example of vague wording and unconvincing generalities. What might be the central thought in the paper? What expressions might better be made more specific and to the point (for instance, "the nature of our life's vocation to be" could just as well read "what we want to be")? Make a list of these expressions and suggest substitutes for them. Also make a list of any words that are incorrectly used.

Choice and Preparation for a Vocation

Remember back to the period of your early years leading to adulthood? Barring exceptions, think of the countless times we have voiced the opinion, in rather salubrious tones, the nature of our life's vocation to be. Think also, of the numerous times this vocational choice has been changed from practically everything from street vendor to chief executive of the land.

Nature is truly the possessor of the ultimate wisdom; for she has endowed man with the ability to think more or less connectedly, and to make his own decisions whether it be for the purpose of self-preservation, the emulation of others, or leadership of one's own fellow-men.

With the unlimited opportunities afforded today, coupled with the fact that our modern civilization is one of specialization, choosing a field of endeavor becomes only a matter of the intellectual and emotional faculties.

This vocational choice, we must remember, is unlocked from within *only* as maturation occurs to the point where one can fully realize his place, not only in society, but in the eyes of his Creator. Also, one, according to his own environment, is constantly molding new ideas concerning his future vocation. These ideas are then integrated and revised with the old, thus bringing about the end-product of his own choosing.

However, nothing can be accomplished without the rigid requirements of special training found in advanced education, necessary to carry out whatever plans one might hold in mind.

6. Bring to class for discussion examples of statements in conspicuously vague words. Some of these you may encounter in conversation or hear over the radio or in newspapers (try the editorials or the columns written by political commentators or the letters to the editor), or perhaps even in some of your textbooks.

7. List the words in the following definitions that have unfavorable connotations. What would be a definition slanted from our point of view? What would be a neutral definition?

Some people feel that progress toward peace among the United Nations is extraordinarily slow, or nonexistent. Part of the trouble seems to stem from that ubiquitous problem, language barriers. Diplomats make endless comments concerning, say "democracy," but no one understands, or appears to understand, the other! In a recent edition of *Slovar Inostrannykh Slov* (Dictionary of Foreign Words) issued in Moscow, appear such definitions (translated) as these:

Boy Scout: "A member of a bourgeois children's organization having a military-political character in capitalistic countries."

Democracy: "A political structure in which power belongs to the people. The Soviet Socialist democracy is a new higher type of democracy, with power actually in the hands of the people. . . . Bourgeois democracy is a form of class supremacy, the dictatorship of the bourgeoisie over the proletariat and the working masses."

Missionary: "A person sent by the ruling church (in the majority of cases with the support of the government) for religious propaganda among backward peoples (for example, in colonial or semi-colonial countries); he is usually an advance espionage agent of the imperialist usurpers."

Wall Street: "A street in New York on which are located the largest banks, financial markets, etc. Wall Street is a synonym for the plundering imperialistic interests of the American financial oligarchy."—"Humpty-Dumpty in Moscow," *Inside the ACD,* November 1951, p. 1. Reprinted by permission of Harper & Brothers.

8. Make a report comparing the wording of headlines for the same story in two newspapers or weekly news magazines with different editorial sympathies. Use a pair from the following list or from publications suggested by your instructor:

The Christian Science Monitor; The New York Times	and	*The Chicago Tribune; The Los Angeles Times*
Time; Newsweek; The Nation's Business	and	*The New Republic; The Reporter; The New Statesman and Nation* (an English publication)
your college paper	and	the paper of a rival school

In your report

a. Show specifically in what way words are used for their connotative rather than for their denotative values ("Federal Officials *Rap* Thornton's *Scheme*"; Washington *Recognizes* Senator's *Proposal*").

b. Suggest changes in wording that might make for more factual or objective writing ("State *Wallops* Midwest" might read "State *Defeats* Midwest, 20-14").

c. Indicate whether the facts in the article support or contradict the wording of the headline.

d. State to what extent the wording of the heading might have influenced the readers' attitude toward the facts reported in the article.

9. In a written report, analyze the writing of a popular columnist for evidence of slanted writing. These names are suggestions, to

which your instructor may wish to add others: Marquis Childs, David Lawrence, Walter Lippmann, Drew Pearson, Westbrook Pegler, Dorothy Thompson, Walter Winchell.

Use at least three or four columns by the writer you select, so that you will have adequate basis for judgment. Discriminate between fact and opinion in the articles, and comment upon the writer's attitude toward his information and toward his readers. Give specific examples of words you believe are intended to convince (or mislead) the readers of the column. Do you think that the articles would be less interesting to read if the words were more specific or more neutral? (Whether you agree or disagree with the columnist, try to make your own comments as unbiased as possible.)

10. Make a list of three to five synonyms for each of the following words and indicate in what kind of context each might be used. Also note any small differences in denotation and in connotation the synonyms show:

artificial	money	student
food	intelligence	teacher
friend	policeman	work

11. Here is a partial list of synonyms for the noun *merchant* in Roget's *Thesaurus of English Words and Phrases.* Describe the different denotations and connotations of these terms and indicate in what context they might be appropriate (or inappropriate) in your own writing:

MERCHANT, trader, dealer, monger, chandler, salesman; money changer, changer [*archaic*]; regrater; shopkeeper, shopman; tradesman . . . RETAILER; chapman, hawker, huckster, higgler; peddler . . . colporteur, cadger, Autolycus; sutler, vivandière; costerman, costermonger . . . canvasser, solicitor [*U.S.*]; cheap Jack . . . faker [*slang*]; vintner; greengrocer, groceryman, haberdasher . . .—C. O. Sylvester Mawson, ed., *Roget's International Thesaurus of English Words and Phrases,* p. 343

22 Appropriate words

. . . no word can be judged as to whether it is good or bad, correct or incorrect, beautiful or ugly, or anything else that matters to a writer, in isolation.—I. A. Richards

Words should be appropriate as well as accurate. That is, they should fit the subject, they should "sound like" the writer, and they should reach the intended reader. The range of words in English is wide and frequently a writer has a choice among several that will convey substantially the same meaning. The differences can be roughly indicated in terms of levels of usage:

> Informal: Johnny's sharp as a tack.
> General: Johnny is unusually bright.
> Formal: Johnny is wise beyond his years.
> Technical: John has an IQ of approximately 130.

Although these four statements tell us much the same thing about Johnny, they are obviously not interchangeable; each would be appropriate only in a certain context.

How should a beginning writer go about finding the words that will best express his ideas and his attitude toward his subject? Dictionaries, unfortunately, are not of much help in putting "proper words in proper places." The definitions in even the largest and most up-to-date ones are of necessity limited to the denotation of words as individual units rather than to their connotation in different kinds of writing. (Is the definition of *glamour* in your own dictionary an accurate description of the way you use the word?)

A writer can, however, make his language more effective in three ways: first, by expressing himself in a manner that reflects his own personality at its best; second, by paying attention to the conversation of the people he meets daily—his classmates, his instructors, his parents—and distinguishing between their Informal and their Formal usage; and third, by reading as widely and as intelligently as possible any and all material that will familiarize him with the range and variety of good current usage—textbooks and fiction, newspapers, magazines, and college publications.

Words from the General English vocabulary can go anywhere but questions of appropriateness arise over words from the more limited parts of the vocabulary, especially Formal, Technical, and Informal words. The various levels of vocabulary are not rigidly bounded, but we can see some broad differences and can guide our choice of words accordingly.

22.1 Formal words   The Formal vocabulary ranges from words that are only slightly more characteristic of writing than of speaking, through such words as *indubitably, moribund,* and *articulation* to quite rare ones like *recherché, educand, genotype,* and *ailurophobe.*

22.1a Appropriate use of Formal words   Formal words are appropriate to writers and to readers who are at home with them, whose experience has made them genuinely familiar. Typically they are found in discussions of ideas. In using them, the writer runs the risk of remoteness, flabbiness, and difficulty for the reader. But a moderate degree of Formality may suggest dignity and vigor, as in this somewhat Formal paragraph (Note *pragmatic, demonstrated, successive, concept, monolithic . . .*):

> The pragmatic value of free criticism was never better demonstrated than in the course of the last war. Successive failures on the part of the administration to mobilize production, for example, were disclosed and ultimately corrected. Precisely the opposite was the experience in Germany. There, where the concept of total war was first developed, it was never, in fact, put into practice. One of the most interesting discoveries of the United States Strategic Bombing Survey, which studied the physical and psychological impact of the American air offensive immediately after Germany's collapse, was the fact that German resources were never fully employed. The most monolithic of all totalitarian states fell far short of the democracies in organizational efficiency.—Alan Barth, "American Freedom: A Method," in *Years of the Modern,* edited by John W. Chase, p. 54

22.1b "Big Words"—inappropriate Formal words

Big W
or
Formal

Big Words. Correction: Change the word or words that are inappropriately Formal to words from the General vocabulary.

"Big Words," as the term is used here, are any and all expressions that are too heavy or too Formal for the subject or for the writer. The words themselves may be short or long, common or uncommon. A typical fault is the use of Big Words for "serious" subjects, perhaps in an effort to sound profound:

> It is difficult to filter out one specific cause for a social problem. Most often there are many minute factors interrelated and closely correlated. Our conception of a social problem today possesses more magnitude than that of twenty or thirty years ago. We now consider the world as a unit rather than as a segregation of component entities.

An extreme use of Big Words has been called *gobbledygook*—the use of words that seem to have lost all contact with the situation—as in "Such obscuration may be effectuated either by blackout construction or by termination of the illumination" for "This darkening can be brought about by blackout curtains or by putting out the lights." That this sort of thing is found in print does not make it Good English.

Your ideas will be easier to understand and hence more convincing if you keep your wording natural. Try to make it exact, not inflated beyond the requirements of the subject or the expectations of your reader.

22.1c Words to watch

It is context rather than the word itself that determines whether or not an expression is appropriate. But certain words deserve particular attention because they occur so frequently in pretentious writing:

	Overelaborate	Direct
conditions:	due to adverse weather conditions	because of rain
conversant:	I wasn't conversant with this viewpoint	this viewpoint was new to me

development:	during the period of his early development	during his childhood
endeavor:	we endeavored to get our candidate elected	we tried to get our candidate elected
factor:	another factor in my choice of State College	another reason I came to State College
metropolis:	in the offing lay the great metropolis	we were nearing the city
nuptials:	her nuptials are scheduled for the month of June	she will be married in June
participation:	the child's active participation in group activities is anticipated	the child is expected to play with other children
reside:	at that period we were residing in upper New York State	we were then living in upper New York State
termed:	a situation that might be termed unfortunate	an unfortunate situation
transpire:	thus it transpired that our trip to Catalina was delayed	our trip to Catalina was delayed
whereas:	whereas, if the truth be known, I have never read a play by Shakespeare	actually, I have never read a play by Shakespeare

22.1d Big Words in student writing College students should be enlarging their vocabularies, including more Formal words. But these words should be the necessary names for ideas, representing an actual growth in intellectual scope, not a translation of simple matters into Big Words.

Heavy wording, as a rule, occurs most frequently in papers written at or near the beginning of a composition course, when writers aren't certain what attitude they should take toward their material or their readers. These are some of the reasons why students think they should use inflated diction instead of their normal form of expression:

1. The mistaken belief that because a paper is written for a composition course (rather than for a course in history, say, or home economics), it should be as Formal and Impersonal as possible.

2. The erroneous impression that Big Words somehow improve a writer's normal manner of expression. Do the authors whose stories or articles you like to read use Big Words?

3. A desire to impress the reader, either by displaying some newly acquired words or by making the subject sound more important than it really is. Big Words used solely for their own sake will do neither.

4. A belief that inflated diction is humorous, perhaps writing "a fair damsel garbed in the mode of the moment," instead of "a fashionably dressed young girl." Such humor unfortunately lies more in the mind of the writer than in that of the reader. Do any noteworthy humorists of our own time—James Thurber, E. B. White, or any others—use this device?

5. In writing done for science courses, confusion of Big Words with the technical terms that the student should acquire and use—when he is discussing scientific topics.

The remedy for too many Big Words is simple: Read aloud what you have written—preferably some time after you have written it—and if you find it conspicuously different from the way you would tell it to a friend, look at the words carefully to see whether you can't find simpler, more General words that are natural to you. Let no others stand in your paper except for a good reason.

22.2 Technical words   In writing intended for a general audience, unfamiliar terms not made clear by the context should be defined or explained in the paper. Technical terms or unfamiliar expressions that often need explaining include:

1. Scientific terms (*isotope, lobotomy, gneiss*), and other expressions restricted to a specialized activity (*a cappella, heroic hexameter, escrow, chiaroscuro, farinaceous, cordon sanitaire*)

2. Words used in special senses rather than in the usual way (the *spine* of a book, to *justify* a line of type, the *recorder* as a wind instrument, a *frog* as a fastener for a jacket)

3. Foreign words and phrases not customarily used by most people (*lex talionis, pourboire, eisteddfod, Walpurgisnacht*)

You can determine which words need explaining by considering as your potential audience not just those friends and acquaintances who share your interests, nor your instructor, but the members of your class. While you may not know them individually, you can, by exercising a little common sense, decide whether you should explain a word like *slalom,* or what is meant by *dummy* in the game of bridge.

The simplest way to define a term whose meaning is not made clear in context is to explain it parenthetically:

> In cold weather the Eskimos wear mukluks (fur boots) and parkas (short fur coats with fur hoods).

It is frequently better tactics to give the definition or explanation first and then use the technical term:

> The ability of the heart to function depends primarily on the state of the heart muscle or myocardium, as it is technically known.

As a rule, do not simply quote a dictionary definition, which is usually stiff and bare, but compose one that fits the style and scale of your own paper. Compare the definition of *oligarchy* in your dictionary with this description of the term:

> I mean by "oligarchy" any system in which ultimate power is confined to a section of the community: the rich to the exclusion of the poor, Protestants to the exclusion of Catholics, aristocrats to the exclusion of plebeians, white men to the exclusion of colored men, males to the exclusion of females, or members of one political party to the exclusion of the rest. A system may be more or less oligarchic according to the percentage of the population that is excluded; absolute monarchy is the extreme of oligarchy.—Bertrand Russell, *The Impact of Science on Society,* p. 43

What matters in a definition of a term of this sort is an adequate description of the way *you* are using it, and the more details and concrete illustrations you can include to clarify the meaning, the better.

A writer should not try to evade the problem of definition by using an inexact or wordy expression in place of a technical term. If, for instance, the subject of a paper is "Mountain Climbing," it is better to define and use a word like *piton* than to say "those little metal gadgets that they tie ropes to." Do not use unfamiliar words just to show off, but use and explain those that are necessary for your subject.

22.3 Informal words

Inf Informal word or expression. **Correction: Change the word or words that are inappropriately Informal to words from the General vocabulary.**

22.3a Inappropriate use of Informal words   It is disconcerting to a reader to encounter an Informal expression in relatively Formal writing or in serious discussion:

> The displaced persons in Europe experienced many *tough breaks* after the end of the war. [More appropriate: *hardships*]
> The natives believe that they can expiate certain offenses against tribal customs *by throwing a feast.* [Better: *by giving a feast*]

In Formal writing, Informal words represent a shift in levels of usage, and they may also suggest that the writer has a careless or flippant attitude toward his subject:

> When Desdemona failed to produce the handkerchief, Othello began to suspect that she wasn't *on the level.*

A writer needs to be particularly careful about certain expressions so widely used that he may not realize (until the slip is called to his attention) that they are considered Informal rather than General usage:

> Alice's *pet peeve* was her roommate's study habits.
> We seldom saw plays of this sort *in our neck of the woods.*
> The proposal sounded like *a good deal,* so I accepted.
> When he admitted that he had never heard of cooperative apartments, I wondered to myself, *how stupid can you get?*

22.3b Appropriate use of Informal words   The Informal vocabulary, including words marked *Colloq.* in dictionaries, and most of these marked *Slang,* are appropriate in Informal writing: in discussions of sports, college dances, summertime jobs, and similar activities. They are often appropriate also in discussions of more important topics, especially by young people. You will find such words used, without apology or quotation marks, in many of our most reputable publications, like those italicized in this paragraph:

What happens to the child who is treated as an adult is that he *gets fresh*—becomes impertinent, disobedient, whiny, and a pest. Nobody enjoys him much any more, beginning with himself. Even to his loving mother he sometimes *gives a stiff pain in the neck*. But if she has read a book . . . she knows that this is because he feels anxious and insecure. Therefore she controls her impulse *to warm his tail* and send him to bed without supper; she treats him, instead, with monumental patience and slightly forced demonstrations of affection. Daddy, who comes home from the office pretty tired, in need of a drink and some peaceful home life, is likely to be less long-suffering. He may even raise the possibility of *cracking down*.—Helen Eustis, "Good-By to Oedipus," *Harper's Magazine*, June 1953, p. 46

When Informal words are appropriate, they should be used without apology. If you are tempted to apologize for them by putting them in quotation marks, ask yourself whether they are genuinely appropriate. If they are, use them, but if not, replace them with words from the General vocabulary.

References

Andrews, Edmund, *A History of Scientific English*, New York, Richard H. Smith, 1947

Fowler, articles titled "Formal words," "Literary words"

Gowers, Sir Ernest, *Plain Words*, London, Her Majesty's Stationery Office, 1948, Ch. 7, Choosing the Familiar Word

Miller, Walter J., and Leo E. S. Saidla, *Engineers as Writers*, New York, Van Nostrand, 1953

Wimsatt, W. K., Jr., "When Is Variation 'Elegant'?" *College English*, 1942, 3:368-383; also in *The Verbal Icon*, Louisville, University of Kentucky Press, 1954, pp. 187-199

Exercises

1. Considering both the subject matter and the kind of readers that the writers had in mind, how appropriate is the wording in each of the following passages? (Unless otherwise indicated, the

examples are from student papers and are intended for a general audience.)

In the examples that you consider unsatisfactory, point out specific instances of unnecessary Big Words and technical terms, of unfamiliar or far-fetched words, and other kinds of inappropriate English. Wherever possible, show how they might be translated into more appropriate language. In the passages you find satisfactory, explain why you think the wording is appropriate.

1) Oft one would see the students who had evaded their classes strolling on the avenue and examining the displays of the different commercial enterprises.

2) Amid printed and broadcasted advance publicity, further stimulated by movie trailers howling the virtues of Hollywood spectacles, one sometimes stumbles upon a good production. Unfortunately, the propaganda generated in behalf of the American product extolling the color, dramatis personae, and general superiority is usually so vociferous that the average individual, with the wool thus pulled over his eyes, is tempted to view them all, the sour with the sweet. In this wise, some of the outstanding films created abroad are relegated to hole-in-the-wall movie houses on forgotten back streets.

3) *Henry James' description of waffles, his favorite food as a child:* ". . . the oblong, farinaceous compound, faintly yet richly brown, stamped and smoking, not crisp nor brittle, but softly absorbent of the syrup dabbed upon it for a finish."—F. O. Matthiessen, *The James Family*, p. 74

4) When observing a person reading the "funnies," one can see the look of felicity or hear the sound of an occasional spontaneous chuckle. Here, one can be sure, is a being who is taking advantage of the momentary escape that comics offer from the adversities and detestations that hobble the daily lives of humans.

5) The radar operator aboard ship must maintain a constant vigil on the radar screen while he is on watch. The screen—usually ten to twelve inches in diameter—contains a small beam of light

that constantly revolves, giving the appearance of a sweeping second hand on a wrist watch. This light works in conjunction with the radar antenna, which is constantly revolving, sending a steady stream of ultra high frequency waves over the ocean. When these waves strike a solid object, they rebound to the antenna. The wave is then relayed from the antenna to the radar screen in the form of a small spot or "blip" as it is called. By means of a guide on the radar screen, the exact direction and the exact distance between the ship and the unidentified object can be determined.

6) *From a technical journal for paint manufacturers:* What are alkyds? Essentially, they are esters of polyhydric alcohols and polybasic acids, usually modified with either straight chain or ring type monobasic acids and reacted to a definite polymer size. An example would be a reaction product of phthalic anhydride as the polybasic acid, glycerine as the polyhydric alcohol, and soya fatty acids as the straight chain monobasic acid.—Benjamin Farber, "Trends in Alkyd Manufacture," *Paint and Varnish Production*, April 1953, p. 34

7) *From catalog notes explaining some paintings on exhibit:* In order to dispel all possibility of obscurity concerning the relationship between the individual and the cosmos as it appears in this text and previous writings, it is necessary to add: The fundamental pseudo-duality of the substantiality of the I indicates its failure the moment the world plunges further into the myth of relative knowledge, and anticipates the approaching decline of the privilege of the real demeanour—the intuitive realization of the vacuity of existence. . . .

8) In the bus station two middle-aged male standees are conversing with the bus driver. Their attitude is one of concern regarding the possible effect of the imminent storm. The rest of the passengers are dividing their audio attention while trying to maintain a very aloof attitude. One septuagenarian is unconcernedly perusing a newspaper.

2. This is the way in which technical terms are explained in a book on psychology written for a general audience:

Word	What it means to the doctor	What it means to the layman
blocking	Sudden cessation of thought, feeling, or action due to strong unconscious emotional interference.	Forgetting
delusion	A false belief, usually incorrigible, due to mental illness; the conviction today that the moon is made of cheese would be a delusion while the conviction before the time of Galileo that the earth was flat was ignorance.	Any mistaken idea
hysteria	A neurotic reaction in which psychological symptoms imitate other illnesses, as in hysterical blindness or paralysis.	Laughing and crying at the same time

—Fritz Redlich and June Bingham, *The Inside Story*, pp. 255, 257, 259

Using a similar form, explain five technical words with which you are familiar—expressions from your major field of study, or from your hobby or some other particular interest. The following words may suggest others to you:

Education: college (within a university), professor, IQ, philosophy

Science: function (in mathematics), epoch (in geology), benign (in physiology), strut (in architecture)

Hobbies and sports: stalemate (in chess), bias (in dressmaking), caller (in square dancing), finesse (in bridge), sacrifice (in baseball)

3. This paragraph is the opening of a short story by Mark Twain. How effective does it seem to you as descriptive writing? Are there any expressions in it that suggest the writer was not wholly serious? Consult your dictionary for the meaning of any terms that strike you as unusual or out of place in this context:

It was a crisp and spicy morning in early October. The lilacs and laburnums, lit with the glory fires of autumn, hung burning and flashing in the upper air, a fairy bridge provided by kind Nature for the wingless wild things that have their home in the tree tops and would visit together; the larch and the pomegranate flung their purple and yellow flames in brilliant broad splashes along the slanting sweep of the woodland; the sensuous fragrance of innumerable deciduous flowers rose upon the swooning atmosphere; far in the empty sky a solitary oesophagus slept upon motionless wing; everywhere brooded stillness, serenity, and the peace of God.

23 Effective words

Nearly always the things a writer says are less striking than the way he puts them; for men in general have much the same ideas about matters that form the stock in trade of all. It is the expression, the style, that makes the difference.—Voltaire

Words should not only convey meaning accurately (§21) and appropriately (§22) but they should appeal to readers; they should be fresh enough and vigorous enough to be readable and perhaps memorable. Instead of using our full range of words to strengthen our statements we often rely too much on certain words and phrases that weaken what we say. Since it is easier to describe these weakening words than to present the whole range of the English vocabulary, this section points out words that are likely to weaken and makes suggestions for replacing them.

23.1 Trite expressions

Trite   Correction: Replace the trite expression with one that is simpler or fresher.

Trite expressions, or clichés, are pat phrases so familiar that, given the first words, we can usually finish the expression without thinking:

Quick as a _____
This is going to hurt me more _____
As brown as a _____
Gone but _____
It isn't the heat but _____

Make a note of the following overworked expressions that occur with depressing frequency in freshman writing:

Cliché	Comment
according to Webster . . .	Did Webster write the dictionary you are using?
history (or science) tells us . . .	A dubious personification, one that often leads to empty generalities.
I would go so far as to say that . . .	Just say it.
the finer things of life . . .	Name two or three; no matter what they are—diamonds, a Beethoven Quartet, Argyle socks—they'll be more convincing to the reader than this nebulous phrase.
last but not least . . .	Is the last item or fact *never* of least importance?
thus I have shown . . .	Not useful unless you aren't quite certain that you *have* shown it.
in conclusion I would like to say . . .	Better to write down what you have to say and forget this introductory phrase

It is impossible to remove *all* trite expressions from writing, but when they become a conspicuous trait of a person's writing, he should take steps to remove them. Secondhand expressions suggest secondhand ideas.

23.1a Worn-out figures of speech Figurative language, when it is fresh and appropriate, is always welcome (see §23.4), but comparisons and personifications that have become stale through overuse will only serve to weaken your writing. You will not make anything seem cooler, steadier, or neater if you describe it as *cool as a cucumber, steady as a rock,* or *neat as a pin.*

Here is a short list of trite figures of speech; you can probably think of a good many similar expressions:

the irony of fate	a watery grave
Father Time	clean as a whistle
sly as a fox	in the arms of Morpheus
rotten to the core	run like a deer
in a nutshell	with bated breath
darkness overtook us	brave as a lion
commune with nature	Mother Nature
to sell like hotcakes	bull in a china shop
trees like sentinels	the crack of dawn

When you find yourself using such expressions, look at them closely to see if they actually mean anything to you; usually you will decide that they really mean very little, and you will make your point another way.

23.1b Frayed quotations Unless they are essential to your discussion, avoid quotations that have lost their vividness through overuse:

a sadder and a wiser man . . .	all the world's a stage . . .
music hath charms . . .	water, water, everywhere . . .

So thoroughly are quotations from Shakespeare woven into our daily speech that some people, when they read or see a play such as *Hamlet* or *Julius Caesar* for the first time, are surprised to find that they have been "talking Shakespeare" all their lives:

to be or not to be . . .
uneasy lies the head . . .
something is rotten in the state of Denmark . . .
lend me your ears . . .
not wisely, but too well . . .

There are many fresh, vivid lines from less-quoted sources —in modern poetry, for instance, and in Shakespeare, too— if you wish to enliven your writing with quotations.

23.2 Euphemisms A euphemism (from the Greek term meaning "fair words") is a polite and often affected expression for some fact or idea that the user feels might offend either himself or his reader if it were said more bluntly or more accurately or in the more common words that may have acquired an unpleasant connotation.

Euphemistic expression	*Direct expression*
financially embarrassed	without money, poor (or in Informal usage, *broke*)
culturally underprivileged persons	uneducated people
inadvertently detained	late
halitosis	bad breath
unmentionables	underwear
our statement that may have escaped your attention	your unpaid bill
pass on, pass away	die

Some of the most common euphemisms are used for jobs or activities that some people consider unpleasant or degrading like *paying guest* for a roomer or boarder, or *mortician* or *funeral director* for undertaker.

When the choice of an expression lies between accuracy and unnecessary politeness, it is better to use the more accurate term. You will seldom offend a reader by using an honest, direct name for an idea or condition, but you may easily annoy him by using a euphemistic substitute.

23.3 Old-fashioned words Certain old-fashioned expressions, whether or not they are obsolete or archaic, no longer represent good current usage, and are incongruous in the writing of young people:

> One may relax on the *greensward* of a Sunday and listen to a rousing band concert.
> The game seemed to have been won, but *alas!* we failed to gain the necessary three yards in four tries.
> Little schooling was required in *days of yore* to get along in life.

Today we say *lawn* or *grass* instead of *greensward; in the past* or *formerly,* not in *days of yore.* Certainly it is difficult to imagine a student crying out "Alas!" at a crucial moment of a football game.

Here are some old-fashioned expressions with their present-day equivalents:

amidst	for	among
befell	for	happened
brethren	for	brothers (or fellow men)
deem	for	think (or consider)
doff	for	take off (as one's hat)
don	for	put on (as one's clothing)
peruse	for	read (or look over)
supped	for	ate
twain	for	two

The best way to judge old-fashioned wording is to read the passage aloud and ask yourself whether you would use such an expression in your ordinary conversation.

23.4 Figures of speech Figures of speech are expressions of comparison, analogy, personification that are used to intensify statements, to make them more expressive and vivid. This is a literal, nonfigurative statement:

> The fewer words a person uses, the more quickly his meaning will be understood.

The same idea can be expressed in a more memorable way by a well-chosen figure of speech:

. . . meaning is an arrow that reaches its mark when least encumbered with feathers.—Herbert Read, *English Prose Style*, p. 16

The most common kinds of figures of speech are comparisons. They are called *similes* when the comparison is explicitly stated, usually with *as* or *like*:

Tropical birds flew swiftly from tree to tree like arcs of many tiny rainbows.

When the comparison is implied rather than explicitly stated, the figure is called a *metaphor*. Typically the writer asserts that one thing *is* another:

Her face was a neon sign that lit up with a single expression for any emotion and then blinked off into rigid obscurity.

We use figurative expressions, both trite and fresh, constantly in our conversation (*dog-tired, a heart of gold, hungry as a bear, at the head of the class*). They are also used in most kinds of writing (with the exception of some impersonal or scientific reports), and are definitely not limited to purely descriptive passages or to "literary" subjects. You will find figurative language used freely in such diverse material as financial articles, literary criticism, advertising copy, sports writing, political discussions.

Don't hesitate to use figurative expressions whenever they seem appropriate: statements that would otherwise be commonplace become interesting and lively when they sound as though they came from the writer's own way of seeing things.

23.4a Consistent figures of speech   A figure of speech should not begin with one kind of picture and switch to another wholly unrelated one:

The nineteenth century *became a door* opened by some of the braver authors, through which many of the earlier ideas of writing for children, which had before been *crushed or discarded,* again *sprang to blossom,* and *spread into the many branches* of children's literature that we have today.

If you can look at your own writing with some degree of objectivity, you can usually determine whether a figure is consistent or not. Sometimes an expression that seemed very vivid at the moment of writing proves on rereading to be confusing or even ludicrous.

23.4b Appropriate figures of speech Figurative expressions should be in keeping with the subject and style, and accurate enough to contribute to the meaning. An inappropriate figure sometimes conveys an impression that the writer never intended:

> When he was sober, he treated his family very well; when he was drunk, he made everyone miserable. He drank up all their savings, their house, their furniture, and their hopes for the future.

Expressions that are too strong for the situation or that strive too hard to be picturesque will distract attention rather than contribute to the meaning:

> As fall comes in with its gentle coolness, Mother Nature *launches her chemical warfare,* changing the leaves into their many pretty colors.
> A shadow from the darkened building fell across him *like a moist towel* and he wriggled his shoulders distastefully.

The appropriateness of a figure of speech is of course often a matter of individual taste. It would be unfair to question the sincerity of this description, because this is undoubtedly the way that it appeared to the student:

> The lake was gorgeous that night. An egg-yolk moon was beaming over the lime-jello and whipped cream waters that were spanked by a dancing breeze.

But in revising the paper, the student might have asked himself whether there wasn't just a little too much food imagery in this moonlit scene, or whether most readers would be hungry enough to appreciate the metaphors he used.

Struggling for original or unusual expressions usually brings on inconsistent figures or inappropriate ones. The figures to use are those that actually come to your mind when you are trying to give an exact account of the subject. They need not be unusual, but they should fit in their context and sound as though you were actually thinking them.

References

Brooks, Cleanth, and Robert Penn Warren, *Modern Rhetoric,* New York, Harcourt, Brace, 1948, Ch. 11, Metaphor

Hunter, Edwin R., and Bernice E. Gaines, "Verbal Taboo in a College Community," *American Speech,* 1938, 13:97-107

Johnson, Wendell, *People in Quandaries,* New York, Harper, 1946, Ch. 11, The Language of Maladjustment, Ch. 12, Language as Technique

McKnight, George H., *English Words and Their Backgrounds,* New York, Appleton, 1923, Chs. 14 to 19, figures of speech becoming parts of the language

Pyles, Thomas, *Words and Ways of American English,* New York, Random House, 1952, Ch. 6, Tall Talk, Turgidities, and Taboo; Ch. 7, Coinages and Adaptations

Quiller-Couch, Sir Arthur, *On the Art of Writing,* New York, Putnam's, 1916, Ch. 5, Interlude: On Jargon

Steadman, J. M., "Affected and Effeminate Words," *American Speech,* 1938, 13:13-18

Sullivan, Frank, "Cliché Expert" papers, in various volumes, e.g., *A Rock in Every Snowball,* Boston, Little, Brown, 1946, pp. 28-36, 51-57, 114-119, 146-152

Exercises

1. According to your understanding of the terms, which of these expressions would you consider clichés or worn-out figures of speech in the situations indicated? Which are polite or conventional phrases appropriate or necessary in certain circumstances?

    1) How do you do? (as a greeting)

    2) "I love you," he murmured, gazing at her with soulful eyes. (in a story)

    3) Can you imagine that! (in conversation)

4) "But first a few words from our sponsor." (prefacing a radio or TV program)

5) Words cannot describe how I felt at that moment. (in a student paper)

6) Kill the umpire! (at a baseball game)

7) You can say *that* again! (as an expression of warm agreement in conversation)

8) The glad news came to us like a bolt out of the blue. (in a student paper)

9) I know what I want to say, but I can't put it in words. (as an excuse in a classroom recitation)

10) "And so it came to pass that at long last Melissa found true happiness. . . ." (transitional phrase in a radio soap opera)

2. Read this article on clichés by a sports writer in a college newspaper. Then answer the questions that follow:

1) Many are the trials in the life of a sports writer. He must always have a plausible explanation for the defeat of the home team, he must steel himself against the same gloomy predictions of coaches that he hears day after day, he must be able to shrug off with a laugh his predictions that go sour.

2) With all these a sports writer can cope, but the most unkindest cut of all is the charge, frequently made by his alleged friends and other wise guys, that his writing style is naught but a collection of clichés. Consider for a moment what a report of a baseball game would be like without the use of good old solid clichés:

3) The Dirt Flats baseball team last night achieved a victory over the aggregation representing Hooper by gaining nine runs while their opponents were unable to get more than seven. A substantial contribution to the victory for Dirt Flats was made by Norman Belcher, who regularly plays at the position of shortstop, in the first inning.

4) When Belcher took his position as the batter, two of his associates were located on base. The first time the ball was thrown to him Belcher smote it mightily, propelling it over the heads of

the astonished Hooper players and beyond the fence that borders the playing field. Belcher was awarded four bases for his stalwart performance and Dirt Flats added three runs which were enough to win the contest. . . .

5) We may as well face the fact that you can't write sports without clichés. Of course, it's possible to go overboard in the other direction:

6) The Dirt Flats Diamond Squad last night blasted out a 9-7 win in their tilt with the Hooper nine. Clouting Norm Belcher, who cavorts at short patch for the Flatters, sewed up the contest in the bottom of the ninth canto, when he drilled the initial offering of fastballing portsider, Lefty Morris, over the right field barrier for a four-master, sending a pair of mates, who were camped on the sacks, across the dish with the winning tallies.—Gary Brandner, "Memo to Soreheads Who Would Purge Sports Writing of Clichés," *University of Washington Daily*, June 10, 1952, p. 3. Reprinted by permission of the University of Washington Press.

Questions:

a. Are there any trite expressions in the first two paragraphs, or in paragraphs 3 and 4, which are supposedly free from "good old solid clichés"?

b. Do you consider the language in paragraph 6 primarily clichés, slang, figurative expressions, or sports jargon? Does such wording represent the language of the baseball players, of the men who write about sports, or of the spectators?

c. Compare both versions of the game (paragraphs 3 and 4, and paragraph 6) with an account of a baseball, football, or basketball game in your own college newspaper. Can you see any justification for the use of slang or clichés in sports writing?

3. Find one euphemistic expression for each of the following terms, and tell under what circumstances or in what contexts, if any, each euphemistic expression might be appropriate.

hairdresser	servant	suicide
clerk	stupid	theft

| saloon | reform school | false teeth |
| lie (noun) | insane asylum | an old house |

4. Write a paragraph of about two hundred words on the qualities of the words in one kind of advertising copy that interests (or amuses) you: automobiles, cigarettes, cosmetics, household appliances, self-improvement courses, life insurance. Is the usefulness of the product or its price stressed? Or is the appeal made to some other buying motive? Translate some of the more obviously euphemistic or indirect phrases into ordinary English to see what is implied rather than directly stated. For example: "Be lovely to love! . . . Use Rosebreath Daily" might actually mean "Use our brand of mouthwash constantly."

5. Some of the figurative expressions in the following examples are effective, others are not. When you have made up your mind about them, be prepared to give specific reasons for your opinions. If a figure is trite, strained, inconsistent, or inappropriate to the subject, explain why. If it is successful, tell what makes it so.

1) When I started to work for the company, I was only a small cog in a big machine, but since then I have scaled a few rungs up the ladder of success, and hope eventually to become at least a medium-sized frog in this big pond.

2) To me a fireroom on a ship is a place of enchantment, with a beauty all of its own. Its intricate fuel lines appear from the bilges like vines creeping up the face of the boiler, putting off branch shoots to each individual boiler assembly.

3) Everyone is now watching the new administration try its wings at running the country's international affairs, while at the same time "sweeping the rascals out of office."

4) A marriage is similar to a corporation in that when two people marry, they form a new unit consisting of the personalities, likes and dislikes, etc., of the married couple. That is, the separate person doesn't lose his individuality, but retains it. In a corporation the stockholders retain their separate individualities, but they

form along with the corporate charter a new unit—the corporation. In marriage, the stockholders, board of directors, and the officers are all one—the married couple. As each officer and director of the corporation has a job to perform, so does each half of a married couple. And as a corporation has a product to sell, so does a successful marriage sell a happy life for all to enjoy if they wish to marry. A corporation sells its goods in order to make a profit for the stockholders; a marriage does the same. It tries to show a profit to its stockholders, be it children, dogs, a home, a new car, horses, or anything else the married couple want.

5) Winter usually comes in like a lion, with its chilly breath from the Great Lakes. Soon everything is clad in white, touched by the artistic fingers of Jack Frost.

6. Discuss the following figurative expressions, considering both their literal meanings and their connotations. Are they used in speaking and writing because we have no adequate substitutes? Which of these expressions do you use? Which do you consider trite or overworked?

a chip off the old block	pretty as a picture
crocodile tears	a bull market
bonehead	to wolf one's food
road hog	an eager beaver
lion's share	a wet blanket
busy as a bee	half-baked

7. These selections represent a variety of styles on different subjects. After you have read them, select two or three for a written report comparing or contrasting the qualities of their words. Suggestions on points to consider in your report follow the examples.

1) Ever since I can remember I have been consistently finding myself up to the neckline in hot water or down to my last friend in number, as the result of an overactive and uncontrollable curiosity. I have often read of the great virtue in having a well-

disciplined and properly directed curiosity, but on much more frequent occasions I have been reminded both verbally and through introspection, of the poor discipline and lack of direction exercised by the writer in such matters. As I understand it, I have not merely approached the state of, but am actively engaged in, being nosey. What is worse, I have as yet found no foolproof method of curbing this virtue-less pastime and so have had to adopt an alternate plan—an attempt at pointing my nosiness in a less critical and more constructive direction: I am becoming water-logged from the neck down and really have to hang on to what friends I have. (Note: Actually my curiosity is not as insatiable as it sounds!)—First paragraph of a student paper entitled "Curiosity Killed the Cat, but I'm No Cat"

2) The fat, white fingers of silver light, beaming from the cones of great searchlights, played tic-tac-toe in the night sky above Hollywood. Wilshire Boulevard, in front of the Ritz Theater, was a happy bedlam. Traffic was backed up for a mile, and in the glare of sputtering arcs sleek Cadillacs pulled up to the curb and discharged elegantly appointed stars and movie-makers, who made their way into the building through an avenue of ropes that held back thousands of breathless fans.

One by one the big names of the movies made the walk past the spectators and each got applause and cheers. Some signed autograph books and hurried inside self-consciously. It was a gala night, for it was the world premiere of 20th Century-Fox's *Call Me Madam*.—Jim Henaghan, "Sex Is Not Enough," *Modern Screen*, June 1953, pp. 49, 97

3) By the time I was twelve, Grandma had taught me how to make beds, scrub the floor, and iron. I scrubbed the floor on my hands and knees—an old Scandinavian custom, I have since learned—ironed stacks of flatwork, and under Grandma's watchful eyes, changed the linen on the beds once a week.

After the housework was finished, which was usually by mid-afternoon, I went to the grocery store. Since Grandma was far from wealthy, I had to shop carefully. She had taught me how to inspect every apple and potato to see that they did not have bad spots; also to squeeze the bread gently to test it for freshness. The other groceries were selected with equal care.

I enjoyed helping Grandma, although there were times when I was pretty tired by evening. She would then take me to the neighborhood movie house, or, if she wasn't feeling well enough, she would give me the money to attend a matinee the next day.

Grandma always thanked me warmly for the work I did, telling me what a good housekeeper I was and that my husband would be a lucky man to have me for a wife, and other kind remarks. I did not realize at the time that I lived with her that I received much more than I gave. She was a true friend and a companion whose memory I will always cherish to my dying day. She taught me, among other things, that it is possible and even gratifying to keep a clean house without a lot of useless gadgets. After I am married, I hope to teach my daughter that keeping house is a worthwhile job for any woman.—Conclusion of a student paper with this central idea: "Grandma taught me the essentials of good housekeeping, for which I shall always be grateful."

4) I could not find anyone to ask whence came this gnarled vine that with each spring bewitched me. The old couple who in their last years made my garden are long since dead; their only child had died before them. The town's rose specialist and its landscape gardner have come and shaken puzzled heads. I sent my mystery rose to experts in southern California; they could not name it. I sent it north to a famous grower of rare old roses; she did not know it. But she advised that I send it to the country's greatest authority on roses, in Massachusetts. June was gone by then, and I had to wait another year for bloom; when my specimens arrived, the great authority was dead. His colleagues at the Arnold Arboretum opined that mine might be some rose long lost to cultivation, a treasure casually unearthed each spring in my old garden, when the pink sprays lift again to the light. So be it. My nameless rose is but one lingerer among the multitude of those that have come, had their bright hour, and gone, leaving the human heart stirred by their fragrance.—Donald Culross Peattie, "Roses," *The Atlantic Monthly*, June 1953, p. 64

5) The strongest motivating force for making a new dress for myself stemmed from the need for economy. From actual experience I can prove to you that it is possible to make a dress for just twice what it would cost in a store.

First of all, since my first venture into dressmaking was not to be my last, I invested in a sewing machine. This machine was, and is, quite a deluxe model with extra gadgets for making buttonholes, hemming, attaching fancy trimmings such as ruffles, pleatings, and rickrack. I have never been able to use any of these attachments, so I have stuck entirely to the plain unadorned garment. This little man-made wonder can also stitch over pins and run forward and backward. It is possible to get a sewing machine for a lot less money than I paid for my electric machine by purchasing a pedal-it-yourself model. Of course, you may develop muscles in the calves of your legs like those of a ballet dancer, but if you want to economize, you'll have to be prepared to sacrifice whatever cheese-cake appeal you may possess.

My next step was to shop for material, a pattern, thread, zipper, seam tape, and several other items listed on the pattern envelope necessary to make the easy-to-make dress. I took my loot home, happy in the thought that I would soon be the best-dressed girl in town. I could just hear an admiring public murmuring, "Aren't her clothes lovely? And she makes EVERY STITCH of them herself!"— First three paragraphs of a student paper titled "Dressmaking Made Easy"

6) To avoid the confusion and uncertainty of various authorities on spelling, the Government Printing Office must of necessity adopt a single guide for the spelling of words the preferred forms of which are not otherwise listed or provided for in this manual. The guide is Webster's New International Dictionary, which, in successive editions, has been the accepted authority for Government printing for more than 85 years. Unless herein otherwise authorized, the Government Printing Office will continue to follow Webster's spelling. Colloquial and dialect spellings are not to be used unless required by the subject matter or specifically requested. —*GPO Style Manual*, 1953, p. 51

7) Since January, 1953, a small group of Weather Bureau personnel have been conducting an artificial rain-making experiment in the Pacific Northwest. That area was selected because it has more rainy days than any other area in the United States. To the layman, such a selection might seem paradoxical but the government rain-makers prefer an area that has many days when it is raining or is practically certain to rain. On some of these days favorable to rain, planes on loan from the Navy will go aloft to seed the rain clouds with one of the two standard weapons of commercial rain-makers: dry ice pellets or silver iodide fumes. On other "favorable" days nothing will be done. In this way it is hoped to discover how much more rain falls, if any, when rainy conditions are present, and thus to find out whether it is possible for man to make rain on a large scale. As a further control, only small areas will be seeded and the rainfall from these areas will be compared with the precipitation from the unseeded areas, and any differences noted. . . .

If the project is successful, it will provide useful data to all interested persons. Other studies have been made proving that it is possible for man to make rain, but there is no data available on how much could be expected, and how it would benefit crops and water supplies, and how it might prevent storm damage. This project will also check the claims of the commercial rain-makers, most of whom will not now release their procedures to private users because they fear exposure of their unethical methods and extravagant claims.—Introductory and concluding paragraphs in a student paper on government experiments in rain-making.

Suggestions for analyzing style:

a. Determine the writer's primary purpose and his attitude toward his subject: to inform, to clarify an idea, to persuade his readers, to amuse them, or any combination of these intentions.

b. Describe the outstanding qualities of the writer's wording: Formal, General, Informal (or a mixture); trite, old-fashioned, wordy, or their opposites; and give examples.

c. Explain in your own words, and as specifically as possible, why you prefer the writing in one passage to that in the others.

Grammar and usage

24 Subjects and verbs

Singular subjects take singular verbs (A *guest arrives*); plural subjects take plural verbs (Five *guests arrive*). Subjects indicating the person speaking, the person spoken to, or the person or thing spoken about may require different verb forms (*I am* satisfied; *You are* satisfied; *He is* satisfied).

This correspondence in form between related words in a statement is called *agreement*. The basic patterns of subject-verb agreement are outlined in the table on p. 302.

Problems of subject-verb agreement rarely arise in typical sentence patterns. But care must be taken with compound subjects, with subjects that are grammatically singular even though they may look to be plural (*politics*), and with subjects that follow the verb or are separated from it.

24.1 Verb with compound subject Two or more words, phrases, or clauses standing as the subject of a verb are called a compound subject (A *boy* and a *girl* were dancing).

24.1a Subjects joined by *and* Subjects joined by *and* usually take a plural verb:

Tschaikovsky, Rimski-Korsakov, and *Shostakovich are* three of the best-known Russian composers.
The text of the poem and *the commentary make* a sizable volume.

Exception: When the words of a compound subject refer to the same person or thing, or are considered as forming a unit, the verb is usually singular:

His warmest admirer and severest critic was his wife.
The Stars and Stripes still *waves* overhead.
The long and short of Brown's argument *is* that higher taxes will mean ruin.

Typical Subject-Verb Agreement

Subject	Present tense typical form	Present tense of be and have
I	believe	am, have
you, we, they, some, these, those; all plural nouns	believe	are, have
he, she, it, one, everyone, each; all singular nouns	believes	is, has

Compound subjects

Plural verb in most instances:
France, Britain, and *Italy agree* to send delegates.
She and *I are* good friends.

Singular verb in some special cases:
A novel or *a biography is* to be read outside class.
For the winner there *was a large cash prize* and *weeks of glory.*

Collective subjects

Singular verb when the group is considered as a unit:
The *majority is* always right.

Plural verb when the group is considered as a number of individuals:
The *majority are* willing to contribute.

24.1b Subjects joined by or, nor   Verbs with compound subjects joined by *or, nor, either . . . or, neither . . . nor* are sometimes singular and sometimes plural. General usage is as follows:

1) When both subjects are singular and felt to be separate, the verb is singular:

One or the *other is* certainly to blame.
Neither *chance* nor political *maneuvering has been* the main factor in the drift of Italy's political situation toward the Left.—Claire Sterling, "Italy: How Far Left of Center?" *The Reporter,* September 29, 1953, p. 16

2) When one or both subjects are plural, or when both are singular but are felt to be plural in meaning, the verb is usually plural:

No artificial *colorings* or *preservatives are used* in this beverage.

One major *accident* or several minor *ones seem* to occur at this corner each weekend.

Since neither *natural science* nor any *form* of manual craftsmanship *are* obligatory . . .—Lancelot Hogben, *Retreat from Reason*, p. 11

The plural is used especially often in questions and when the subjects are pronouns of different persons:

Are either *Fred* or *Larry* really good friends of hers?

Neither *he* nor *I are* going.

3) When the first of the two subjects is plural and the second is singular, Formal usage often, but not consistently, has a singular verb:

Formal: Neither the *revolutionists* nor their *leader was* to blame for the slaughter.

General: Neither the *revolutionists* nor their *leader were* to blame for the slaughter.

References: Because of conflicting statements in stylebooks and handbooks, this construction has been much studied: Adeline C. Bartlett, "*Neither* with Plural Verb," *College English*, 1951, 13:161-162; Curme, *Syntax*, pp. 52, 56-57, 60; Dorothy J. Hughes, *College English*, 1941, 2:697-699; Marckwardt and Walcott, pp. 70-71, 74-75; Pooley, pp. 82-84; Roberts, pp. 276-278

24.1c Pronouns as compound subjects Pronouns of different persons used as compound subjects take plural verbs when they are joined by *and:*

You and *she seem* to be in disagreement.

Do you and *he* intend to stay here all night?

When pronoun subjects are separated by *or* or *nor*, in Formal usage the verb agrees with the pronoun nearer the verb:

Neither *you* nor *she is* [General: *are*] using the proper backstroke.

This problem of agreement is usually avoided by using some other construction:

You are both using the wrong backstroke.

24.1d **Verb after *together with* and similar phrases** In Formal usage, a singular subject followed by a phrase using an expression like *with, together with, as well as, in addition to* ordinarily takes a singular verb:

Specialization in the undergraduate colleges, combined with the growth of college and university populations and our desire for efficiency, *has* fostered rigid departmentalization of the teaching function.— Emerson Shuck, "Cold War in the Graduate Schools," *School and Society,* September 29, 1951, 74:194

But a plural verb is often used in these situations when the added phrase is clearly intended as a compound subject:

Both the demand for the competent serious literature, as well as the ability to read it intelligently, *have* seriously depreciated.—Seymour Betsky, "The Teaching of Literature," *Sewanee Review,* Autumn 1949, 47:646

A simple solution—and one that may make the statement more direct—is to use *and* rather than such phrases wherever appropriate:

The main feature *and* the short subjects *last* about three hours.

rather than

The main feature, *together with* the short subjects, *lasts* about three hours.

24.2 **Verbs with collective nouns as subjects** Words that refer to a group of people or objects but are singular in form are called collective nouns: *army, audience, choir, committee, crowd, faculty, gang, group, government, jury, mob, orchestra, public, team,* etc. Verbs and pronouns used with collective nouns are either singular or plural depending upon the meaning of the group word.

24.2a Collective nouns referring to the group as a unit   Singular verbs and singular reference words are used with collective nouns that refer to the group as a unit:

> *Class is* dismissed.
> The *committee has* already held *its* first meeting of the year.
> The *audience is* requested to remain seated during intermission.

24.2b Collective nouns referring to the individuals   When the reference is to the individuals of the group, especially when they are represented as acting individually, collectives take plural verbs and plural reference words:

> The graduating *class have* all agreed to have *their* pictures taken in caps and gowns.
> The *committee are* arguing among *themselves.*
> The *audience have* now returned and are taking *their* seats.

24.2c Measurements and figures   Expressions signifying quantity or extent (*miles, gallons, years, pounds*) take singular verbs when the amount is considered as a unit:

> *Five dollars is* too much to pay for a book in that condition.
> *Four quarts* of oil *is* all the crankcase holds.
> *Three months passes* in no time at all when you spend your vacation on a dude ranch.

When the amount is considered as a number of individual units, a plural verb is used:

> *Two* more *dollars are* missing from the till this morning.
> There *are three quarts* of milk in the refrigerator.
> The last *three months have been* the driest in California's history.

In expressions of addition, subtraction, and multiplication, usage is about evenly divided:

> Five and seven *is* [or *are*] twelve.
> Five times seven *is* [or *are*] thirty-five.

24.2d *Data, number, public*   *Data* is a plural form (and is generally so considered in scientific writing), but since the singular *datum* is rarely used, *data* is used for both singular and plural.

Singular idea: The actual *data* of history [a body of facts] *consists* of contemporary facts in the form of remains and documents.—Morris R. Cohen, *Reason and Nature,* p. 381

Plural idea: When the *data* [the individual facts] *have* been secured the task is to analyze, to sift, to select and to arrange *those* data which *bear* upon each particular phase of the object or event examined until at the end the scientist has what one might call a logical construct.— G. D. Higginson, *Fields of Psychology,* p. 10

Number as a collective noun may be either singular or plural: preceded by *the,* it refers to the total sum and takes a singular verb; preceded by *a,* it refers to the individual units and takes a plural verb:

The number of pages assigned for daily reading *was* gradually increased to twelve.

A number of pages *are* badly torn.

Public takes a singular verb if the writer wishes to signify the whole group (The *public is* invited); it takes a plural construction if the writer is considering the individual members (The *public are* invited).

24.2e Words ending in -ics *Physics, mathematics, economics, civics,* and similar *-ics* words that refer to a science, art, or body of knowledge are usually considered singular; other words ending in *-ics* that refer to physical activities or qualities (*athletics, acrobatics, tactics*) are generally treated as plurals.

Singular forms

Physics was my most difficult subject in high school.

Ballistics is the study of the motion of projectiles.

Plural forms

Athletics have been virtually abolished from some smaller schools.

His motives may be good, but his *tactics are* deplorable.

Some words ending in *-ics* (*ethics, politics, acoustics*) may be used either in a singular or plural sense:

Singular idea	Plural idea
In almost every group, *politics* *is* a subject that will arouse controversy.	Radical *politics* *were* offensive to the Federalists.
Acoustics is a branch of science that is growing fast.	The *acoustics* in this room *are* not all they might be.

When you are in doubt about the number of a word ending in *-ics,* consult a dictionary.

References: Curme, *Syntax,* Ch. 26 and index entries; Fries, pp. 48-50, 54, 57-59; Pooley, pp. 85-88

24.3 Blind agreement The tendency to make a verb agree with a nearby expression rather than with its actual subject is called "blind agreement."

24.3a Plural nouns between subject and verb A singular subject followed by a phrase or clause containing plural nouns is still singular:

Here and there a *man* [subject] such as Columbus, Galileo, and others *has* [not *have*] ventured into the unknown physical and intellectual worlds.

The *lumberman* [subject] who previously sold only to carpenters and builders now *finds* [not *find*] hundreds of amateurs eager to build their own homes.

I decided to go to see exactly how *one* of those new cars *is* [not *are*] put together.

24.3b One of those who In written English, the verb in clauses that begin *one of those who* (or *that*) is plural:

He is one of those men who never *care* how they look. [The verb is plural because its subject *who* refers to *men,* not to *one.*]

"The Lottery" is one of those stories that *leave* you more puzzled when you finish than when you began. [*Stories* is the antecedent of *that.*]

Although a singular verb is common in spoken English ("one of those girls who *talks* all the time") and in a good deal of published material as well, the plural verb is customarily expected in these constructions and should therefore be used in college writing.

Reference: Russell Thomas, "Concord of the Verb in Relative Clauses After *one of*," *College English*, October 1951, 13:43-44

24.3c *There is, there are*   When a sentence begins with the introductory (or "dummy") word *there*, the number of the verb is determined by the subject which follows:

> There *are* conflicting *opinions* [subject] about smoking in the classrooms.
>
> There *were* at our camp at least a dozen *men* [subject] who were familiar with the mountain trail.
>
> There *is* great narrative and dramatic *power* [subject] in the first part of this novel.

There is frequently is used before a compound subject, especially when *are* would be unidiomatic, as in this statement from *The New Yorker:* "There *is* no telephone, no Frigidaire, no gas, no use of electricity. . . ."

Reference: Robert J. Geist, "There Is One And . . ." *College English*, November 1952, 14:115-116; Robert J. Geist, " 'There Is' Again," *College English*, December 1954, 16:188-189

24.3d **Verb and complement**   A verb agrees with its subject and not with its complement or its object:

> The *material* [subject] that was most interesting to me when I worked on my reference paper *was* [not *were*] the books that stated the facts forcefully.
>
> Our chief *trouble* [subject] *was* [not *were*] the black flies that swarmed about us on the trip.
>
> The *black flies* [subject] that swarmed about us on our trip *were* [not *was*] our chief trouble.

24.3e **Inverted order**   When the word order is inverted, care must be taken to make the verb agree with the subject and not with some other word:

Throughout the story *appear* thinly disguised *references* [subject] to the author's own boyhood.

Is any *one* [subject] of these pictures for sale?

Accompanying the publisher *were* his secretary and two members of his legal staff. [*Secretary and two members* is a compound subject.]

24.3f Type, part, series Subjects like *type, part, portion, a series* before a phrase with plural nouns take singular verbs:

The best *part* of the summer concerts, most people agree, *was* the second and third performances.

A third *type* of religious festival among these primitive people *was* the annual harvest feasts.

A *series* of panel discussions *is* scheduled for the convention.

Exercises

1. Copy down the italicized verbs in the following paragraphs and then opposite each verb write down its subject. If the subject is a pronoun (*it, that, they, which,* etc.) indicate in parentheses what noun or phrase it refers to.

1) One of the most fascinating games to watch—from the standpoint of psychology—*is* that venerable device, the high striker. This *is* spectacular, noisy and *provides* plenty of action. A standard, between 25 and 30 feet in height, *is set up* and guyed out. At the top *is* a bronze gong. Running its length, from ground up to gong, *is* a wire and along this wire *slides* a small cylinder of tough rubber, set in motion by a teeter board, balanced in the center. The other end of the board *carries* a rubber striking cushion. The customer *pays* ten cents, takes a heavy wooden maul and slams down on the cushion, sending the rubber weight sliding up the wire. If it *is* done properly the cylinder slides all the way up and *rings* the gong, whereupon the operator gives the customer a cigar.—William Lindsay Gresham, *Monster Midway*, p. 265

2) A much larger group of students, with more fighting spirit, *express* their rebellions, repressions, and frustrations through a fierce determination to reform the world immediately. Most of these students *come* from a comfortable and prosperous background, and very often from a home where one or both the parents *have achieved* a conspicuously successful place in society. Literature, of course, *is* full of examples of dominating parents and rebellious children, but writers usually *manage* their conflicts artfully and dramatically enough to make a somewhat tragic ending seem inevitable. They also, perhaps unintentionally, *give* the impression that these are exceptional cases. Only one who *has followed* some such routine as interviewing parents and children before college entrance and during the college years *has* an idea of the amount of pent-up rebellion against fathers and mothers, and can understand the attractiveness of any ideas which *justify* the individual in revolt.—Everett Hunt, "The Dean and the Psychiatrist," A.A.U.P. *Bulletin*, Spring 1953, 39:25

2. Copy the subject of each of the following sentences and the form of the verb in parentheses that agrees with it. If there is any problem of agreement, explain your choice of verb in terms of the points made in this section:

1) The principles on which Henry Ford thought as well as acted (*was, were*) one of his outstanding traits.

2) To a large class of specialists, the rest of mankind (*is, are*) made up of ignorant laymen.

3) Professor Dodd's analysis of the emotions, which (*seem, seems*) to follow Plato, is loose, inexact, and wholly superficial.

4) The kind of movies that I see on TV these days (*bore, bores*) me.

5) Neither expensive lotions nor frequent massaging (*have, has*) proved successful in the treatment of baldness.

6) As every baseball fan knows, three strikes (*is, are*) out.

7) Gradually the reader comes to suspect that the tone of most of the letters that both newspapers publish (*is, are*) favorable to the editorial policies of the papers.

8) The Class of 1954 (*requests, request*) your presence at a reception to be given Thursday, June 3, at eight o'clock in the ballroom of the Hotel Geneva.

9) One of the main reasons for the rapid decline of Spain as a sea power (*was, were*) the series of naval defeats she suffered at the hands of the English.

10) Critics of adoption agencies claim there (*is, are*) too much red tape and delay, partiality and various unnecessary obstacles.

3. Recast the following sentences according to the directions given for each. Make whatever changes are necessary in the verb form and other wording.

1) Change *one mile* to *three miles:* I generally take the bus home, since one mile is too far to walk after standing on my feet all day.

2) After *children* add *together with a sense of humor:* An interest in children is an absolute necessity if a person intends to be a playground director.

3) Add *of England and Wales* after *Association:* The Youth Hosteling Association takes special pains to enable young people of limited means to explore the countryside.

4) Change *lighting* to *acoustics:* Several speakers have suggested that the lighting in our auditorium is not as good as it might be.

5) After *you* add *and she:* Your sister told me that you intend to study ceramics at night school.

6) Change *money* to *riches:* Too many people still think that money is the sole standard of success.

7) Begin with *Neither* instead of *One:* One of the books you asked for last week has been returned.

8) Make *what worried him most* the subject: Unforeseen medical expenses were what worried him most.

9) Add *one of those parents who* after *is:* I can now see that my father is almost always right.

10) Change *their* to *its:* By the end of the second mile it was obvious that the crew were not rowing their best.

25 Adjectives and adverbs

Ad **Adjective or adverb form. Correction: Use the proper or the more appropriate form of the adjective or adverb marked.**

Adjectives and adverbs are modifying words used to make the meaning of other words clearer or more exact. Modifiers are essential because the subject, verb, and object by themselves do not ordinarily convey the full meaning a writer wishes to give to his ideas. Thus in place of "War (S) brought (V) suffering (O)," a person might write "The *recent* (M) war brought *untold* (M) suffering *throughout Europe* (M)." Modifiers may add descriptive details (a scene of *pleasant* memories), limit or make more definite the meaning of a key word (*Mary's* books; He laughed *loudly*), qualify statements (*However,* you may do as you wish).

The following sections deal with single word modifiers. For clauses used as adjective and adverb modifiers, see §15, Subordinate clauses, p. 187. For verbal phrases as modifiers, see §16, Infinitives, participles, and gerunds, p. 197.

25.1 Forms of adjectives and adverbs The form of an adjective or adverb should be appropriate to the passage in which it occurs. Particular care should be taken to distinguish between the forms that end in *-ly* and those that do not. While many adverbs end in *-ly* (*really, particularly, sincerely*), some of the more common ones do not (*now, quite, too, there*). In addition, some adjectives also end in *-ly* (*friendly, lonely*).

25.1a Adjectives and adverbs of identical form Some adjectives and adverbs have identical form, including:

	Adjective	*Adverb*
better:	a better book	try to do better
early:	an early bird	leave early
fast:	a fast car	drive fast
much:	waste much time	a much better plan
straight:	a straight line	go straight to bed
well:	all is well	runs well when oiled

312

An *-ly* ending should not be added to adverbs of this kind:

> She types *fast* [not *fastly*].
> I appreciate your kindness very *much* [not *muchly*, an archaic or Vulgate form].

25.1b Long and short forms of adverbs Some adverbs have two forms: one with an *-ly* ending (long form), the other without (short form):

Short form	Long form
Go *slow*.	Go *slowly*.
Don't talk so *loud*.	Don't talk so *loudly*.
The rope was drawn *tight*.	The rope was drawn *tightly*.

Other adverbs used with and without the *-ly* ending include:

bright	deep	loose	smooth
cheap	even	second	straight
close	fair	sharp	wrong

When two forms of an adverb are in common use, the choice usually depends upon appropriateness. Formal English tends to prefer the *-ly* form (The motor runs *smoothly*); General usage, the short form (The motor runs *smooth*). The tone of the passage, the sound of the word, and the level of usage are the determining factors.

Caution: Do not drop *-ly* from words like *sincerely, really, considerably*, when you are using them as adverbs. Substituting an adjective for an adverb form is Vulgate usage and should be avoided:

> It was a *really* outstanding performance [not: *real* outstanding].
> Our trip took *considerably* longer than we expected [not: *considerable* longer].

As an adverb, *badly* is the proper form in General writing (He danced *badly*); in such constructions *bad* is Vulgate usage. For the use of *bad* as a predicate adjective, see §25.2c.

25.1c Most, almost In Formal and General English *most* is not used for *almost* in the sense of "nearly." *Almost* is an adverb, and *most* is an adjective:

I *almost lost* my mind. [adverb, modifying the verb *lost*]
The train was *almost* always on time. [adverb, modifying the adverb *always*]
Most fishermen are optimists. [adjective, modifying *fishermen*]
Almost all fishermen are optimists. [adverb, modifying the adjective *all*]

In Informal English, *most* is frequently used for *almost:*

Most everybody used the reverse pedal quite as much as the regular foot brake—it distributed the wear over the bands and wore them down evenly.—Lee Strout White, "Farewell, My Lovely!" *The New Yorker,* May 16, 1936, p. 22

In this sense, *most* is spoken usage and inappropriate in all but Informal writing.

Reference: Pooley, p. 156

25.1d *This kind, that sort* *Kind* and *sort* are singular nouns and should be preceded by singular modifiers (*this* kind of clouds, *that* sort of people). In spoken English *these* or *those* is often used with these words when a plural noun occurs in the following phrase (I like *these* kind of *records* best; *Those* sort of *jokes* annoy me). But in General usage both words should be treated as singular forms:

I like *this* kind of records best.
That sort of jokes annoys me.

References: Curme, pp. 544-546; Fries, p. 58; Jespersen, p. 202

25.2 Position of adjectives and adverbs Adverbs and adjectives should be clearly related by their position in a statement to the words they are intended to modify. Few problems arise with single-word adjectives because they usually appear immediately before the word they modify. The position of adverbs, however, is much more flexible and needs to be watched in writing to prevent ambiguous or confusing wording.

25.2a Typical position of adjectives The typical position of adjectives in English is ̣immediately before the words they modify:

> Some of the *island* species have, at best, the most *tenuous* hold on life. The *Laysan* teal is found nowhere in the world but on the *one small* island of Laysan. Even on *this* island it occurs only on *one* end, where there is a seepage of *fresh* water. Probably the *total* population of *this* species does not exceed *fifty* individuals.—Rachel L. Carson, *The Sea Around Us,* p. 95

In some set phrases or conventional expressions the adjective occurs after the noun (accounts *receivable,* attorney *general,* bride-*elect,* battle *royal*).

Two or more adjectives are often placed after the words they modify to gain emphasis or to avoid clumsy or wordy expressions.

> Everywhere among this swarming crowd gleamed the bright raiment of blood and glory: the sailors thronged the streets in flapping blues and spotless whites—*brown, tough,* and *clean.*—Thomas Wolfe, *Look Homeward, Angel,* p. 512

25.2b Predicate adjectives Predicate adjectives are separated from the nouns they modify by linking verbs. The common linking verbs are *be, (is, was, were, am, has been), seem, appear, become, grow, prove* and verbs describing sensations like *taste, feel, smell, look, sound.*

Some of these forms may also be modified by adverbs (The weeds grew *rapidly*). To determine whether a predicate adjective or an adverb should be used, see what word is being modified: when the modifier refers to the subject, use a predicate adjective; when it modifies the verb, use an adverb.

> The children looked *unhappy.* [predicate adjective describing *children*]
> As the rain continued to fall, the children looked *unhappily* out the window. [adverb, modifying *looked*]
> He turned *abruptly* when he heard his name called. [adverb, describing the way in which he *turned*]
> Overnight the weather turned *cold.* [predicate adjective modifying *weather*]

A simple method of determining whether a predicate adjective should be used is to see if the word following the verb can be combined with the subject as an adjective: thus *the unhappy children, the cold weather;* but not *the unhappily looking children* or *abruptly he.*

References: Curme, *Parts of Speech,* pp. 66-69, *Syntax,* pp. 26-28

25.2c *Good, well; bad, badly* **as predicate adjectives** *Good* is an adjective (a *good* time; This cake tastes *good*). *Well* is either an adjective (Are you feeling *well?;* All is *well*), or an adverb (He writes *well*). Either *good* or *well* may be used as a predicate adjective in the expression *to feel well* (good), but with different connotations:

Don't you feel *well?* [referring to a state, "not ill"]

It made him feel *good* to pack his own bag and get into the front seat and drive his own car. [referring to a general attitude or bodily sensation]—John Dos Passos, *The Big Money,* p. 319

The use of *good* for the adverb *well* is Vulgate and should be avoided in writing: The team played *well* [not *good*] for five innings.

As an adjective, *bad* is the usual form after linking verbs (She feels *bad;* The milk tastes *bad;* The situation looks *bad* to me). *Badly* is also used when the emphasis is on the verb (I feel *badly* [or *bad*] about your troubles; The decaying fish certainly smelled *badly* [or *bad*]).

References: Lillian M. Feinsilver, "How Bad(ly) Do You Feel?" *American Speech,* 1949, 24:161-170; Curme, *Syntax,* p. 37

25.2d Position of adverbs The position of an adverb, particularly one that modifies a verb or a complete statement, may vary within a sentence, depending upon the emphasis desired:

Perhaps he was *once* the most popular writer in America.
He was, *perhaps,* the most popular writer in America *once.*
Perhaps once he was the most popular writer in America.

This flexibility makes it possible to shift the position of many adverbs for sentence variety and movement as well as for emphasis.

25.2e **Only and similar adverbs** Limiting adverbs like *only, merely, hardly, just* are placed immediately before the element they modify in Formal usage: I need *only* six more to make a full hundred; The audience seemed *hardly* to breathe when the girl began speaking.

In General usage the adverb usually stands immediately before the verb: I *only* need six more to make a full hundred; The audience *hardly* seemed to breathe when the girl began speaking. This pattern, typical of spoken English, is often found in writing, when no misunderstanding of the author's meaning will occur:

> When the brilliant lightweight boxer, Kid Lewis, stood for Parliament in his native borough, he *only* scored a hundred and twenty-five votes. —George Orwell, *The English People*, p. 11

> He *only* remembers one verse of the song and he has been repeating it.—Eugene O'Neill, *A Moon for the Misbegotten*, p. 72

But a writer should be careful not to misplace a modifier so that the meaning of a statement becomes ambiguous or even ludicrous:

> Ambiguous: Using several pen names, the two editors have *almost* written every article in the magazine. [Obviously *almost* should modify *every article*.]

> Clear: Using several pen names, the two editors have written *almost* every article in the magazine.

> Nonsensical: He had *only* a face a mother could love.

> Accurate: He had a face *only* a mother could love.

In some constructions, misplacing the modifier may alter the intended meaning:

> The way I can stand in front of a store window and persuade myself that I need useless articles *even* surprises me. [intended meaning: *surprises even me*]

25.2f Split infinitive   A phrase with an adverb between *to* and an infinitive (I don't want *to ever see* him again) is called a *split infinitive*. A writer should avoid split infinitives that are obviously awkward or that call undue attention to themselves:

Awkward	*Better*
I will not describe the circumstances of our meeting, or even attempt *to* physically *describe* her.	I will not describe the circumstances of our meeting, or even attempt *to describe* her physically.
After a while I was able *to,* although not very accurately, *distinguish* the good customers from the sulky ones.	After a while I was able *to distinguish*—although not very accurately—the good customers from the sulky ones.

But constructions of this sort are by no means always awkward. When the normal position of the adverb is after the word *to*, a split infinitive is Standard usage (The receptionist asked them *to please sit* down). Putting the adverb modifier immediately before or after the infinitive would be unnatural or misleading in some statements:

. . . we know of no better way *to quickly glimpse* the range of rhetoric than to read, in succession, the articles on "Property" and "Propaganda" in *The Encyclopaedia of the Social Sciences.* [*Quickly* belongs before *glimpse*, not after it or before *to*.]—Kenneth Burke, *A Rhetoric of Motives,* p. 24

References: Curme, *Syntax,* pp. 458-465; Fowler, "Split infinitive" (for overprecise distinctions); Fries, pp. 132, 144; Roberts, pp. 204-206

25.3 Comparison of adjectives and adverbs   Most adjectives and adverbs have three different forms to indicate degrees of the characteristic they name. The positive degree (or simple form of the modifier) expresses no comparison (*red, slow, serious*); the comparative degree represents an increase of the positive form, or makes a specific comparison between two things (*redder, slower, more seriously*); the superlative indicates the greatest (or least) degree among three or more things (the *reddest* apple of all, the *slowest* runner on the team, the *most*—or *least*—seriously presented argument).

25.3a Regular forms of comparison Most adjectives and adverbs are compared in one of two ways: by adding *-er, -est* to the positive form, or by prefixing *more, most* (or *less, least*).

	Positive	Comparative	Superlative
Adjectives	hot	hotter	hottest
	brilliant	more brilliant	most brilliant
	expensive	less expensive	least expensive
Adverbs	near	nearer	nearest
	sincerely	more sincerely	most sincerely
	often	oftener, more often, less often	oftenest, most often, least often

In general, the *-er, -est* forms are used with words of one syllable (*longer, driest*), and *more, most* with words of more than two syllables (*more interesting, most rapidly*). With two-syllable words a writer usually has a choice of either form (*abler, more able; easiest, most easy*); the sound of the expression may determine which form is used:

> His step was *steadier* and *more elastic.* Even his bloodshot eyes looked *fresher,* and his hair and beard were *softer.* . . .—Eyvind Johnson, *Return to Ithaca,* p. 260

25.3b Irregular forms of comparison A few common modifiers have irregular forms in comparisons:

bad	worse	worst
good ⎫ well ⎭	better	best
far	farther, further	farthest, furthest
little	less, lesser, littler	least, littlest
many ⎫ some ⎬ much ⎭	more	most

Worse, worst: Worst is the appropriate form for the superlative: That was the *worst* [not *worse*] show I have ever seen.

Farther, further: In Formal English a distinction is sometimes made between *farther,* referring to physical distance (It was six miles *farther* to town) and *further* referring to abstract degree (We will study these suggestions *further*). In General English this distinction is not made.

25.4 Use of comparatives and superlatives

Comp Comparison of adjectives and adverbs. Correction: Change the construction of the comparison marked to one more accurate or more appropriate (§§25.4, 25.5).

25.4a Use of the comparative The comparative form of an adjective or adverb is ordinarily used when two things are compared:

> You're a *better* man than I am, Gunga Din!
> Blood is *thicker* than water.
> She works *more diligently* than her roommate.

But in some expressions the comparative form is used when no actual comparison is mentioned (higher education, the lower depths, Better Business Bureau). In others, the reader is left to supply the comparison (Look younger, live longer). Writers of advertising copy are particularly fond of this absolute use of the comparative: Smoke a *milder* cigarette; *More* protection for *fewer* dollars; Suds gets clothes *cleaner*. In Formal writing, it is better to avoid this construction.

Reference: Esther K. Sheldon, "The Rise of the Incomplete Comparative," *American Speech,* 1945, 20:161-167

25.4b Use of the superlative for the comparative The superlative form ordinarily indicates the greatest degree among three or more persons or things:

> He was voted the member of his class *most likely* to succeed.
> Many critics consider *King Lear* the *greatest* of Shakespeare's tragedies.

The superlative is sometimes used for comparing two things in spoken English (May the best man [of two opponents] win), and the same construction is occasionally seen in writing:

> Of the two Mr. Weidman's book is the *most* ambitious—which is appropriate enough since his hero is most furiously concerned with ambition.—Orville Prescott, "Books of the Times," *The New York Times*, February 17, 1948

But this usage is regarded as distinctly Informal, and it is better to keep the superlative for comparisons among three or more units.

References: Russell Thomas, "The Use of the Superlative for the Comparative," *English Journal* (College Edition), 1935, 24:821-829; Fries, p. 101

25.4c Absolute use of the superlative Superlative forms occur in expressions in which no direct comparison is implied (*best* wishes, *deepest* sympathy, *highest* praise, *most* sincerely yours). The form with *most* is frequently used as an intensive to signify a high degree:

> For example, Herbert Spencer (1820–1903), a *most* influential English philosopher, contended that man is an animal subject to the general laws of evolution and that human progress results from the stern discipline of nature which eliminates the unfit.—Melvin Rader, *Ethics and Society*, p. 46. Reprinted by permission of Henry Holt and Company, Inc.

The colloquial use of a heavily stressed superlative to indicate nothing more than general approval (the "feminine intensive") should be avoided in serious writing:

> Hasn't she the *sweetest* voice?
> I saw the *loveliest* lamb chops at the butcher's.

Reference: Curme, *Syntax*, pp. 506-508

25.4d Unique and similar words Words such as *unique, perfect, dead, empty* are sometimes regarded as logically incapable of comparison or qualification because their positive forms express absolute states. But in actual usage these terms are often qualified or modified by comparative forms:

> We the people of the United States, in order to form a *more perfect* union. . . .—Preamble to the Constitution of the United States

> . . . the *more unique* his nature, the more peculiarly his own will be the coloring of his language.—Otto Jespersen, *Mankind, Nation, and Individual from a Linguistic Point of View*, p. 204

Whether words like these should or should not be qualified is a matter that can be determined only by appropriateness. In General writing an expression such as "That was the *most perfect* meeting I ever attended" would be appropriate, but in Formal usage, "the *most nearly perfect* meeting" would be preferable.

References: Curme, *Syntax*, p. 504; Roberts, pp. 99-100

25.5 Constructions in comparisons   In writing, expressions of comparisons should be more carefully and more fully stated than they usually are in speaking. Expressions that might pass unnoticed in conversation (such as *all the higher the ladder will reach* or *the slowest of any runner on the team*) are too slipshod to be used in careful writing (where the same ideas would be *as high as the ladder will reach* and *the slowest runner on the team*).

25.5a Comparable terms   Things compared should be of the same kind and actually comparable:

Terms not comparable	*Comparable terms*
The rhinoceros has a hide almost as tough as an alligator [*Hide* and *alligator* are not comparable].	The rhinoceros has a hide almost as tough as that of an alligator [or *as an alligator's*].
One reviewer compared these short stories to O'Henry.	One reviewer compared these short stories to those written by O'Henry [or *to O'Henry's*].

25.5b As . . . as   Double comparisons with *as . . . as, if . . . than* should be filled out in writing:

> He is *as* tall *as, if* not taller *than,* his brother. [not: He is as tall if not taller than his brother.]
> The styles vary *as* much *as, if* not more *than,* the colors.

Since the *if . . . than* construction tends to interrupt sentence movement, it is often preferable to complete the first comparison and then add the second:

> He is as tall as his brother, if not taller.
> The styles vary as much as the colors, if not more.

25.5c Other   *Other* is used when the comparison involves things of the same class, but not when the things belong to different classes:

> She is a better dancer than the *other* girls.
> She dances better than any [not *any other*] boy in school.
> *Blithe Spirit* was more successful than the *other* plays we produced last year.
> I think movies are more entertaining than any [not *any other*] book.

Other is not used with superlative comparisons:

> Jerry was the best cook of all the [not *all the other*] cooks in the surrounding camps.
> The Egyptians had attained the highest degree of cultivation in medicine that had up to that time been achieved by any [not *any other*] nation.

25.5d Like   To introduce a prepositional phrase of comparison, *like* is Standard usage:

> It may of course be argued, as it has often been argued, that foreign languages, *like* mathematics, are too difficult for students generally, and should be reserved only for those with the ability to profit by their study.—Norman P. Sacks, "A Linguist's View of the Current Public School Controversy," A.A.U.P. *Bulletin,* Spring 1953, 39:79

In phrases like this, *as* should not be substituted for *like* or *such as:*

Some writers *like* Faulkner and Caldwell take their material from a particular region. [not *as*]

To introduce a clause of comparison with a definite subject and verb, Formal English prefers *as, as if, as though* to *like:*

These big monopolies, taken as a single group, are in devastating competition with the not yet grouped, much *as* the fair-trade economy competes against the free-trade economy.—David Riesman and others, *The Lonely Crowd,* p. 247

Although still regarded as "disputable" usage, *like* as a conjunction introducing a clause is gaining respectable status in current writing:

The author of "Stranger and Alone" looks a little *like* he might have been both of these things at one time or another.—Harvey Breit, "Talk with J. Saunders Redding," *The New York Times Book Review,* March 5, 1950, p. 12

More and more we are treating children *like* a rich man incapable of love might treat his wife—trying to fob off on them material things in place of the vital things that they have a right to.—Henry Steele Commager, "When Majors Wrote for Minors," *The Saturday Review,* May 10, 1952, p. 46

Like is a more definite word than the overworked *as* and it may become as acceptable in these constructions as it is in prepositional phrases. Except where *like* is the Standard idiom, as in the South, the preferred forms *as though* or *as if* should be used, especially in Formal English.

References: Curme, *Syntax,* pp. 281-282; Pooley, pp. 153, 155; Marckwardt and Walcott, pp. 46-48, 113-114

25.5e Completing comparisons Statements involving comparisons should be written out in full, particularly if any misunderstanding might arise through shortening one of the terms:

Ambiguous	*Clearer*
I owe him less than you.	I owe him less than I owe you. Or: I owe him less than you do.
That cat liked milk more than most children.	That cat liked milk more than most children do.

Exercises

1. First determine what word or statement each of the numbered forms modifies. Then identify each form according to its function as adjective, adverb, or predicate adjective.

1) . . . Greek is a (1) *very* subtle language, full of (2) *delicately* (3) *modifying* words, capable of the (4) *finest* distinctions of meaning. Years of study are needed to read it (5) *even* (6) *tolerably*. Small wonder that the writers of other countries left it (7) *alone*, and unlike their brother artists in stone (8) *never* imitated Greek methods.—Edith Hamilton, *The Greek Way to Western Civilization*, p. 38

2) (1) *Thus*, the boys had gone out to work, after (2) *school* hours and in the vacations, since they were very (3) *young*. (4) *Unhappily*, neither Eliza nor Gant were at any pains to examine the kind of work their children did, contenting themselves (5) *vaguely* with the comfortable assurance that all work which earned money was (6) *honest, commendable and formative* of character. —Thomas Wolfe, *Look Homeward, Angel*, p. 112

2. Select the adjective or adverb form that seems appropriate in each of these sentences and give the reason for your choice. If both forms are possible, indicate the level at which each would be acceptable.

1) Near the picnic grounds was a (*new, newly*) painted lunch stand.

2) Everyone should drive extremely (*careful, carefully*) when dusk sets in.

3) Reno may be the "biggest little city in the world," but it's a long way from being the (*wickedest, most wicked*).

4) With deft fingers the cowboy rolled his cigarette (*tight, tightly*).

5) You take the white chessmen and I'll take the black, and may the (*better, best*) man win.

6) This sweater must be much more (*close, closely*) knit.

7) Several people have been kind enough to tell me that for a beginner I play the piano pretty (*well, good*).

8) Confronted by the same temptations, a less conscientious person might have acted (*different, differently*).

9) Writing comes (*easy, easily*) to students who like to read.

10) When you first bite into a mango, it may taste (*peculiar, peculiarly*), but after a few more bites you'll probably like it.

11) The senator's arguments always sound (*convincing, convincingly*) over the radio but they don't stand up very (*good, well*) when you study them in the papers.

12) Either sandpaper or steel wool may be used to remove the rust, but of the two I prefer steel wool because it's (*easiest, easier*).

13) Even after he bought a hearing aid, he complained that he heard (*more badly, worse*) every day.

14) Without additional machinery, the factory can now turn out parts (*more quickly, quicker*) than ever before.

15) With high octane gas the motor starts (*easy, easily*) and runs (*smooth, smoothly*) even in sub-zero weather.

3. Some of the adjective and adverb forms and expressions of comparisons in these sentences would be inappropriate in Formal English. Change these to Formal English and briefly tell why.

1) After exams I was real concerned about my grades.

2) There were other problems confronting the settlers, as education, law enforcement, and sanitation.

3) My parents were always arguing about which one was the best qualified to supervise the raising of the children.

4) These kind of scissors are called pinking shears.

5) The hours of work in public health nursing are not the same as any other business or industry.

6) The junior varsity has been playing as well if not better than the first team.

7) Da Vinci's "Mona Lisa" is probably the most perfect portrait of its kind.

8) The investigations should have been carried on further.

9) Following the withdrawal of the occupation troops, a series of riots harassed the newly independent country.

10) One of the most annoying things about double features is that the worse picture is always shown first.

11) Her skin was soft like a baby.

12) Experienced stamp collectors value those sort of stamps more highly than these.

13) We started our march early, but the underbrush was so thick that eight miles was all the farther we could go.

14) Key West is the southernmost city in the United States.

15) The old Ford tri-motor monoplane was used because the space for the smokejumpers was greater than the other planes.

4. Study the following sentences carefully and state where you would place the modifier within each sentence. Explain any change of emphasis or meaning that would result from shifting the modifier.

1) Add *definitely:* Should a student try to determine his future career before coming to college?

2) Add *scarcely:* He found he had enough money to last him over the weekend.

3) Add *more or less:* Our teachers told us what to do and what to think.

4) Add *better:* They are thus able to orient themselves in a changing society.

5) Add *almost:* The snowflakes seemed to melt before they touched the ground.

6) Add *half:* There's no need to kill yourself on this job.

7) Add *even:* This sonata is too difficult for a concert pianist to play.

8) Add *only:* After fishing all day, they caught five small trout.

9) Add *almost* to the dependent clause: I must confess that in the last year I have come to like ROTC.

10) Add *even* to the main clause: Since everything is important in our cultural history, there is a place for that domestic symbol, the bathtub.

26 Verbs

The italicized words in these sentences are verbs:

The hunter *shot* a deer.
Our next speaker *will be introduced* by the chairman.
My sister *has* measles.
Are you ready?

Terms used in describing verbs

Principal parts (§26.1)

English verbs have three principal parts:
The *infinitive*, or base form: *ask* (*to ask*), *go* (*to go*)
The *past* tense: *asked, went*
The *past* participle: *asked, gone*

Tense (§26.2)

The "time" of a verb's action as expressed in the form of the verb:
    Past: I *went*   *Present:* I *go*   *Future:* I *will go*
(For other tenses, see the table on pp. 332-333.)

Transitive and intransitive

A verb is *transitive* when it has an object to complete its meaning:
    The teacher *demanded* (V) *order* (O).
A verb is *intransitive* when it does not have an object: He *slept* (V).

Active and passive voice (§26.9)

A verb is in the *active* voice when its subject is the actor:
    The President *delivered* (V) a speech.
A verb is in the *passive* voice when the subject receives the action:
    A *speech* (S) *was delivered* (V) by the President.

Mood (§26.10)

The manner in which a statement is expressed:
    The *indicative* mood expresses a fact or a statement: I *am* thrifty.
    The *imperative* mood expresses a command or request: *Be* thrifty!
    The *subjunctive* mood is used in some conditions and in clauses like:
It is necessary that he *be* twenty-one.

In meaning, verbs indicate action (*run, manufacture, write*), condition (*am, feel, sleep*), or process (*become, grow*). In form, they may consist of one word or more (I *should* not *have done* it), and may indicate person, number, tense, voice, and mood.

The table on these two pages lists the terms used to describe the principal characteristics of verbs.

Terms used in describing verbs

Auxiliary verb (§26.2)

A verb used with another verb form in a phrase to show tense, voice, or mood:

    I *am* going.   He *will* go.   They *had* gone.
    The work *should have been* completed earlier.

Linking verb or copula (§§13.1d; 24.3d)

A verb that "links" its subject to a predicate noun or an adjective:
    She *is* a teacher   The days *became* warmer.

Regular and irregular verbs (§26.1)

Regular (or "weak") verbs form their principal parts by adding *-ed, -d,* or *-t* to the infinitive: *asked, engraved, dealt*
Irregular (or "strong") verbs change or retain the vowel of the infinitive and do not add *-d, -ed,* or *-t*:

    sing, sang, sung   *put, put, put*

Finite and infinite verbs (§10)

A finite verb (from the Latin *finis*, meaning "end" or "limit") can be limited:

    In person by a pronoun or subject (I *sing*, she *sings*)
    In time by a tense form (she *sings*, she *sang*)
    In number, singular or plural (he *sings*, they *sing*)
Finite verbs can be main verbs in sentences and clauses:
    I *had gone* before he *came*.
Participles, infinitives, and gerunds are infinite or "non-finite" verb forms because they are not limited in person or number and are ordinarily used in subordinate constructions:
    Before *leaving* I thanked our host.   She needed a hat *to wear*.

26.1 Principal parts The appropriate form of a verb should be used to indicate each of its tenses. With regular verbs problems seldom arise because their forms do not change, except for the endings *-ed, -d,* or *-t.* But errors may occur in the formation of certain tenses of the irregular ("strong") verbs, because of a confusion in spelling (*choose, chose*), or because of an inappropriate use of a Vulgate form (He *seen* the show last week).

The following list contains the principal parts of common verbs that sometimes raise questions. The *past tense* in the second column is used in the simple past (She *wrote* a letter). The *past participle,* third column, is used to form compound tenses (The bird *had flown* away; Soon this *will be forgotten;* The chimes *are being rung*).

Where two forms are given, both are acceptable (He *lighted* a cigarette; He *lit* a cigarette). But those forms in parentheses labeled NS (*Nonstandard*) should not be used in General writing. For verbs not given here, consult a recent dictionary. Caution: If your dictionary labels a form in question *Vulgate, obsolete, archaic,* or *rare,* it is not suitable for college writing.

Principal parts

(Forms marked NS [Nonstandard] should not be used in writing.)

Infinitive	Past tense	Past participle
arise	arose	arisen
bear	bore	borne (carried)
		born (given birth to)
begin	began (NS begun)	begun
bite	bit	bitten, bit
blow	blew (NS blowed)	blown (NS blowed)
break	broke	broken
burst	burst	burst (NS bursted)
catch	caught	caught
choose (chōoz)	chose (chōz)	chosen
come	came (NS come)	come
dig	dug	dug
dive	dove, dived	dived

do (see §26.8)	did (NS done)	done
drag	dragged (NS drug)	dragged
draw	drew	drawn (NS drawed)
dream	dreamed, dreamt	dreamed, dreamt
drink	drank (NS drunk)	drunk
eat	ate	eaten
fall	fell	fallen
fly	flew	flown
forget	forgot	forgotten
freeze	froze	frozen
get (see §26.7)	got	got, gotten
give	gave (NS give)	given
go	went	gone
grow	grew (NS growed)	grown
hang (as a murderer)	hanged	hanged
hang (as a picture)	hung	hung
know	knew (NS knowed)	known
lay (see §26.6a)	laid	laid
lead	led	led
lend	lent	lent
lie (recline; see §26.6a)	lay	lain
light	lighted, lit	lighted, lit
pay	paid	paid
prove	proved	proved, proven
ride	rode	ridden
ring	rang, rung	rung
rise	rose	risen
run	ran (NS run)	run
see	saw (NS seen)	seen
set (see §26.6b)	set	set
shine	shone, shined	shone, shined
show	showed	showed, shown
sing	sang, sung	sung
sink	sank, sunk	sunk, sunken
sit (see §26.6b)	sat (NS set)	sat
spring	sprang, sprung	sprung
steal	stole	stolen
swim	swam, swum	swum
take	took	taken
throw	threw (NS throwed)	thrown
wake	waked, woke	waked
wear	wore	worn
wring	wrung	wrung
write	wrote	written

26.2   Use of tenses

T   **Tense. Correction: Make the tense of the verb marked conventional in form (a) or consistent with the others in the passage (b, c).**

By means of the different tenses, a writer sets the time of the situation he is describing (as happening in the past, going on at the present time, or occurring in the future), and also indicates for the reader the continuity of the action or explanation. It is important, therefore, to see that the verb tenses are consistent and easy to follow.

26.2a   Tense forms

Except for the simple present and past tense forms, English verbs show distinctions of time by various phrase combinations, often supported by adverbs (for example, "he is *about* to go" as a future).

The following table lists the names of the most frequently used tenses and the verb phrases most commonly associated with time distinctions:

	Active	*Passive*
Present tense	he asks he is asking he does ask	he is asked he is being asked
Past tenses		
Past (time in the past not extending to the present)	he asked he was asking he did ask	he was asked he was being asked
Perfect (past time extending to the present; past participle plus *have* or *has*)	he has asked he has been asking	he has been asked
Past perfect (a time in the past before another past time; past participle plus *had*)	he had asked he had been asking	he had been asked
Future tenses		
Future (future, extending from the present)	he will ask he will be asking he is going to ask	he will be asked

Future perfect (past time in some future time; future tense of *have* plus past participle)	he will have asked he will have been asking	he will have been asked

26.2b Consistent use of tenses

Unnecessary or careless shift in tense (as from the present to the past, or the past to the future) should be avoided:

Unnecessary shifts

[Mixture of present and past]:

I *sit* down at my desk early with intentions of spending the next four hours studying. Before many minutes *passed*, I *heard* a great deal of noise down on the floor below me; a water fight *is* in progress. Studying *was forgotten* for half an hour, for it *is* quite impossible to concentrate on Spanish in the midst of all this commotion. After things *quieted* down I *began* studying again, but *had* hardly *started* when a magazine salesman *comes* into my room.

Consistent

[Past tense throughout]:

I *sat* down at my desk early with intentions of spending the next four hours studying. Before many minutes *passed*, I *heard* a great deal of noise down on the floor below me; a water fight *was* in progress. Studying *was forgotten* for half an hour, for it *was* quite impossible to concentrate on Spanish in the midst of all that commotion. After things *quieted* down I *began* studying again, but *had* hardly started when a magazine salesman *came* into my room.

In single sentences inconsistencies in verb tenses often occur when a writer shifts the form of two or more verbs that should be parallel:

Shifted

For years I *have been attending* summer camp and *enjoyed* every minute of it.

Consistent

For years I *have been attending* summer camp, and *enjoying* every minute of it.

26.2c Sequence of tenses

When the verb of a main clause is in the past or past perfect tense, the verb in a subordinate clause is also past or past perfect:

They slowly *began* to appreciate what their teacher *had* [not *has*] *done* for them.

Up to that time I *had* never *seen* Slim when he *hadn't* [or *didn't have;* not *hasn't*] a wad of tobacco in his mouth.

Exception: A present infinitive is usual after a past verb:

I *would have liked* very much *to attend* [not *to have attended*] her wedding, but I was out of town.

26.3   Be   The verb *be* has eight forms, three more than any other verb in English. In addition to the infinitive there are three forms in the present tense (I *am;* he *is;* we, you, they *are*), two in the past tense (I, he *was;* we, you, they *were*), the present participle (*being*), and the past participle form (*been*).

Since *be* is the verb used most frequently in English, its forms are not troublesome in ordinary situations. Writers should, however, be careful not to use Nonstandard forms.

26.3a   You was, you were   In the past tense, *you, we, they* are followed by *were,* not *was:*

Nonstandard	*Standard*
You *wasn't* fooling me, *was* you?	You *weren't* fooling me, *were* you?
We both joined the army when we *was* eighteen.	We both joined the army when we *were* eighteen.

26.3b   Ain't   *Ain't* is a Vulgate contraction; *aren't* and *isn't* are the Standard forms. In questions with *I, am I not* is Formal. *Aren't I* is often used, but displeases many people. Fortunately the forms are rarely needed in writing except in dialog, in which the one most natural to the speaker would be used.

References: Curme, *Parts of Speech,* p. 248; Marckwardt and Walcott, pp. 48, 95–96

26.4   Shall—will, should—would   In current American usage, *will* is generally used with all persons of the verb for the future tense (I *will* leave tomorrow; He *will* arrive at six; We *will* return later). To express determination or for emphasis, usage is divided about *will* and *shall*, although *shall* is perhaps the more common form for all persons (I *shall* return; They *shall* not pass). Some Formal writers make the following distinctions between *shall* and *will*:

Simple future

First person:	I shall ask	we shall ask
Second person:	you will ask	you will ask
Third person:	he, she, it will ask	they will ask

Emphatic future

First person:	I will ask	we will ask
Second person:	you shall ask	you shall ask
Third person:	he, she, it shall ask	they shall ask

It doesn't hurt to know about these distinctions, but you need not follow them unless you want to or are expressly told to do so.

26.4a **Shall and will in questions** In questions, *will* is used in all persons, but *shall* is often used if there is a notion of propriety or obligation:

Will I go? Where will we go next? What will you do now?
Obligation: Shall I go? What shall she wear?

In the negative, *won't* is the regular form: What *won't* they think of next?

26.4b **Overuse of shall** *Shall* should not be used in statements where *will* is the Standard form:

Whether or not Congress *will* [not *shall*] pass laws against lynching is not for me to guess.

Some people apparently think that *shall* is a more correct (or elegant) form than *will*. It isn't.

26.4c **Should and would** *Should* and *would* are used in statements that carry a sense of doubt or uncertainty:

They *should* be here by Tuesday. (Contrast with the meaning of: They *will* be here by Tuesday.)

I wasn't ready as soon as I thought I *would* be.

In polite or unemphatic requests both *would* and *should* are used for the first person, and *would* for the second person:

I *would* be much obliged if you could help me.
I *should* be much obliged if you could help me.
Would you please give this your earliest attention?

In indirect discourse *would* and *should* serve as the past tenses of *will* and *shall* and are usually equivalent in meaning to *ought to* or *wish to*:

Direct discourse	*Indirect discourse*
Mary said, "I will go."	Mary said that she would go.
"Shall we adjourn?" the chairman asked.	The chairman asked if they should adjourn.

References: Much has been written about the use of these words. For a good short summary of actual usage, see Fries, pp. 150–168. Other discussions appear in Curme, *Syntax*, pp. 362–371; Jespersen, Chs. 25, 26; Marckwardt and Walcott, pp. 23, 24, 83, 84; Adeline C. Bartlett, "*Shall* and *Will*," *College English*, October 1953, 15:55–56.

26.5 ***Can and may*** In all levels of usage *can* is used for ability (This car *can* do better than 80 miles an hour; He *can* walk now with crutches), and *may* for possibility (That *may* be true; We *may* get there before dark).

To express permission, Formal English uses only *may* (*May* I go now? You *may* have any one you like); Informal and General English increasingly use *can* in such expressions (*Can* I go now? You *can* have any one you like), but many people object to this. To be on the safe side, in writing use *may*.

References: Marckwardt and Walcott, pp. 37, 126; Gladys D. Haase, "*Can* and *May*," *College English*, January 1950, 11:215–216

26.6 Lay——lie, set——sit   The forms of these words should not be confused in writing.

26.6a Lay——lie   *Lie,* meaning to recline, does not take an object. Its principal parts are *lie, lay, lain:* You *lie* down for a rest, or *lie* down on the job; The farm *lay* in the valley; The log had *lain* across the road for a week.

Lay, meaning to put or place, takes an object. Its principal parts are *lay, laid, laid:* You *lay* linoleum, *lay* a book on the table; She *laid* her purse on the desk; The cornerstone was *laid* by the mayor a year ago. Egg laying is *lay, laid, laid.*

Informal English uses *lay* for both these verbs, but this is inappropriate for General usage.

26.6b Set——sit   The verb *sit* (as in a chair) does not take an object. Its principal parts are *sit, sat, sat:* I like to *sit* in a hotel lobby; He *sat* there an hour; I have *sat* in the same chair for three semesters.

The verb *set,* meaning to put something down, takes an object. Its principal parts are *set, set, set:* Set the soup on this pad; They *set* the trunk in the hall; She has *set* candles in the windows.

However, a hen *sets* on her eggs, and the sun *sets* in the west.

26.7 Get, got, gotten   The principal parts of the verb *get* are *get, got,* and *got* or *gotten.*

26.7a Got, gotten   Both forms are used in America as the past participle:

> He could have *gotten* [or *got*] here by now.
> In the past I have *got* [or *gotten*] good meals here.

The choice between *got* and *gotten* in such expressions depends largely upon the emphasis and rhythm of the particular sentence and on the user's speech habits. *Gotten* is probably the more common.

26.7b Have got, have got to   *Have got* in the sense of possession
(I *haven't got* a black tie) or obligation (We *have got* to finish this experiment today) is widely used in speech and is
acceptable in most kinds of writing. Some writers of Formal
English avoid the expression, regarding *got* as redundant
(I *haven't* a black tie; We *have* to finish this experiment
today).

While *have* alone would carry the meaning, it is less emphatic, particularly when contracted, and anyway is so frequently used as a mere auxiliary of tense that most people
do not consider it as a verb of full meaning. Unless you have
been instructed otherwise, use either form in General or Informal writing, and avoid *have got* in Formal papers.

26.7c Idioms with get   In many common idioms (set expressions)
get is Standard usage for all levels of speaking and writing:

get up in the morning	get over (an illness)
get cold	get tired
get ahead	get away (as in the start of a
get along with (someone)	race)

In other expressions *get* is considered as Informal or slang;
the last four on the following list would not be appropriate
in General writing:

get thrown out
get away with (escape punishment)
get it across (information or a point of view)
A stray bullet got him in the shoulder.
Get the look on her face!
This modern music gets me.
How silly can you get?
Get [understand] me?

When you are in doubt about the standing of other expressions with *get*, consult a recent dictionary.

References: Adeline C. Bartlett, "*Get, Have Got,* and *Have Got
To,*" *College English,* February 1949, 10:280–282; Curme, *Parts
of Speech,* p. 218; Pooley, pp. 148–151

26.8 **Do; don't, doesn't**   The Standard forms of the verb *do* should be used in writing, with particular attention to the past tense and the past participle:

Present tense: I, you *do*; he, she, it *does*; we, you, they *do*
Past tense: I, you, he, she, it *did*; we, you, they *did*
Past participle: *done* (He knew he had *done* wrong; They have *done* their best)

Forms like "He *done* his best" and "I have *did* what I could" are Vulgate.

26.8a **Don't, doesn't**   *Don't* is the contraction for *do not* (I *do not*, I *don't*), *doesn't* is the contraction for *does not* (he *does not*, he *doesn't*). It is Vulgate usage to substitute carelessly one form for the other: *Doesn't* [not *Don't*] she look pretty?

26.8b **Idioms with do**   *Do* is used in many standard idioms (do without, do away with, make do, do one's fingernails). Writers should be careful, however, not to use in Formal English, Informal or Vulgate expressions made with *do*:

When the Dean of Women arrived, she seemed *done in.* (exhausted)
Leaving the game, I realized I had been *done.* (cheated)
Hearing the police knock at his door, Simms knew he was *done for,* because he had already *done time* at Sing Sing.

Expressions with *do* and *done* are so numerous in current speech that a writer should consult a dictionary whenever he is uncertain about the standing of any form in question.

26.9 **Active and passive verbs**

Pass **Passive. Correction: Change the passive verb or verbs to active.**

We frequently have a choice of whether a noun will be the subject or object in a sentence, with a resulting difference in the verb form:

Active verb: Jim's father *gave* him a car.
Passive verb: Jim *was given* a car by his father.

The great majority of verbs in English sentences are active.

26.9a   Appropriate passives   Passive verbs are natural when the active subject is unknown or unimportant for the statement (A leak *was found* in the main pipe), or obvious (This topic *is treated* in the following section), or for some reason of emphasis (Our house *was painted* last year; We *were taken* there by boat).

26.9b   Inappropriate passives   Passive constructions are sometimes awkward and should be changed to the more direct active form:

Awkward passive	*Active*
All the glories of an early Canadian sunrise *were enjoyed*.	We enjoyed all the glories of an early Canadian sunrise.
When he is *conversed with*, I learn a great deal.	When I converse with him [Or: Talking with him], I learn a great deal.

It is usually awkward to combine an active and a passive verb in the same sentence:

Awkward	*Revised*
With fewer games and shorter practice hours, the subjects could be kept up and we would not have to cram for final examinations.	With fewer games and shorter practice hours, we could keep up in our subjects and not have to cram for final examinations.

26.10   Subjunctives   Certain instances of untypical verb forms are known as the subjunctive mood: he *ask* instead of *asks*; I, he, she *were* instead of *was*; I, he, she *be asked* instead of *is* or *was asked.* The use of these forms in current English is quite limited and inconsistent, even in Formal English. There is almost always an alternative construction in General usage and students hardly ever need to use a subjunctive.

26.10a   In conditions   In contrary-to-fact, impossible, or improbable conditions, the subjunctive is sometimes used, especially in Formal English.

If I *were* in your position [I'm not], I wouldn't accept his offer. (More common: If I *was* in your position. . .)

He said if he *were* President [he isn't], he would remove them. (More common: He said if he *was* President. . .)

"If I were you" is a formula that is common in all levels.

The subjunctive is sometimes found in simple conditions (If the subject of a verb *be* impersonal, the verb itself may be called impersonal). This use does not contribute to meaning and should be avoided.

26.10b In *that* clauses The subjunctive is used in many set expressions (usually in a Formal, often legal context) for recommendations, demands, and so on:

Formal	*General*
It is required that the applicant *be* under twenty-one.	The applicant must be under twenty-one.
It is necessary that every member *inform* himself of these rules.	Every member should inform himself of these rules.
	Or: It is necessary for every member to inform himself of these rules.
I ask that the interested citizen *watch* closely the movements of these troops.	I ask the interested citizen to watch the movements of these troops closely.

References: Ballard, pp. 12–23; Fowler, article "Subjunctives"; Fries, pp. 103-107; Jespersen, Ch. 27; Marckwardt and Walcott, pp. 30, 37, 88, 89; Pooley, pp. 55–59

Exercises

1. Correct any faults in verb forms that you find in the following sentences. Write "C" after the number of a sentence if the verb form is correct.

1) Imagine that you—or anyone else, for that matter—was faced with a similar situation.

2) When I was a child, the summer months use to seem much longer than they do now.

3) The chairman recommended that the meeting be adjourned until the following day.

4) Sam kept pumping more and more air until I thought the inner tube would surely bust in his face.

5) Years later, when she returned to her home town, every-thing—the buildings, the streets, even the people—seem to have shrank.

6) No sooner had he examined the flimsy evidence than the judge throwed the case out of court.

7) The campus looks deserted today, don't it?

8) Educational programs have been regularly broadcast by at least two local radio stations.

9) Our "Meet Your Neighbor" program would of been more successful had we received more cooperation from the new mem-bers of the community.

10) I am raising a perfectly valid question, aren't I?

2. Supply the proper form of the verb in parentheses in each of these sentences. If more than one form is acceptable, explain in what circumstances each might be used.

1) If you had (go) by plane, you would have arrived five hours earlier.

2) Pictures should be (hang) slightly above eye level.

3) He was suddenly (wake) by the wail of sirens.

4) I wish now I had (choose) my courses more carefully when I registered.

5) The mile was first (run) in less than four minutes by Dr. Roger Bannister, an Englishman, in 1954.

6) The moment after the engine caught fire, the pilot (dive) the plane to extinguish the blaze.

7) In recent years the annual Harvest Festival has not (prove) to be as successful as we hoped.

8) The senator suggested that the mistakes of the past be now (forget).

9) Virginia had just (begin) to study when someone knocked at the door.

10) When they finally returned from the ice rink, their faces were nearly (freeze).

3. Correct any shifts or errors in tense that you find in the following sentences by rewriting the sentence and underlining the changes you have made. Write "C" after the number of any sentence that is correct as it stands.

1) But whenever it comes time to vote, you always heard Perry complain, "My vote won't mean a thing."

2) Statistics made public at a recent medical convention indicate that excessive cigarette smoking had tended to shorten life.

3) Everyone in town knew or should have known by this time that the Geyers are visiting us.

4) They intended to have stayed only a week at Miami.

5) A year ago I knew I would never marry; today I am not so certain; and in three more years I'll probably have a wife, a child, and a heavy mortgage on a home.

6) If Mary's inherent goodness had ever been pointed out to her, she would be the first to deny it.

7) He was about to sink for the third time, when one of the members of our fishing party suddenly sees him.

8) Even though the President should veto the bill, the minority party undoubtedly intends to bring it up in the next session of Congress.

9) Liz would have like to have had her hair cut in a more popular fashion, but her mother wouldn't let her.

10) Although this essay was written two hundred years ago, the facts are as true today as they were then.

4. This exercise will test your knowledge of grammatical terms frequently used in discussing verb forms. Make up two sentences

of your own (ten in all) illustrating clearly and briefly the terms indicated. You may use any tense of the verb, but be sure to underline the verb in each of your sentences.

1) Two sentences, using *sing* in the first as a transitive verb, in the second as an intransitive verb

2) Two sentences, with the main verb *eat* in the active voice in the first, in the passive voice in the second

3) Two sentences, using *grow* as a linking verb in the first, and as a verb with an object in the second

4) Two sentences, with the verb *be* in the indicative mood in the first, and in the subjunctive mood in the second

5) Two sentences, using a form of *go* as a participle in the first, and as a gerund in the second

5. Rewrite the following sentences, using *have, has,* or *had,* with the proper form of the italicized verb in each sentence, and making any other necessary changes.

1) The newsboy complained that the same dog *bit* him twice before.

2) For centuries the treasures of the Pharaohs *lay* buried.

3) Old Pete *wrings* sympathy and money from almost everyone by his pitiful stories.

4) A few members of the club *swim* the straits every year on New Year's Day.

5) Polls show that popular opinion *is swinging* toward daylight saving time.

6) After the bread *rises,* it is ready to bake.

7) *Did* you ever *see* anything as spectacular as the Grand Canyon?

8) Once each year the village bells *ring* in memory of the Liberation.

9) Two hens, both Plymouth Rocks, *lay* more eggs than the rest of the flock combined.

10) Mrs. Greene *bears* her misfortunes with great fortitude.

27 Nouns

A noun names a person, place, thing, quality, action, idea: *George Washington, Spain, home, beauty, hunting, justice.* The tables on the following page show the different forms of nouns (as *boy, boy's, boys*) and their functions (as subject, as objects, and so on).

27.1 Genitive case In English, nouns have two case forms, the common form (*Jacob, lambs, dictionary*) and the genitive, which can be made by an apostrophe (*Jacob's, lambs', dictionary's*) or by a phrase with *of* (*of Jacob, of the lambs, of the dictionary*).

27.1a Uses of the genitive The genitive case of nouns is commonly called the "possessive," because its most frequent function is to show possession (a *student's* books; a mannerism *of the professor*). But the genitive case also shows other relationships:

> Description: a *day's* work, a suit *of wool,* last *night's* newspaper.
> Doer of an act (or "subjective genitive"): the *wind's* force, with the permission *of the dean,* the *dean's* permission.
> Recipient of an act ("objective genitive"): the *bill's* defeat, the execution *of a spy.*
> Subject of a gerund: the *doctor's* warning, the *play's* closing.

27.1b Apostrophe with genitives When a noun is pronounced with an added *s* or *z* sound, the spelling for the genitive case is *'s: man's, men's, horse's, ship's, George's.*

When there is no added sound the apostrophe alone is generally used, as in singular nouns ending in an *s, sh,* or *z* sound, and in regular plurals ending in *s:*

Singular	*Plural*
hostess'	hostesses'
princess'	princesses'
Jones'	Joneses'

Noun forms

Case forms: Nouns in English have only two distinguishable case forms: the basic or "common" form (*boy, Harriet, gentleman*) and the genitive or "possessive" form, usually made by adding *'s* to the basic form (*boy's, Harriet's, gentleman's*). See §27.1.

Singular and plural: The plural of most nouns is formed by adding *-s* to the singular: *book, books; mother, mothers.* For other forms, see §27.2.

Compound nouns: Two or more nouns that function as a single unit are called a compound noun (or group word): *bookcase, pine tree.* Some are written solid (*football*), others as two words (*high school*), and some are hyphened (*father-in-law*). See §39.1.

Gender: A very few nouns in English show gender, with one form for the masculine and another for the feminine: *actor, actress; comedian, comedienne; aviator, aviatrix.*

Functions of nouns

Nouns are used in statements in the following ways:

As subjects of verbs (§13.1a): The *tires* (S) squealed (V) as the *car* (S) skidded (V) around the corner.

As objects of verbs and prepositions (§§13.1c, 13.3b): man bites (V) *dog* (O); inside (P) the *tent* (O); among (P) *friends* (O).

As complements (predicate nouns) after linking verbs (§13.1d): A whale is (LV) a *mammal* (C); He became (LV) *president* (C) of the firm.

As indirect objects, words that name the receiver of something after verbs like *ask, tell, give,* and that come before the direct object (§13.1c): He gave the *church* (IO) a memorial window (O).

As appositives, nouns that describe or further identify the expression to which they are added (§13.4b): Mr. McDermott, *the insurance agent* (A), is here; The term *unilateral* (A) means affecting one side only.

As modifiers of other words or of statements: *Mrs. Tyler's* car; a *cigaret* holder; *Each year* we make new resolutions.

See §15.3 for noun clauses.

The apostrophe is not used in some expressions in which the plural noun may be considered as an adjective: *teachers* college, *Veterans* Administration, *United Nations* program.

27.1c Apostrophe with nouns in series and group words To show individual possession with two coordinate nouns (joined by *and, but, or, nor*) the genitive form is used for both nouns (*Barbara's and Tommy's* bicycles). To show joint possession the genitive is used for the last term only (*Barbara and Tommy's* mother).

With group words or compound nouns the *'s* is added to the last term: the King of England's duties, his mother-in-law's address, sisters-in-law's attitude, the attorney general's responsibility.

27.1d Of phrases and 's forms The *'s* form of a noun modifier is customarily used with living things (my *uncle's* house, a *cat's* paw, a *robin's* nest) and an *of* phrase with inanimate objects (the door *of the room,* an angle *of inclination,* the beginning *of the end*). But in many instances either form may be used, the choice depending largely upon the sound of the expression.

> The *doctor's* visiting hours *or* The visiting hours *of the doctor*
> The *book's* cover *or* The cover *of the book*
> The *ship's* log *or* The log *of the ship*

Some idiomatic expressions are stated in one form only (a *week's* wages, a *moment's* hesitation; an embarrassment *of riches,* the wages *of sin*). In a few statements both forms (called the "double genitive") are used, a practice of long and respectable standing in General English:

> that boy *of Henry's,* some friends *of father's,* those hobbies *of my cousin's*

27.1e Awkward use of genitive forms An *of* phrase is sometimes preferable to an *'s* form to avoid a clumsy or unidiomatic expression, or a statement that may be ambiguous. When the modifying noun is separated from the word it refers to by a phrase or a clause, an *of* phrase should be used:

The hat *of the man* who got on the bus was obviously not his.
Not: The man who got on the bus's hat. . . .
Nor: The man's hat who got on the bus. . . .

The *of* phrase is useful in distinguishing between the recipient and the doer of an act (between the subjective and objective genitive), particularly if the meaning isn't made clear in context. *Miss Rutherford's picture* might mean either a picture of her or a picture belonging to her; but *a picture of Miss Rutherford* would ordinarily mean a portrait of her.

A writer should be careful when using an *of* phrase for the genitive to place it near the word that it modifies; otherwise strange results may occur:

Inaccurate	*Accurate*
Wanted: High school girl to care for children of some experience.	Wanted: High school girl of some experience to care for children.

27.2 Plurals of nouns The typical plural of a noun is made by adding -*s* or -*es* (*cats, bushes*). Nouns ending in -*y* preceded by a consonant change the -*y* to -*i*, as in *babies, caddies, enemies*. The plural of words ending in -*o* or -*f* varies (*dynamos, Negroes; beliefs, halves*); these words are discussed in §§45.3g and 45.3h, pp. 468–469.

There are three groups of exceptions to the -*s* ending, preserving older methods of forming the plural:

1. A few nouns ending in -*en*, as in *children, oxen*
2. A few with change of vowel, as in *feet, geese, mice*
3. Some nouns with the same form for both singular and plural: (a) all words ending in -*ics*: *athletics, civics, mathematics*; (b) names of some animals: *deer, fish, mink, sheep*; (c) a number of words rarely or never used in the singular, such as *barracks, headquarters, measles, pants*

The following sections present other groups of plurals likely to raise questions.

27.2a Group words and compound nouns Most compound words and group words form their plurals by adding -*s* to the last word of the group, whether the expression is written as one word or two:

Singular	Plural
baby sitter	baby sitters
cross-examination	cross-examinations
high school	high schools
major general	major generals
vice-president	vice-presidents

But when the significant word is the first term (as it often is in hyphened compounds), the plural sign is added to it:

daughters-in-law	mothers-in-law
kings of England	passers-by
men-of-war	presidents-elect

The plural of nouns ending in -ful is made by adding -s to the last part of the word: two *cupfuls*, three *tablespoonfuls*.

27.2b Words with foreign plurals Some nouns have two forms for the plural: the foreign plural and the Anglicized form ending in -s or -es. The foreign plural is characteristic of Formal usage, particularly in scientific and academic writing:

Singular	Formal plural	General plural
antenna	antennae (zoology)	antennas (radio, TV)
apparatus	apparatus	apparatuses
appendix	appendices	appendixes
cactus	cacti	cactuses
curriculum	curricula	curriculums
formula	formulae	formulas
index	indices	indexes
medium	media	mediums
radius	radii	radiuses
sanatorium	sanatoria	sanatoriums
stratum	strata	stratums
syllabus	syllabi	syllabuses
vertebra	vertebrae	vertebras

Certain nouns derived from Greek or Latin and ending in -is form their plurals by changing -is to -es:

Singular	Plural	Singular	Plural
analysis	analyses	neurosis	neuroses
axis	axes	parenthesis	parentheses
basis	bases	psychosis	psychoses
crisis	crises	synopsis	synopses
diagnosis	diagnoses	thesis	theses

27.2c Alumnus, -ni, -na, -nae   The word for a person who has been graduated from a college has four forms:

One male graduate is an	alumnus	(ə lum′nəs)
Two or more male graduates are	alumni	(ə lum′nī)
One female graduate is an	alumna	(ə lum′nə)
Two or more female graduates are	alumnae	(ə lum′nē)

The simplest way out of this confusion of forms is to use the term *graduate* or *graduates.*

27.3 A and an with nouns   *A* is used before words beginning with a consonant *sound:*

a car	a European country	a *D*	a used car

An is used before words beginning with a vowel *sound:*

an ape	an *F*	an hour	an honor	an oar

27.4 Unidiomatic noun modifiers   When an adjective is the customary form in an expression, it should be used in place of a clumsy or unidiomatic noun modifier:

> Price took his *doctor* training at Northwestern. [better: his *medical* training]
>
> After sparking his team to victory in the city [not *civic*] championship, Les went on to play with a *Canada* team. [better: a *Canadian* team]

But for words that do not have exact adjective equivalents, the noun forms are freely used as modifiers: a *murder* mystery, *kitchen* utensils, *radio* reception, *prison* walls. In some expressions either the noun or adjective form may be used: *atom* bomb, *atomic* bomb. Notice that noun modifiers—particularly when used as units of measurement—are treated as singular forms: a ten-*ton* truck, a six-*foot* jump. (Used as nouns, the forms would be plural: ten *tons* of coal, a jump of six *feet*.)

Exercises

1. Indicate which of the italicized nouns in these sentences are correctly written with -s endings and which should have -'s or -s' endings, and briefly explain why.

1) When I told mother I wanted a sweater just like *Pats,* she exploded, "For *goodness* sake, why?"

2) The Legislative *Councils* subcommittee agreed that certification of *teachers* is in need of revision.

3) Keeping up with the mythical *Joneses* puts too great a strain on most *peoples* pocketbooks.

4) For the accurate spelling of little known geographical place *names* within our borders, the *United States* Postal Guide is most helpful.

5) Parents too often fail to understand the problems confronting *boys* in their early *teens.*

6) The bus line was only a two *minutes* walk from the sorority house, but most of the *girls* preferred to take taxis rather than wait for the *buses.*

7) The *Hells* Canyon project was argued for months in the editorial pages of many leading *newspapers.*

8) I prefer *Keats* poetry to *Shelleys* because it is closer to my own experiences.

2. Read each sentence and then select the form you consider appropriate. If the choice is optional, explain in what contexts both forms might be used. Consult your dictionary, if necessary, to see what plural forms are in use.

1) These all-band television (antennae, antennas) with either eight- or ten-(foot, feet) masts are no more difficult to install than aerials for most (radios, radioes).

2) While it isn't difficult to get (synopsis, synopses) of the classics, it is much better to read the works themselves if you wish to have adequate (basis, bases) for comparison.

3) The sudden flowering of countless varieties of (cactuses,

cacti) is a (phenomena, phenomenon) that never fails to delight those who visit the Southwest deserts in the spring.

4) None of the (stadia, stadiums) I saw at various (campuses, campi) throughout the nation were half as attractive as ours.

5) The (hanger-ons, hangers-on) down at the City Hall this time of year are thick as (leaves, leafs) in fall.

6) A recent (analysis, analyses) of medical directories shows that (woman, women) doctors are twice as numerous today as they were twenty years ago.

7) My fraternity (brothers, brethren) had planned an elaborate stag party for some of the more distinguished (alumnus, alumnuses, alumnae, alumni) on the eve of the homecoming game.

8) The girls were cutting graceful figure (eight's, eights) on the ice, their (scarfs, scarves) whipping like pennants.

9) Stan had an enormous appetite and would eat as many as five (platesful, platefuls) of (calf's, calves, calf) liver and bacon.

10) Women interested in home (economic, economics) research may follow one of two (curricula, curriculums).

3. Rewrite the following sentences, making the changes indicated in the directions and whatever others are necessary as a result of the first one. Underline each noun form that you change.

1) Make *baby* plural: The next task of the nurse is to prepare the baby's formula.

2) Change *brother* to *brother-in-law*: My brother's favorite poem is "Dover Beach."

3) Use *the hostess* in place of *her*: When the guests arrived, her table was already set.

4) Change *This* to *These*: This belief found little sympathy among the general public.

5) Change *A* to *A series of*: A crisis occurred just before the performance.

6) Change *children* to *Kathy and Jimmy*: Every Saturday night Dad would shine the children's shoes.

7) Omit *a*: Then as now, a congressman's mail included hundreds of letters from cranks.

8) Change *Neither* to *Both:* Neither chairman had any adequate basis for such a change in procedure.

9) Change *one* to *three:* I next add one cupful of crushed tomato and bring the mixture to a boil.

10) Omit *the:* Tim became curious about the mongoose after reading Kipling's *Jungle Books.*

4. See how well you understand the grammatical terms in the table "Functions of nouns" on page 346 by identifying the function of each of the italicized nouns in these sentences (as subjects of verbs, as objects of verbs or prepositions, as predicate nouns, and so on).

1) The first settler, *Thomas Sanborn,* later became the *leader* of the colonists.

2) Other *arguments* for lowering the voting age might have been mentioned, but they weren't discussed in *Congress.*

3) Judo as a spectator sport will probably never attain the *popularity* of boxing or wrestling in this *country.*

4) The object that Bob found was not a *flying saucer* but only a *hub cap.*

5) Sally gave her *escort* a cold *glance.*

6) The registrar's office was as crowded as a *New York* subway at *five o'clock.*

7) As I watched the parent who was punishing his *child* in public, I wondered what the *child's* reaction was.

8) A *look* at some Eastern colleges will illustrate this *problem.*

9) The hotel offers its *guests* a *choice* of daily or weekly rates.

10) Art also built his own *television set,* using a neon lamp in place of a cathode-ray *tube.*

28 Pronouns

A pronoun refers to a person, object, or idea without naming it: *He* has arrived; Put *it* there; *Who* is coming? *This* interests me; *Somebody* is listening; *Three* will be enough.

Kinds of pronouns

Personal pronouns

	Subject	Object	Possessive
First person			
Singular	I	me	my, mine
Plural	we	us	our, ours
Second person			
Singular	you	you	your, yours
Plural	you	you	your, yours
Third person			
Singular			
masculine	he	him	his
feminine	she	her	her, hers
neuter	it	it	its (of it)
either gender	one	one	one's
Plural	they	them	their, theirs

Relative pronouns

who	whom	whose
that	that	
which	which	whose, of which

Interrogative pronouns

who	whom	whose
which	which	whose, of which
what	what	

Reflexive pronouns (referring back to the subject)
myself, yourself, himself, herself, itself, oneself
ourselves, yourselves, themselves

Demonstrative pronouns: this, this one, these; that, that one, those

Indefinite pronouns

all	both	everything	nobody	several
another	each	few	none	some
any	each one	many	no one	somebody
anybody	either	most	nothing	someone
anyone	everybody	much	one	something
anything	everyone	neither	other	such

Reciprocal pronouns: each other, one another

Numeral pronouns: one, two, three . . . first, second, third . . .

Pronouns are used more exactly in writing than in speaking and should be checked carefully for proper form and reference in revising a paper. The table on the opposite page lists the various kinds of pronouns and their forms.

28.1 Pronouns referring to specific nouns

Ref **Reference of pronouns. Correction: Change the pronoun marked (or revise the sentence) so that its reference will be exact and obvious (§§28.2, 28.3).**

When the meaning of a pronoun is completed by referring to an antecedent (a specific noun for which the pronoun stands), the reference should be exact and obvious:

> The first hundred miles, *which* we covered before lunch, were rough, but *they* seemed to go faster than the sixty we did in the afternoon. [*Miles* is the antecedent of the pronouns *which* and *they*.]

28.1a With clearly stated antecedent   The antecedent of a pronoun should be a definite noun, not one that is implied:

Inexact	*Accurate*
The other fellow enlisted for four years and spent one year of *it* in Korea. [no antecedent for *it*]	The other fellow's enlistment was for four years and he spent one year of *it* in Korea. [*Enlistment* is the antecedent of *it*.]

Instead of changing the antecedent, it is often better to substitute a noun for the inexact pronoun:

Inexact	*Accurate*
When we heard that the game was being televised, we turned *it* on, but the game was already over.	When we heard that the game was being televised, we turned on *our set,* but the game was already over.

A simple test for accurate reference is to see whether the antecedent could be substituted for the pronoun:

Inexact	*Accurate*
She talked a lot about the technique of horsemanship, although	She talked a lot about the technique of horsemanship, although

as a matter of fact she had never ridden *one* [horsemanship?] in her life.	as a matter of fact she had never ridden *a horse* in her life.

The antecedent of a pronoun should not be a noun used as an adjective or a noun in the possessive form:

Inaccurate: When building a stone wall, you should select *them* all of the same size. [*Stone* is used as an adjective; for clear reference, substitute a noun for *them*: ". . . select *stones* all of the same size."]

Inaccurate: Bill provided more excitement one afternoon when he was skipping rocks across the swimming hole and cut open a young girl's head *who* was swimming under water. [For clear reference, this should read ". . . and cut open the head of *a young girl* who was swimming under water."]

28.1b With two possible antecedents   When a pronoun seems to refer to two different antecedents, the reference should be made clear, either by substituting a noun for the pronoun or by clarifying the antecedents:

Confusing	*Clear*
When Stanton visited the President in February, *he* did not know that *he* would be dead within two months.	When Stanton visited the President in February, *he* did not know that *Lincoln* would be dead within two months.

Sometimes ambiguous reference may be avoided by making one of the antecedents singular and the other plural:

Ambiguous	*Clear*
In the nineteenth century many business men [plural] exploited the mass of workers [plural] at every point, not caring whether *they* were making a decent living wage, but only whether *they* were getting a lot of money.	In the nineteenth century many business men [plural] exploited the working man [singular] at every point, not caring whether *he* was making a decent living wage, but only whether *they* were getting a lot of money.

Using the same pronoun for different implied antecedents is particularly annoying to a reader and should be avoided:

Confusing	Revised
We pulled out our spare, which was under the seat, and put *it* on. *It* dampened our spirits for a while, but we decided to try *it* again. [The first *it* refers to the tire, the second to the mishap, the third to the trip.]	We pulled out our spare, which was under the seat, and put it on. The mishap dampened our spirits for a while, but we decided to go on.

Identifying the antecedent by repeating it after the pronoun is a makeshift practice, and should be avoided by revision.

Clumsy	Revised
Boswell first met Johnson when he (Johnson) was fifty-four.	Johnson was fifty-four when Boswell first met him.

28.1c Reference clear from context   The antecedent of a pronoun may be obvious from the meaning of a statement (Craig asked the dean for permission to be absent for the first part of the week, but *he* refused to give it to *him*). In such instances it is unnecessary to repeat the antecedent.

28.1d *He or she*   When reference is made to a noun or pronoun that includes persons of both sexes (*student, teacher, clerk, everyone, anyone, somebody*), the most satisfactory method is to use the pronoun *he* or *his*:

Each entering freshman is required to report promptly for *his* scheduled physical examination.

It is the duty of everyone who is eligible to vote to make certain that *he* has registered before the national election.

When practically all of the group referred to are women, *she* is used:

A home economics major often finds that more work is expected of *her* than *she* anticipated.

The phrase *his or her* is almost always clumsy and no more accurate since the meaning is determined by the antecedent.

Clumsy: Every student wants to participate in some activity authorized by *his or her* college. ["By *his* college" would be better even if
the reference is to a coeducational school.]

Clumsy: I am sure that every reader of this book will find *his or her*
time well spent.

Revised: I am sure that every reader of this book will find *his* time
well spent.

28.2   Referring to indefinite pronouns   A number of words of
greater or less indefiniteness often function as pronouns:
some, all, none, everybody, somebody, anybody, anyone.
Some of these words are considered singular in form; others
may be singular or plural, depending upon the meaning of
the statement. A writer should be careful in revising his
papers to see that the verb and other reference words agree
in number with indefinite pronouns.

28.2a   Everyone, anybody, somebody   *Everyone, everybody,
anybody, somebody, nobody* are singular forms and are used
with singular verbs (Everybody has left; Somebody was here;
Nobody ever calls).

There is frequently a difference between spoken and written usage in the form of the pronouns used with these words.
A singular reference word is Standard usage in writing
(Everyone brought *his* book), but in spoken usage where
agreement is based upon meaning more than on form, a
plural reference word is often used.

Spoken	*Written*
Not everyone is as prompt at paying *their* bills as you are.	Not everyone is as prompt at paying *his* bills as you are.
Someone has forgotten *their* hat and coat.	Someone has forgotten *his* hat and coat.

In some statements, however, a singular reference word
would be puzzling or nonsensical with the indefinite pronoun:

When I finally managed to get to my feet, everybody was laughing
at me, and I couldn't blame *them* [*him* would be impossible] because I
was a funny sight.

References: Marckwardt and Walcott, pp. 38, 74; Fries, p. 50; Roberts, pp. 86-88

28.2b ***All, some, none*** *All, any, some, most, more,* are either singular or plural, depending upon the meaning of the statement:

> All of the turkey *has* been eaten.
> All of these questions *need* restating.
> Some of the dialog *is* witty.
> Some of the farmers *have* refused to sell their crops until the price is stabilized.

None may be either singular or plural, but in current usage it is more often used with a plural verb:

> Of all the national parks in this country, none *are* [or *is*] more unspoiled than Glacier.
> The council made headlines with a series of shocking charges, none of which *have* [or *has*] been substantiated.
> I looked at half a dozen books on the subject but none *were* of any use to me.

28.2c ***Each*** *Each* is a singular pronoun and takes a singular verb and singular reference words:

> *Each* of the so-called modern composers *has his* own ideas about the principles of tonality.
> Every June a thousand brides wear identical gowns and *each thinks hers* is somehow unique.

The use of the plural form to refer to *each* is considered Informal (*Each* of the boys ran as fast as *their* legs could carry *them*), but this construction is sometimes found in writing when the plural idea is uppermost:

> *Each* of these peoples undoubtedly modified Latin in accordance with *their* own speech habits.—Albert C. Baugh, *History of the English Language,* p. 35

But unless a writer is prepared to justify his use of plural forms with *each*, he should use singular verbs and pronouns with it.

Reference: Russell Thomas, "Concord Based on *Meaning* Versus Concord Based on *Form*," *College English*, 1939, 1:38-45

28.3 Pronouns referring to ideas and statements   *This, that, which,* and *it* are regularly used to refer to ideas or situations expressed in preceding statements:

> Always do right. *This* will gratify some people and astonish the rest. —Mark Twain

> Bits of thread were still dangling from the front of my gown, but we did not bother about *that*.—David Daiches, "A Matter of Degree," *The New Yorker*, May 10, 1952, p. 64

> For "human relations," unfortunately, had generally applied only to relations below that rather vague level called "management," *which* is, in a sense, going at the problem backwards.—William W. Whyte, Jr., *Is Anybody Listening?* p. 111

The thing to watch when using pronouns for general reference in these situations is that the ideas to which they refer are clearly indicated.

Pron   Pronoun. Correction: Change the form of the pronoun marked to the one required by the construction (§§28.4, 28.5).

28.4 Subject and object pronouns   Most personal pronouns and the relative pronoun *who* have one form when they are used as subjects (*I, she, he, we, they, who*) and another when they are used as objects (*me, her, him, us, them, whom*). The distinction between these forms is often disregarded in speech (There were no secrets between Mother and *I*), but writers are expected to follow conventional use (There were no secrets between Mother and *me*).

28.4a After prepositions   The object form of a personal pronoun is used after a preposition (a letter for *him*; among *us* three). When a pronoun immediately follows a preposition, there is seldom any question about the proper form, but when there are two pronouns, or when a noun is used with the pronoun, writers are sometimes tempted to use a subject form, as Vulgate usage frequently does.

Nonstandard	*Standard*
After all, those men are human beings like you and *I*.	After all, those men are human beings like you and *me*.
The same is no doubt true of what European and Asiatic nations have heard about *we* Americans.	The same is no doubt true of what European and Asiatic nations have heard about *us* Americans.
The work was divided between *she* and *I*.	The work was divided between *her* and *me*.

In Formal English *than* is considered a conjunction, not a preposition, and is followed by the subject form of a pronoun, whether or not a verb appears in the construction (I am older than *she* is; I am older than *she*). In speech the object form is common with *than* when the pronoun stands alone (I am older than *her*; My roommate was taking more courses than *me*).

In college writing the subject form is preferable in these constructions, but the object form is by no means uncommon among reputable writers.

Although he was two years older she had grown faster than *him*, and in the summer they used to wrestle and fight out on the plot of grass by the street.—Carson McCullers, *The Heart Is a Lonely Hunter*, Part II, Ch. 1

References: Marckwardt and Walcott, pp. 40, 42, 79; Jespersen, p. 133

28.4b *It's me, it is I* Formal English prefers using the subject form after the linking verb *be* (It is I). But educated as well as uneducated people usually say and write "It's me."

Me is more natural in this expression because the pronoun stands in the object position, immediately after the verb. All authoritative grammars and dictionaries consider *it's me* acceptable General usage.

The notion that *I* is somehow more "correct" or polite than *me* sometimes leads people to use the subject form even when the pronoun is the object of a verb: Father promised to take you and *I* to the game. The object form should be used in such constructions: Father promised to take you and *me* to the game.

28.4c Who, whom *Whom* is the Standard form when it appears immediately after a preposition (To *whom* were you speaking?; He was a man in *whom* we placed great trust). In other constructions, usage is divided:

Formal: *Whom* are you taking to the concert? [*Whom* is the object of the verb *are taking*.]
General: *Who* are you taking to the game? [Since it stands first, in the subject position, *who* seems the natural form to use.]
Formal: No matter *whom* one meets, the first thing one mentions is the weather. [*Whom* is the object of the verb *meets*.]
General: No matter *who* you meet, the first thing mentioned is the weather.

Often *whom* is misused for *who* (*Whomever* can that be phoning at this hour?). A writer should use *who* when it serves as the subject of a verb:

He made a list of all the writers *who* [subject of *were*] he thought were important in that century.
There was little doubt about *who* [subject of *contributed*] contributed most to the campaign.

The distinction between *who* and *whom* has practically dropped from speech (the *Oxford English Dictionary* says *whom* is "no longer current in natural colloquial speech"), and it may eventually disappear in writing. But here, as elsewhere in matters of disputed usage, college students are expected to know which form is considered more correct, and not to follow Informal usage except in distinctly Informal papers.

References: Fries, pp. 88-96; Pooley, pp. 72-77, 221

28.4d Reflexive pronouns   Reflexive pronouns are used to refer back to the subject (He shaves *himself*) and as intensives for emphasis (We were met at the door by the governor *himself*).

In certain constructions *myself* is mistakenly considered by some people as more polite than *I* or *me* (My wife and *myself* accept with pleasure), but in Standard English the reflexive form is not used as the subject, or as a substitute for *me*:

> Another fellow and *I* [not: *myself*] saw the whole thing.
> Sam invited John and *me* [not: *myself*] to dinner.

Himself and *themselves* are Standard English forms. *Hisself* and *theirselves* are Vulgate.

References: Josephine Burnham, "The -*self* Forms as Personal Pronouns," *American Speech*, December 1950, 25:264-267

28.5 Possessive pronouns   In writing, the chief problem in the use of possessive forms of pronouns is the apostrophe. Writers should remember that an apostrophe is not used with the possessives of personal pronouns (a relative of *ours*; the tree and *its* leaves), nor with the relative pronoun *who* (a boy *whose* name was Tom).

28.5a My or of mine   Personal pronouns have two forms for the possessive (see p. 354): one used as a modifier before the noun (*my* roommate, *her* favorite hat) and the other, after the noun by itself or in a phrase (That pencil is *mine*; a friend of *hers*).

While either form may be used in many statements (*our* government, this government of *ours*), there are some constructions in which one form is obviously better than the other:

Clumsy	*Standard*
I picked this college because of the location *of it*.	I picked this college because of *its* location.
We decided to pool *their* and *our* resources.	We decided to pool their resources with *ours*.

Careless use of the possessive may lead to ambiguous statements, when, for example, the doer of the action seems to be the receiver:

Mrs. Hurst was a very popular woman and *her accusation* scandalized everyone in town [either: *the accusation she made* or *the accusation made about her*].

28.5b Its, it's *Its* without the apostrophe is the possessive form of *it; it's* with the apostrophe is the contraction for *it is:*

Everything should be in *its* proper place.
It's an ill wind that blows no good.
It's a pretty good car, but *its* motor could stand overhauling.

One of the mistakes most frequently marked on student papers is using *it's* for *its*. It is a good idea for writers who habitually confuse these two forms to check each instance of *its* (*it's*) when revising papers.

28.5c Possessive of indefinite pronouns Several of the indefinite pronouns, (*all, any, each, few, most, none, some*) are used in *of* phrases for the possessive:

They were both happy when things were going well, but adversity brought out the best side *of each*. [not *each's* best side]

The apostrophe and *-s* are used with the possessive forms of other indefinite pronouns, just as they are with nouns:

Anyone's guess is as good as mine.
One man's meat is *another's* poison.
Somebody's books were left in the classroom.

When indefinite pronouns are used with *else*, the apostrophe *-s* is added to *else* and not to the preceding word:

These notes are somebody *else's*.
Anyone *else's* offer would have been accepted.

28.5d Whose, of which While *whose* most often refers to persons and *which* to things, *whose* is regularly used to refer to inanimate things when *of which* would be awkward.

In the 'twenties Hemingway brought to the language of the novel a style *whose* originality no contemporary can match. . . .—William Barrett, "American Fiction and American Values," *Partisan Review,* November-December 1951, p. 684

. . . we would cross a room in which no one ever sat, *whose* fire was never lighted, *whose* walls were picked out with gilded mouldings. . . . —Marcel Proust, *Remembrance of Things Past,* 1:55

The possessive form of the relative pronoun *who* is *whose. Who's* is the colloquial contraction for *who is* and it is not used in most writing.

Best known of American primitives is Grandma Moses, *whose* paintings are familiar to thousands.

It is the white-collar worker *who is* [colloquial: *who's*] least likely to be affected by seasonal unemployment.

28.6 Use of personal pronouns Personal pronouns indicate the person or persons speaking (first person: *I, we*), the person spoken to (second person: *you*), or the person or thing spoken of (third person: *he, she, it, one; they*). In writing, the choice of form may be a problem since the writer can refer to himself as *I, one,* or *we.* Some questions that frequently arise in using these pronouns are considered here.

28.6a I, we There is no reason to avoid using the pronoun *I* in any situation where it is needed. Some writers, perhaps through excessive modesty, try to get around the natural use of *I* by devices that only call attention to themselves.

Although believing in the value of work, the writer does not believe [better: I do not believe] in labor for labor's sake.

After examining several college catalogs, the decision was reached [better: I decided] to apply at the state university.

We is useful for general reference (*We* are living in an atomic age), but as a substitute for *I,* the "editorial" *we* is out of place in most writing.

We [better: *I*] have stated earlier in our [*my*] paper that *we* [*I*] firmly believe in the present economic system with its competition and free enterprise.

28.6b **One**   In current American usage, it is standard practice to refer to *one* (meaning the writer or anyone) by *he* and *his* (or *she* and *her*):

> *One* is warned to be cautious if *he* would avoid offending *his* friends and thus bring down their displeasure upon *his* head.

One is used, particularly in Formal English, to refer either to people in general or to the writer:

> *One* can't be too careful, can *one?*
> Watching the scene on television, *one* senses the drama of the situation.

But *one* is impersonal, rather stiff, and not characteristic of General English:

> *You* [or *We*] can't be too careful, can *you* [*we*]?
> Watching the scene on television, *I* [or *you*] sense the drama of the situation.

28.6c **Consistent use of we, you, one**   When using pronouns for general reference, a writer should be consistent and not make unnecessary shifts from singular to plural forms or from *we* to *you* or *one*.

Inconsistent	*Consistent*
After *one* has selected the boat *he* is going to learn in, it would be a good idea if *you* would first learn the theory of sailing. Most of *us* have at least seen a sailing boat, but seeing one and sailing one are two different things. *One* might think that a boat can sail only with the breeze and not against it. Or *they* might think that a stiff breeze is needed to sail.	After *you* have selected the boat *you* are going to learn in, it would be a good idea if *you* first learned the theory of sailing. *You* have probably seen a sailing boat, but seeing one and sailing one are two different things. *You* may think that a boat can sail only with the breeze and not against it. Or *you* may think that a stiff breeze is necessary to sail a boat.

The pronoun *one* is more likely to lead to shifted constructions than are the other forms. Unless a writer intends to be impersonal and also feels confident in his use of *one*, he should use *you*, *we*, *he*, or a noun substitute in these situations.

28.6d Avoiding the use of pronouns Because it is easy ᵗ mistakes in using pronouns, some people try to avoiᵈ But this, in itself is a more serious mistake because th is stiff and unattractive writing:

The speaker was Senator Smith, who was here for a reception in connection with a book written by *the Senator*. [better: in connection with a book *he* had written]

Avoiding pronouns not only results in repetition of nouns but also loses the effect of continuity of thought that pronouns give to sentences. Notice how the italicized pronouns in this passage bind the statements together:

If the history of the earth's tides should one day be written by some observer of the universe, it would no doubt be said that *they* reached *their* greatest grandeur and power in the younger days of Earth, and that *they* slowly grew feebler and less imposing until one day *they* ceased to be. For the tides were not always as *they* are today, and as with all that is earthly, *their* days are numbered.—Rachel L. Carson, *The Sea Around Us,* p. 157

Exercises

1. Revise each of the following sentences in which the reference of pronouns seems to you inexact, misleading, or otherwise faulty. If you leave a sentence unchanged, explain why you think it is satisfactory as it stands.

1) Some of the classes are so large that it is impossible for the professors to remember their names or even their faces.

2) Polonius gives this pompous advice to his son just before he leaves Denmark.

3) International law was profoundly affected by World War II in all its phases.

4) The bookcase shelves should be adjustable so that the tall ones will fit as neatly as those of standard size.

5) In most campaign speeches it isn't what you say but how loudly you can say it that counts.

6) Today most people are so accustomed to flying that they seldom look up when one of them flies overhead.

7) The rules governing freshman dances are always a target for criticism, those directly concerned being the most vociferous.

8) One waitress would wipe the lipstick off the glasses with her fingers, and then, without washing them, put them in the steam sterilizer.

9) Anyone who likes to spend his vacation climbing mountains can get more than his share of it at Camp Kill-Kare.

10) My liking for my roommate soon developed into a warm friendship and today she is one of the best that I have.

2. Follow the directions for the preceding exercise.

1) He mastered dancing with ease and soon became an expert ~~one.~~

2) While sailboats have the right of way over motor boats, this shouldn't be carried to extremes.

3) By this time they had very little food left, but the summit of the mountain looked so near they decided to eat it all up.

4) Science may have cures for almost everything, but they haven't yet come up with one for hiccups.

5) Les told his father that a bill collector was looking for him.

6) The moment after my trousers began to smoulder, it blistered the skin on my legs wherever it touched them.

7) Children can't be expected to take a real interest in school work when they put so much emphasis on grades.

8) Danny glared for a moment at the mirror, then hurling his electric shaver at it, smashed it into a thousand pieces.

9) A swimming pool is available for guests during the summer season, which is one of the most beautiful in this area.

10) At the last moment we were given an extra week to finish our term papers, which was all right with me.

3. Correct every needless shift in the person or number of pronouns in these examples by revising the sentences in which the shifts occur. Put "C" after the number of any sentence that does not need to be revised.

1) Although a rumor may contain some truth, they should never be accepted as fact.

2) The blaze was probably caused by either a careless hunter or a thoughtless fisherman who forgot to extinguish their campfire.

3) My grades, I now realize, will be no better than the amount of time and effort that you are willing to put into your schoolwork.

4) The Army has its problems, just as the Navy and the Air Force have theirs, but they are not so effectively presented to the public.

5) After one has been confined to a hospital bed for six months as I was, you are certain to be a cautious driver for the rest of your life.

6) Next year the Class of '49 will hold its annual reunion at the Broadmoor Hotel on May 1, and everyone who plans to attend should send their reservations as early as possible.

7) The clerk must also be able to give the correct rate for any one of a hundred different items the moment a customer telephones for it.

8) Someone is always taking the joy out of other people's lives by their thoughtless remarks.

9) The trio bowed, cleared their throats, and then announced that for its final number, they would sing "Honeysuckle Rose."

10) One should always keep in close touch with one's distant relatives, for you never can tell when you may be mentioned in someone's will.

4. Select the pronoun form you consider the most appropriate in these sentences and be prepared to justify your choice.

1) If everyone would keep (*his, their, his or her*) wits about (*them, him, him or her*) when someone shouts "Fire!" there would be fewer panics and catastrophes in public meeting places.

2) When we were about to get on the plane, we found that no less than half of the squad had brought more than (*their, its, his, our*) limit of luggage.

3) Some people think that a brisk cold shower before breakfast is the right way to begin the day, but not (*I, me*).

4) By inquiring at the information desk, anyone can find the location of the encyclopedia (*he is, they are, one is*) looking for.

5) There was little doubt about (*who, whom*) would be pledged and (*who, whom*) wouldn't.

6) The first assignment required each of us to prepare a three-minute talk based upon (*his, their, our*) own personal experiences during the summer.

7) It is the duty of every voter, a duty most people avoid, to acquaint (*himself, themselves*) with the candidate's past record.

8) Although there was not the slightest resemblance between (*she and I, her and me, I and her*), people were constantly mistaking us for sisters.

9) Just before the game, the coach had decided to start me at forward without (*me, my*) knowing anything about it.

10) By the end of the day everybody had picked (*his, their*) quota of peas and all that remained was for the supervisor to pay (*them, him*).

5. Rewrite these sentences, changing the italicized words as indicated. Make all other changes which would naturally follow, including those in pronoun, noun, and verb forms. Follow Formal usage throughout.

1) Change *Each* to *All:* Each freshman is asked to indicate the church of his preference on his registration booklet.

2) Change *a person* to *people:* When a person drives on the wrong side of the road, he is endangering the lives of oncoming motorists as well as his own.

3) Change the first *her* to *them:* I considered her a friend of mine, even though I disagreed with her opinions on many subjects.

4) Change *anyone* to *everyone:* Father would greet anyone who knocked at the door, and would make him feel welcome, no matter who it happened to be.

5) Omit *a:* Such a phenomenon can usually be explained if its causes are fully understood.

6) Change *An excuse* to *Excuses:* An excuse of that sort was not acceptable because it had been used before.

7) Change *child* to *children:* The child of divorced parents may feel that he has no real home of his own if he is shunted from one parent to another for six months of each year.

8) Change *Another* to *Other:* Another theater also reports that its receipts have fallen off.

9) Change *One* to *Two:* One of the boys admitted that he was ashamed of himself for the trouble he had caused his parents and friends.

10) Change *This* to *These:* This is the kind of play I prefer because of its happy ending.

6. Correct any errors in the case of pronouns in these sentences according to General usage. Indicate any instance in which another form might be preferred in Formal English. Write "C" by the number of any sentence you consider appropriate at either level.

1) Arrangements have now been made for her and I to attend the State Convention.

2) It is easy for an inexperienced person like me to be confused by such elaborate directions.

3) Just between you and I, Mary considers herself a little better than ordinary people like us.

4) The "common man" is a person who each of us talks about as if we knew him well, but do we really know what we mean by the term?

5) It was then Sheila realized that Trent loved another girl more than he did she.

6) To us citizens of the United States, communism has not the slightest appeal.

7) If you were I, would you accept the position?

8) My family expressed doubts about me earning my own living in a strange city.

9) Some people always think of their own selves and never of others.

10) The prize will be given to whoever submits a correct answer first.

7. This exercise is a general review in pronoun usage, involving reference, case, shifts, and general effectiveness. Revise each sentence in which you think pronouns are inaccurately or awkwardly used, and explain why you made the changes.

1) Miss Pearson was one of those unsympathetic teachers about which my friends had warned me.

2) It says on page 86 that Tasmania exports most of its precious metals.

3) Two months after I borrowed the lawnmower, I received a curt note asking me to return same.

4) Lee is one of those kind of people that always tells a better story than the one you just finished.

5) After the war, the United States replaced Amsterdam, who had a monopoly on the diamond cutting industry of the world for centuries.

6) The sophomores turned out in full force for the tug of war but they didn't have the enthusiasm of we freshmen.

7) After setting Tom's broken leg, the doctor told his father that he wouldn't be able to play football for at least a year.

8) There is an inclination to procrastinate in me that accounts for my low grades.

9) Whether it was the heat or the listless crowd, it certainly had an adverse effect on Chuck's pitching.

10) Mr. McNeir asked Mr. Steele to attend a meeting at his (the former's) office.

11) I enjoy reading Wordsworth's poetry, who was a contemporary of Coleridge.

12) Each day he would go out with his expensive fishing gear, hoping to catch himself a tuna.

13) Not everyone who is employed by the government will find it to their liking.

14) When it was completely folded, the machine resembled a small suitcase having a handle on it, which made it easy to carry it from house to house.

15) Everyone should love his neighbor and do his best for them.

[handwritten annotations: Idiom = a group of words meaning different. Study 373-379. Idiom is a way of expressing a particular idea]

29 Idioms

Id Idiom. Correction: Revise the construction marked to make it idiomatic English.

In English, as in other languages, a great many expressions are stated in fixed phrasal patterns, in words that "go together," such as a particular preposition with a noun or a verb to express a certain idea. We say for example that a person *looks up* a number in the phone book, but that he *looks through* the papers in his wallet, *looks into* a situation, *looks after* his children, and *looks down* his nose at someone.

Expressions like these are called idioms. An *unidiomatic* expression is one that is not typical of the language as it is spoken or written; for instance, *you are right* is idiomatic English, but *you have right* (a literal translation of the French equivalent *vous avez raison*) is not.

The problem in the use of idioms is often not their form but their appropriateness in different levels of writing. An expression may be idiomatically "correct" (like "to go whole hog"), but more characteristic of spoken usage than of General or Formal writing.

Dictionaries list under the key words the accepted or preferred forms of most common idiomatic phrases. However, instead of laboriously checking each time to see whether it is *comply with* or *comply to, acquiesce in* or *acquiesce to,* a writer should learn the idioms by being attentive to the speech and the writing of those who use the language accurately.

29.1 Idiomatic prepositions The appropriate preposition should be used in idiomatic phrases. Avoid redundant prepositions in expressions that do not require them. Following is a list of some common expressions in which the prepositions sometimes cause trouble. Some are appropriate on one level of usage but not on another; those that are Vulgate should be avoided. For expressions not given here, consult a dictionary.

agree to, agree with: You *agree with* a person; you *agree to* a plan or proposal.

as to, about: *About* is the preferred form in expressions like this: "There is no question *about* [or *of* rather than *as to*] the boy's innocence."

beside, besides: *Beside* is a preposition meaning *by the side of*, as "Gretel stood *beside* her mother." *Besides* is an adverb or a preposition meaning *in addition* or *furthermore*: "*Besides* these financial gifts the church also received several baskets of food." "I couldn't afford the trip; *besides*, I had already visited Mexico."

between, among: *Among* implies more than two objects: "For once there was agreement *among* the members of the United Nations." *Between* is typically used with two objects (*between* you and me), but in many expressions it is appropriately used with three or more objects: "What is the difference *between* apt, liable, and likely?"
Reference: Pooley, pp. 135-137

compare to, compare with: *Compare to* means to point out likeness, and *compare with* to find both likenesses and differences: "Who wouldn't be pleased to have his stories *compared to* Maupassant's?" [to have it said that they were like his]; "We were asked to *compare* O'Henry's stories *with* those of Maupassant" [to point out similarities and differences].

correspond to, correspond with: *Correspond to* indicates similarity: "Scotland Yard *corresponds to* our FBI." *Correspond*, meaning to exchange letters, is followed by *with*: "Holmes *corresponded* for many years *with* Lasky."

different from, different than: In writing, *different from* should ordinarily be used since many people consider *different than* Informal usage: "Reynolds' latest book is considerably *different from* others." But *different than* is common when a clause follows: "Army life was *different than* I had expected."
Reference: Gladys D. Haase, *College English*, 1949, 10:345–347

due to: *Due* was originally an adjective, as in "The epidemic was *due* to the brown rat," in which *due* modifies *epidemic*. But rather recently *due to* has come to be used as a preposition (like *owing to*) and is General usage in expressions like "*Due to* the continued tensions of the Cold War, many people live in a state of fear."
Reference: John S. Kenyon, *American Speech*, 1930, 6:61–70

in, into, in to: *In* generally shows location (literal or figurative); *into* generally shows direction: He was *in* the house. He came *into* the house. He was *in* a stupor. He walked *into* the alley. (*In to* is the adverb *in* followed by the preposition *to*: They went *in to* dinner.)

jealous of, jealous about: The proper form is *jealous of*: "Tom was *jealous of* his brother's success."

kind of, kind of a: In General usage *kind, sort, type of* are not followed by *a*: an odd *kind of* hat, this *sort of* boot, my *type of* man. "A new *kind of a* stove" is Informal usage.

on account of: An idiomatic preposition (She stayed home *on account of* her mother's illness) but Vulgate as a conjunction (She didn't wear the dress because [not *on account of*] she couldn't wear green).

prior to: Usually an unnecessarily stiff substitute for *before*: "Before coming here [rather than "*Prior to* coming here"] he had attended Stanford."

regard, in regards to: The appropriate form is *in regard to* or *with regard to*: "What shall we say *in regard to* the innocent bystanders?" *In regards to* is Vulgate.

such as, such that, such a: *Such as* is used to introduce examples with no comma after *as*: "He was interested in outlandish subjects *such as* palmistry, phrenology, and numerology."

Such is used with *that* in clauses of degree or result: "There was *such* a crowd that [not: *so that*] we couldn't get to the door." As an intensive not followed by a *that* clause, *such* is Informal: "It was *such* a lovely day." Because many people object to this construction, it is usually better to use another word or to omit it: "It was a very lovely day" or "It was a lovely day."

Adding the article *a* to *such* in expressions like "no such a word" is Vulgate usage. In writing, the appropriate form is "no such word."

superior to, superior than: The standard idiom is *superior to*: "His early poems are *superior to* [not *superior than*] his later ones."

type of, type of a: See *kind of, kind of a* above.

without, unless: *Without* is a preposition, and is Vulgate when substituted for the adverbial conjunction *unless*: "The pipes will freeze *unless* [not *without*] the water is left running all night."

The use of a doubled preposition where one preposition would be sufficient (as "to arrive at around noon" rather than "to arrive around noon") is more characteristic of spoken than of written usage. Whether a writer should try to avoid all such expressions depends upon his typical style and the general tone of the paper he is writing. But a conspicuous number of doubled prepositions obviously suggests wordiness.

Here are some examples of prepositions that are frequently doubled in speech and in Informal writing:

about, around, and similar words: In expressions such as "about this time" and "around two dollars a yard," another preposition is often added in speech: "*at about* this time," "*at around* two dollars a yard." The extra preposition is superfluous and may just as well be omitted in writing.

off: In a statement like this the *of* is superfluous: "The soldier stepped *off of* the sidewalk." It is better to say "off the sidewalk."

outside of, except: *Outside of* is Informal for *except* or *besides*: "No one cared *except* [not *outside of*] her mother."

A special nuisance is the careless repetition of a preposition at the beginning and end of a construction: She is the one *to* whom I am supposed to look up *to*. One of these should be crossed out, preferably the first.

29.2 Idiomatic verbs Verbs and verb phrases should be both idiomatically correct and appropriate to the general level of a writer's usage. Some of the idiomatic verb forms in this list should be avoided because they are Nonstandard or clumsy. Others are acceptable in Informal or General usage, but are sometimes frowned upon in Formal English.

able to: A clumsy and unidiomatic expression when used with a passive infinitive: "This shirt *can be* [not *is able to be*] washed without shrinkage."

aggravate, irritate: In General usage *aggravate* means to intensify or make worse; *irritate* means to vex or annoy: "The seriousness of his crime was *aggravated* by the prisoner's implication of innocent people." "Stop *irritating* me with those silly questions." Informally *aggravate* is used in the same sense as *irritate*: "I was never so *aggravated* in my life." The distinction between the two words should be observed in college writing.

being that: To introduce a dependent clause of reason or cause, *being that* is a clumsy or unidiomatic substitute for *because, since,* or *for*: "Randy decided to major in pharmacy *because* [not: *being that*] his uncle was a successful pharmacist."

bust, bursted: The verb *bust* is Nonstandard in the sense of smashing, exploding, or losing one's money: "He *busted* out of jail." "I was flat *busted* a week before payday." It is the accepted word in a few idioms like *busting a bronco, to bust a trust,* but in practically all expressions *break* is the General form.

complected: Informal when used for *complexioned*: "He was a dark-*complexioned* [not dark-*complected*] man."

contact: Many people dislike this verb as a substitute for "get in touch with someone," although it is widely used in business: "Will you *contact* our Mr. Hubble?" In General and Formal writing another expression, "call" or "see," is usually used.

enthuse: Dictionaries label this verb colloquial, and prefer *be enthusiastic about* or *to show enthusiasm*. While *enthuse* is in fairly common use, it is usually better to use another form in college writing.

fix: In General usage *fix* commonly means repair or prepare (*fix* a broken clock, *fix* lunch for three). It also means to make fast or establish (*fix* the tent to its pegs, *fix* tariff prices). *Fix* is Informal in the sense of to *get even* with (I'll *fix* you for that). The noun *fix*, meaning a difficult situation, is also Informal: "How did you ever get into such a *fix?*"

leave, let: *Leave* means to depart or to abandon; *let* means to permit: "*Let* us *leave* this place." *Leave* for *let* is Vulgate and should be avoided.

predominate, predominant: *Predominate* is a verb: "The captain's will *predominated* throughout the voyage." *Predominant* is an adjective: "The *predominant* feature of the landscape is the swamplands."

suspect, suspicion: *Suspect* is the verb meaning to distrust or imagine: "The police *suspected* foul play." *Suspicion* is a noun, and when used for *suspect* is a localism.

try and, try to: Both are accepted idioms: *Try and* is the more common in General English (*Try and* get your work in on time), *try to* is the preferred form in Formal English (*Try to* get your work in on time).

want, want to, want that: In the sense of *ought* or *should*, *want* is Informal: "You *should* [rather than: *want to*] review your notes before the test." In statements of desire or intention, *want to* is the Standard idiom: "I *want* you *to* get [not *for you to get* or *that you get*] all you can from this year's work." In such constructions *want that* and *want for* are Nonstandard.

29.3 Double negatives

A statement in which a second negative needlessly repeats the meaning of the first negative is called a *double negative*: "The trip will *not* cost you *nothing*." Such constructions, once acceptable in English, are now Vulgate idioms and should be avoided: "The trip will cost you *nothing*" or "The trip will *not* cost you anything."

Usually what writers must be careful about are not the obvious double negatives like *not* and *nothing*, but the concealed ones, when *not* is combined with *but* or with adverbs of negative meaning such as *hardly, barely, scarcely.*

29.3a *Can't hardly, couldn't scarcely*   The Nonstandard expressions "I can't hardly hear you" and "There wasn't scarcely enough money left to pay the taxes" are double negatives, because *hardly* and *scarcely* in this sense mean *almost not.* The Standard idioms that should be used in writing are "I *can* hardly hear you," and "There *was* scarcely enough money left to pay the taxes."

29.3b *Can't help but*   Three idioms are currently used for this construction:

> Formal: I *cannot but* feel sorry for him.
> General: I *can't help feeling* sorry for him.
> Informal: I *can't help but feel* sorry for him.

29.3c *But what*   Nonstandard idiom in negative expressions such as "I don't doubt *but what* he will come." Standard English would be "I don't doubt *that* he will come."

29.3d *Irregardless*   Nonstandard for *regardless.* The suffix *-less* is a negative ending; adding the negative prefix *ir-* doubles the negative.

29.4 Idioms with infinitives and gerunds   Some expressions are regularly completed by infinitives (privileged *to attend*), others by gerunds (the privilege *of attending*). When one form is substituted for the other, the result is an unidiomatic construction: for example, "anxious *to increase*" is a Standard idiom, but "anxious *of increasing*" is not.

Here are typical expressions, some that call for a gerund, others for an infinitive. You will find others in your dictionary under the key (main) word of the construction.

Gerund	Infinitive
cannot help doing	compelled to do
capable of working	able to work
desirous of writing	the desire to write
the habit of giving	the tendency to give
hopeful of continuing	hoped to continue
ignore saying	neglect to say
my object in paying	my obligation to pay
satisfaction of doing	satisfying to do

References

Marckwardt and Walcott. See the index entries for current standings of some common idioms.

Fowler, "Idiom," "Cast-Iron Idiom"

Smith, Logan Pearsall, *Words and Idioms*, Boston, Houghton Mifflin, 1925. Chapters 4 and 5 list hundreds of idioms based on figurative expressions.

Vizetelley, Frank H., and L. J. de Bekker, *A Desk-Book of Idioms and Idiomatic Phrases*, New York, Funk and Wagnalls, 1923. Somewhat outdated, but very thorough

Exercises

1. On a sheet of paper, write down the numbers 1 to 10, corresponding to the numbers of the following sentences. Then after each number, write the preposition or conjunction in parentheses which you consider most appropriate in the expression. If more than one preposition seems to you idiomatic, state briefly under what circumstances each might be used.

1) Helen had a craving (*about, toward, for*) sweets.

2) Several critics mentioned that the portrait bore a noticeable resemblance (*to, at, with*) one painted by Reynolds two centuries ago.

3) Saul's version of the accident is considerably different (*from, than, with*) that of the victim's.

4) If I were asked to compare communism (*with, to, against*) democracy, I would find it difficult to begin with the greatest differences (*among, between, in respect to*) the two opposing systems.

5) "Scrabble" was a new kind (*of, of a, of this*) word-building game to me (*on account of, because, since that*) the rules were so much more complicated (*then, than, as*) any I had seen before.

6) It took me a long time to realize why Shelley's poetry was superior (*to, than, with*) Edgar Guest's.

7) He developed a strong distaste (*against, about, for*) publicity after his home was overrun (*with, by*) curiosity seekers.

8) During my first two years in high school, I failed to make good grades (*due to, because of, on account of*) my interest in sports.

9) (*In regards to, In regard to*) your recent letter, I regret to say I cannot comply (*to, with, in*) your request.

10) Speaking (*off, off of*) the record, the governor admitted that many of his views were the same as those of his opponent.

2. Supply a preposition for each of the blanks in the following sentences to complete the idiom. If more than one preposition is appropriate, give both or all of them.

1) My roommate is one of those persons who always jump _____ conclusions.

2) Napoleon never did become reconciled _____ his exile on Elba.

3) When flying saucers were first reported, the Air Force hastened to tell the public that there was no cause _____ alarm.

4) Johnson vowed to himself that if he were acquitted _____ this charge, he would never again meddle _____ his neighbor's affairs.

5) Spanish is not so different _____ Italian, but at first I found it difficult to distinguish _____ the singular and plural forms.

6) Throughout his short life Keats had a deep interest _____ and a warm appreciation _____ the literature of antiquity.

7) The union failed to agree _____ the proposition offered by the management.

8) No wonder we were angry _____ him; he considered himself superior _____ us in every way.

9) Lines parallel _____ each other will never meet.

10) You seldom meet anyone who is prejudiced _____ Scandinavians, Scots, or Swiss.

3. Point out any expressions in these sentences that are not idiomatic English and show how you would revise them.

1) Fire prevention measures may take time, but in a long run they will save you money.

2) Some young married couples think that they can live in the world on love, but the husband soon finds that he has to work hard to make the payments of his house.

3) Before the war broke out, my father was a prosperous Korean man of business, what people in America call a white collar.

4) Our city planning commission is far behind step with the needs of the community.

5) When the Texans tried to lord over these veteran Indian fighters, a full scale feud started.

6) I didn't want to write a paper pro or con to the subject.

7) When he was out of office, Churchill sought a hobby that would satisfy his want of something to keep himself occupied, and he turned to painting to fulfill his need of a hobby.

8) Beauty contests, to my opinion, are a waste of time.

9) Sailing, sailing over the bouncing main! Ah, but to be sailing—to have the wind rushing through my hair—the harp of seagulls overhead—that is the life. To have not sailed is not to have lived.

10) Since I came over here as an exchange student, it has passed two years and I still have trouble of the language.

4. Which of the verb forms or phrases in these sentences would be inappropriate in Formal English? Which would you consider Vulgate and how would you revise them for General usage?

1) Students who intend to register in evening classes may contact the Department of Extension Classes by telephone.

2) It's possible to teach any puppy a few simple tricks if you got patience, but if you give up in disgust after two or three tries, you won't learn him anything.

3) Whenever I buy a new book, the pages of which want cutting, I use a sharp letter opener so's not to leave jagged edges on the pages.

4) Because of its special rear springs and low center of gravity, this sports car has excellent "cornering"—that is, it is able to be driven around sharp corners at high speeds.

5) Nothing aggravated the boss more than to find a misspelled word in one of his dictated letters.

6) Before arthritis laid him low, Doc Winters used to would walk five miles every day, come fair weather or foul.

7) A clerk at one of the teletype machines quickly tore off a long strip of the message and walked it down to the administration office.

8) Willy could fix anything that needed fixing; even a busted cuckoo clock didn't faze him.

9) The governor told the reporters that he aimed to study the measure, even though he wasn't enthused about increasing the sales tax at this particular time.

10) Leave us not fool ourselves on this point: when you ask a friend to borrow you as little as $5, that friend becomes your creditor.

5. Select the verbal form in parentheses—an infinitive or a gerund —that is idiomatic.

1) All Owen asked was a chance (*for proving, to prove*) his innocence.

2) Our teacher tried in every way possible (*of seeing, to see*) that we understood the purpose of the experiments.

3) There are many good reasons why people prefer (*the buying of, to buy*) books rather than to borrow them from the public library.

4) The walls of the stockade were sturdy enough (*to repel, for repelling*) any Indian attack.

5) By the time she was ten, Maryon's skill (*to imitate, in imitating*) screen stars was known throughout the city.

6) All citizens share an obligation (*of voting, to vote*) intelligently in every election.

7) Mrs. Gleason had the annoying habit (*to forget, of forgetting*) a guest's name the moment after he was introduced to her.

8) In every man's life, the time comes (*for his making of, for him to make*) his last will and testament.

9) No one was less happy at the prospect (*to leave, of leaving*) Bermuda than the newlyweds.

10) The author took great pains (*to see, at seeing*) that his message would be clear to his readers.

6. In the following sentences, point out which expressions are "double negatives" and show how they should be corrected. Explain why the negatives in other sentences are correct.

1) Recent public opinion polls haven't shown nothing that any intelligent citizen didn't know before.

2) I can't truthfully say that I don't believe you.

3) For the most part, our college newspaper contains hardly nothing of news to the students.

4) There wasn't scarcely a trace of sediment in the retort when I took it off the bunsen burner.

5) Obviously, no one can live on nothing a year.

6) No more than four parcels may be shipped overseas in a six-month period, irregardless of what the sender wants to do.

7) Hartley wasn't exactly the least intelligent member of his class.

8) German officials had no doubt but what their proposals would be turned down by the French.

9) It was not for nothing that Mr. Chew was known as the most civic-minded citizen in our community.

10) Although Bessie is given to wild statements, you can't really help but not like her.

Conventions of writing

30 Appropriate punctuation

> Good punctuation is possible only in good writing. If sentence struc-
> ture is lame or stiff, punctuation is only patchwork, helping after a
> fashion but also showing how bad the word pattern is.—George Sum-
> mey, Jr.

Pn
or
No Pn
**Punctuation or No punctuation. Correction: Correct the punctuation
error marked. If the correction to be made is not clear, consult the
following sections for the specific punctuation mark or marks in
question.**

The most important use of punctuation is to help make the
meaning of written statements clear and easy for the reader
to understand. Practices have grown up that indicate to a
reader the groups of words that are to be understood as
units, and often the punctuation shows the relationship between these units. Misused marks or too few marks may make
the reader go over a passage two or three times to get its intended meanings; too many marks may keep him from grouping words that belong together, or they may slow the speed
of reading down to the point of exasperation.

The table on the opposite page lists the principal punctuation marks and gives their main uses. (The numbers following the marks indicate the sections in which each mark is discussed in detail.) Most of the uses are standard, like a period
at the end of a sentence or after an abbreviation (Mr.), or the
comma after *He said* introducing a quotation. These seldom
cause anyone difficulty because they are followed as a matter
of habit.

Most questions in punctuation arise when a writer has a
choice of one mark or another, or perhaps of using no mark
at all. Hard and fast rules are not very helpful in such situa-

Principal punctuation marks

Internal marks
Used to separate, to inclose, or to indicate the relation between elements within a sentence:

,   *Comma* (§31), the most common mark, basically a mark of slight separation between words, phrases, and clauses

;   *Semicolon* (§33), separates constructions of equal rank, not with the finality of a period, but more definitely than a comma

:   *Colon* (§34), a mark of anticipation pointing to what follows: formal quotations, series too long or too complex to be prefaced by commas, and occasionally before explanatory statements

—   *Dash* (§35), a mark of separation or interruption, more emphatic than a comma and much less frequently used

( )   *Parentheses* (§38.1), used to inclose explanatory statements not built into the structure of the sentence

End stops (§36)
Used principally to mark the end of sentences:

.   *Period,* at the end of statements, after abbreviations, in decimals, and in dollars and cents

?   *Question mark* (or interrogation point), after direct questions (How are you?) but not after indirect questions (He asked me how you were)

!   *Exclamation mark* (or exclamation point), at the end of an exclamation or a vigorously stressed sentence

Quotation marks " " (§37)
Used to inclose speeches in conversation and words or statements quoted from other sources.

tions because we find different practices in the books, magazines, and newspapers that we read. It is helpful, however, to know the characteristic differences between General and Formal styles.

Formal English generally uses *close* punctuation—more marks and often heavier marks, such as a semicolon in place of a comma—because the sentences in this style are longer and have more involved constructions. In addition, Formal writing tends to follow older practice in punctuation.

In General English today, with simpler sentences and more rapid movement, the punctuation is usually *open,* or relatively light. This style uses the marks that are conventionally required and as many more as readers will need for ready understanding.

The same passage punctuated in two ways will show typical differences between open and close punctuation:

Open punctuation

Now the chief literary and dramatic vice of the scientists and philosophers is that they seldom begin at the point of the reader's or hearer's interest. Here for example is a book on botany. It begins with a long account of the history of botany and continues with an even longer account of the general principles of the science. But what do you or what do I want to know about the feeble beginnings of botany? We want to know, provided of course that we want to be something more than the ladylike botanists who know only the names of flowers, we want to know what the problems of botany are, in what direction botanical research is tending, what difference all this research makes anyway, why it is worth studying.

Close punctuation

Now, the chief literary and dramatic vice of the scientists and philosophers is that they seldom begin at the point of the reader's or hearer's interest. Here, for example, is a book on botany. It begins with a long account of the history of botany, and continues with an even longer account of the general principles of the science. But what do you, or what do I, want to know about the feeble beginnings of botany? We want to know—provided, of course, that we want to be something more than the ladylike botanists who know only the names of flowers—we want to know what the problems of botany are; in what direction botanical research is tending; what difference all this research makes anyway; why it is worth studying.

Reading first one and then the other version aloud will bring out the difference in movement. The first version is more in line with general punctuation practices today. While perhaps less emphatic than the second, it is equally clear and can be read more rapidly.

Punctuation should be appropriate to the movement and other qualities of a writer's style, and it should put the emphasis where he wants it to be. For example, the punctuation in each of the following four versions of the same statement is equally correct; the difference lies in the emphasis placed on the phrase *but actually turns out to be a help:*

1) One thing which at first seems to be an obstacle for an athlete but actually turns out to be a help is the fact that he usually has less spare time than a nonathlete. [This "open" punctuation, while appropriate for Informal writing, obscures the phrase.]

2) One thing which at first seems to be an obstacle for an athlete (but actually turns out to be a help) is the fact that he usually has less spare time than a nonathlete. [The parentheses suggest that the idea is relatively unimportant.]

3) One thing which at first seems to be an obstacle for an athlete, but actually turns out to be a help, is the fact that he usually has less spare time than a nonathlete. [Setting the phrase off with commas brings it more clearly to the reader's attention than in the first version.]

4) One thing which at first seems to be an obstacle for an athlete— but actually turns out to be a help—is the fact that he usually has less spare time than a nonathlete. [The dashes compel the reader to pause and to consider the phrase as important as the main statement.]

Which of these versions is preferable? The answer depends upon the writer's intention. If the phrase is unimportant, either the first or second example would be satisfactory; but if he wanted to emphasize the idea that less spare time is helpful for the athlete, he might use either the third or fourth versions.

Since most students' writing falls within the range of General English, open punctuation is usually appropriate unless there is some special reason for using close.

See pp. 403, 409, 415, 435, 452 for exercises involving open and close punctuation.

References

George Summey, Jr., *American Punctuation,* New York, Ronald, 1949, is the most thorough study of current punctuation practices and the only one with authority.

Albert H. Marckwardt, "Punctuation," pp. 21-24 of the Thorndike-Barnhart *Comprehensive Desk Dictionary,* stresses the functions of punctuation marks. All dictionaries summarize punctuation practices.

GPO Style Manual, 1953, pp. 127-139 and elsewhere, gives detailed practices in punctuation, compounding words, abbreviations, and so on.

31 Commas

An experienced writer means a point as definitely as he means a word.—Arlo Bates

C Comma. Correction: Insert or remove a comma at the place marked.

Commas mark a slight separation between ideas and grammatical units, similar to very brief pauses in speech:

No, you may not go to the movies tonight.
The performance of the machine, on the other hand, is relatively easy to estimate.

Commas are highly important both to the meaning and to the movement of all kinds of writing. They account for two-thirds of all punctuation marks used.

The table on the opposite page lists the places where commas are used and where they should not be used. In some situations commas are conventional and are handled the same way in almost all writing (see §31.6). But in other situations the question of whether to insert commas or leave them out must often be answered by the writer himself.

31.1 Commas to separate clauses and phrases

31.1a Between main clauses joined by conjunctions   With *and*: A comma is generally used between main clauses joined by *and* if the clauses are long (especially when they have different subjects) or if it is desirable to emphasize their distinctness:

Commas

Commas should be used:

1. Between clauses and phrases (§31.1):
   a) Between long or distinctly separate main clauses joined by *and, but, for, or*
   b) After dependent clauses and long phrases preceding the main clause
   c) Before a dependent clause or phrase following a main clause but not closely related to it
2. In lists and series (§31.2):
   a) In lists with conjunctions
   b) In lists without conjunctions
3. To set off nonrestrictive modifiers (§31.3): *Two* commas are used when the modifier occurs within the sentence
4. Around interrupting and parenthetical elements (§31.4): *two* commas are used when the construction occurs within the sentence
5. For clearness (§31.5)
6. In conventional places (§31.6):
   a) In dates
   b) In addresses
   c) After salutations in informal letters
   d) With figures
   e) After weak exclamations
   f) With degrees and titles
   g) With nouns in direct address

Commas are usually optional:

1. Between short main clauses joined by *and* or *but*
2. After introductory dependent clauses or phrases closely related to the main clause
3. Before *and* in last item in a series
4. Around modifiers that may be considered either restrictive or nonrestrictive (§31.3c)
5. With most introductory adverbs and phrases, depending upon the emphasis desired (§31.4)

Commas are not used:

1. To separate subject and verb or verb and object
2. To separate two words or phrases joined by *and*
3. To separate a single-word adjective or adverb from the word it modifies
4. To set off restrictive modifiers

I was standing knee-deep in the water near the tail end of the pool, and my observations were limited to an area of possibly forty or fifty square yards.—Fred S. Gibbs, "The Salmon of Labrador," *The Atlantic Monthly*, June 1953, p. 66

When the clauses are short or closely related in thought, a comma is not necessary:

The bitter cold of winter had descended [   ] and the northern seas were frozen.—*Ibid.*, p. 67

With *but* and *yet*: A comma is usually used between main clauses joined by *but* or *yet* to indicate contrast:

In a month of fishing, my largest salmon in hand was eighteen pounds, but many much larger fish combined their fighting frenzy with the powerful currents of the rushing stream to defeat my best efforts. —*Ibid.*, p. 68

With *for*: A comma is needed between main clauses joined by the conjunction *for* (equivalent to *because*) to avoid confusion with the preposition *for*:

Conjunction (comma): Sharon felt extremely homesick, for neither her family nor her friends had written her in weeks.
Preposition (no comma): Sharon felt extremely homesick [   ] for her family and her friends.

31.1b   After dependent clauses and long phrases   A comma is usually used after a dependent clause or a long phrase preceding the main clause:

Preceding clause: Although grandfather could and did behave in an extraordinary way toward his own children, he was charming to the children of others.—Joyce Warren, "The Black Monkey," *The New Yorker*, June 20, 1953, p. 62
Preceding phrase: In this lovely landscape, at a point visible for miles around, Grandfather erected the ugliest church I have ever seen. —*Ibid.*, p. 60

When the preceding clause or phrase is short or closely related in thought to the main clause, commas aren't needed:

Related clauses: When Roy asked the author of a flattering review to lunch [   ] it was because he was sincerely grateful to him for his

good opinion, and when he asked the author of an unflattering one [   ]
it was because he was sincerely concerned to improve himself.—W.
Somerset Maugham, *Cakes and Ale*, p. 12

  Short phrase: In his mind's eye [   ] he saw a book, in royal octavo,
slim and light in the hand, printed with large margins on handsome
paper in a type that was both clear and comely, and I think he saw
a binding in smooth black cloth with a decoration in gold and gilt
lettering.—*Ibid.*, p. 97

**31.1c Before a dependent clause or a phrase that follows the
main clause** A comma customarily separates a nonrestrictive dependent clause or a long phrase following the main
clause when the relationship isn't close or if it would be read
with a distinct pause:

> Clause: His eyes had a bland, kindly look about them, and his mouth
> was set in a sort of serene half-smile, as though he had just pronounced
> grace before a seven-course dinner.—Albert R. Kitzhaber, "Götterdäm-
> merung in Topeka," *Kansas Historical Quarterly*, August 1950, pp.
> 249-250

> Phrase: These men were already in Washington, enormously eager
> to unburden their hearts before the committee.—*Ibid.*, p. 259

But if the connection is close and no misreading will result,
the comma is frequently omitted:

> He added that he wouldn't think of giving so much for one man's
> vote [   ] if he didn't know that York had a reputation for being a
> truthful man. . . .—*Ibid.*, p. 263

31.2 Commas in lists and series

31.2a In lists with conjunctions Usage is divided over the use of a
comma before the *and* of the last item in a series. The punctuation may be either

> celery, onions, and olives *or* celery, onions [   ] and olives.

Formal usage regularly uses the comma before *and* or *or,*
and it is usually expected in college writing; Informal usage,
especially in newspapers, often omits it.

  Commas are not used when each of the items is joined by
and or *or*:

Fire insurance [ ] and life insurance [ ] and accident insurance [ ] and all other forms of insurance are bets placed on odds more or less scientifically determined.

When the items themselves contain commas, they are separated by semicolons.

See §33.2, Semicolons to separate elements containing commas, p. 407.

References: Summey, pp. 69–71, 75f.; R. J. McCutcheon, "The Serial Comma Before 'and' and 'or,'" *American Speech*, 1940, 15: 250–254

31.2b In lists without conjunctions Commas are used to separate the items of a series of three or more elements not joined by *and* or *or*:

The typical freshman's program includes English, social studies, a science, physical education.

When to get up, when to eat, when to work, when to have fun, when to go to bed were all laid down in the regulations.

31.2c With adjectives in series Commas are used in a series of adjectives modifying a single noun when the adjectives are coordinate—that is, when each could be thought of as modifying the same noun separately:

It was a *long, exciting, well-played* game.

A simple test to determine whether adjectives in a series are coordinate is to see if *and* could be put between the adjectives without changing the meaning (a long and exciting and well-played game). Notice that a comma is *not* used between the last adjective in the series and the noun.

Commas are not used with adjectives in series when the first adjective qualifies the one that follows or the entire expression:

He spoke longingly of the *good* [ ] *old* [ ] *prewar* [ ] days.

Since the order of the adjectives cannot be changed, nor can *and* be inserted between them, commas should not be used.

31.3 Commas to set off nonrestrictive modifiers   Modifiers which do not limit or define the meaning of a noun or a verb but add only descriptive or explanatory details are called *nonrestrictive* (or *loose*) modifiers, and are set off from the rest of the statement by a comma or commas:

> Our coach, *who had never played football,* failed to understand our anxiety before the final game.
> The renovation program includes those two buildings, *both of which were constructed in 1912.*

Modifiers which define or limit the meaning of words are called *restrictive* (or *close*) and are not set off by commas:

> Coaches *who have not played football* fail to understand the anxiety of the players before the final game.
> The renovation program does not include buildings *constructed after 1921.*

Whether a modifier is clearly nonrestrictive or restrictive often depends upon the context of the passage. But a conventional test for individual sentences is to see if the modifier could be omitted without a significant change in meaning. If it could be omitted, the modifier is nonrestrictive; if not, it is restrictive and essential to the meaning of the statement. Compare these versions of the two examples given above:

> Our coach failed to understand our anxiety before the final game [the omitted modifying clause does not change the essential meaning of the sentence].
> Coaches fail to understand the anxiety of the players before the final game [omitting the modifying clause changes or extends the meaning].

31.3a Adjective clauses   The most common problem in punctuating both nonrestrictive and restrictive modifiers concerns adjective clauses beginning with *who, which,* and *that.* Three tests may be applied in such situations: (1) If the word modified is one that cannot be further limited (such as *Harvard University, Asia, my mother, her first party dress*), the modifier will be nonrestrictive. (2) If the clause is essential to the meaning of the statement, it is restrictive; but if it could be expressed in a separate sentence, it is nonrestrictive. (3) If the reader would pause momentarily before or after the modifier when reading the sentence aloud, the clause is nonrestrictive (hence commas); if not, the clause is probably restrictive and is not preceded or followed by commas:

Nonrestrictive: Frank introduced his father, *who immediately dominated the conversation.* [Obviously Frank could have but one father, so the clause cannot limit the word.]

Restrictive: Frank's father was one of those people *who try to dominate the conversation.* [There are many kinds of people; the adjective clause shows what kind of people are meant.]

Nonrestrictive: London, *which I hadn't visited since before the war,* had changed greatly in fifteen years. [A pause would be normal after *London* and *war.* In addition, the same statement could be expressed in two sentences: I hadn't visited London since before the war. It had changed greatly in fifteen years.]

Restrictive: Most European cities *which were heavily bombed during World War II* have now repaired the damage. [No pause after *cities* or before *have.* The clause is also essential to explain which cities and what damage.]

Most adjective clauses beginning with *that* are restrictive:

The book *that you sent me* wasn't the one I needed.

Notice that any clause in which *that, who, which* could be omitted is restrictive:

The book *you sent me* wasn't the one I needed.

None of the students [*whom* or *that*] *I knew in high school* are attending this university.

31.3b Appositives   An appositive—a word or a phrase which identifies or enlarges upon the expression which it immediately follows or precedes—is punctuated in the same way as other kinds of modifiers. If the appositive is nonrestrictive, it is set off by commas; if it is restrictive, no commas are used:

Nonrestrictive appositives (commas used): It was difficult for me to believe that Joan, *my best friend,* had made such a statement about me.

The landlord tactfully suggested that we get rid of Mei-Mei, *our Siamese cat.*

Restrictive appositives (no commas needed): The word *appositive* means "putting beside."

I thought the question referred to Lewis *the novelist* rather than to Lewis *the union leader.*

Words used as titles are not separated by commas (Julian the Apostate, William the Conqueror, former President Truman).

31.3c Commas optional Not all modifiers are clearly restrictive or nonrestrictive; there are degrees of closeness. Notice in this sentence that while the two *which* clauses both perform similar functions, the first is set off by commas and the second isn't:

The cities of Provence, which (except for Marseilles) are small ones, are mostly ancient, crumbling medieval centers [   ] which have grown out of the very stones of Provence itself.—Winthrop Sargeant, "Provence in Stone," *Life,* July 13, 1953, p. 75. [A comma after *centers* would mark an unnecessary pause.]

Commas around modifiers emphasize a slight relationship; no commas suggest a closer relation. These italicized modifiers might or might not be set off by commas:

These physicians *who so vigorously oppose state medicine* have definite bases for their opinion.

They had *of course* more experience by then.

The sound of swing music reached my ears from a room down the hall *even before I heard the tramping feet that seemed to go with it.*

In open punctuation fewer commas are used, tending to bind the parts of a sentence closer together. The decision in any particular situation depends on whether the punctuation in the whole piece of writing is open or close, and also on the writer's sense of the closeness of the relationship.

References: Summey, p. 50; W. Paul Jones, "Punctuating Nonrestrictives," *College English,* 1948, 10:158-162

31.4   Commas with interrupting and parenthetical elements

A word, phrase, or clause that interrupts the direct movement of a sentence may be set off by commas (or other appropriate marks). Whether the degree of interruption is sufficient to require commas or not is usually a matter of appropriateness. Formal English uses commas more frequently than General English for this purpose:

> In Shakespeare, for example, the tradesman or the merchant is honored for the most part. [A comma before *for the most part* would give the sentence an awkward seesaw effect.]—Howard Mumford Jones, "Looking Around," *Harvard Business Review,* January-February 1953, p. 136

> Now what is remarkable in the literary treatment of the tradesman, at least until the nineteenth century was well along, is that even when good-natured fun was poked at him the tradesman was on the whole regarded by the literary world with considerable respect.—*Ibid.,* p. 136 [Notice that the phrase *on the whole* is not set off by commas because it closely modifies *was regarded.*]

Two commas, not one, are needed to set off such expressions (as in these examples) when they occur within a statement.

Adverbs that compare or contrast the idea of the preceding sentence (*however, therefore, too, furthermore, also*) are generally set off by commas (*two* commas when they do not come first or last in the construction):

> At the end of the seventeenth century, moreover, we find a notable prose writer, Daniel Defoe, presenting himself as a propagandist for business.—*Ibid.,* p. 136

> This retort, however, is more ingenious than sound.—*Ibid.,* p. 140

(Note: this form of punctuation should not be confused with the stronger punctuation that is required when these words are used as conjunctive adverbs between main clauses. See §33.4, Semicolon with conjunctive adverbs, p. 408.)

When connective adverbs appear at the beginning of a sentence, they may or may not be followed by a comma, depending upon the emphasis desired and the relationship of the word to the rest of the statement:

Thus [   ] by way of a hat the ancestry of the Wharton School at the University of Pennsylvania acquires an air of respectable antiquity in American terms.—*Ibid.*, p. 133

Nevertheless, the difference between the tradesman and the businessman is not sufficiently radical to disturb the comparison. . . .—*Ibid.*, p. 136

Adverbs that modify the verb or the statement closely (*yet, perhaps, so*) should not be set off when they appear at the first of the sentence:

Perhaps we won't feel the wind so much on the other side of the street.

Short connective phrases like *of course, for example, generally speaking, on the other hand,* may or may not be set off from the rest of the statement, depending upon emphasis and clarity:

Of course [   ] there is a difference between the connotation of a word like tradesman and that of a term like businessman.—*Ibid.*, pp. 136-137

Of course, such an emphasis also results in a one-sided picture.— Leonard R. Sayles and George Strauss, "Conflicts Within the Local Union," *Harvard Business Review*, November-December 1952, p. 84

After that [   ] the *Flyer* wasn't always on the Seattle-Tacoma run she had made famous.—W. J. Granberg, "Galveston," *Ships and the Sea,* July 1953, p. 49

Worse than that, ships could not get in to shore, and there were no wharves. . . .—*Ibid.*, p. 42. [The comma is essential here to prevent misreading.]

31.5 Commas for clearness   A comma should always be used wherever necessary to prevent misreading or confusion of meaning:

She had a gruff manner, but underneath, [comma needed] her only thought was the welfare of her students.

Writers should be careful to use commas in the following situations:

1) When the subject of a clause may be mistaken for the object of a verb or a preposition:

> As far as I can see, the whole bunch of them acted childishly. [to prevent misreading "As far as I can see the whole bunch . . ."]
> After the tension of passing the perilous island is over, the passengers again breathe normally. [not "is over the passengers"]

2) When a word has two possible functions: *For* and *but* may be used either as conjunctions or as prepositions. To prevent confusion, put a comma before either one when it is used as a conjunction:

> The surgeon's face showed no emotion, but anxiety and a little nervousness must have been hiding behind that impassive mask. [to avoid reading "no emotion but anxiety"]
> When Billy finally returned home, he was thoroughly ashamed, for his parents treated him as if nothing had happened.

As a connective, *however* (equivalent to *but*) is usually followed by a comma to distinguish it from the simple adverb *however* (equivalent to *no matter how*):

> Connective (comma): However, that may be just the answer we are looking for.
> Simple adverb (no comma): However [   ] hard we tried, we couldn't get the students interested in the election.

3) When one expression might be mistaken for another:

> On the other hand, writing on a subject in which you can express your own opinions is relatively easy. [to prevent reading "hand writing on a subject"]

4) When the same word occurs twice consecutively in a statement:

> What the reason for her refusal is, is of no interest to me.

31.6 Commas in conventional places   Current practices should be followed in the use of commas in dates, addresses, and similar places. While these uses are routine or conventional rather than meaningful, writers are expected to observe them.

31.6a In dates Commas are used in dates to separate the day of the month from the year: June 18, 1954. When the day of the month is not given, a comma may or may not be used: open punctuation, which omits the comma, is becoming more common:

> *Open:* June 1954
> *Close:* June, 1954
>
> *Open:* June 1954 [   ] was the hottest month of the year.
> *Close:* June, 1954, was the hottest month of the year.

The form favored in military usage—18 June 1954—is more common in British writing than in American.

Reference: Howard Hoving, "Commas in Dates," *College English*, February 1951, 12:286–287

31.6b In addresses Commas are used in addresses to separate the town from the state or the county when they are both written on the same line:

> Chicago, Illinois
> Hamilton, Madison County, New York
> Washington, D.C., is too hot and humid to be a nation's capital.

Notice that a postal zone number is separated from the state, but not from the city: Chicago 11, Illinois.

31.6c In informal letters Commas are conventional after salutations (Dear Sam, Dear Uncle Joe,) and after the complimentary close (Very truly yours,).

31.6d With figures and numbers Commas are used to separate thousands, millions, etc.:

> 18,529,632 $1,325.15

Commas are not used in serial numbers or in round numbers of four figures:

The serial number of my typewriter is 11-6445793.
There were about 1500 words in the article.

31.6e After weak exclamations Weak exclamations like *well, why, oh* are followed by a comma when they are not stressed.

Well, read it and judge for yourself.

An introductory *yes* or *no* is customarily followed by a comma:

Yes, those were the days when an advertising man was a poet.

31.6f To separate degrees and titles from names:

Will Rogers, Jr.
Alexander Stockdale, A.B.
Gen. Carl Spaatz, U.S.A.F., Ret.
Ruth Minto, A.B., Ph.D.
H. M. Pulham, Esq.

31.6g To separate nouns in direct address:

Professor Morris, I have no excuse, but I'll try to think of one.
All right, Sam, you answer the next question.
Do you mind if I share your table with you, sir?

31.6h With phrases introducing direct quotations A comma is the customary mark after expressions like *he said* followed by a direct quotation:

Robert said, "I should think that by this time you would have learned what is expected of you."

If the phrase interrupts the quotation, it is set off by two commas:

"I should think," Robert said, "that by this time you would have learned what is expected of you."

No comma is necessary with very short quotations, exclamations, or quoted phrases closely built into the structure of the sentence:

Danny yelled "Hi!" as he entered.

He annoyed me by adding "See what I mean?" to nearly everything he said.

See p. 403 for exercises on commas.

32 Unnecessary commas

No C **No comma. Correction: Omit the comma at the place marked.**

When units that should run consecutively are broken up by commas, or when the movement of a passage is unnecessarily interrupted, the effect can only be annoying.

Long sentences may be perfectly clear without any commas at all, as in this example of over fifty words:

> The manner in which their grandfather began the tremendous task of giving away substantial parts of the world's greatest fortune and the way in which their father expanded the business of philanthropy had a significant role in guiding the five brothers into new ventures intended to help make the world a better place in which to live.—Joe Alex Morris, *Those Rockefeller Brothers*, p. 133

Students frequently use too many commas at the beginning of a composition course because of a mistaken notion that all punctuation has to be close. Too many commas are as bad as too few.

These suggestions are of necessity negative, but it will pay you to follow them if your papers are marked for unnecessary commas.

32.1 Commas between main sentence elements Do not separate a subject from its verb, a verb from its complement or object, or a preposition from its object:

> Subject-verb: The divers' disappointment on finding that the cargo wasn't gold [   ] was soon ended when they learned it was worth $50,000.
> Boys who are supposedly wild [   ] should not be sent to a strict preparatory school.
> Verb-object: They were told [   ] that the ship was a total loss. [*That* introduces a clause, the object of *were told*.]

Preposition-object: The library is well stocked with collections of [   ] maps, monographs, diaries, and other material relating to the early days of the Southwest.

I was especially fond of the works of [   ] Dickens, Mark Twain, Willa Cather, and J. P. Marquand.

If a loosely related element comes between any of these elements it should be set off by commas—*two* commas:

This brief synopsis of the plot, *it should be said,* does not do full justice to the book.

32.2 Commas between two elements joined by *and*   Do not separate two words or short parallel phrases joined by *and*:

The canoe was paddled by a young man [   ] and two boys about Tommy's age. [two nouns]

When teeth are extracted [   ] and not replaced immediately, there is nothing to prop the jaws apart. [two verb phrases]

32.3 Commas between modifier and keyword, conjunction and clause   Do not separate a short adverb from the words it modifies, or a conjunction from the clause it introduces:

Women are also [   ] interested in sports and even in business.

It was a cold, dismal day, yet [   ] no one had the heart to complain of the weather.

But and other light conjunctions are part of the clauses which they introduce and should not be followed by a comma:

But [   ] the milkman insisted on leaving a dozen eggs every day.

32.4 Commas setting off restrictive modifiers   Do not use commas to set off restrictive or close modifiers. See §31.3, Commas to set off nonrestrictive modifiers, p. 393.

If you are in doubt about using a comma or not in situations where the usual principles do not apply, try reading the passage aloud. Unless a pause is clearly indicated, a comma is probably unnecessary. Or you can try omitting the comma to see whether the clearness or the emphasis of the statement is in any way altered.

Exercises

1. In which of the lettered spaces in the following sentences do you consider commas essential? unnecessary? optional? Give specific reasons for your choice of punctuation in each instance.

1) Professor Ames __a__ who is now on leave for a year __b__ is perhaps __c__ the most popular lecturer on the campus.

2) In the small town where we used to live, __a__ there were dozens of men and women all with the same family name __b__ who never finished high school at all.

3) The closet was filled with all those useless, __a__ cherished toys a child saves: a board game __b__ without the counters, __c__ one roller skate __d__ part of a block set __e__ a Halloween mask __f__ and other objects too worn to identify.

4) According to the few and quite dull __a__ psychology books I've read, __b__ most people can be conveniently placed in certain categories __c__ such as __d__ introverts __e__ extroverts __f__ and those who make up the happy medium __g__ that is supposed to lie between these two extremes.

5) It certainly seems practical to me __a__ that the more we can learn about the people around us __b__ and of the world in which we live, __c__ the better prepared we will be to cope with our own problems __d__ and to understand those of the people we meet in our daily lives.

2. Follow the instructions given for the preceding sentences:

1) As it turned out __a__ Mr. Brebner __b__ who owned the car __c__ was fully covered by insurance.

2) In more than 300 of our cities __a__ the water that comes out of the tap already contains about one part per million of added fluorine __b__ which is a highly toxic element __c__ that generally retards tooth decay in young children, __d__ but isn't enough to affect adults' health.

3) So __a__ I decided to write to 187 E. 89th Street __b__ New York __c__ N. Y. __d__ the address given in the ad __e__ to

see whether the editor, __f__ a person who called himself __g__ "Kit Carson, Jr. __h__ " was actually interested in cowboy stories by young writers.

4) When two speeding motorists meet at an intersection of a busy highway __a__ and neither is willing to give the other the right of way __b__ something unpleasant is bound to happen.

5) As a child grows, __a__ his toys __b__ whether they are expensive __c__ or bought from the dime store, __d__ should become increasingly complex __e__ so that he learns while he plays.

6) However, __a__ Mr. Pineo, __b__ our next advisor, __c__ was a man __d__ who didn't care the least bit about a student's previous accomplishments.

7) What we can do, __a__ and should try to do, __b__ is to show the South Koreans __c__ who have lost their families, __d__ homes, __e__ and businesses __f__ that we are anxious and willing to aid them.

8) But these situations were never difficult __a__ for David, __b__ who had had a great deal of experience __c__ handling similar cases of hysterical men during World War II.

9) In July __a__ 1864 __b__ when General Sherman was about to lay siege to Atlanta, __c__ my great-grandfather, __d__ aged sixteen, __e__ left his father's plantation to join the Confederate forces.

10) My father was always kind __a__ and generous __b__ and I have some wonderful childhood memories to look back upon because of him, __c__ but it was not until I became an adult __d__ that he was able to understand my point of view.

3. Indicate where you would put commas in the following sentences and give your reasons. If commas are optional in any instance, explain whether you would use them or not.

1) It seems logical, therefore, that if the number of accidents on the highways is reduced, the number of fatalities will decrease.

2) When the first atomic bomb was dropped on Hiroshima, August 6, 1945, and the reports were issued about the death and destruction there, many people the world over lost hope for the future.

3) If you are looking for a cotton or washable dress, first check to see that the material is sanforized so that it won't shrink.

4) Regeneration, the ability of animal life to overcome or repair damage to parts of the organism is best illustrated by the lower forms of life such as sponges, hydroids, and planarias.

5) Robert Sherwood's first play, *The Road to Rome,* a comedy written in 1927, did not receive the critical acclaim of his later plays.

6) Yes, such are the experiences that each nervous expectant father has to endure before he hears the joyful news "It's a boy!"

7) The new recruit in the armed forces, before he sees the rifle range, knows his gun inside and out and all the safety practices involved.

8) The chief advantages of this model, which is called "The Comet", are its low operating costs, its simplicity of design, and its extremely light weight.

9) From then on, we left the selection of our camp sites entirely to Ken, who had had years of experience in the woods.

10) Seen from outside, the house, a one-story frame structure, looked commonplace enough; but within its appearance was breathtaking.

See pp. 415, 452 for further exercises involving commas.

33 Semicolon

Semi
;
Semicolon. Correction: Use a semicolon to separate the sentence elements at the place marked, or change the misused semicolon.

The semicolon is a mark of separation much stronger than a comma and almost as full as a period:

Our haunted house was not strictly in the best haunted-house tradition. It was not a ramshackle pile standing at a lonely crossroad; it was on a street inside the town and was surrounded by houses that were cheerfully inhabited. It was not tumble-down; it was a large, well-built mansion of brick, and it still stands, good as new.—Frank Sullivan, *The Night the Old Nostalgia Burned Down*, p. 133

This mark gives many student writers trouble, either because they feel they should use it to avoid "comma faults" or because they use it in places where lighter marks (commas or perhaps dashes) would be more appropriate.

Actually the semicolon should be much less difficult to use properly than the comma, since its functions are more clearly defined and considerably fewer: less than five percent of the total marks used within sentences in current writing are semicolons. Some sentences because of their structure obviously require semicolons. But aside from the constructions listed below, the use of a semicolon is in large part a matter of style, more appropriate in Formal writing with close punctuation than in General writing with open.

33.1 Semicolon between main clauses without connectives

Semicolons are used to separate main clauses not joined by *and, but, or, for*:

> We all like to listen to stories; this is just because we are human.

In such constructions both statements could be punctuated as separate sentences, but they are combined because the writer wishes to have them considered parts of one idea. Contrasting statements are often separated by semicolons:

> Literature, in itself a very valuable thing, is nevertheless not all of life; literature and language both derive from life as a whole, not life or language from literature.—Robert A. Hall, Jr., *Leave Your Language Alone!* p. 51

But commas are usually sufficient marks of separation with short clauses in series, parallel in form, and closely linked in thought. In this statement about a young boy's reasons for going fishing, semicolons would be too heavy as marks of separation for the series of clauses following the colon:

> If he decides to go with the boys, he may give himself many good reasons to justify his decision: he hasn't been fishing for a long time,

his parents will appreciate the fish, he can do the chores later.—William F. Ogburn and Meyer F. Nimkoff, *Sociology*, p. 227

Writers should distinguish clearly between main clauses that may be linked by commas and those that should not. (See §14.2, Comma faults, p. 181.)

33.2 Semicolon to separate elements containing commas
Semicolons are the most appropriate marks for separating elements in lists and series which themselves contain commas:

> Greenfield Village has over 100 separate exhibits illustrating 19th century America, including the laboratory and other buildings used by Edison at Menlo Park, N. J., where he invented the incandescent light; a silk mill, a grist mill, a cooper shop, a blacksmith's shop, a shoemaker's shop, a Cape Cod windmill, etc., moved from the original sites; the Logan County, Ill., courthouse in which Lincoln practiced, containing relics such as the chair in which he sat when shot; the Wright Bros. cycle shop. . . .—*The World Almanac*, 1952, p. 540

A sentence like the one above is perhaps encountered more frequently in punctuation tests than in actual writing situations, but the same principle applies in less involved series:

> Her reading should include the stories children love; the traditions, history and folklore of her part of the country; the stories of history, and of great men and women.—Mary S. Switzer, "Is a Woman's Work Never Done?" *The Wonderful World of Books*, p. 135

33.3 Semicolon with coordinate conjunctions A semicolon is sometimes used between main clauses connected by coordinating conjunctions (*and, but, for, or, yet*) in any of these situations: (1) if the clauses are long, (2) if the connection isn't close, (3) if each clause contains several commas, or (4) if the writer wishes to show an emphatic contrast between them:

> After all, if a reader is genuinely interested in what he is reading, he may be able to work his way through long sentences and difficult words; but if you write primer style, he may not look at your stuff at all if your presentation is as dull as dishwater.—Rudolf Flesch, *How to Test Readability*, p. 41

In college this would be an evil, and in fact it is; but even the high school student is nagged until he declares what he wants to do when he grows up. The boy who knows that much is one out of a thousand.—Mark Van Doren, *Liberal Education*, p. 168

Reference: Summey, pp. 97-101

33.4   Semicolon with conjunctive adverbs   A semicolon is used between two main clauses linked by conjunctive adverbs (*however, therefore, nevertheless, consequently* . . .):

The investigative jurisdiction of the FBI is limited to those cases in which the stolen automobile has been transported from one state to another; *however,* through cost-free services provided by the FBI Laboratory and Identification Division, the FBI has been able to assist state and municipal law enforcement agencies in identifying and convicting numerous auto thieves whose operations have not yet extended across state lines.—J. Edgar Hoover, "Auto Theft Is Big Business," *Motor Trend*, December 1952, p. 17

If the decisions or the rules of the Board permit the use of either the local official form or the conventional English form, it is the prerogative of the originating office to select the form which is most suitable for the matter in hand; *therefore,* in marking copy or reading proof, it is required only to verify the spelling of the particular form used.—*GPO Style Manual*, p. 62

These two sentences are long, 65 and 64 words, and distinctly Formal in style. Shorter sentences requiring punctuation of this sort are rare in current writing—except in student papers. Professional writers are more likely to use the conjunctive adverb as a link between two sentences rather than between the clauses of a single sentence:

One could ask a hundred questions of this kind, but the reader is not to imagine that I am going to provide a universal key to answer them all. I think, *however,* that this problem of the relations of personality to character does provide the right setting for such questions. . . . —Herbert Read, *Form in Modern Poetry*, pp. 24–25

Students who have difficulty remembering whether or not they should use a semicolon will save themselves a good deal of trouble—and will write better sentences—if they use conjunctive adverbs for transitions *between sentences* rather than as connectives between short main clauses.

33.5 Unnecessary semicolon When semicolons are used in places other than the four situations described above, they disrupt the movement of a sentence or sometimes make the meaning difficult to grasp:

33.5a Semicolon for colon or other marks Don't use a semicolon for a colon or other marks of punctuation:

> The following books were required reading for the course: [*not ;*] *Pamela, Tom Jones, Tristram Shandy,* and *The Vicar of Wakefield.*
> "Now that we have been admitted to the conference," the coach continued, [*not ;*] "what are we going to do about it?"
> On the last day of the State Fair, everyone was there: [or a dash or comma, but *not ;*] old people, middle-aged people, young people, children, and babes-in-arms.

33.5b Semicolon between parts of unequal rank A semicolon should not ordinarily be used to separate a phrase from a clause or a main clause from a dependent clause:

> After the crowd had waited for five long hours, milling impatiently in front of the auditorium, [*not ;*] the loudspeakers announced that they might as well go home.
> Engineers have been working on this problem in Los Angeles for the past four years, [*not ;*] hoping eventually to eliminate the smog.
> Senator Chadwick might have succeeded in getting the bill passed, but he failed [no punctuation] because public opinion was against it.

Reference: Summey, pp. 44-45, 97-101

Exercise

Some of the semicolons in these sentences are used correctly, others are not. Indicate in what places a semicolon should be used instead of another mark of punctuation, and in what places a comma, a colon, or no punctuation would be more appropriate than the semicolon.

1) Occasionally the illustration on the jacket of a pocketbook may give a clue to the contents; more often, however, it only proves that you shouldn't judge a book by its cover.

2) For several years Hoffman worked as a reporter in Springfield, Ohio; then he was called to Washington to serve as a consultant to the Office of War Information.

3) The author didn't intend his short essay to be considered a complete discussion of marriage, although the title certainly gave me that impression.

4) Most of the major dams in the United States are located in the West: Hoover Dam in Arizona-Nevada, Fort Peck and Hungry Horse Dams in Montana, Grand Coulee in Washington, and Shasta Dam in Northern California.

5) You couldn't get Sammy to admit he had been fibbing; however, even if you questioned him for hours on end.

6) Every gift the clerk suggested cost too much: a set of monogrammed towels, "suitable for bath or beach," was $13.50; a leather-bound diary, complete with automatic pencil, $15.00; a crystal bowl with a sterling silver spoon ("something every bride needs") for $21.50, plus tax; and so on.

7) Some large libraries have separate catalogs for special collections; for example, doctoral dissertations and manuscripts may be listed in a file by themselves.

8) If you work hard enough, you may succeed; if you don't work at all, you will surely fail.

9) Five years ago the population of Brownville was 16,500; today, according to conservative estimates, the figure is in excess of 24,000.

10) When I was in high school, I thought that writing would be a pleasant occupation—thinking, I suppose, as most young people do, of the finished product and not of the work that went into it.

See pp. 415, 452 for exercises involving the semicolon and other marks of punctuation.

34 Colon

Colon   **Correction: Use a colon in the place marked, or change the misused**
:   **colon.**

A colon is a mark of anticipation, directing attention to a series, a quotation, or a statement that follows: *Introduces something that follows.*

> A complete reading program, therefore, should include four factors: one good book each week, a newspaper or news magazine, magazines of comment and interpretation, and book reviews.—Atwood H. Townsend, "How to Use *Good Reading*," *Good Reading*, p. 97

Colons are not used very much in most writing, and perhaps the main thing students should watch when using them is that they are not substituted for semicolons. The distinction between the two marks is simple: a semicolon separates; a colon introduces or indicates what is to follow:

> On the way back to Roqueville Raoul talked nursery French to Ricky and Troy, pointing out the places of interest: the Alpine monastery where, in the cloisters, one might see many lively pictures executed by the persons of the district whose relations had been saved from abrupt destruction by the intervention of Our Lady of Paysdoux; villages that looked as if they had been thrown against the rocks and had stuck to them; distant prospects of little towns.—Ngaio Marsh, *Spinsters in Jeopardy,* p. 72.

34.1   Colon to introduce a series or an example   A colon is used after a main clause to indicate that an enumeration or an illustration is to follow:

> The printed credentials pour out in a multitude of colors and shapes: one badge for the main press box, another for the roving reporter, a field pass, a runner's pass, a photography pass, a radio pass, a television pass, a newsreel pass, and from time to time a technician's pass—enough to reduce to absurdity the life work of the late One-Eyed Connally.—Charles Einstein, "Covering the World Series," *Harper's Magazine*, September 1954, p. 36

> Many other "grammar rules," although not derived from Latin grammar, are still quite inaccurate and unfounded: the best example of this is the "shall" and "will" rules that we are taught with regard to the

future of English verbs.—Robert A. Hall, Jr., *Leave Your Language Alone!* p. 23

A colon is the mark to use before a series or list of items when the preceding statement is a main clause ending in expressions that definitely point to what follows, like these:

. . . including the following examples:
. . . to name but a few:

34.2   Colon between clauses   A colon is an appropriate mark of separation between two main clauses when the second clause is an illustration, a restatement, or an amplification of the first:

Lazy minds give up in despair: "I can't write anyhow," say students to me year after year; they mean they won't think.—Barrett Wendell, *English Composition,* p. 136

Taste and style of poet-librettist and composer were thus well matched: each is a finished craftsman; each is able to adapt to his purposes the material at hand.—Peter Yates, "Music," *Arts and Architecture,* June 1953, p. 38

Punctuation of this kind is not characteristic of General writing, which might use periods rather than colons in both of these examples.

See §41.2c, After a colon, p. 440, for capitalization of the first word following a colon.

34.3   Colon in conventional places   A colon is the customary mark of punctuation in the following places:

1) After an introductory expression, as after *places* in the preceding statement.

2) Between an introductory statement and a quotation if the quotation is long or paragraphed separately. You will notice in this book that colons are used after most sentences that introduce illustrative examples, as after *of the first* in the first sentence of §34.2 above, and after *and its object,* §34.4 below. (A comma is the usual mark after phrases like *he said* to introduce direct discourse.)

3) Between hours and minutes expressed in figures (11:30 a.m.), between volume and page in formal footnotes and bibliography (*Nation,* March 19, 1914, 98:295), between chapter and verse of the Bible (Matthew IV:6), and between the title of a book and its subtitle (*China: The Land and the People*).

4) After a formal salutation in a letter (Dear Sir: Dear Professor Martin:).

References: Summey, pp. 104–106; *GPO Style Manual,* p. 128

34.4 Unnecessary colon A colon should *not* be used between a verb and its object or complement, or between a preposition and its object:

Romance languages are languages derived from Low Latin, most prominent among which are [ ] French, Italian, Spanish, and Portuguese.

The magazine features colorful ads for all popular means of travel, such as [ ] railroads, buses, planes, and ships.

The community song festival attracts music lovers of all sorts, including [ ] those who can sing, those who know they can't, and those who don't know they can't but think they can.

See pp. 415, 452 for exercises on the colon.

35 Dash

The dash is a mark of separation or interruption between units in a sentence, similar to a comma but more abrupt and emphatic:

Always a mobile people by comparison with the peoples of Europe, now Americans followed the economic tides more readily than ever before, moving by automobile—and before long by trailer—wherever there might be a call for construction workers, or fruit pickers, or airplane mechanics.—Frederick Lewis Allen, *The Big Change,* p. 129

On a typewriter the dash is made with *two* hyphens with no space between the words it separates:

Two hyphens--the hyphen is the mark on
the same key as the asterisk--are used to
make a dash in typed copy.

The dash is a useful mark of punctuation, but teachers—
and editors and proofreaders and others—do not always agree
on its appropriateness. According to Professor Summey, the
dash has been described as

the interruption, the mark of abruptness, the sob, the stammer, and
the mark of ignorance. The last name—which might be equally well
applied to the comma as crude writers use it—records the fact that the
uninformed mistake the dash for an all-purpose mark for every possible
occasion. . . . Though condemned by some as a nuisance, the dash is
so useful that it has come into wide use for a variety of purposes.

35.1 Dash to mark a sharp turn in thought   A dash or dashes
may be used to indicate a sharp turn in the thought or construction of a sentence:

After I had followed the real Allison to high school, I wrote a story
about the fictional Allison that was admired by my English teacher and
was read aloud to the class—but that marked the beginning of a third
stage in the future writer's career.—Malcolm Cowley, "Psychoanalysts
and Writers," *Harper's Magazine,* September 1954, p. 90

A conviction that is genuine will always come through—that is, if one's
work is sound.—Edmund Wilson, *Shores of Light,* p. 671

35.2 Dashes to set off parenthetical material   Dashes are
used to set off parenthetical material when commas might be
confusing or when parentheses might not be sufficiently
emphatic:

Naturally, a moderator is on hand—a panel program without a mod-
erator is as inconceivable as a set without an aerial—but in this instance,
Ben Grauer, the moderator, performs his task with tact and humility.
[Parentheses might have been used here, but not commas.]—Philip
Hamburger, "Television," *The New Yorker,* June 28, 1952, p. 58

She went on to say that this summer had been a complete and
hideous fiasco, that he could not have shown more plainly his boredom
and distaste for her, that all her efforts—her patience, her cheerful front,

her willingness to forgive—had gone for nothing.—Rosamond Lehman, *The Echoing Grove*, p. 142

Note that dashes *inclose* the inserted statement when it occurs within the sentence, as in the last example. One dash comes before the parenthetical expression, another after it.

35.3 Dash before added phrase or summarizing expression
A dash is often used to set off or to emphasize a phrase that summarizes or illustrates the preceding statement:

That is the miracle of Greek mythology—a humanized world, men freed from the paralyzing fear of an omnipotent Unknown.—Edith Hamilton, *Mythology*, p. 17

While other marks may be used in place of the dash (commas, parentheses, colons, periods), they would change the movement or the emphasis of the statement. Dashes are becoming more and more popular in current writing, and there is no reason why a student should avoid them in his own papers. But he should be careful not to overuse them so that they lose all their force as in an example like this:

Marlene Dietrich was turned into a static image of lorelei charm, frozen in a lovely pose—and to bring that image again to life, there seems to be no proposal except to point again to its over-publicized legs, and its—by this time—rubber-stamp "allure."

Reference: Summey, pp. 101-104

Exercise
(Semicolons, colons, dashes, and commas)

In each space in the following student sentences, which of these marks would you consider most appropriate in General English: a semicolon, a colon, a dash, or a comma? If more than one of these marks would be appropriate or if no punctuation is needed, list the possibilities in order of your preference.

1) Let us first consider the method proposed by the council _____one-way streets.

2) In many cases, a person will become an alcoholic as a way of escaping from reality_____for drinking is essentially a neurotic escape mechanism.

3) At first I felt insulted by his remark and eager to defend myself publicly_____then, as I cooled down a bit, I could see that he had not intended to injure me in any way.

4) After the meeting adjourned, our conversation turned to two topics_____the futility of working hard for a raise in pay or position, and the stupidity some men showed when it came to choosing a wife.

5) The records we kept on the propellers that were unsatisfactory rarely showed any troubles with the governors_____however, we knew that all propeller failures could not be charged to structural flaws or battle damage.

6) Often we would confide in our house-mother things we would never dream of telling each other_____such as_____our secret hopes and ambitions.

7) Sooner or later a true test of friendship was to come and it came too soon for me_____a week before the junior-senior ball, to be exact.

8) The secretary in the movies is usually pictured as either of two extremes in physical appearance_____a girl with beautiful long hair, which is blond, black, or red_____never the in-between everyday shades_____large eyes, perfectly shaped lips painted dark red, and an hour-glass figure_____or as a girl who wears horn-rimmed glasses, with dull, straight hair, a hopeless figure, and a face that would be lost in any crowd.

9) There is an old rule about human relationships_____always treat the other person as you would like to be treated yourself _____that certainly applies to the success of any fraternity or sorority.

10) All sorts of excuses are given in the business world for women's unequal opportunities and salaries_____women have homes and children to care for and so cannot give their full attention to a career_____women are inclined to take more time off from

work and can't therefore expect the same wages as men＿＿＿women en can't be advanced regularly as men can because they usually quit to get married just when they learn their jobs＿＿ and so on.

See pp. 452-457 for further exercises involving all marks of punctuation.

36 End stops

A terminal mark (. ? or !) is needed at the end of every sentence to show that the statement is completed. Put a period at the end of all declarative statements, a question mark after a question, an exclamation mark after an exclamation or emphatic command or especially vigorous statement.

36.1 Period

36.1a After declarative sentences A period is used to mark the end of all sentences that are not questions or exclamations:

Madagascar is an island off the southeast coast of Africa.
Please answer yes or no. Yes.
"Why don't you wear brighter colors?" she asked.

36.1b After abbreviations:

| Mt. Everest | I.O.O.F. | Oct. | Dr. | William Green, Jr., M. A. |
| St. Augustine | W. Va. | etc. | *i.e.* | *ibid.* (in footnotes) |

For the use of abbreviations in writing, and abbreviations without period, see §44, Abbreviations, p. 448.

When an abbreviation occurs at the end of a sentence, only one period is used:

Mr. and Mrs. Samuel Hopkins will arrive at 10:30 p.m.

36.1c In sums of money A period (decimal point) is used between dollars and cents:

$3.95 $1,268.50

The period is not used unless the dollar sign is used:

66 cents   66¢ $0.66

36.1d In figures with decimal fractions A period (decimal point) is used before decimal fractions or between the whole number and the decimal:

.750   99.98% pure   .05   3.14159

36.2 Question mark A question mark is used after a clear cut question:

What was the real reason that she left?

When a sentence begins with a declarative statement but ends with a question, the ending determines the punctuation:

It is possible that these skills may be taught in one course, but how shall they be integrated?

36.2a A question within a sentence A question mark stands immediately after a question that is included within a sentence:

Someone once remarked (wasn't it Mark Twain?) that old second-hand diamonds are better than no diamonds at all.
The neighbors kept asking me, "Who is moving into your house?" but I said I didn't know.

36.2b With an indirect question or request A question mark is *not* used after an indirect question:

The gamekeeper asked us if we knew that we were fishing on private grounds.
Ask yourself if you are satisfied with your present income. [The direct question would read: *Are you satisfied with your present income?*]

A question mark is not necessary after a polite request phrased as a question:

Will you please return this copy as soon as possible.
Would you please fill in the questionnaire and return it at your earliest convenience.

See §37.5, Quotes with other marks, p. 426, for question marks inside or outside quotation marks.

36.2c **Question mark to indicate doubtful statement** A question mark with or without parentheses is used to show that a statement is approximate or questionable, as with dates:

Geoffrey Chaucer, 1340 (?)-1400
Geoffrey Chaucer, 1340?-1400

A question mark in parentheses to indicate a humorous or mildly sarcastic comment is usually crude and better omitted:

Dubious punctuation

No fashionable woman would think of going to a football game unless she looked like a giant squirrel or some other innocent (?) furbearing animal.

Standard punctuation

No fashionable woman would think of going to a football game unless she looked like a giant squirrel or some other innocent furbearing animal.

36.3 **Exclamation mark** An exclamation mark is used after an emphatic interjection (*Oh! Ouch! Fire! Help! No, no, no!*) and after statements that are genuinely exclamatory:

Caligula wished his enemies had but a single head; how he would have envied Hitler the scientific lethal chambers of Auschwitz!—Bertrand Russell, *The Impact of Science on Society*, p. 46

Exclamation marks are far less common in factual writing than in fiction, where the dialog may require strong marks of emphasis:

The Duke's gloved hands shook and shimmered. "I'll throw them up for grabs betwixt the Todal and the geese! I'll lock them in the dungeon with the thing without a head!"—James Thurber, *The 13 Clocks*, p. 94

Don't use an exclamation mark when the statement itself isn't emphatic. An exclamation mark (once described as "the period that blew its top") won't make a simple statement of fact any more impressive (The water looked inviting in the moonlight!), nor will two, three, or more of them add anything to the meaning of a passage:

My first job, as an elevator operator, was the most thrilling I've ever had! To me it was almost as if I was an actor, waiting my cue to speak and move!! My audience responded! (How could they help it? They had to get off!!)

Punctuation like this is better left to advertising copy that must attract attention by mechanical means. In student papers in which dialog is not used, there is seldom any need for exclamation marks. If many are used, the reader will probably wonder what all the unnecessary excitement is about.

See §37.5, Quotes with other marks, p. 426, for the use of exclamation marks with quotation marks. For exercises involving the use of end stops, see p. 452.

37 Quotation marks

Quot   **Quotation marks. Correction: Use quotation marks in the passage**
"   **marked in accordance with the usage described in this section.**

A quotation mark is usually a double mark (") as on a typewriter. Single quotation marks, an apostrophe (') on the typewriter, are used by some publications in place of double marks, but in most material printed in this country their use is restricted to quoted material within quotations:

"If you acted like a 'progressive' you could get food, cigarettes, the run of the camp, less work details—almost anything," one sergeant explained.—*U.S. News & World Report,* August 21, 1953, p. 31

Whether double or single, quotes are always used in *pairs,* before the quoted material (the *open-quote*) and after it (the *close-quote*). There are no half-quotes: a statement, a phrase, or a word is either a quotation with quotation marks around it, or else it is not a quotation and so has no quotes.

37.1   Quotation marks to inclose conversation   Statements representing actual speeches or conversation are inclosed by quotation marks. This passage illustrates typical punctuation for conversation or *direct discourse* (notice also the punctuation before and within the quotation marks):

One morning when I was passing the entrance stairway, I saw Mark Twain coming in alone, with a half-smoked unlit cigar in his mouth. He called out to me, "Young man, have you got a light?"

I fumbled in my pocket for a match, eager to be of service. He bent his head toward the flame, and my hand shook with anxiety, for the mustache stuck out so far, and the cigar was so short, that I feared I might go down in history as the man who burned off Mark Twain's mustache.

But we got it lit, and then he looked at me sternly and barked, "Young man, do you smoke?"

I said, "Yes sir; not very much sir."

He said, "Don't do it; it's a filthy expensive habit. I've got so I can smoke only dollar cigars." Then he frowned at me and turned to go to Colonel Harvey's inner office. I stood there a moment and he called back to me over his shoulder, "Dollar a barrel."—Burges Johnson, "A Ghost for Mark Twain," *The Atlantic Monthly*, May 1952, p. 65

In written dialog the words of each speaker are customarily indented like paragraphs (as in the above example). But when the speeches or statements are not given for their own sake but to illustrate a point, they are usually included in the same paragraph:

To these little girls, Dodgson used to tell stories, teasing them by breaking off in the middle with "And that's all till next time." Whereupon the "cruel Three" would cry, "But it *is* the next time!"—May Hill Arbuthnot, *Children and Books*, p. 290

37.1a **Direct and indirect discourse** *Direct discourse* represents the actual words of the speaker and is inclosed by quotation marks. *Indirect discourse,* the substance but not the exact words of the speaker, is *not* inclosed by quotation marks:

Direct discourse	*Indirect discourse*
The coach said, "Get in there and fight."	The coach told us to get in there and fight.
"At the present time," the senator replied, "I haven't yet made up my mind about the bill."	The senator replied that he had not yet made up his mind about the bill.

"Nope, Jones ain't sick," the proprietor told me; "just not working here any more."	No, Jones wasn't sick, the proprietor told me; he just wasn't working there any more.

Direct discourse represents actual speech, with the speaker referring to himself as *I*: Joe asked, "May I bring a friend home for dinner tonight?" Indirect discourse is a restatement of the quotation in the writer's words: Joe asked if he might bring a friend home for dinner that night.

The words *quote* and *unquote* are not used before or after direct discourse in writing because the quotes themselves show clearly the beginning and ending of the quoted statement.

37.1b Quotation within a quotation Use single quotation marks around quoted material that appears within a quotation which is itself inclosed by double marks:

> If they depended solely on economic theory to guide them, they would be in the position of the man John Williams mentions: "About the practical usefulness of the theory, I have often felt like the man who stammered and finally learned to say, 'Peter Piper picked a peck of pickled peppers,' but found it hard to work into conversation."— C. Hartley Grattan, "New Books," *Harper's Magazine,* August 1953, p. 98

In the rare instances when a third quotation occurs within a second, double and single marks are alternated, like this:

" ' "   " ' "

37.2 Quotation marks around quoted material

37.2a Short quotations Quotation marks are used around phrases and short statements to show that they are being quoted from other writers. The quoted material may be worked into the structure of a sentence or may stand by itself:

> Another immortal pun is Eugene Field's comment on the actor, Creston Clarke, that "he played the king as though he were in constant fear that somebody else was going to play the ace."—Max Eastman, *The Enjoyment of Laughter,* p. 111

I felt as a treasure-hunter might feel had he tripped over the locked chest that belonged to Captain Kidd. "Oh, my America, my new-found land!"—Phyllis McGinley, "The Consolations of Illiteracy," *The Saturday Review*, August 1, 1953, p. 39

37.2b Long quotations　When quoted material is relatively long—more than one full sentence from the original source or more than four lines in your paper—it is usually indented (and single spaced on the typewriter) but not inclosed in quotation marks. (The quotations throughout this book are examples of this style.)

See §49, The reference paper, p. 516, for other examples of quoted material.

37.2c Verse　A phrase or a portion of a line of verse may be inclosed by quotation marks, as is this phrase from *Romeo and Juliet:*

"A plague on both your houses" was the general attitude toward the parties in any conflict, no matter what the outcome.—Percy Finch, *Shanghai and Beyond*, p. 240

But when a full line or more is used, it should be indented, lined off exactly as in the original, and *not* inclosed in quotation marks. If typed, the lines are single spaced:

A century or so ago a Harvard graduate wrote a hymn whose opening line, plausible enough when written, turned out to be one of the most inaccurate forecasts ever set down:

The morning light is breaking, the darkness disappears.

The final couplet of that stanza, however, would—with the omission of a single word—be a fairly accurate picture of the world today:

Each breeze that sweeps the ocean brings tidings from
　afar
Of nations in commotion, prepared for Zion's war.

—Elmer Davis, "Are We Worth Saving?" *Harper's Magazine*, August 1953, p. 23

37.3 Quotation marks around titles　Titles of books, plays, and poems, and names of magazines, newspapers, and ships may be either set off by quotation marks or underlined (italicized). (Formal style, usually expected in college writing, uses italics for the titles of books and the names of periodicals, and quotation marks for titles of written works shorter than volume length, like single poems, short stories, magazine articles:)

The *Oxford Book of English Verse* contains but two poems by Oliver Goldsmith: "Women" and "Memory."

A rule can't be given about which form to use, since current editorial practices differ, some publications (like *Harper's Magazine*) preferring italics, others (like *The New Yorker*), quotation marks. While a writer may ordinarily use whichever form he prefers, he should be consistent, avoiding changes in style (such as writing "The San Francisco Chronicle" in one paragraph, *The San Francisco Chronicle* in the next, and The San Francisco Chronicle in the third). And he should not use the same form for different purposes where such punctuation might be confusing:

Confusing	*Clearer*
"O.K." is labeled "Orig. U.S. Colloq." in "The American College Dictionary."	*O.K.* is labeled "Orig. U.S. Colloq." in *The American College Dictionary.*

Quotation marks and italics are not used for the same expression; use one form *or* the other, but not both. (See §42, Underlining for italics, p. 443.)

A few titles are neither set off by quotation marks nor underlined: the Bible, Old Testament; the Constitution of the United States, Lincoln's Gettysburg Address; Montgomery Ward Catalog, the Denver Telephone Directory (or any other catalog or telephone directory).

37.4   Quotation marks to set off words used in special senses

37.4a   A word used as a word   A word used as a word or as an example rather than for its meaning in a passage is either

inclosed by quotation marks or (as in this book) italicized to set it off from the other words in the passage. Quotation marks are widely used for this purpose:

> When the word "hemlock" is used, it is bound to carry certain literary associations.

37.4b Slang and colloquial expressions used out of context
In Formal writing, an expression from a conspicuously different level of speech may be put in quotation marks if the writer feels that he should apologize for it:

> The disheartening outcome of recent international conferences has convinced some of our statesmen that certain nations consider us as little more than "fall guys."

The trouble with apologetic quotes is that they focus the reader's attention on the expression and make him wonder why the writer didn't use another term. If a writer is certain of the appropriateness of a word, he will use it without apology and without quotation marks regardless of the level of his own usage, as with the word *highfalutin* in this passage:

> I suspect that this kind of transition was easily acceptable to an Elizabethan audience, to whose ears both prose and verse came naturally, who liked highfalutin and low comedy in the same play; and to whom it seemed perhaps proper that the more humble and rustic characters should speak in a homely language.—T. S. Eliot, *Poetry and Drama,* p. 13

In General writing there is seldom any need to use apologetic quotes about a word or expression. If the word is appropriate, use it without quotes. If it isn't, use another.

When a real or imaginary person is frequently referred to by his nickname, it is not set off by quotes:

Abe Lincoln   Huck Finn   the Brown Bomber   Ivan the Terrible

37.5 Quotes with other marks   The following are the conventional ways in which other punctuation marks are used with quotes:

1) Comma and period are placed *inside* the final quotes:

"Yes," Roger agreed, "it's too late to worry about that now."

Her watch case was described as "waterproof," but "moisture-resistant" would have been more accurate.

2) Semicolon and colon are placed outside quotes:

This critic's attitude seems to be "I don't like any movie"; on a few occasions, though, he has said kind words for a travelog or a documentary film.

Fully a third of the railroad passengers were what trainmen call "deadheads": people who ride on passes and never tip.

3) Question marks, exclamation points, and dashes are placed inside *or* outside the final quotes depending upon the situation. They come *inside* the final quote when they apply to the quotation only:

"Why do you say that?" Mother asked me.

He gave me a skeptical look which seemed to mean "Look who's talking!"

Terence interrupted, "No, listen to this—" and proceeded to recite a poem none of us had ever heard before.

They are placed *outside* the final quotes when the marks apply to the entire statement:

Who can deny that this is indeed "the best of all possible worlds"? [The whole statement is a question.]

And to top it all off, she refers to her automatic dishwasher as "essential equipment for gracious living"!

End punctuation marks are not doubled, the mark within the quotes also marking the end of the inclosing statement or question:

Every successful politician knows when to say "No comment." [Not .".]

Did you hear him say, "Are you crazy?" [Not ?"?]

Exercise

Make the following passage of conversation from a short story in conventional form by copying it with appropriate use of paragraphs, capital letters, and punctuation marks:

hey clyde his name pushed him back like a brute hand howd you make out his eyes fled from one face to another i i did pretty good his voice was muffled whatd you get oh i i got a one of those erector sets the big one the one with the three motors my father gave me that my mother gave me a microscope a microscope they were impressed its got three lenses five hundred magnification he pleaded its a its a nice one that was absorbed what else dyou get oh i i got some other stuff quite a bit of stuff i got some skis too but that compulsive integrity that tyrannizes children made him add from my uncle his voice dwindled book of knowledge his voice was a husk a whisper my other uncle how about your other mother they asked didnt she give you anything clyde shook his head she didnt gee they were sympathetically surprised i dont have another mother clyde said how about your other father they asked helpfully i dont have another father clyde cried i only have one mother and one father from the smallest the least of them a runty drip nose he could have knocked over with the flat of his hand came the shrill sapient cry holy cow hes still got the same parents he was born with—David Goldknopf, "Christmas Twice," *Harper's Magazine,* January 1953, p. 51. Reprinted by permission of *Harper's Magazine.*

See p. 452 for further exercises on quotation marks.

38 Parentheses, brackets, and ellipsis

38.1 **Parentheses**   Parentheses are curved marks used chiefly to inclose incidental or explanatory remarks (the singular form is *parenthesis*).

38.1a To inclose details and examples that add to the clearness of the statement:

For seven long years (1945–1952) austerity was the key word in British economic life.

Thousands of GIs enrolled in college courses under the United States Armed Forces Institute (USAFI) program.

The few verb endings that English now retains (*-s, -ed, -ing*) are being still further reduced in ordinary speech.

In some business letters and in legal documents, figures are repeated in parentheses after a sum that has been written out: The contract shall be completed in ninety (90) days. This repetition is unnecessary and inappropriate in most other kinds of writing.

See §49.8c, Footnote form, p. 545, for the use of parentheses in footnotes.

38.1b To inclose incidental remarks and asides, either within a sentence or set apart as a separate statement:

He was adored (I have spent some time looking for the right verb, and that's it) by the members of the *Journal* staff, who greeted him each afternoon, in a sudden silence of typewriters, as if they hadn't seen him for a long time.—James Thurber, "Photograph Album," *The New Yorker,* May 3, 1952, p. 34

It does not mean that religion started with some definite thing, as when man first perceived the vastness of the universe. (Always read through narrowed lids a sentence which begins "When man first. . . .") —William Howells, *The Heathens,* p. 291

Parentheses for added remarks should be used sparingly in General English. They are more characteristic of Formal expository writing, reference works, and so forth. Frequent parentheses may suggest that the material inclosed isn't important enough to deserve mention, and they are likely to seem clumsy if they don't fit in well with the structure of a sentence.

38.1c Around figures or letters to enumerate points:

The main questions asked about our way of life concern (1) the strength of our democracy, (2) our radical practices, (3) our concept of modern economy, and (4) the degree of materialism in our culture.—Vera Micheles Dean and J. B. Brebner, *How to Make Friends for the U.S.,* p. 22

38.1d With other marks   No punctuation marks are used before a parenthetical statement that occurs within a sentence. If a comma or period is needed after the parenthetical material, it is placed after the closing curve:

> The jodhpur, because of its close fit and lack of boot (it is worn with a special pull-on shoe), is certainly not the garment for the bandy-legged man or one who can't "show a good leg."—*Amy Vanderbilt's Complete Book of Etiquette*, p. 151. Copyright 1952, 1954 by Amy Vanderbilt, reprinted by permission of Doubleday & Company, Inc.

When the parenthetical statement comes between sentences, the appropriate end punctuation is placed *inside* the closing parenthesis:

> The first signs of the ersatz should be treated in a relaxed manner and with some such words as these: "I see you have been smoking corn silk. It doesn't taste very good, as I remember." (Surprise on the child's part.)—*Amy Vanderbilt's Complete Book of Etiquette*, p. 536. Copyright 1952, 1954 by Amy Vanderbilt, reprinted by permission of Doubleday & Company, Inc.

38.2 Brackets   Brackets are used to insert explanations or brief comment in material quoted from other writers:

> Lest it be thought that I am exaggerating, listen to Mencken: "The impact of this flood [of common-speech, non-fashionable Americanisms] is naturally most apparent in Canada whose geographical proximity and common interests completely obliterate the effects of English political and social dominance."—Eric Partridge, *Slang To-day and Yesterday*, p. 293

Comments or directions may be bracketed in conversation or in any other quoted material to show that the speaker didn't actually say the inclosed words:

> For the first few minutes the practiced speaker, therefore, fills in time with his "Thank you" to the chairman introducing him. . . . Then come his formal salutations, "Mr. President, honored guests [if there are any], ladies and gentlemen."—*Amy Vanderbilt's Complete Book of Etiquette*, p. 582. Copyright 1952, 1954 by Amy Vanderbilt, reprinted by permission of Doubleday & Company, Inc.

In quoting material, *sic* (Latin for *thus* or *so,* pronounced sik) in brackets is sometimes used to mark an error in spelling, usage, or fact which occurred in the quotation:

> The author's next letter was headed "Danbury, Conneticut [*sic*] Oct. 6, 1854."

Brackets are rarely used and are not on the standard typewriter keyboard. If you have to use them (as you may in a reference paper) put them in with pen and ink. You will sometimes see brackets used for parenthetical material within parentheses, thus ([ ]), but the occasions for such constructions are rare in most writing.

38.3 Ellipsis   A punctuation mark of three spaced periods is called an ellipsis (plural: *ellipses*), and indicates that one or more words have been omitted from material that is quoted:

> Fourscore and seven years ago our fathers brought forth upon this continent a new nation . . . dedicated to the proposition that all men are created equal. Now we are engaged in a great civil war. . . . We are met on a great battlefield of that war.

In the second ellipsis above, there are four periods because the omitted matter is at the end of the sentence and the sentence period is added to the usual three.

Ellipsis periods are sometimes used, especially in narrative, to indicate interruptions in thought, incompleted statements, or hesitations in speech, as in this description of the dying words of John Wilkes Booth, the assassin of Lincoln:

> Water was poured into his mouth. He blew it out feebly, opened his eyes and moved his lips to shape the words: "Tell . . . mother. . . ." Then he fainted again. When he came to, he finished his sentence: "Tell . . . mother . . . I . . . died . . . for . . . my country."—Eleanor Ruggles, *Prince of Players,* p. 194

It is inadvisable to follow the practice of some advertising copywriters who use a series of dots in place of conventional punctuation marks: Keep your hands lovely . . . soft . . . beautiful to see . . . and to touch. . . .

39 Hyphen

Hyphens are used to connect two or more words used as a single expression (*heavy-hearted, will-o'-the-wisp*) and to keep parts of other words distinct (*anti-inflation, re-examine*).

Hyphens are needed in some instances to prevent misreading (*un-ionized*) or to differentiate between the same words used in different ways (*a drive in* the evening, *a drive-in* theater). But generally they are used as a matter of convention and for better appearance (*brother-in-law, hocus-pocus*).

In printed matter the use of hyphens varies considerably: newspapers and General English use relatively few hyphens, Formal and somewhat old-fashioned writing use more. This section lists the most common uses of hyphens.

39.1 Hyphen in compound words A hyphen is used between two or more words considered as a single unit in certain expressions:

39.1a With some names for family relationships:

Hyphened: father-in-law, great-grandfather, sister-in-law, great-aunt
One word: stepson, stepmother, grandfather
Two words: half brother, second cousin

39.1b In compound numbers from twenty-one to ninety-nine, and in fractions, especially when used as modifiers:

thirty-three	four-fifths of a box
one hundred twenty-eight	one thirty-second of an inch
twenty-first birthday	one-half inch

In General usage, compound numbers are frequently written without hyphens when the figure is easily understood from the context (at the age of *sixty five*; the correct answer is *thirty eight*).

39.1c In compounds with *self* Some group words beginning with *self* are written with hyphens (*self-contained, self-pity, self-*

support, self-government); some may be written with a hyphen or without (*self support, self government*). A very few words beginning with *self* are written as one word: *selfsame, selfless, selfhood.* Consult a recent dictionary to find out which form is preferred.

39.1d Standard compound nouns   A number of compound nouns are regularly written with a hyphen: *bull's-eye, good-for-nothing, jack-o'-lantern, secretary-treasurer.* Other similar compounds are written as one word (*beeswax, newsprint, policyholder*) or as two words (*intelligence test, labor union, shipping point, water cooler*).

Since practice is likely to vary with these forms, a writer often has the option of using or not using a hyphen. Where no confusion of terms is apt to arise, most writers would omit the hyphen except in conspicuously Formal style. When questions arise, a good recent dictionary should be consulted.

39.2 In group modifiers   When two or more words act as a closely linked modifier immediately before another word, they are often hyphened to suggest the close relationship:

gray-green eyes   a ninety-pound tuna
a well-kept lawn   an all-out effort
two two-hundred-pound fullbacks   tongue-in-cheek comment

A hyphen should always be used to prevent a possible misreading:

a *slow-motion* picture   a *pitch-dark* room
a *navy-blue* uniform   some *reclaimed-rubber* plants

When the first word of a group modifier is an adverb ending in *-ly*, no hyphen is used after it:

richly deserved praise   openly antagonistic attitude

Single syllable adverbs are often hyphened with past participles, especially in Formal style:

a well-planned attack   a short-lived magazine

A group of words used as a modifier to describe a situation for which there is no single word equivalent is hyphened:

> . . . and he offers dramatic recitals about guerrillas (whom he didn't meet) and possible ambushes (which he didn't find), all of it pretty much in the gosh-we-could-even-hear-the-guns-in-the-distance school of war reporting.—George Barrett, "Korean Scenario," *The New York Times Book Review*, July 12, 1953, p. 14

39.3 With prefixes Hyphens are used between certain prefixes and the root word either as a matter of convention or to prevent ambiguity. Dictionaries list most of these forms.

1) Between prefix and a proper name:

pre-Renaissance   post-Civil War
anti-Communist   un-American
ex-President Truman   pro-Eisenhower

2) Between some prefixes that end with a vowel and a root word beginning with a vowel, especially if the root word begins with the same vowel:

re-elected   re-ink
semi-independent   micro-organism

When the parts have become merged in General use, no hyphen is necessary, though it is often still found:

cooperation   coordinate   preexistent

3) To prevent possible ambiguity with a similar term, or when the prefix is stressed:

to *re-cover* a sofa (to *recover* from an illness)
a *run-in* with the police (a *run in* her hose)
to *re-sort* buttons (a seaside *resort*)

Stressed prefixes include terms like *ex-wife, all-American, do-gooder, anti-religious, co-author*.

39.4 Suspension hyphen The suspension hyphen is often used to carry the modifying expression from one word over to the next:

Two-word forms first acquire the hyphen, later are printed as one word, and not infrequently the transition is from the *two-* to the *one-word* form, bypassing the hyphen stage.—*GPO Style Manual,* p. 63

As you pass *shorts-* and *slacks-clad* women in the street stop to bless the memory of Amelia Jenks Bloomer, who invented the plus fours that sent her name down to posterity.—Richardson Wright, "Female Fighters," *The Saturday Review,* September 12, 1953, p. 42

39.5 Unnecessary hyphen Don't hyphen a term that is currently written as a single word or as two words. Even if your dictionary lists as alternatives such old-fashioned forms as *to-night* and *post-man,* use the first or preferred form.

Here is a brief list of words that students are sometimes tempted to hyphen:

One word	Separate words
anybody (pronoun)	all right
basketball, baseball, football	class president
bookkeeping	grade curve
footnotes	high school
himself, myself, ourselves	"How do you do?"
nevertheless	motion picture
outdoor	no one
outwit	press agent
overlooked	report card
percent (or per cent)	school days
roundabout	second in command
semicolon	six o'clock
taxpayer	tax rate
today, tomorrow	water pressure
throughout	
uphold	
whatever	

References: *GPO Style Manual,* pp. 63-120; Summey, Ch. 10, Compound Words and Open Compounds

39.6 Hyphen for word division For the use of a hyphen to divide a word into syllables at the end of a line, see §7.3, Division of words, p. 87.

Exercise

1. Make three columns, writing in the first one the expressions in this list that should be written as separate words; in the second column those written as one word; and in the third, those that are customarily hyphened. The parenthetical expressions indicate the sense in which the expression is intended.

1. a lot (of work to do)
2. bath tub
3. daughter in law
4. every one (is present)
5. fly by night (unreliable)
6. good night (a farewell)
7. high school
8. in so far as
9. intra mural (sports)
10. kilo watt hours
11. left overs (food)
12. man made
13. man of war (a ship)
14. may be (perhaps)
15. never the less
16. no one (is at home)
17. not with standing (a conjunction)
18. over look (to slight or neglect)
19. our selves
20. pocket book (a purse)
21. re written
22. school board
23. self satisfied
24. semi colon
25. some body (has been eating my soup)
26. south south west (a compass point)
27. ten word (telegram)
28. three quarters (of an inch)
29. un American
30. where abouts (at what place)

See p. 452 for further exercises involving the use of the hyphen.

40 Apostrophe

Apos **Apostrophe. Correction: Insert an apostrophe where it belongs in**
' **the word marked, or take out the unnecessary apostrophe.**

An apostrophe (') is used in contractions, to mark the plural form of some expressions, and to indicate the genitive (possessive) case of nouns. Although it is a minor mark of punctuation that seldom affects the reader's interpretation of a statement, its omission or wrong insertion is very noticeable.

40.1 In contractions An apostrophe is used in contractions to indicate the omission of one or more letters:

can't	I'll	it's (it is)	we're
don't	I'm	o'clock	won't
haven't	isn't	shouldn't	

An apostrophe is *not* used as an apologetic mark with shortened forms:

altho	bus	phone	tho	thru

An apostrophe is used with dates from which the first figures are omitted (the class of '59, the spirit of '76).

40.2 For plurals of letters and figures An apostrophe is generally used before an *s* to form the plurals of figures, letters of the alphabet, and words considered as words:

the early 1900's [or 1900s]
several size 16's [or 16s]
a .44 pistol and two .22's [or .22s]
There are four *s*'s, four *i*'s, and two *p*'s in *Mississippi*.

40.3 For letters dropped in representing speech An apostrophe is commonly used to indicate the omission of sounds in representing speech:

"But J. C. he wouldn't let me be until I brought him over. Just kept on sayin', Mamie I'm not a-goin' to move until I see where I'm goin'."
—Ann Petry, *The Narrows*, p. 120

It is not necessary in representing conversation to indicate all such omissions, and frequent apostrophes make for difficult reading.

40.4 With genitive (possessive) case forms An apostrophe is used with the singular and plural forms of nouns to mark the genitive case:

John's car	children's games
New York's Parks	your parents' permission
a stone's throw	

An apostrophe is *not* used with the possessive forms of the pronouns *his, hers, its, ours, yours, theirs*:

the city and *its* suburbs	these seats are *ours*

See §27.1b, Apostrophe with genitives, p. 345, and §28.5, Possessive pronouns, p. 363.

Exercises involving use of the apostrophe can be found on p. 452.

41 Capital letters

Cap **Capital letter; no capital letter (or lower case). Correction: Capitalize**
No Cap **the word marked; or if the word marked is written with a capital,**
(or lc) **make it a small (lower case) letter.**

Most uses of capital letters are standard conventions that every writer is supposed to follow (such as for the first word of a sentence and for proper names). In a few situations words may be capitalized or not, according to the writer's taste or the type or level of writing: Formal English tends to use more capitals, General and newspaper style fewer.

The following description of conventional practices in capitalization is intended as a general guide rather than a complete listing of all forms. For expressions not covered here, consult a dictionary.

41.1 **With proper names** All proper names are capitalized, including names of

1) People, their nicknames and titles:

John Quincy Adams	Bill Jones	Grandma Moses
Monsignor O'Brien	Professor Ames	Congressman Greene

2) Places, and the names for people who live there:

Boston	Yellowstone Park	Asia	Irishmen
Bostonians	Cape Cod Bay	the Asiatics	Middle West
The Dalles, Oregon	the Bowery	Ireland	Midwesterners

3) Racial, religious, and political groups (whether singular or plural):

Negroes	Moslem	Swedes	Democrat
Indians	Protestant	Scots	Socialist
Catholics	Christian Scientist	South Koreans	Communist
Jews	Baptist	Republican	Farmer-Laborite

Names of social and economic groups are not capitalized (except for stylistic emphasis):

the middle class	the bourgeoisie	the ruling class
the proletariat	the intelligentsia	the station-wagon set

4) Languages:

English	Latin	Esperanto
French	Greek	Basic English

5) Days of the week, months, holidays:

Monday	January (Jan.)	Labor Day
Sunday (Sun.)	Thanksgiving Day	Easter

Names of the seasons need not be capitalized:

winter	summer	spring	fall	autumn

Names of centuries are sometimes capitalized in Formal writing (the Seventeenth Century) but are usually not in General writing (the twentieth century).

6) Names of organizations and their abbreviations:

Phi Beta Kappa	National Association of
the Elks, BPOE	Manufacturers, NAM
Sigma Chi, the Sigma Chis	General Motors, G.M.
the Democratic Party	Boy Scouts
DAR	

The words *freshman, sophomore, junior, senior* are not capitalized when they refer to a member or members of a class (The committee consists of one freshman, two sophomores, four juniors, and a senior). Capitals are used when these words are used to designate organizations (the Freshman Class, an invitation to the Junior Prom).

7) Names of historical events and documents:

the Battle of Bull Run	Magna Charta
the American Revolution	Monroe Doctrine
the Constitution	the Middle Ages
the Renaissance	the Treaty of Vienna

8) Names of ships, planes, specific buildings and other structures:

the *Enterprise*	Grand Coulee Dam
S. S. *America*	Golden Gate Bridge
four-engine Constellations	Highway 99
Bodleian Library	the Empire State Building

41.2 For the first word of a sentence Capitalize the first word of every sentence:

Won't you come again soon? Yes.

41.2a In quotations The first word of a direct quotation that is in itself a complete sentence is capitalized:

He said, "The first time I came this way none of the roads were paved."
"That was your last chance," she said. "Don't ever ask me again."

But no capital is used when the quotation is fragmentary or built into the structure of the sentence or is the second part of a quoted sentence interrupted by an expression such as *he said*:

According to the advertisement, it was the "most spectacular picture of the year."
"The first time I came this way," he said, "none of the roads were paved."

41.2b In parentheses A complete sentence inclosed in parentheses is always capitalized when it stands alone, but when inclosed *within* another sentence, it usually is not:

> The broadcast, sponsored by a local bank, was frequently interrupted by lengthy commercials. (Apparently the sponsor doesn't believe that silence is golden.)
>
> The broadcast was interrupted by frequent commercials for the bank (apparently the sponsor doesn't believe that silence is golden), but we enjoyed it nevertheless.

41.2c After a colon A complete sentence standing after a colon is not capitalized when the connection with the preceding clause is close:

> We observe a great diversity of phenomena: changes in luminosity and color take place which seem to be capricious and unpredictable. —Philipp Frank, *Relativity: A Richer Truth*, p. 126

The sentence after the colon is often capitalized when it is distinctly separate:

> Quite a few teachers in the departments of science would tell the student: We scientists deliver the laws of nature to the philosopher, who has to interpret them.—*Ibid.*, p. 84

41.3 With principal words in titles of books and articles The first word, the last word, and all important words (nouns, pronouns, verbs, adjectives, and adverbs) are capitalized in the titles of books, magazine articles, themes, and so forth:

> The Battle Hymn of the Republic   Of Mice and Men
> How To Tie Dry Flies   A Man and His Dog

See §7.5, Titles of papers, p. 88.

41.4 For names of specific academic courses The names of specific high school or college courses are capitalized:

> Naval Science
> Psychology 101 (all courses with numbers after them are capitalized)
> General Anatomy
> French Literature of the Eighteenth Century

The names of languages (German, English, Chinese, French) are proper adjectives (see §41.7) and are always capitalized. Other branches of study that are not specific course names need not be capitalized:

> Physics and chemistry I found almost as baffling as analytic geometry —a form of mental torture in which I distinctly recall having achieved a 17 per cent grade out of a possible 100.—J. Donald Adams, "Speaking of Books," *The New York Times Book Review,* July 12, 1953, p. 2

For listing specific courses with general subjects, this form may be used:

> My program this quarter is biology, chemistry, European history, English composition, and of course P. E. 100.

In referring to the various departments of an institution, all names should be capitalized:

the Department of Applied Psychology
the English Department
the School of Biological Sciences
the Graduate School

The words *high school, college,* and *university* are not capitalized unless the name of the institution is also used or the reference is clearly to one specific institution:

> When I was in high school, I never thought I would get to college.
> After leaving Jefferson High School, Warner attended a business college for three months and then enrolled at Riverside Junior College.
> The University also acknowledges an anonymous gift of $5000 for the aid of needy foreign students.

41.5 For titles of people and names of relatives A person's title should be capitalized when it is used with his name:

Professor Prins	Pfc. A. L. Marston
Sheriff Cooper	Coach Lou Little
Vice-President Nixon	County Assessor Mable Poole

The title *President* referring to the President of the United States is always capitalized, whether or not the officeholder is named. A few other titles of high rank are similarly capitalized: the Pope, the Queen of England, the Chief Justice of the United States.

Other titles referring to a position or an office rather than to the person holding it, are not capitalized:

> Barbara refused to run for class president.
> An infantry sergeant should have a voice that will command respect.

Names of family relationships like *mother, father, sister, brother, uncle,* are capitalized when used with the person's name (*Aunt Letty, Grandma Moses*) and usually when they may be considered as proper nouns standing for the name of a person:

> "May I have the car tonight, Dad?" Tim asked.

> Perhaps the greatest shock to Ruth and me was that Father and Mother seemed to take it for granted we should be unhappy. "School is always like that at first," wrote Mother blithely.—Rumer Godden, "The Little Fishes," *The New Yorker,* September 18, 1954, p. 85

These names are not capitalized when used as common nouns (She had three *brothers*) or when used with possessives (their *father,* Sarah's *grandmother*):

> Now our mother wrote to Sister Laura Mary asking for us to be excused from the services.—*Ibid.,* pp. 85-86

41.6 In references to deity *God, Jesus,* the *Virgin Mary,* and nouns like *Saviour* are capitalized. Pronouns referring to these names are usually capitalized also, although usage varies:

> God has fashioned man in His own image.

41.7 With adjectives derived from proper nouns Adjectives derived from proper nouns (the *Roosevelt* era, *Parisian* styles) are capitalized except when the adjective has been so frequently used that it has lost its relation to the noun from which it came (*pasteurized* milk, a *jersey* sweater).

Usage differs about the capitalization of many proper adjectives: some publications for example capitalize *Levis* (referring to jeans) and *Diesel* engine. Others use lower-case letters for these forms. An up-to-date dictionary will usually help you in your selection of the proper form.

41.8 For geographic areas and directions Words used to designate geographic areas and words that refer to these areas are generally capitalized:

the old West	the Far East
Eastern oysters	the Midwestern states
the South	the Pacific Northwest
Southern fried chicken	a Southerner

A word indicating direction only is not capitalized (We traveled *north* for several hours; The sun always rises in the *east* and sets in the *west*).

41.9 I and O The pronoun *I* and the exclamation *O* are always capitalized to prevent reading them as parts of other words:

Give a man a girl he can love,
    As I, O my love, love thee. . . .
—James Thomson, "Gifts"

The exclamation *oh* is not capitalized unless it stands first in a sentence.

See p. 452 for exercises involving the use of capital letters.

42 Underlining for italics

Ital   **Italics. Correction: Underline the words marked.**

Words are set off or emphasized in many published works by printing them in slanting type called italics, like this: *Encyclopedia Americana.* In handwritten or typed papers they are underlined:

    The article first appeared in Harper's
    Magazine and was later reprinted in The
    Reader's Digest.

42.1 Underlining titles   The names of newspapers and magazines and the titles of books, plays, and other complete works published separately are conventionally italicized (underlined):

Newsweek
The Caine Mutiny
the novel *Huckleberry Finn*
Webster's New Collegiate Dictionary

The Chicago Tribune (or: the Chicago *Tribune*)
Hamlet, Act III
the movie *High Noon*
Longfellow's *Evangeline*

Titles of articles, short stories, poems, and other short pieces of writing that are part of a larger work are usually inclosed in quotation marks:

"The Easy Chair" is a regular feature in *Harper's Magazine.*

See §37.3, Quotation marks around titles, p. 423.

42.2 Underlining words and phrases as illustrations   Words used as examples rather than as parts of a sentence should be underlined if they are not set off by quotes:

Even on a sophisticated level there is some variation in word usage. For instance, what in other parts of the country is called a *sidewalk* was and may still be called in my native section of Maryland a *pavement,* and what is elsewhere called a *pavement* was in our usage the *street* if in town and the *road* if in the country.—Thomas Pyles, *Words and Ways of American English,* p. 70

42.3 Underlining foreign words   Words from foreign languages that are not considered as English should be underlined, not set off by quotes:

The wave of rich whipped cream (*Schlagober* is what you ask the waiter for) that rolled in about 1948 has grown and been reinforced by rebuilt dairy herds on Austria's own Tyrolese Alpine slopes.—Josef Israels II, "The Schlags of Vienna," *Gourmet,* September 1953, p. 8

Foreign words that would ordinarily be underlined include terms like *coup d'état, Weltschmerz, lex talionis, mañana.* In books and Formal writing, the accents and other marks would also be used.

Scientific names for plants, insects, and so forth are underlined:

The mistletoe (*Phoradendron flavescens*) is the state flower of Oklahoma.

Words from other languages that are now widely used in General English are not considered foreign terms and so are not underlined or otherwise set off:

blitzkrieg	chic	fiancée	status quo
bourgeois	debut	laissez faire	vice versa
chalet	debutante	slalom	

Although dictionaries designate which words are now Anglicized (have become part of the English language) and those that are not, their usage tends to be conservative. If a writer is certain that an expression marked "foreign" is familiar to his readers, he should not underline it.

Abbreviations of some Latin words and phrases used mainly in reference works are generally italicized (*ibid., et seq.*), but Latin abbreviations in common use are not:

e.g.	et al.	etc.	i.e.	vs.	viz.

42.4 Underlining to emphasize words or statements Italics are used in printed material to indicate an emphatic word or a stressed statement:

The food, clothing, and shelter of this vast rural population add up to one fact—*poverty.*—Gerald F. Winfield, *China: The Land and the People*, p. 82

I had never seen the play since then, but as I remember it, one of the young men dressed up as Charley's Aunt, and ran across the stage, lifting up his petticoats, and *showing his trousers underneath.* No thing since then has ever shocked me so much.—Gwen Raverat, *Period Piece*, pp. 113-114

Underlining should be used sparingly for emphasis. When a word or statement is underlined that does not actually deserve stress, the effect may be just the opposite of what the writer intended:

What I <u>really</u> mean is that <u>most</u> students
are mature enough by the time they enter
college to select <u>their</u> <u>own</u> <u>courses</u> without
an adviser's help.

43 Numbers

Num   **Numbers. Correction: Revise the number or numbers indicated according to the principles in this section.**

Usage varies considerably in writing numbers that are parts
of consecutive sentences: some scientific and technical publications use figures exclusively for sums that might be expressed in words in other kinds of writing. But in general,
figures are used for numbers over ten, and words for smaller
numbers and round numbers:

> College freshmen listened to a series of recorded quotations or state-
> ments varying in length from approximately *50* to *125* words.—Arthur
> Heilman, "Critical Listening and the Educational Process," *Education,*
> March 1952, p. 483

> Young found oral presentation superior to reading at grade *four,* but
> by grade *six* this superiority had disappeared.—*Ibid.,* p. 483

Except in situations in which figures are customary (such
as dates, street addresses, page numbers), a writer should use
the form that is appropriate for his material and for his audience. He should also be consistent in his usage, not changing
needlessly from words to figures for the same kind of sums:

Inconsistent	*Consistent*
When I was 15, I thought that a person over thirty-five was old.	When I was fifteen, I thought that a person over thirty-five was old.

43.1 Numbers written in words   Write out as words all simple
sums and round numbers that can be easily read. Whether a
figure or its spelled-out form should be used depends largely

upon its appearance on the page. A writer's reading experience and his common sense should tell him that "There were *three* of us in the front seat" is a more appropriate form than "There were 3 of us in the front seat."

Words appropriate	*Figures appropriate*
He shot three quail and one rabbit.	The next ship unloaded 3500 pounds of king salmon, 947 pounds of chinook salmon and 200 pounds of crab.
Five votes were cast for the class president's proposal, twenty-one against it.	In Colorado 10,547 farmers voted for controls; in Indiana, 17,003; in Minnesota, 10,750. The nation-wide total was 87.2% in favor.
If I had ten dollars for every time I've broken one of my resolutions, I would have at least a thousand dollars by now.	We were shown two 6-room houses, about a dozen 4-room houses, and two 2-room houses.

43.2 Numbers written in figures

1) Dates and time:

January 1, 1956	Jan. 1, 1956	January 1

The forms *1st, 2nd, 3rd,* are sometimes used in dates, but generally without the year (October 10th; October 10, 1815).

Hours are written in figures when *a.m.* or *p.m.* are used, but are spelled out before *o'clock*:

7 a.m.	twelve noon	one o'clock
11:35 p.m.	1800 hours (military usage)	

2) Mathematical and technical numbers:

3.14159	longitude 74° 02′ E.
99.8 percent, 99.8%	318th Bomb Group
the 38th parallel	.410 gauge shotgun

3) Page numbers and similar references:

pp. 183–186	page 12
chapter iv	Genesis 39:12
Ch. 19	Act III, scene iv, line 28 (III, iv, 28)

4) Sums of money except in round figures:

Figures　　　　　　　　　　　　　*Words*

a bargain at $4.98　　　　　　Can you live on two thousand a year?

The British pound was once worth $4.85.　　　　Coffee was then selling for about a dollar a pound.

5) Street numbers (with no commas between thousands):

2027 Fairview North　　　　Apartment 3C, 1788 Grand North

43.3 Numbers at the beginning of sentences　　Numbers at the beginning of sentences are written out unless they refer to a year:

Two to 3% of loading and up to 10% is common and 20 to 30% in specially surfaced papers. . . .—"Paper Manufacture," *Encyclopaedia Britannica*, p. 234

1953 was a year of spectacular heat waves in the central and eastern states.

44 Abbreviations

Ab Abbreviation. Correction: Write in full the abbreviation marked or change the incorrect abbreviation.

Abbreviations are useful and appropriate in business and legal documents, in reference works (dictionaries, catalogs, footnotes), and other places where space saving is important. But in most other kinds of writing—including freshman papers—ordinary words and phrases should be written out in full. The space that might be saved by abbreviations isn't important.

The situation and the writer's common sense should determine whether an expression is better written out in full or abbreviated. Forms that might be used in notes or in letters to close friends (*chem* for *chemistry*, *L. A.* for *Los Angeles*) are obviously not appropriate in General usage.

Dictionaries list most abbreviations used in current writing, but they don't indicate in what situations these forms should be used. A safe rule is to use only a few standard abbreviations (Mr., i.e., FBI) and to write in full all other words.

The following sections list abbreviations most often found in General usage as well as some forms that should be avoided.

44.1 **Titles and names** *Mr., Mrs., Dr.* are the proper abbreviations to use before a name: *Mrs.* Eleanor Roosevelt, *Dr.* Christian. They are *not* used in combination with academic degrees or honorary titles following names:

Mr. Logan Rice or Logan Rice, Ph.D. [not Mr. Logan Rice, Ph.D.]
Dr. William Carey or William Carey, M.D. [not Dr. William Carey, M.D.]
Mr. James T. Holloway or James T. Holloway, Esq. [not Mr. James T. Holloway, Esq.]

In Formal writing, titles like *Reverend, Professor, President, Senator, Admiral* are usually written out in full, but in most other styles these words may be abbreviated when the first name or the initials of the person are used:

Forms to avoid	*Standard forms*
Rev. Shaw	The Reverend Mr. Shaw
The Rev. Shaw	Rev. James Shaw
The Reverend delivered a sermon.	Rev. J. T. Shaw delivered a sermon.
Prof. Moore	Professor Moore
	Prof. John Moore
	Prof. J. R. Moore
Gen. Washington	General Washington
	Gen. George Washington
Hargrove was a sgt. in the army.	T. Sgt. Hargrove
	Hargrove was a sergeant in the army.

Christian names are not as a rule abbreviated:

| Charles Wilson | rather than | Chas. Wilson |
| Robert Burns | rather than | Robt. Burns |

44.2 Names of places, dates   Names like the following are usually written out in full:

United States   Ghent, Belgium   November   Christmas (rather
South America   Portland, Oregon   Wednesday   than *Xmas*)

In reference work and journalistic writing, well-known place names are often abbreviated:

U.S. Representative Henry Cabot Lodge
Captain Austin J. King of San Rafael, Calif.

A few place names are customarily abbreviated to avoid unnecessarily long expressions: The *USSR*, Honolulu, *T.H.* (for Territory of Hawaii), Washington, *D.C.*

44.3 Units of measurement   In consecutive writing most expressions for time, weight, and size are customarily written out:

a pound   rather than   one lb.
four ounces   4 oz.
weight   wt.
a half inch   a half in.
in a minute   in a min.
hour   hr.

These units are abbreviated in directions, recipes, references, and technical writing when they are used with figures: ¼ lb. butter, 16 ft. 3 in.

The expressions *a.m.* and *p.m.* (for *ante meridiem,* "before noon," and *post meridiem,* "after noon") and B.C. and A.D. ("before Christ" and "anno Domini") are always abbreviated.

Expressions of combined measurements and certain technical terms are abbreviated when they are used with figures (mph, rpm, kwh or K.W.H., ft-lb):

Tests show the car's best speeds to be 34 mph in low gear, 58.7 mph in second, and 93.5 mph in third.

Such expressions are not abbreviated when no specific figures are given:

The speed of a ship is usually given in knots rather than in *miles per hour.*

Abbreviations of this kind are usually written with three periods or none (*m.p.h., mph*).

44.4 Names of organizations Names of organizations and governmental agencies may be abbreviated when they are frequently referred to by their initials and the form is one that most readers are familiar with:

GOP TVA ROTC AP SPCA UNESCO CIO FBI 4-H Club

Abbreviations that are pronounced as words (called *acronyms*) are written as they are pronounced:

WAVES (rather than "women accepted for volunteer emergency service")
WAC (a Wac)

Amvets   UNRRA   CARE   NATO

44.5 Scientific words, trade names Some scientific words, trade names, and other expressions are referred to by their abbreviations when they are familiar to most people and would be needlessly long if written out:

DDT (in place of *d*ichlora-*d*iphenyl-*t*richloro-ethane)
ACTH
Rh factor
NBC Network
MGM Studios
c.o.d.
FM radio
PMLA (*P*ublications of the *M*odern *L*anguage *A*ssociation)
GPO (*G*overnment *P*rinting *O*ffice) Style Manual
OED (*O*xford *E*nglish *D*ictionary)

44.6 Capitals with abbreviations Abbreviations are capitalized when the words they stand for are themselves capitalized and when the abbreviations represent a person's title:

DAR (*D*aughters of the *A*merican *R*evolution)
USAF (*U*nited *S*tates *A*ir *F*orce)
Lt. Col. Brown
St. Matthew, St. Thomas Aquinas
100 degrees F. (Fahrenheit)

When an abbreviation stands for words that would not be capitalized if they were written out, no capitals are needed unless it stands at the first of a sentence:

i.e. (*id est,* "that is")
etc. (*et cetera,* "and so forth")
ibid. (*ibidem,* "the same"—used in footnotes)
p. (page)

44.7 Periods with abbreviations   A period should be put after the abbreviation of a single word and between the letters of a term that isn't written solid:

p.	doz.	N.Y.	c.o.d.
ch.	Lt.	Ph.D	A.T. and T.
Nov.	hp.	e.g.	P.S.

Usage is divided about the punctuation of abbreviations of many words of two or more letters written as a unit, some publications preferring periods and spaces (*P. T. A., B. B. C.*), others the solid form (*PTA, BBC*). Most dictionaries list the optional forms.

It doesn't make much difference which form a writer uses as long as he is consistent, using the same form for the same abbreviation throughout his paper.

44.8 Ampersand   The ampersand (&) should not be used in General writing unless it appears in an expression which the writer is copying:

U.S. News & World Report
Abercrombie & Fitch Co.
Doubleday & Company, Inc.

Exercises for §§30-44

1. The punctuation marks (including hyphens and apostrophes) and the capital letters have been removed from the following

passages. First read each selection for its meaning and general movement, then put in the punctuation you consider appropriate and necessary for an easy understanding of the passage. The statements at the beginning of each passage describe briefly the original punctuation. While the punctuation you use need not follow the original, be prepared to explain the marks you have put in.

1) This paragraph was originally written in three sentences with close punctuation:

whatever may be said against us most foreigners would agree on one thing americans are friendly people perhaps because of the loneliness of early frontier days when neighbors were scarce and therefore valuable perhaps because of our democratic upbringing which makes us feel free to talk with everyone we meet americans are quick to break the ice wherever they go our howdy stranger attitude which is alien to the english and french the germans and the japanese strikes visitors to our shores as refreshing and sometimes even as overwhelming in its all embracing hospitality to peoples and ideas—Vera Micheles Dean and J. B. Brebner, *How to Make Friends for the U.S.*, p. 3

2) This paragraph was published in three sentences, with a minimum of internal punctuation:

in his report to the nation last week the president spoke of difficulties encountered when a party takes over after 20 years of opposition the difficulties are compounded when a president is elected by the greatest of majorities but his party controls congress by the slimmest of margins they are still further compounded when some of that partys rank and file find it difficult to alter the stiff necked old habits of opposition—*Life*, August 17, 1953, p. 20

3) This paragraph was written in four sentences with one quoted statement:

the simplest pun is based on the re use of a word with a slight shift in meaning s j perelmans doctor i ve got brights disease and hes got mine a pun involving not the slightest verbal distortion may have great richness take sidney smiths famous remark observing two housewives screaming at each other across a court-yard he remarked that they would never agree because they were arguing from different premises—Clifton Fadiman, "Party of One," *Holiday*, August 1953, p. 8

4) This passage was written in two paragraphs. The first paragraph contained three sentences, the second, two:

punctuation is the visual inflection the marks should clarify meaning and like shouting should be employed sparingly skillful phrasing avoids ambiguity insures correct interpretation and lessens need for punctuation when punctuation is used it should be employed solely to bring out what is intended if punctuation does not clarify it should be omitted—*The Associated Press Style Book*, p. 17

5) This paragraph was written in three sentences, with an interrupting remark in the third sentence:

when the great depression struck our family i was ten my brother freddy nine my sister aggie five i had long ago lost interest in dolls and was concerned with collecting marbles especially glassies and prying my way into roller skate hockey with the boys on main street freddy was engrossed in model airplanes and aggie it was a shame aggie had to come out of the name angela for aggie looked more like an angel than any child ive ever seen aggie occupied herself with burying dead birds in the tulip bed and digging them up the next day to see if they had turned to dust yet—Mary Bolté, "The End of the Depression," *Stories of Sudden Truth*, edited by Joseph Greene and Elizabeth Abell, p. 103

2. Study the punctuation in the following passages. Explain briefly the purpose of each mark and comment on any that you think might be changed or omitted.

1) Lord Chesterfield advised his son to learn spelling, saying that he knew a man of quality who never recovered from the shame of having spelled "wholesome" without the *w*. On the other hand the Duchess of Gordon, a miserable speller, justified her want

of learning when she told a friend: "You know, my dear, when I don't know how to spell a word I always draw a line under it, and if it is spelled wrong it passes for a very good joke, and if it is spelled right it doesn't matter."—H. Allen Smith, *Smith's London Journal*, p. 79

2) He was slumped in the leather chair fumbling for the cigar-clipper in his vest pocket when the portly man in the next chair looked up from a bluecovered sheaf of lawpapers he was poring over. Charley looked into the black eyes and the smooth blue-jowled face and at the bald head shaped like a bird's wing, without immediately recognizing it.—John Dos Passos, *The Big Money*, p. 355

3) Here, at the corner, in 1908, took place the murder of King Carlos and his elder son. King Manuel and his Mother, Queen Amélie, who died in 1951, were riding in the fatal carriage, driving back from a shooting party, south of the Tagus. Now, all is forgiven and forgotten, and the present Pretender to the Throne of Portugal has just returned to the land of his ancestors, at the invitation of the Republic.—Sacheverell Sitwell, "Portugal," *House and Garden*, June 1953, p. 98

4) When our government negotiates with the government of the Soviet Union, it is not dealing with individuals; it is not even dealing just with heads of State; it is dealing with those who, in addition to being heads of State, are heads of a Party which has a clearly enunciated creed and a membership which adheres to that creed with almost religious fervor.—John Foster Dulles, *War or Peace*, p. 15

3. Correct every error or inconsistency in punctuation that you find in these sentences. Notice apostrophes, capital letters, and quotes as well as other marks. If the punctuation of a sentence is satisfactory as it stands, write "correct" after the number.

1) When our Junior class decided to produce the play, the Man Who came to Dinner, I was chosen to play the role of "Sheridan Whiteside."

2) Before examining these three view-points, lets first admit that many of our friends wont take our advice, that different people have different opinions—that neither your efforts—nor mine, can achieve a perfect World.

3) Many of the school officials are of course concerned about methods of financing an educational television program, but no one has as yet offered a practical solution which would be acceptable to the taxpayers as well as to the members of the school board.

4) For the past 6 years, I, too, have wanted to become a nurse, an "angel of mercy", and thus help those in pain or in need of care.

5) There are certain terms that telephone operators use when talking to each other; such as, By (for busy), Da for "Dont Answer," and Nf for "no telephone number.

6) The wail of an ambulance siren, the smell of anesthetic, the gleaming instruments in the operating room, the cry of a new-born baby, these are some of the dramatic incidents in the daily life of a nurse.

7) Among those who objected most loudly to daylight saving time, however, the noisiest were those associated with such night time recreation businesses as theaters, bowling alleys, dance halls, and indoor skating rinks.

8) Perhaps the most widely-known graduate of Spokane's Gonzaga university is the world famous Actor and singer, "Bing" Crosby.

9) "At that price, a leading businessman told me, "I couldnt afford to stay in business very long, could I."

10) To every rule there is an exception, parents who have a complete understanding of the bases of racial prejudice can prevent these feelings from becoming a part of their children's attitude by teaching tolerance in the home.

4. Read the following sentences and then write down what mark or marks (if any) should be used in each of the lettered spaces. Be prepared to give reasons for each mark you use, to explain possible optional marks, or to justify the omission of a mark.

1) After reading this story __a__ one is led to believe that it is unwise to marry __b__ that is __c__ if one believes all that he reads.

2) Without warning __a__ a uniformed stranger __b__ obviously a guard from some industrial concern __c__ stopped and asked Sam if he would like to make fifty dollars __d__

3) Tucker said __a__ I was right as usual __b__ Tucker was an admirable yes man __c__ but he wondered if he might do it his way for once __d__

4) Another field of investigation __a__ which promised to be fruitful __b__ but which I had to abandon __c__ was the origin of public opinion polls.

5) Northcott pleaded guilty six years after the murder __a__ to a reduced charge of manslaughter __b__ and was sentenced to fifteen years in prison __c__ but was paroled after less than a year __d__ to go on to greater things.

6) The boss was utterly aloof from the office help __a__ he would call __b__ Here boy __c__ or __d__ Here girl, do this __e__

7) Almost every statement Mrs. Taine made was qualified __a__ for example __b__ the weather was never __c__ very pleasant __d__ it was always __e__ somewhat pleasant __f__

8) It wasn't until our housemother gently took my hand __a__ and asked __b__ Are you perhaps a little bit homesick __c__ that I realized I was homesick __d__ very homesick.

9) The boss __a__ a pudgy __b__ little man __c__ with an almost expressionless face __d__ asked me if I would be willing to work on Sundays and holidays __e__

10) When Younger finally returned home __a__ he found that the family plantation had been put to the torch __b__ all livestock driven away or killed __c__ all family treasures __d__ except those carefully hidden __e__ stolen or destroyed.

45 Spelling

> The man who writes with no misspelled words has prevented a first suspicion of the limits of his scholarship or, in the social world, of his general education and culture.—Julia Norton McCorkle

Sp Spelling. Correction: Correct the spelling of the word marked on your paper, looking it up in your dictionary if necessary. Learn the correct spelling so that you won't repeat the error.

Why is correct spelling considered important? You can answer this question for yourself. What would your reaction be if you found your name misspelled in a list of students elected to an honor society or to class offices? Would you willingly register for a course that was listed in the college catalog as "Sosial Science 101"? How reliable would you consider a textbook that bore the title *Hanbook of Curent English*?

Standardized spelling is a convenience for reminding a reader of the words he knows orally and is useful in conventional situations like alphabetical lists; but the chief motive to regular spelling is the fact that the majority of people consider it a sign of literacy and even of social respectability. It is taken for granted that the spelling of educated people will be accurate; even persons who are careless about their own spelling are quick to detect and to condemn misspelled words in the writing of others. If you are one of those who have not acquired good spelling habits, now is the time to begin by making an intelligent analysis of your errors and by trying conscientiously to remove them from your writing.

45.1 Causes of misspelling   Spelling would not be so difficult if each sound that we use in speaking was represented by a single letter or combination of letters. But the way we pronounce a word and the way it is spelled do not always coincide. The same letter or combination of letters may represent a variety of sounds, as the *a* in *aha, fare, hat, many, lay, far, was, idea,* or the *ou* in *though, bough, enough, through.* And one sound

may be represented in a variety of ways: b*ee,* bel*ie*ve, pre-
c*e*de, s*ea.*

In addition, a number of words are written with letters that
are not pronounced, and others (called *homonyms*) sound
alike but are spelled differently:

Silent letters	*Homonyms*
lam(b)	meat, meet, mete
(p)sychology	sight, site, cite
(k)nife	capital, capitol
r(h)ythm	write, right, rite
s(w)ord	its, it's
(w)rote	peace, piece

Such inconsistencies are explained by the history of the
individual words—but that does not make them easier to
spell today.

Absolute correctness in spelling isn't easy to achieve in
English; it is, in fact, attained in printed matter only by careful and repeated proofreading. But certainly every college student should be able to achieve an acceptable level of accuracy. If spelling is still a major problem for you, find out which
of the common causes of misspelling are responsible for your
difficulties, so that you can concentrate on them.

45.1a Carelessness   Be as careful about your own spelling as you
would expect other writers to be about theirs. Carelessness
undoubtedly accounts for the majority of misspelled words in
student papers. It may result from too rapid writing (as in papers written in class), or from failure to check the finished
copy carefully.

Every misspelled word that you actually know how to spell
is an example of carelessness. Typical examples are *their* for
there, to for *too, whose* for *who is, it's* for *its, fourty* for *forty—*
basic words that you learned before entering high school.

In themselves, such errors are trivial and cannot lead to any
misunderstanding in writing. But if a writer persists in making
them, it certainly indicates carelessness.

45.1b **Failure to visualize words**   If you aren't absolutely certain how a word is spelled, letter by letter, consult your dictionary. The trial and error method of writing a word several ways until it "looks right" (*curiousity? couriousity? curosity?*) isn't a reliable guide to accurate spelling. Unless you have a clear mental picture of the word to start with (*cu-ri-os-i-ty*), it is better to be safe and look it up.

Because reading is better taught by complete words and groups of words than by separate letters or syllables, many people do not see the individual letters in a word as it appears on the printed page. For example, everyone has seen the name "Eisenhower" in print a great many times, yet not everyone has noticed the individual letters: it begins with an *E*, of course, and contains an *h*, but how many letters are there in the first two syllables? And is the last part spelled *-hour, -hauer,* or *-hower?* The careful writer, when he needs to write the word, will look it up and fix it in his mind for future use.

45.1c **Faulty pronunciation**   Words should be spelled as they are written, not as they are sometimes mispronounced. Although faulty pronunciation is not a major cause of misspelling, it is responsible for some very common mistakes:

Correct spelling	*Misspelled because pronounced*
a*th*-*let*-ics	ath*a*letics
priv-*i*-lege	priv*v*lege
en-vi-*ron*-ment	enviro*m*ent
ac-ci-den-*tal-ly*	acciden*tly*
tem-per-*a*-men-tal	temper*mental*
dis-gust	dis-c*ust*

You will find that it helps to pronounce each syllable to yourself when you are writing longer words (*ac-com-pa-ny-ing, par-tic-u-lar-ly, stud-y-ing*). You should also notice that even though many people say "I *use* to go there every summer" or "He was *prejudice* against red-headed people," these forms are in the past tense and should therefore be written "I use*d* to go . . ." and "He was prejudice*d*. . . ."

45.2 Improving spelling A writer's own attitude is the main consideration for improving spelling. If he isn't really interested in bettering it, or if he feels that his spelling is hopeless, no amount of general advice or of "rules" to memorize will do him any good. Spelling, like most other aspects of writing, is only as important as the writer wishes to make it. A few people, in fact, seem to enjoy poor spelling habits in much the same way that a person might derive a certain pleasure in being the victim of an interesting allergy or a spectacular run of bad luck.

This is a list of the ten most frequently misspelled words compiled by several high schools in one city. If you can spell these and distinguish between similar forms, your spelling isn't hopeless:

too (to, two)	principal (principle)
its (it's)	writing (written)
believe	therefore
together	separate
their (there, they're)	pleasant

Some useful practices for improving faulty spelling are discussed in the sections that follow.

45.2a Proofreading Check all written work for spelling errors before you hand it in. Careful proofreading doesn't take long—ten or fifteen minutes should be sufficient for a 600 word paper—and the time will be well spent if you can find and correct most of your errors.

For papers written outside class, spelling should be checked in *revision.* It isn't a good practice when writing a first draft to stop to look up the spelling of every doubtful word; if you do so, you may lose the flow of thought, or at least interrupt the sentence movement. Put a check in the margin or over the word as you are writing; then when you are ready to revise, look up each word you have marked.

Accurate proofreading requires careful word-by-word reading. If you have difficulty checking your own writing, try following each line with a pencil point, so that you are obliged to see every word as you have written it. Or start at the end of the paper, reading backwards and covering the line directly above with a sheet of paper. Some people find it helpful to read their papers aloud, pronouncing each word distinctly. Any method is useful if it makes it easier for you to see the way that the words have actually been put down on paper.

45.2b Spelling lists   In your notebook, keep a list of words you have misspelled or that you have trouble spelling. The words should be spelled correctly (not as they may have been misspelled in your papers) and should be easy to find so that you can refer to them when proofreading future work.

The following list contains common words frequently misspelled in student papers, and may be used as a check list when you are correcting your own errors. Each word is divided into syllables so that you can see more clearly how it is put together. Less common forms are given in parentheses.

1. ac-com-mo-date	24. de-pend-ent
2. ac-quaint-ed	25. de-scrip-tion
3. a-cross	26. de-vel-op (de-vel-ope)
4. a-gree-ment	27. din-ing room
5. all right	28. dis-ap-pear-ance
6. al-read-y	29. dis-ap-point
7. a-nal-y-sis	30. dor-mi-to-ry
8. ap-pear-ance	31. em-bar-rass
9. ar-ti-cle	32. en-vi-ron-ment
10. ath-let-ics	33. e-quip-ment
11. at-tend-ance	34. ex-ag-ger-ate
12. be-lieve	35. ex-ist-ence
13. ben-e-fit-ed	36. ex-treme-ly
14. Brit-ain	37. fa-mil-iar
15. bus-i-ness	38. fas-ci-nate
16. change-a-ble	39. for-eign
17. choose	40. for-mer-ly
18. com-par-a-tive	41. for-ty
19. con-ceive	42. gram-mar
20. con-science	43. height
21. con-tin-u-ous	44. hin-drance
22. de-ci-sion	45. im-ag-i-nar-y
23. def-i-nite	46. im-me-di-ate-ly

47. in-ci-den-tal-ly
48. in-de-pend-ent
49. in-tel-li-gent
50. ir-re-sist-i-ble
51. judg-ment (judge-ment)
52. knowl-edge
53. lei-sure
54. li-brar-y
55. lik-a-ble (like-a-ble)
56. main-te-nance
57. man-u-fac-tur-er
58. mis-spelled
59. mo-not-o-nous
60. mys-te-ri-ous
61. nec-es-sar-y
62. no-tice-a-ble
63. oc-ca-sion-al-ly
64. oc-cur-rence
65. o-mit-ted
66. op-por-tu-ni-ty
67. par-tic-u-lar-ly
68. pas-time
69. per-form
70. pre-ced-ing
71. prej-u-dice
72. priv-i-lege
73. prob-a-bly

74. pro-ce-dure
75. pro-nun-ci-a-**tion**
76. pro-por-tion
77. psy-chol-o-gy
78. quan-ti-ty
79. re-ceive
80. re-fer-ring
81. rep-e-ti-tion
82. re-sem-blance
83. sched-ule
84. sec-re-tar-y
85. seize
86. sep-a-rate
87. sim-i-lar
88. soph-o-more
89. suc-ceed
90. sym-pa-thize
91. tem-per-a-ment
92. tend-en-cy
93. there-fore
94. trag-e-dy
95. tru-ly
96. un-doubt-ed-ly
97. un-til
98. u-su-al-ly
99. val-u-a-ble
100. writ-ing

See also the list of words in §45.4, Words that sound alike, p. 460.

A spelling list of your own, however, will be more profitable to study than those made by others, because it will help you to concentrate on your individual problems. The purpose of such a list is to prevent the same mistakes from occurring in one paper after another. When the same word occurs more than once in your list, print it in large capitals (FAS-CI-NATE), write it in red ink, spell it over and over to yourself, or use any other system that will call it to your attention.

45.2c **Writing the word** Master the spelling of troublesome words by writing them until you spell them right without thinking. If you aren't certain about the spelling of *embarrass*, for example, write or type the word, ten, twenty, or more times, in its various forms, until the spelling becomes automatic: *embarrass, embarrassed, embarrassment, embarrassing.*

Separate into syllables words that you find difficult to spell (consult your dictionary for the proper divisions). Stress those letters or combinations of letters that trouble you:

em-baR-Rass
oC-Ca-sion-al-ly
o-MiT-Ted
op-tI-mist

par-aL-Lel
preJ-U-dice
rep-E-ti-tion
sep-A-rate

It helps to say the word as you write it, either aloud or to yourself. The combination of (1) seeing a word letter by letter, (2) writing it carefully, and (3) pronouncing it at the same time will overcome most spelling problems.

45.2d Learning new words   Learn to spell new words correctly as you meet them in your college courses. A new or unfamiliar expression isn't a useful part of your writing vocabulary until you can spell it with confidence.

Make a note of the words you will probably have to write in reports or in examinations. Underline key words in your textbooks, and observe their spelling when they are written on the blackboard. Then write them out in syllables, pronouncing them as you do so:

ba-cil-lus
bi-par-tite
car-bon-if-er-ous
de-men-tia prae-cox

Gen-ghis Khan
me-tath-e-sis
pro-pri-e-tar-y
u-ni-cel-lu-lar

When instructors in various courses complain that their students can't spell, they are referring either to very common words of the language or to the words that make up the essential vocabulary of their subject.

45.3 General principles of spelling   Use whatever rules will help you to overcome your personal spelling problems. Chaotic as spelling is in English, there are some principles that are helpful for spelling common words.

Rules would be the best answer to spelling problems if they did not have any exceptions, but as everyone knows who has memorized spelling aids since the fourth grade, it is the exceptions that make the rules only partially helpful in the spelling of the most troublesome words.

Listed below are guides to spelling that you have probably heard before. If you *know* that you know them, you might better spend your time on some other aspect of writing. But if you aren't quite certain about these general principles, review them and perhaps also consult the spelling section in the front pages of your dictionary for more detailed information.

45.3a **Final -e** Words ending in silent *-e* generally retain the *-e* before additions (called *suffixes*) beginning with a consonant (*-ment, -ly, -some, -ness*), but drop the *-e* before additions beginning with a vowel (*-ing, -able, -ous, -ary*).

-e retained before a consonant

arrange	arrangement	nine	ninety
awe	awesome	require	requirement
definite	definitely	shape	shapeless
hope	hopeless		

Exceptions:

argument	awful	duly	ninth	truly

-e dropped before another vowel

argue	arguing	imagine	imaginary
arrive	arrival	shape	shaping
conceive	conceivable	value	valuable
grieve	grievous	write	writing

Exceptions: In a few words silent *-e* is retained before a vowel to avoid confusion with other forms:

dye	dyeing (compare *dying*)
line	lineage (compare *linage*)
singe	singeing (compare *singing*)

Words ending in -ce or -ge retain the final -e before additions beginning with a, o, or ou (so that the final -c or -g will not suggest the "hard" sound):

changeable   outrageous
courageous   unmanageable
noticeable   vengeance

45.3b -ei- and -ie- This jingle learned by most school children may help you to spell -ei- and -ie- words:

> Write i before e
> Except after c,
> Or when sounded as a
> As in neighbor and weigh.

Words with -ie- are more common than words with -ei-. The typical sound of -ie- is ē:

achieve   chief   grievous   niece
believe   field   hygiene   siege

Other -ie- words include the plurals of nouns ending in -y (companies, enemies); the third person singular present tense form of verbs ending in -y (defy, defies; fry, fries); and mischief, sieve, view.

After c, and also to spell the sound ā, -ei- is used:

ceiling   perceive   eight   reign
conceive   receipt   freight   sleigh
deceive   receive   neighbor   vein

Exceptions (long ē sound spelled -ei-): *either, leisure, neither, seize, weird.* Other sounds spelled -ei-: *counterfeit, foreign, height, heir.*

45.3c Doubling the final consonant Double the final consonant before a suffix beginning with a vowel (-able, -ed, -er, -ing) with (1) words of one syllable ending in a single consonant after a single vowel (brag, hit, sit) and (2) with words of more than one syllable, ending the same way and accented on the last syllable (commit, forget, prefer).

One-syllable words		Words of more than one syllable	
bat	batter, batting	commit	committed, committing
din	dinned, dinning	control	controllable, controlled
grip	gripping, gripped	occur	occurrence, occurred
hit	hitting, hittable	omit	omitted, omitting
spot	spotty, spotted	prefer	preferred, preferring

The consonant is *not* doubled (1) in words with two vowels before the final consonant (*daub, daubing; keep, keeper; spoil, spoiled*), or (2) in words ending with two consonants (*help, helped; peck, pecking; lurk, lurked*), or (3) when the accent of the lengthened word shifts to an earlier syllable (*infer', in'ference; prefer', pref'erence; refer', ref'erence*).

Usage is divided about doubling the final consonant of some words not accented on the last syllable, but American spelling generally favors the single consonant.

bias	biased	quarrel	quarreling
counsel	counseled, counselor	travel	traveler, traveled
diagram	diagramed	worship	worshiped, worshiping
kidnap	kidnaping, kidnaper		

45.3d Final -y Nouns ending in *-y* preceded by a consonant change *y* to *i* and add *-es* to form the plural:

apology	apologies	library	libraries
company	companies	study	studies
curiosity	curiosities		

Exception: in forming the plural of proper names, the *-y* is retained and *s* added: all the *Kellys*, both *Marys*.

A final *-y* preceded by a consonant regularly changes to *i* before all suffixes except those beginning with *i*:

body	bodies	happy	happiness
busy	business	lonely	loneliness
carry	carried, carrying	marry	marriage
duty	dutiful	mercy	merciful
easy	easily	study	studious, studying

Final *-y* preceded by a vowel remains unchanged when a suffix is added:

boy   boys, boyish
delay   delayed, delayer
enjoy   enjoyable, enjoyment, enjoying
play   playful, playing, played

45.3e -cede, -ceed, -sede Only one word ends in *-sede*: *supersede*. Only three end in *-ceed*: *exceed, proceed, succeed*. All other words of this sort end in *-cede*: *precede, recede, intercede, secede*, etc.

45.3f -able, -ible; -ance, -ence Words with these endings should be carefully checked in a dictionary unless the writer is certain of their correct spelling. Words ending in *-able* (like *advisable, desirable, improbable, suitable*) are much more common than those ending in *-ible* (such as *audible, divisible, horrible, visible*). But since no rules govern the formation of these endings, the individual words should be looked up in every case of doubt.

A few words are spelled with either *-able* or *-ible* endings. Dictionaries indicate the more common or preferred spelling by putting it first (*collapsible, collapsable; preventable, preventible*).

The spelling of words ending in *-ance, -ant; -ence, -ent* must also be watched since there is no difference in the pronunciation of either endings (attend*ance*, confid*ence*; defend*ant*, exist*ent*).

45.3g Words ending in -o Nouns ending in *-o* preceded by a vowel form the plural by adding *-s*:

cameo	cameos	studio	studios
folio	folios	tattoo	tattoos

Most nouns ending in *-o* preceded by a consonant form the plural by adding *-es* (*heroes, Negroes, potatoes, tomatoes, vetoes*). A few add *-s* only:

dynamos	Filipinos	silos	sopranos
Eskimos	pianos	solos	tobaccos

(handwritten in margin: check dictionary or memorize)

A few nouns ending in -o add either -s or -es to form the plural (*cargos, cargoes; hobos, hoboes; zeros, zeroes*). Because no rule can be given for adding -s or -es, a writer must either memorize the plurals or look them up in a dictionary.

45.3h Words ending in -f The plural of many nouns ending in -f is regular (*belief, beliefs; chief, chiefs; fife, fifes; roof, roofs*). But some common words ending in -f or the sound of -f form their plurals by changing -f to -ves:

calf	calves	loaf	loaves
half	halves	self	selves
knife	knives	thief	thieves
leaf	leaves		

The plural of a few nouns ending in -f may be either -s or -ves:

elf	elfs, elves	staff	staffs, staves
hoof	hoofs, hooves	wharf	wharfs, wharves
scarf	scarfs, scarves		

45.4 Words that sound alike Be careful to distinguish between the spelling of words of identical or similar sound. It is easy for anyone when writing rapidly to put down *their* for *there, its* for *it's, maybe* for *may be,* but the writer who is conscientious about his finished work will check it closely for errors of this sort. The confusion of one form for another may suggest an idea that the writer did not intend:

> Psychiatric treatment changed Bobby's entire personality from a withdrawn, unhappy child to a normal, happy boy *excepted* by his group.

The following pairs of words are often confused in writing. Check this list to see if you can distinguish between the meaning of each form:

accept	except	beside	besides
advice	advise	capital	capitol
affect	effect	choose	chose
aisle	isle	cite	site
allusion	illusion	conscience	conscious
birth	berth	coarse	course

credible	creditable		principal	principle
desert	dessert		quiet	quite
its	it's		stationary	stationery
lead	led		than	then
loose	lose		their	there
passed	past		to	too
peace	piece		weather	whether
personal	personnel		who's	whose

If you have trouble keeping any of these forms clear in your mind, try making up sentences that will illustrate plainly the differences in meaning:

Everyone *except* Sam *accepted* the invitation.
It's difficult for the leopard to change *its* spots.
The ceremonies will be held *whether* or not the *weather* is fair.

45.5 Separate words and combined forms

Observe the distinctions between expressions that are written as one word or as two. These forms frequently need to be checked in revision:

all ready (adjective phrase):
The girls were at last *all ready* to leave.
already (adverb of time):
It was *already* dark when they arrived.

all right (adjective phrase, conventionally written as two words):
The seats seemed *all right* to me. (The forms *alright* and *alrite* are not accepted in Standard usage.)

all together (adjective phrase):
There were six trout *all together.*
altogether (adverb, meaning *wholly*):
That's *altogether* another matter.

a while (noun):
They talked for *a while.*
awhile (adverb):
Can't you stay *awhile* longer?

may be (verb phrase):
He *may be* the next mayor.
maybe (adverb, short for *it may be*):
Maybe you'll have better luck next time.

Certain phrases may be mistakenly written as one word through analogy to other forms or because they are often run together in speech:

> The assignment was *a lot* more difficult than I expected. [not: *alot*]
> Will you be able to go? [not: *beable*]
> The puppy was always there at his owner's *beck and call*. [not: *beckon call*]

See §39.1, Hyphen in compound words, p. 431, for further material on word division.

45.6 Variant spellings   When a word is currently spelled in two ways (*extol, extoll*), it is usually a good idea to use the more common form.

Many words have secondary spellings, usually British or simplified forms which are labeled in dictionaries as *Brit., Variant, Archaic,* and so on, so that you can choose the form most appropriate to your subject and your style. Most people writing today, and certainly anyone who has difficulty with spelling, will ordinarily prefer:

1) The more modern of two equally reputable spellings of common words: *catchup, mold, plow* instead of *catsup* (or *ketchup*), *mould, plough.*

2) The simpler form of a specialized word if it has attained currency among the people who use it most: *anesthetic, catalog, medieval, program, sulfur* rather than *anaesthetic, catalogue, mediaeval, programme, sulphur.*

Although many common words can be and undoubtedly should be spelled in simpler ways (as *thoro* for *thorough, enuf* for *enough*), conventional spelling is expected in most kinds of writing. Three forms are gradually gaining wider acceptance and may be used in Informal papers if your instructor doesn't object: *tho, altho, thru.* Other shortened forms sometimes seen in advertisements and Familiar writing are not accepted by most people and should therefore be avoided: *nite, naborhood, alrite, brot, laff, ruf.*

In this book the spelling *inclose* is used rather than *enclose* because it appears to be gaining popularity in General American usage.

3) American rather than British spellings: *center, judgment, labor, pajama* rather than *centre, judgement, labour, pyjama.*

For the spelling of proper names (the British *Labour* Party) and for direct quotation (the Prime Minister described it as "a *humourless* situation"), British spelling is appropriate, but in other situations the American forms should be used.

References: Discussions of English spelling may be found in the front pages of most good desk dictionaries. A great deal of information is given in the section "Orthography," at the front of *Webster's New International Dictionary* (unabridged), available in all college libraries. Other sources are:

Baugh, Albert C., *A History of the English Language*, New York, Appleton, 1935, Chs. 9, 11, and Appendix II

Craigie, W. A., *English Spelling*, New York, Crofts, 1927

GPO Style Manual, pp. 51-62

Kennedy, Arthur G., *Current English*, Boston, Ginn, 1935, Ch. 7 and section 128

McCorkle, Julia N., *Learning to Spell: An Informal Guide for College Students*, New York, Heath, 1930

Pyles, Thomas, *Words and Ways of American English*, New York, Random House, 1952, Chs. 4, 5

Exercises

1. What words are misspelled in the following sentences? The words used as examples are correctly spelled in the preceding section on spelling. Without referring to the text, point out which

words are misspelled in each sentence and write down the correct form.

1) President Eisenhower accepted an invitation to be the principle speaker at a convention of the governors of the fourty-eight states.

2) When he was only a sophomore, Mike was all ready the outstanding athlete in school.

3) The child's outrageous curiosity was quiet as embarrassing to it's parents as it was to there neighbors.

4) Mathematics is alot easier for me than foreign languages, probably because I am prejudice against grammar in any form.

5) Looking down from that awesome heighth, the courageous climbers felt a definate sense of loneliness.

6) A temperamental person maybe one whose not well adjusted to his environment.

7) The judgment of the labor relations board benefited the skilled laborers more then it did the white-collar workers.

8) My advice to the beginning skier is to buy equiptment that is adequate, but not to expensive.

9) Old timers still remember the argument over the original site of the state capital.

10) What woman wouldn't be embarassed if the contents of her overstuffed purse were unexpectedly revealed to the gaze of the public?

2. Compose sentences that will illustrate clearly the differences between these pairs of words of similar sound (for example: "The *morale* of the troops overseas has never been higher"; "You would look in vain to find a *moral* in this story"). Pay particular attention to those words that give you trouble in writing:

advice	advise	conscience	conscious
affect	effect	its	it's
beside	besides	loose	lose
capital	capitol	personal	personnel
choose	chose	principal	principle
coarse	course	quiet	quite

to : prep
too : more than necessary - adv of quantity

stationary	stationery	there	their
than	then	to	too

3. Keep a list of words in your spelling notebook that you will have to use in writing for the different courses you are taking. To fix the spelling in your mind, divide the words into their proper syllables (consult your dictionary for this purpose). Use the names of your subjects for headings, in this manner:

economics: guar-an-tee; de-ben-ture; per-son-nel . . .
history: me-di-e-val; Med-i-ter-ra-ne-an; Ren-ais-sance . . .
psychology: ap-per-cep-tion; cor-re-la-tion; he-red-i-tar-y . . .
"general": dor-mi-to-ry; soph-o-more; sched-ule; cur-ric-u-lum . . .

4. The words in each of the following groups are to be copied down with the correct letters filled in the blanks as indicated.

1) Supply -ei- or -ie- as required for correct spelling:

1. ach _ _ ve	8. l _ _ sure
2. bel _ _ ve	9. n _ _ ghbor
3. c _ _ ling	10. sc _ _ nce
4. counterf _ _ t	11. s _ _ ze
5. for _ _ gn	12. sl _ _ gh
6. fr _ _ ght	13. y _ _ ld
7. hyg _ _ ne	14. w _ _ rd

2) Add -ed to the following verbs to show whether the final consonant is doubled or not. If there is a choice of forms, explain why you used the one you did:

1. benefit	8. kidnap
2. bias	9. light
3. chafe	10. play
4. clot	11. quarrel
5. dine	12. repay
6. drop	13. travel
7. handicap	14. worship

3) Add *-ing* to each of these words, making any necessary changes in the root form of the word:

1. become	6. hope
2. control	7. hurry
3. decide	8. prove
4. dine	9. use
5. endure	10. write

4) Change each of these words to an adjective ending *-ous:*

1. continue	6. grieve
2. courage	7. humor
3. courtesy	8. mischief
4. disaster	9. outrage
5. fame	10. ridicule

'5. Write the plural forms of the following nouns. If there is a choice of spelling, indicate which is the more common form:

alley	bus	Eskimo	play
alto	diary	Macy	quiz
ax	duty	motto	radio
belief	enemy	Negro	tomato

6. Add *-able* or *-ible* to the following words, changing letters wherever necessary to conform with accepted spellings:

admire	justify
advise	laugh
contempt	profit
digest	sense
force	size

Add *-ance, -ant,* or *-ence, -ent* to these words, making any other necessary changes:

attend	exist
compete	expect
confide	revere
descend	vigil

7. This is a "demon" spelling list compiled at Purdue University, on which the highest score made by four English teachers was 92%. Without looking at the words, have someone dictate them to you to see how many you can spell accurately without the use of a dictionary. Which words should you know how to spell for the purposes of general writing?

ecstasy	battalion	Chautauqua	diphtheria	rarefy
heinous	Eskimos	maintenance	exhilarate	seize
liquefy	meringue	perseverance	mosquitoes	siege
naphtha	mortgage	questionnaire	picnicking	sieve
villain	sergeant	sacrilegious	supersede	weird

—List compiled by George S. Wykoff, quoted in *Inside the ACD*, November 1951, p. 2

8. This paragraph explains and illustrates one kind of simplified spelling as used by *The Chicago Tribune*. Do the changes seem reasonable and consistent to you? Would you be willing to see spelling such as *sofomore* become general?

From now on, proclaimed the *Trib*, words of more than one syllable ending in "ff" will end simply in "f," *e.g., distaf, sherif, tarif, midrif, balif, mastif, rifraf.* (One syllable words like *cuff, scoff,* and *fluff* will keep the "ff.") Also doomed to *Trib* extinctions: the letters "ph" within a word, which will be replaced by "f," *e.g., anglofobe, sofistry, sofomore, sofisticate, biografy.* Magnanimously, the *Trib* granted "ph" the right to continue to exist at the start of words, *e.g., philosofy, photografer.* Explained [the education editor]: "It is a wise policy to recognize the universally valid principle of *festina lente* (hasten slowly). To abolish 'ph' at the beginning of words would mean to be out of line with the dictionary. . . . Where, for instance, would a foreigner or student find '*fthisis*' to learn that it meant tuberculosis?"—*Time,* July 18, 1949, p. 56

Study and reference

46 Study habits

Thinking means shuffling, relating, selecting the contents of one's mind so as to assimilate novelty, digest it, and create order.—Jacques Barzun

In spite of the agreeable competition of social life, of athletics and a multitude of other activities, and often the less agreeable necessity of earning money, the central occupation of a college student is studying. As in other work there are more profitable and less profitable ways of going about studying, and either can become fixed into habits.

The suggestions usually given for studying are based on the habits of successful students. These habits can be cultivated by those who may have to work hard in their courses so that they will get the maximum results for energy spent and will steadily increase their skill. Suggestions in the pages of a book are of little use by themselves, but they can help you examine your practices. Since they are likely to remind you of what you already know you should do, they may help reinforce your good intentions.

46.1 Conditions of study   It is only good sense for you to make it as easy as possible to carry out these good intentions by having conditions and habits that will prove effective.

46.1a Physical conditions   Although the important part of studying is mental activity—attention, interest, concentration—proper physical conditions can help. These include a desk or table of convenient height (making it easy to focus eyes on the book or paper), a chair that suits the body but is not too comfortable, and light that is adequate but does not tire the eyes with glare. It is worth experimenting to find the combination of conditions that calls for a position of slight tension (lolling is not conducive to concentration) but that will not waste energy in combating actual discomfort.

46.1b Time   Looked at as a job, college work usually calls for more than a forty-hour week: fifteen or more hours in class with the theoretical allotment of two hours preparation for each class hour (probably approximated by most serious students) means forty-five hours at least. The class hour is fixed but you arrange your own periods of preparation. These should be as regular as other circumstances allow. Obviously not everything can be left for evening but it is often hard to make efficient use of the afternoon. Lunch period should not be allowed to stretch out indefinitely, and it is especially useful to form a habit of doing work for one or more classes in the afternoon, before the natural time off for relaxation.

Usually the best time for working on a particular subject is as soon after the class hour as possible. Preparation for subjects that meet on alternate days can be divided into shorter daily periods, with a longer period on the day preceding the class. Programs that are very heavy on some days and conspicuously light on others require careful advance planning.

It is wise to have the time of studying for specific courses as regular as possible, because expecting to attack a subject at a definite time helps to focus attention on it in advance. It is better if written assignments or any unusually long or complex assignments are started early to allow for revision and rounding out at a second period.

Most people cannot concentrate profitably for more than an hour at a time, so that it is necessary to allow for breaks. Get up and stretch, walk around, chat—but try not to get absorbed in anything that will be a distraction when you return to study.

46.1c Attention   In psychological terms, studying is first a matter of attention. Because we cannot see the mind in action we sometimes forget that it can be directed, as more observable action can be.

There is always competition for our attention—and our minds cannot go in two directions at once. Consequently one of the conditions of attention is reducing distractions as far as possible. Pictures of family and friends on the desk are a natural temptation; it is better to put them in a position of honor on the wall or dresser. If you have other duties, try to get them out of the way first or postpone them to a definite time after studying, noting them on a scratch pad or calendar. Worries, financial or personal, are the greatest handicap, and if they can't be disposed of, you just have to learn to live with them and try to keep them in perspective.

There is naturally a tendency for previous lines of thought to continue. Sports and other activities not only take energy but are so interesting that they may absorb attention when they shouldn't. Many students don't seem to realize that a preoccupation with football or some other activity simply prevents attending to study. Talk about these things at mealtime or before your study period, and then try to forget them for a bit. A commonly given bit of advice is to do some mental arithmetic—adding, multiplying—as a transition to a period of study.

Interruptions by others are perhaps the hardest to handle. To escape them, some students have to go to a library or some other quiet place to study. But often an open understanding can be arrived at, even with talkative roommates or neighbors: an agreement to study at certain times and to respect each other's habits. One defense against interruptions is building a reputation for taking your studies seriously. Most people will respect this, and it needn't mean that you are a grind.

The point to remember is that among the varied competitions for your attention you have to make a choice. The competition is real and sometimes intense, but you are responsible for apportioning your time, for reducing distractions to a minimum, so that you can concentrate on the main job.

46.2 Adjustments required in study   Although we talk about "methods of study" in general, they vary with the particular subject. Actual accomplishment depends not only on time and attention but even more on your attitude and adjustment to the individual course.

46.2a General attitude   Your attitude in a particular course depends on a number of matters: the hour the class meets, its size, what others say about the course and the instructor, the reasons you are taking it (especially whether it is elective or required), the effort it requires of you, your past experience with the subject or lack of experience, the way the instructor conducts the class.

If you find yourself "fighting" a course, try to find out why; bring the causes into the open and examine them. If you can't remove them, resign yourself to making the best of a bad matter. But often the sources of discontent are superficial. If the course is required, why is it? Are you giving it a fair chance or handicapping yourself by repeating clichés about it? A hard course may be a challenge, new subject matter becomes familiar with practice, and it is always possible to make progress or to turn over a new leaf.

More important still is your idea of how useful and interesting the course is going to be. The usefulness of a particular course may be as preparation for other college work, for eventual application in some job, or for general information— for conversation, for understanding what goes on in the world, or for the general cultural background proper for an educated person. Beginning students sometimes object to courses outside their immediate, already formed interests; seniors almost always wish they had had more of them. It is natural that some courses should interest you more than others, but interest can be cultivated and ordinarily will grow if you do not set up barriers to your natural curiosity.

You are likely to feel somewhat confused in a new situation, and the start of every college course is a new situation. Psychologists call this stage "the undifferentiated blur." Soon some particular facts stand out clearly, and finally with luck they fall into a pattern that is understandable. It is often a help to study the outline of a course, if one is given out, or the whole table of contents of the textbook to get a frame within which the particulars fall.

It is a good thing to examine occasionally what you do in a particular course, to intensify your successful efforts, to find difficulties, understand them, and find ways of removing them. Instructors are glad to discuss such matters with students, with those who are doing reasonably good work as well as with those who are doing poorly. You should bring up questions of this sort early in a course, not wait, as so many do, till the last two weeks when it is too late.

46.2b Special methods Each subject requires somewhat different methods of work. These are usually suggested by the instructors in the courses. Some general suggestions for studying textbooks, the largest part of the work in most courses, are made in §47, Reading, and some comments on lectures in §46.3, Lectures. Suggestions for writing the "papers" frequently required in courses are the principal subject of this whole handbook, with general suggestions for composition especially in §5, Writing a paper, and §49, The reference paper. Here are comments on a few specific matters of adjustment to particular courses:

1) Many students have made harder work of a foreign language than they need to. As a people, we do not take easily to languages, though they have become increasingly important as our world contacts have increased, and they have always been a means of adding to a person's experience and general development. Probably no other college subject profits so much by incidental study, by being looked at often for short periods outside the time of preparation for a specific class. It takes only a few minutes to glance over a paragraph, to read a little aloud, to look through a conjugation table. Copying out brief passages, like reading aloud, helps give the feel of the language. And best of all, you can actually use the

language with others, seriously or for fun. Such small contacts added to regular preparation of assignments can build a familiarity with the language.

2) Laboratory work is partly for training in handling the apparatus and materials of a science, partly for emphasizing its general principles, and partly for practice in interpreting and reporting on specific data. Although ordinarily a laboratory period has no outside preparation, if there is a prepared manual, you should read the directions for the day's work before going to the laboratory, to see what the problem is and what principles are involved. Try to visualize in advance what you will do. This will often save time in doing the actual experiment and make it more meaningful. The work requires a clear understanding of directions, which sometimes have to be read several times and broken down into clearly seen stages: accurate observation, careful recording of observation, interpretation of the data, perhaps calculations of some sort, and perhaps diagrams. Often the most important part is applying principles. All these skills grow with practice. The final stage of writing up the experiment calls for accuracy and neatness, and when there is interpretation or discussion the report is a profitable exercise in clear, concise composition.

3) In courses in which working problems is important, the instructor gives special directions and hints that apply to the subject. In general the first problems are simple but they grow in complexity as the course goes on, so that it is very important to master each as it comes and to keep up with the assignments. Most problems are very compactly stated and often have to be read through several times to be understood. The essential thing is to grasp the actual "problem," what is demanded, and to see what principles, formulas, or methods might apply.

Orderly, neat work is usually a sign of clear thinking and may even encourage it. Comparing work with that of other students is often helpful—and most students who do well with problems usually work more of them than are actually assigned. As with laboratory reports, many problems give an opportunity for clear expression in words as well as in figures and symbols.

46.2c Special devices Some students work out special helps for themselves, such as cards with vocabulary or word forms of a foreign language, tables of dates, formulas. There is some value in the act of copying things of this sort. But if the cards are made without thinking through the material as it is copied, or if they are not actually used in review, they may become just busy work. Use any devices that your experience shows can be of help, but don't let them become ends in themselves.

46.3 Lectures Lectures are an important part of a good many introductory courses in college. Sometimes they present separate material but more often in beginning courses they are related closely to other work in textbooks or the laboratory and are intended to show the general plan of the course, to add to or interpret or re-emphasize topics that are also treated in the course reading. It is necessary for you to learn how to get facts and ideas from listening and to keep a record of them in notes.

46.3a Materials The best materials for taking lecture notes are the usual loose-leaf (ring) notebooks of whatever size you like. These allow for moving pages about, adding pages, and taking them out for convenient study. The wirebound notebooks are fixed and should not be used unless you are going to copy the notes. Notes should be taken in ink because it doesn't smudge and is clearer to read.

46.3b Preparation for the lecture Probably the main reason that some students do not profit from lectures is that they think the lecturer does all the work. A lecture usually is related to a reading assignment or some other work and frequently cannot be understood without this reading. It is a waste of time to sit through a lecture that is meaningless or almost meaningless because you have put off the reading and so cannot understand terms that are used in it. One lecture is usually related to the preceding one, so that it is helpful to glance over the last notes in order to connect the two. And as in all study, you should come prepared to pay attention, with your mind at work on the subject of the course.

46.3c   Form of notes   The form of the notes depends on your thought habits and on the lecturer's method. A lecture that proceeds by numbered points, 1, 2, 3, can be taken down in outline form. Often it is more satisfactory to use a block form—instead of separate lines for topics, a group of sentences or phrases following each other in an informal sort of paragraph. The important thing is to have main points stand out, starting from the left margin, with subtopics or examples or reasons indented under them. Leave good margins and frequent blank lines to add material from other sources or your own comments.

You should not take down too much, just the main points and important details. Every good lecture has quite a bit of incidental matter and repetition that make it more understandable but do not add content. Learn how your lecturer emphasizes important points—by saying they are important, by tone of voice, or by pause. Summarize rather than record exactly what is said. Phrases are usually more efficient than full sentences, and abbreviations or symbols (standard ones in the subject or some of your own invention) help you keep up with the speaker. The material should be put into your own words so far as possible, as you understand it and relate it to what you already know. Special care has to be taken in copying diagrams and formulas accurately from the blackboard. As a rule a demonstration can be briefly summarized with emphasis on the point actually demonstrated.

It is a good habit to go over the notes of a lecture soon after they have been taken to see that you really can follow and understand them, and to add essential bits while you still recall them. It is not necessary and usually a waste of time to copy notes unless they are on material that you will want to use after the course is over or unless you really improve them by adding related points from the textbook or other source. Early in a course it is a good idea for two or three students to compare their notes on a lecture soon afterwards (not waiting for the threat of an examination) and to discuss how well they represent the lecture. It is possible to improve your note taking by giving it a little thought, but there is no single perfect system of notes for a lecture. Notes are for your own use and they should fit around and supplement your other work in the course.

46.4 Progress in a course Your progress in a course is a steady addition of knowledge and increased skill in using that knowledge—a growth in thinking, in discussion, in doing problems, in laboratory work, in papers.

46.4a Increasing confidence Confidence comes from your own use of the material and from recognition and encouragement by others, both the instructor and students. Taking part in class by asking and answering questions, by giving bits of extra information, is a sign of, and encourages a feeling of, *belonging* to the class. The proper attitude is somewhere between indifference and apple polishing, but closer to the latter than the former.

If you are not gaining confidence and do not have a sense of accomplishment in a course, you should do something about it. If you have been putting a proper amount of time and effort on the work but with unsatisfactory results, it is best to talk with your instructor. One device that often helps is to concentrate for two or three days on the particular course, going over the textbook and notes from the beginning.

46.4b Grades Although it is possible to think too much about grades—and sometimes a fraternity or one's family stresses them more than is reasonable—a healthy regard for grades is a proper incentive. Though there is some element of chance in them, they are usually a fairly accurate sign of progress in a course. Know the general policy on grades: in most large courses about half the grades are C. Don't worry about "curves" and instructor's crotchets. Don't take any one grade too seriously—there will be others—and try sometimes to get a better grade than you usually do by extra concentration on the work. And try to see the reasons for your grades, both the high and the low ones.

46.4c   Retention of material   Above all, expect to remember what you study and try to retain a sense of the direction of the whole course and as many details as possible. You are taking several courses, all competing for attention. Some move fast and later material tends to blot out earlier. This is one reason why frequent quick reviews from the beginning help you retain both the general line and the particular facts. Don't turn immediately from studying one subject to another. Wait a few minutes to let the first one sink in.

Learn to review lecture notes and your reading as soon afterwards as possible, and remember that frequent short reviews will increase retention. Try to recall points when you are at rest, walking, or riding on a bus. Use the material in conversation if it is appropriate. But nothing helps like a determination to remember as much as possible and to build the mass of details into a growing body of related, associated particulars within the general frame of the course.

46.4d   End of the term   Work in all courses piles up toward the end of a term. There comes a time when things can't be postponed any longer and many students find themselves swamped just when they should be getting ready for examinations. The last themes in a composition course are consequently often not the best ones, and examinations usually show that the last readings have been slighted. Look ahead and try to keep up along the way so that you can give the tasks of the last week or two a fair chance.

46.5 Preparing for examinations All study prepares for examinations and the best preparation is steady day-to-day work. But since examinations are conspicuous and important parts of most courses, it is only good sense to make a little extra effort and go to them as well prepared and as confident as circumstances allow.

Examinations have several functions in a course: to encourage students to look at a part or the whole of the course in one view; to emphasize important material; to give students a chance to *use* the material, often to see it in new relations; to let a student see his grasp and progress in the course; and to give the instructor information for grading a student in comparison with others in the class and in preceding classes. Grading is by no means their only function.

46.5a Practice questions It is a good idea to make up and ask yourself some questions of the sort that are likely to be on the examination. This is not to try to outguess the examiner but to practice for the examination, as for any other contest. Often questions from previous examinations are good for practice. It is important to make full answers to these trial questions and to check them for correctness.

Do not make them all of one type but get some practice in the various activities that may be called for on the actual examination:

Recall, remembering and producing both particular facts and general principles from the course

Selection, shutting out matters that don't belong and picking out details that relate to each other or to a general principle

Application, fitting a general idea to some particular situation, applying principles in working out a problem

Interpretation, showing the meaning or the implication of facts

Relationships, seeing causes and effects, similarities, differences

Reaction, your attitude toward something (a story, an idea, a social situation), your response to or opinion of it

Organization, arranging the discussion so that one part follows another and they all add up to a full answer

Reflection, thinking through to some conclusion on the basis of facts given

46.5b Preparing for essay questions   Essay questions, usually beginning "What are . . . " or "Discuss . . . " or "Describe . . . , " name a specific topic for which you must recall and organize the subject matter. They call for discussing a rather general topic of the course, and so depend on knowing the principal topics, seeing their relations, and remembering at least a sample of the specific data (facts, reasons, results, and so on) by which they were developed in the textbooks or lectures. Outlines and summaries are especially useful in preparing for essay questions and so is a good notebook, made clearly so that the notes can be reviewed rapidly. In a textbook you would ordinarily underline or check headings and topic sentences as a guide to review for essay questions.

Two other types of question that depend on your recall of material are *short answer* questions, for which you are allowed a few lines on the question sheet or are told to write "not over three sentences" in a bluebook, and *completion* questions, in which statements are presented on the examination with blanks that are to be filled in with a word or two.

Working problems, drawing diagrams, and so on call for much the same preparation as essay questions.

46.5c Preparing for objective questions   In an objective examination you do not as a rule produce the answer but select among statements given: statements to be marked true or false, or from three to five possible answers from which you are to select the most accurate. Although objective questions call for "thinking" and sometimes for quite complex thinking, typically they depend on rapid spotting of particular points. In review for this type of examination you would mark or note not only the main points but particular details, definitions, words, phrases, or sentences that focus and emphasize material.

Objective questions usually come in fairly large numbers and not much time is allowed for each one. Consequently any practice that makes you shift rapidly from one topic or part of a course to another and encourages you to recall points quickly and accurately will help.

46.5d Final preparation   Anyone who takes an approaching examination seriously is going to put some concentrated effort on preparing for it. If you lose too much sleep or study too long at a time or do not bother to think about the subject as you go over it or see how the parts fit together, you may become more confused. You may naturally emphasize areas in which you feel weakest, but you should try to distribute your time and energy over the whole body of material to be covered. Try to increase your *understanding* as well as your memory. Intelligent final preparation, whether you call it cramming or not, usually pays dividends.

46.6 Taking examinations   As a rule if you are well prepared you will make good use of the actual examination period. A feeling of general readiness and an intention to make the best of the period help, as does thinking about the actual material of the course rather than about yourself or others.

46.6a Reading the questions   It is a good idea to read first all the main questions of an examination (though not the detailed questions of an objective part if there is one) and perhaps to read them through twice. You will certainly find some that you can do well on. This quick reading will let you lay out your time for each, allowing more for the harder ones; it will let you see if some are more important than others (often indicated by a suggested time allotment); it will perhaps let you decide which of various allowed choices you will take; and most important it will start your mind working on the topics you will treat. See what proportion of the whole examination a particular question is—a half, a fourth, a tenth—and if an amount of time is allotted to individual questions, try to approximate it in making your answers.

Underline key words in the questions, the specific matters called for. Get the pattern of the questions in mind and note their use of typical examination vocabulary: *illustrate* (give examples of), *enumerate* (make a list), *compare, contrast,* and directions like *outline* or *in not more than three sentences.* Be careful of questions that have more than one part and do not omit one unintentionally.

46.6b   Order of answers   Do first the questions that you feel sure of, to get full credit for them and to get in the swing of writing. But don't spend so much time on them that you won't have a fair amount left for the others.

Keep the answers in the same order as the questions, leaving space for the ones you are going to fill in later. This is a great help to the reader—as is making the answer numbers correspond to the question numbers. In general don't crowd the pages, and leave some space for afterthoughts.

46.6c   Objective questions   Be sure you understand the directions for objective questions because they tell exactly what you are to do. Use accurately the system of marking, whether it calls for check marks or crosses or numbers or letters or lines. If a sample answer is given, study that. Do the ones you are sure of first and then go back to the ones you need to think longer about. Often when several possible answers are given you will work by elimination, discarding one and then another till you are left with the most likely. Often the right choice is not a completely accurate answer but is the most accurate of the ones given. Watch for little words of strong meaning, like *only, always, never, all,* which make statements to which there are no exceptions, and for words calling for evaluation, like *main, principal, most important.* If the objective questions form only one part of the whole examination, do not spend more time on them than the part deserves. Usually a time (say, half an hour) or a fraction of the examination (say, one-fourth) will be indicated, though you may have to estimate this for yourself.

46.6d Essay questions   Since an individual essay question is likely to be an important part of the total examination, often one-fifth or more, it is necessary to see exactly what is called for, to note parts and subdivisions if there are any, and any special directions for the form of the answer. Since you have to recall the material, it is wise to make notes of points as they come to you and when you have enough for a satisfactory answer to arrange them in a rough outline. Very few people can write consecutively for fifteen minutes or longer without a plan of some sort. Since by its nature and by the time allotted to the question you are expected to say quite a little, this preliminary work is very important—and sometimes takes longer than the actual writing.

As a rule start the actual answer with a general or summary statement and develop it with the appropriate details. The suggestions on writing paragraphs in §9, Writing paragraphs, p. 107, can well be applied in examinations.

Make your answers as full as your knowledge allows, be as specific as you can, and show the relationships between your statements. Be concise and compact. Keep out material that you know is irrelevant, because writing it will take time from more important statements and having to wade through it will irritate the reader.

46.6e Revising the examination   If possible save a few minutes to read over and revise your examination or at least some questions on it. Probably you can add some small facts that you remembered after writing the answer. If time allows you to search your mind for further material, try to figure things out and use association: with the topic under which the question falls, with the part of the textbook or lecture from which it comes, with related facts.

Touch up your writing, especially checking on spelling and the punctuation of sentences. Check your use of the technical words of the course for meaning and for spelling. Draw a horizontal line through any matter you do not want read. In short, do anything that will make the examination an accurate and clear representation of your knowledge of the course.

References

Barzun, Jacques, *Teacher in America*, Boston, Little, Brown, 1945, Ch. 2, Pupils into Students

Chapman, Seville, *How to Study Physics*, Cambridge, Addison-Wesley Press, 1949

Cole, Luella, *The Background for College Teaching*, New York, Farrar and Rinehart, 1940, Ch. 11, Study Methods; Ch. 12, Learning and Forgetting; Ch. 19, Examinations

LeCount, Samuel N., and Henry A. Bamman, *How to Improve Your Study Habits*, rev. ed., Palo Alto, Pacific Books, 1953

Wrenn, C. Gilbert, and Robert P. Larsen, *Studying Effectively*, Stanford, Stanford University Press, 1941

Exercises

1. On a notebook page keep a record of exactly how you spent your waking time on two consecutive days, breaking the time into half-hour intervals. Then on the basis of this record and your consideration of how your time could be most profitably spent, lay out on a notebook page a time schedule for a typical week. Be specific, naming courses to be studied at specific times and be realistic, allowing time for fun and recreation.

2. Under each of the following headings list in order all the subjects you are taking, putting at the top of the first column the one

you find most interesting, at the top of the second, the one you find most useful, and so on:

Interest   •   Your past success
Usefulness   Your present standing
Effort required

Taking these lists into account, write a short discussion of your attitudes toward your courses and of your study habits, noting both satisfactions and problems and giving suggestions for meeting the problems.

3. Make out questions for a half-hour examination based on §§1-4 of this book, or on a section in another of your textbooks, or on some other material indicated by your instructor. Then make a key to any objective questions you used and a model answer to any essay question or questions.

47 Reading

The art of reading consists in getting from the printed page as nearly as possible a sensation equivalent to the real thing. . . . Ideally, at every stage, the reader should use printed matter to reinforce his experience of life, to organize it, to extend it.—Jacques Barzun

The amount of reading expected in college, some of it quite difficult, requires effective reading habits. It is a good idea to examine early in your college course the way you read and see if you need to improve. Though actual improvement comes only from practice, some general suggestions may be helpful.

47.1 The activity of reading   Although you can read for pleasure in almost any circumstances, serious reading calls for concentrated attention, freedom from distraction, and the general conditions required for successful study (§46.1). Though different people read at different rates, it has been found that speed and understanding tend to go together, that fairly rapid readers comprehend better than conspicuously slow readers. College students usually read material of average difficulty, like a magazine article, at 250 to 300 words a minute. (There are about 415 words on a solid page of this book.) If you are a conspicuously slow or inaccurate reader, you should make an effort to increase your speed and comprehension. If your efforts to improve in reading do not bring results, it would be wise to go to a reading class. Most colleges have such classes or clinics and they have helped thousands of students to better reading habits.

47.1a Avoid vocalizing   A symptom of slow reading is forming the sounds in your throat, "vocalizing." Sometimes though you make no sound, you can feel the movement of your vocal cords with your finger. Sounding out new and difficult words may help master them but ordinary material should be read silently. If you find yourself vocalizing as you read, try to force yourself to go faster and to get the meaning just from seeing the words.

47.1b Read by sense groups   A second symptom of slow reading is being conscious of individual words, even of the incidental ones like *in, be, the.* Meaning is conveyed by small groups of words, "sense groups," and efficient readers are not conscious of the individual letters or words of which they are made. Your eye can take in five or six words up to a total of thirty letters in one glance. Here is the first paragraph of this section with the sense groups marked:

The amount of reading | expected in college, | some of it quite difficult, | requires effective reading habits. | It is a good idea | to examine early | in your college course | the way you read | and see if you need to improve. | Though actual improvement comes only from practice, | some general suggestions | may be helpful.

Practice in seeing the sense groups in what you read is one of the best ways you can improve both the speed and the comprehension of your reading.

47.1c Read actively   Reading as a skill involves not only the use of your eyes but the full use of your mind. Somewhat arbitrarily this can be analyzed into these activities:

Understanding, seeing beyond the words on the page to the things, situations, ideas they represent

Associating, tying these facts and ideas to others you already have, most closely to those from the course in which you are working but perhaps more importantly to the rest of your experience

Evaluating, seeing the rightness and relative importance of what you are reading as compared with other ideas, its place in your general development, its meaning to other people, its value in the life of our time

Applying, using what you learn not only in the course but in conversation, in your work, in your thinking

Enjoying, for though this discussion may make reading and study seem like work, your college reading, as well as your voluntarily selected reading for pleasure, can be enjoyed. Progress in reading will be a source of satisfaction.

47.2 Types of reading   How you read depends on the kind of material, on your purpose, on the time you have, and on other factors. For efficiency you should be able to adjust your reading to at least these five types:

47.2a Browsing   In browsing you allow your eyes to wander down the column or page, perhaps pausing when something strikes your fancy. Browsing is primarily for passing the time, going through a book or magazine you have picked up casually, and is of little use in college work—though occasionally of course you pick up a few random facts in this way.

47.2b **Skimming**   In skimming you cover material rapidly, passing your eye down the center of the page or column, or perhaps moving from the upper left corner to the lower right. You are usually looking for some particular item or kind of material that you need. Skimming is useful in picking up particular details, in seeing if a work has something of importance to you, and in making a preliminary survey of an article or chapter or book to get its general scope, plan, direction. Skillful skimming is useful in college and worth practicing.

47.2c **Rapid reading**   In rapid reading your eye follows each line across at the fastest rate you are capable of. It should give you the general progress of thought without many details. It is the appropriate type of reading for articles of general interest, for most fiction, and for reviewing material with which you are somewhat familiar. Though it is not a satisfactory substitute for more thorough reading, it is sometimes necessary because of lack of time, and skillful rapid reading is useful under pressure.

Rapid reading is also a way of keeping up your rate of reading. Because you have so much difficult reading to do in college, your rate tends to slow down. If you do a certain amount of rapid reading in magazines and fiction along with your study, it will have an effect on your whole reading skill. Occasional rapid reading, going as fast as you can, should help your efficiency in the following two types.

47.2d **Ordinary reading**   Typical or general reading is somewhat slower: The goal for most people is from 250 to 300 words a minute. You follow across the lines, getting the sense groups clearly and understanding the general content and important details, so that you could write a fairly good summary of the content. You are definitely reading to absorb the material presented. You should be able to handle a good deal of textbook and outside reading in this way. Often two "ordinary" readings of a passage will give a better idea of the material than one slower reading.

47.2e Close reading Compact or difficult material or the need to completely master the material requires slower reading. This is largely because you have to reflect, figure things out as you go. Close reading is often necessary for a new subject, especially if it is compactly written; for literature written in the past or written in a difficult idiom, like some poetry; for understanding directions and problems; and usually for evaluating, judging what you read. This might actually be called study rather than reading. When you must read thoroughly, go as rapidly as you can and still understand the material, but don't fight it or make short cuts. You will usually be helped by examining the form of the piece, noting the introduction or keynote, the way the central theme is repeated and developed, the closing paragraphs in relation to the whole; and rereading of important passages will often be necessary. Give it the concentration it deserves and feel satisfaction in mastering its substance.

47.3 Reading textbooks Textbooks vary in their readability. Some can be read at your typical rate, others require close, thorough reading. Often an instructor will make specific suggestions on how you should read a textbook; but even if he doesn't, a rapid survey of the book and your knowledge of the course requirements should indicate the degree of thoroughness needed.

Before beginning to read the text, you should know the general purpose, plan, and main topics of the book from reading the table of contents and perhaps the introduction, and you should know any special parts it contains—the index, glossary, and appendix, if it has these. This preliminary survey is especially important if you are reading only part of the book or are not reading its parts or chapters in the order in which they come in the book.

The following suggestions apply to particular assignments:

47.3a Preliminary skimming Skimming the chapter or assigned part before actually reading it is a good practice. Note the title and the paragraph or section headings if there are any; read the introductory paragraph and the conclusion; look at the illustrations; let your eye glance over the pages. Four or five minutes spent in this way will give you an inkling of what is to come, introduce you to the key words, and focus your attention, perhaps raise some questions that you will want to answer as you read.

47.3b   Reading by sections or paragraphs   You are looking for the ideas in your reading, and in a carefully written book these are developed in paragraphs and short groups of paragraphs. Be sure you understand one section before going on to the next. Pause and think over the subject of a section, ask yourself questions about it and see if you can restate the ideas in your own words. This is the time to underline important points or check them or summarize them in the margin. If after the first close reading you go back over a section two or three times rapidly, you are much more likely to remember its content than if you go over it only once. If you become confident that you know one topic before going on to the next, it is less likely to be blurred or buried by the later material.

47.3c   Sentences   The style of sentences varies noticeably from one book to another, and for efficient reading you have to accustom yourself to their movement. Learn to spot automatically the subjects and main verbs and see how the modifiers fit. If the sentences are long or interrupted, read very slowly at first, perhaps reread or even read a page or so aloud, until you feel at home with them. After this practice you can usually go faster.

47.3d   Vocabulary   Every college subject has its special vocabulary and sometimes at the start new words come fast. It is necessary for you to know what the words stand for. Pronounce new words so that you can use them and can recognize them if they turn up in lectures.

Most textbooks carefully define technical terms when they

first appear. If a word is not defined directly, get the meaning so far as you can from the passage (the "context" as described in §20.3, Words in context and situation, p. 248).

Use the glossary if the book has one, or through the index find the places where the word is discussed. Consult a dictionary if necessary, but remember that your book will usually give a fuller definition than a dictionary can, and may be using the words in a special sense. It is useful to underline definitions of words that are important for the subject, or even to make a glossary of your own in your notebook if the textbook does not have one.

47.3e Diagrams and charts   Diagrams, charts, maps, tables, pictures supplement the text. Often they give a great many facts in a small space. The writer expects you to "read" them or he would not put them in. Look at them especially to see how they are related to the text, what they add to the subject, or how they summarize it. Do not try to understand charts or diagrams without reading what the text has to say about them. If you are visual-minded, you will often remember facts presented by these devices better than from the sentences.

47.3f Underlining   Many students try to keep their textbooks clean to sell them. This is usually shortsighted policy. The two or three dollars you may get for a secondhand book is a small sum compared to what the course is costing you. A textbook is a tool, and if it is to be of greatest use to you, you should adapt it to your needs. Some—not too much—underlining or checking of important general ideas and key details keeps you alert as you read, forces you to understand what is being said, actually impresses it in your mind, and in addition makes it possible for you to review rapidly. Sometimes marginal notes added—a definition, reference to a lecture or outside reading, another example or application—will make the book more useful, more your own.

It may be useful to write a summary, or even to make an outline of a textbook in your notes. If you find this useful or if you are by nature extremely thorough, by all means do it. But the book is already organized so that it or your lecture notes (or both) will make a record of your experience with the course.

47.4 Outside reading   In many courses supplementary reading, usually in library books or periodicals, is part of the work. The process of reading is the same, but there are a few special points to consider.

Since the reading is in books you do not own, you will have to take notes. The sort of notes will depend on the purpose of the assignment and the nature of the book or article. Often the assignment is to report on some special, detailed investigation. For this you would probably take notes on the method of the study, on what was actually done (whether a laboratory experiment, questionnaire, interview, or what); you would also need to give sample data and the principal conclusions, as they relate to the topic of the course.

Sometimes the reading is extensive, a whole book, a biography, one man's interpretation of a social or political situation (the presidency, labor relations in an industry, a detailed history of a war or of an industry or a part of the country). The important point is to see the relationship of the outside reading to the topic of the course and how it expands the text or lectures. Perhaps you might make a condensed summary followed by some important details. Many of the suggestions for taking notes in §49.4 apply here, certainly the ways of keeping track of the exact title and pages. Since these books usually have fewer helps than textbooks (summaries, topical headings, and so on), the preliminary skimming is especially helpful. Practice will improve your judgment of what to take notes on.

In reading a long play or novel for a literature course, you would not skim first but would read carefully the first part, until you were at home with the tone, style, and general direction, and then you would read more rapidly. The best way to review a book of this sort is to run over your notes on it and then reread a section of the book itself to bring it vividly to mind.

The notes on outside reading should be filed in your notebook with other notes on the topic it relates to. And above all, the reading should be done when it can be of immediate use in the course, and not be allowed to pile up.

References

Altick, Richard D., *Preface to Critical Reading*, New York, Holt, rev. ed., 1951

Barzun, Jacques, *Teacher in America*, Boston, Little, Brown, 1945, Ch. 4, How to Read and Be Right; Ch. 11, The Classics off the Shelf

Brown, James I., *Efficient Reading*, New York, Heath, 1952

Gray, William S., ed., *Growth in Maturity Through Reading*, Chicago, University of Chicago Press, 1952

Gray, William S., ed., *Reading in an Age of Mass Communication*, New York, Appleton-Century-Crofts, 1949

Wilking, S. Vincent, and Robert G. Webster, *A College Developmental Reading Manual*, Boston, Houghton Mifflin, 1943

Wrenn, C. Gilbert, and Luella Cole, *How to Read Rapidly and Well*, Stanford, Stanford University Press, 1935

Wrenn, C. Gilbert, and Robert P. Larsen, *Studying Effectively*, Stanford, Stanford University Press, 1941, pp. 9-15

Exercises

1. By drawing slant lines between expressions, divide the sentences of the following paragraph into sense groups:

The odor of a flower can be compared to radio advertising that calls to customers from a considerable distance, at least in the dimensions of the insect world. The color of a flower is like the store front or neon sign. When the right insect customer arrives at the right flower a variety of attractions and devices are provided at the point of sale. These are especially important in the hidden nectar flowers where a visitor must tread in precisely the right places to operate the pollinating gears. Many petals and sepals which act as landing stages have white or yellow streaks, or bright dots, called nectar guides, that converge for the entrance of body or head or proboscis. We find these guides in such flowers as the iris, speedwell, violet, lady's slipper and countless others. Sometimes the nectar guide is a bright circle, as the red center of certain pinks and mallows and the little yellow circle at the center of bluets and blue-eyed grass. The tall blue lobelia has two white patches at its portal. The tiger lily has red glands that not only converge as nectar guides but also glisten deceptively as though with nectar drops. The lip of the snapdragon is colored red where the bee enters.—Reprinted by permission of Dodd, Mead & Company, from *This Green World* by Rutherford Platt, p. 140. Copyright 1942 by Dodd, Mead & Co., Inc.

2. In your own words make a note of the general idea of the paragraph in exercise 1 with sample details.

3. Compare the way you read two textbooks in your present courses, or two selections in the volume of readings for your composition course. Illustrate how the format of the book (section divisions, headings, and so on), the development of paragraphs, the sentences and words affect your speed and understanding. Make your report in the form of notes and be prepared to discuss in class the factors of reading involved.

4. (For a class exercise) Your instructor will select a passage and give the class five minutes in which to read as much as possible. When time is called, mark the point at which you stopped. Then your instructor will ask you to write the answers to four or five questions. How many words did you read and at the rate of how many words a minute? Did you answer the questions correctly?

48 Using a dictionary

Dictionaries are like watches; the worst is better than none, and the best cannot be expected to go quite true.—Samuel Johnson

Every college freshman should buy a good dictionary and know how to use it. A reputable, up-to-date dictionary is an indispensable reference not only in composition courses but in most other courses as well.

Dictionaries answer questions about the meanings, spellings, origins, and pronunciations of words. What, for example, does *unilateral* mean, or *aphorism*, or *ganglion*? Is the preferred American spelling *judgement* or *judgment*? Should you say *Him a la'yas* or *Hi mal'yas*? Dictionaries give a good deal of information about the forms of words (plurals, past tenses) and constructions (which preposition goes with a given noun or verb). In addition, they help a writer to distinguish between closely related words, like *childish* and *childlike* or *imply* and *infer*. One of the most valuable habits the college student can acquire is that of checking the dictionary for meaning, pronunciation, and spelling of words, especially during the revision of his papers.

48.1 Evaluating dictionaries There is no such thing as *the* dictionary, a supreme authority which can be quoted to settle all arguments about words. Instead, there are numerous dictionaries, differing in purpose and in three general characteristics: date, size, and responsibility of editing.

48.1a Date An up-to-date dictionary is essential because new words are constantly being added to the language (*orlon, wetback*); other words are used in new senses (*alert,* for an air-raid warning); spellings and pronunciations change. In buying a dictionary, see that you get the most recent printing or edition of the one you prefer. (Copyright dates and printing dates are listed on the back of the title page.)

48.1b Size   For everyday use the most practical dictionaries for students to own are the "college" dictionaries that cost from five to six dollars (a recommended list is given below). Pocket dictionaries may be helpful to check spelling, but they are obviously not adequate for college work. The larger, unabridged dictionaries, such as *Webster's New International Dictionary* and the *Standard Unabridged,* are available in all college libraries.

48.1c Editing   Responsible editing makes the dictionary really useful, gives it what "authority" it may possess. It should be a compilation from a vast accumulation of actual recorded uses of words, not a patchwork from existing word books. This raw material then should be worked over by specialists in various subjects and by trained editors who digest the evidence and compose the dictionary's brief entries.

The following dictionaries are currently available and composition courses usually recommend certain ones for student use:

American College Dictionary (1947). Simplified pronunciation key and pronunciations based on current usage; comprehensive treatment of technical words; good synonym studies; all words (general words, proper names, abbreviations) in one alphabetical list; common meanings of each word come first in entry; frequently revised.

Webster's New Collegiate Dictionary (1949). Long established; careful treatment of usage problems and the general vocabulary; four alphabetical lists of words: (1) common and technical words and foreign words and phrases, (2) biographical names, (3) geographical names, (4) abbreviations; synonym studies; oldest meaning of a word stands first in each entry; frequently revised.

Webster's New World Dictionary of the American Language (1953). (Not a Merriam-Webster dictionary) Emphasizes simplified definitions even for technical terms; includes many Informal words and phrases; common meanings first in entry; etymologies unusually full; all words in one alphabetical list; new words added annually.

New College Standard Dictionary (Emphatype edition, 1947). Intelligent handling of technical definitions; greatly simplified pronunciation key with few diacritical marks; no synonyms; common meaning first.

Thorndike-Barnhart Comprehensive Desk Dictionary (1951). Contains 90,000 entries as contrasted with the 120,000 to 140,000 in the usual "college" dictionaries; synonym studies; simplified etymologies; simplified pronunciation key and pronunciations based on current educated usage; usage notes; common meanings first in entry; one alphabetical list of all words; frequently revised.

Since dictionaries differ in various features, as the notes just made show, it is important for you to know your own thoroughly to make it of maximum use to you. Look through the table of contents to see what units of material there are besides the main alphabetical list of words. You may find a grammar of the English language, a discussion of punctuation, a guide to letter writing, a table of signs and symbols, perhaps a list of the colleges and universities in the United States.

See if your dictionary has a supplement of new words or if new words are incorporated in the regular list. Are proper names and foreign words listed separately? Read a page or two consecutively to see how words and phrases are handled. Try pronouncing some familiar words, looking only at the respelling for pronunciation, to see how the pronunciation key works.

A little time spent in learning your dictionary will make it really useful to you. The next subsections describe in some detail the main features of a typical dictionary, and the exercises at the end of the section will give you practice in the actual use of your own dictionary.

48.2 Definitions   The most important use of a dictionary is as a guide to the meanings of words, making you sure of words you partially know and giving you some idea of the meaning of words that are new to you.

Definitions begin with an abbreviation showing whether the word is being defined as an adjective, adverb, noun, an intransitive verb, a transitive verb, and so on. All of these abbreviations are explained in a table at the front or back of the dictionary. If the word is used in some special sense, as in music, chemistry, baseball, etc., it may be so labeled. The definitions then follow, as in these examples:

flaunt (flônt; flänt), *v. i. & t.* [Of Scand. origin.] **1.** To wave or flutter showily. **2.** To move or display ostentatiously; to display boastfully, brazenly, or the like; to parade. — **Syn.** See SHOW. — *n.* Act of flaunting; display; something flaunted. — **flaunt′er,** *n.* — **flaunt′ing·ly,** *adv.* — **flaunt′y,** *adj.*

stance (stăns), *n.* [OF. *estance* a standing, position.] **1.** *Scot.* Station; position, as for a building; site. **2.** Mode of standing or being placed; posture. **3.** *Golf.* A player's position after he places his feet preparatory to making a stroke.

By permission. From *Webster's New Collegiate Dictionary,* copyright, 1949, 1951, 1953, by G. & C. Merriam Co.

To a writer, the dictionary definitions are most useful in checking the meanings of words he is almost sure of but not quite—perhaps such a word as *flaunt,* above. When revising a paper he should make sure that such doubtful words mean what he thought they meant when he put them in his first draft. To a reader, a dictionary is useful not only for meanings of unfamiliar words but also for unusual senses of familiar words. It is most valuable for finding the exact sense in which a word is used in a particular passage.

In using a dictionary either for your writing or your reading, it is usually necessary to read *the whole definition entry.* Some dictionaries put the oldest meaning first and others the most common one. Often you will need neither of these but a more specialized meaning that comes late in the entry.

Three points should be remembered in using dictionary definitions: (1) A dictionary does not *require* or *forbid* a particular meaning of a word but *records* the uses that have been found for it. (2) The dictionary definition is for the most part a record of the *denotation* of a word, although the usage label or illustrative phrase or synonym entry may suggest also its *connotation* (see §§20.1, 20.2, pp. 245, 246). For this reason it is safest not to use a word until you have read it or heard it and so know at least in part what suggestions it may carry if it is not a simple factual word. (3) Finally and most important, the words in the definition are not the meaning of the word but phrases suggesting their referents, which, often with the aid of an example, will indicate to you what objects, ideas, or acts that particular word refers to.

48.3 Spelling   Learn how to use your dictionary to check the spelling in your papers. Dictionaries divide words into syllables by means of spaces or small dots between the syllables (*de light ful*) (*de·mar·ca·tion*). You can thus see each part of the word clearly and correct any omitted or transposed letters in the word as you may have written it.

If you can't immediately find a word because you aren't certain how it starts (is it *gibe* or *jibe?*), keep in mind other spellings for the same sound.

48.3a Division of words   Words should be divided at the ends of lines according to the syllable divisions shown in the dictionary entry. Thus *dis·par·ag·ing·ly* could be divided at any one of the four breaks. Hyphened words should be divided only at the hyphen to avoid more than one hyphen in the same word.

Accurate division at the ends of lines will prevent such blunders as dividing *bedraggled* into *bed-* and *raggled*. (See §7.3, Division of words, p. 87.)

48.3b Optional spellings   When usage is divided, two spellings will be given for a word. The one the editors believe is more common is given first: *hemoglobin, haemoglobin; although, altho.* Use the spelling you are accustomed to, though since there is a tendency toward uniform spelling, you will certainly be safe if you use the spelling put first in the dictionary.

Spellings labeled British (such as *colour, gaol, judgement*) should be avoided in favor of the usual American spelling.

48.4 Pronunciation   To show how they are pronounced, words are respelled (in parentheses) in specially marked letters. The letters of our alphabet are directions to say sounds. Because their directions are often confusing (there are over 250 letters and combinations of letters to spell some forty sounds of English), dictionaries use a uniform system of symbols, usually specially marked letters, to represent the sounds of words. The sounds represented by the symbols are usually shown at the bottom of the page and are more fully explained in the discussion of pronunciation in the front of the book.

ar·chi·tect (är′kə·tekt), *n*. **1.** person whose profession is to design buildings and superintend their construction. **2.** person skilled in architecture. **3.** maker; creator. [< L < Gk., < *archi*– chief + *tekton* builder]

dé·cor (dā·kôr′), *n*. **1.** decoration. **2.** scenery on a stage. [< F, < *décorer* DECORATE]

suave (swäv), *adj*. smoothly agreeable or polite. [< F < L *suavis* agreeable] —**suave′ly**, *adv*. —**sua·vi·ty** (swä′və·ti; swav′ə–), **suave′ness**, *n*.

Copyright, 1955, by Scott, Foresman and Company

The accented or stressed syllable is indicated by a heavy mark (′); secondary stress is usually indicated by a lighter mark (′): ev′er last′ing.

Dictionaries list two or more pronunciations when usage is divided, as in this example:

ad·ver·tise·ment, *esp. Brit.* **ad·ver·tize·ment** (ad′vər·tīz′mənt; ad·ver′tis·mənt; –tiz–), *n*. a public notice or announcement, as in a newspaper or magazine, or over the radio.

Copyright, 1955, by Scott, Foresman and Company

While the first pronunciation given is usually preferred, a person should use whichever pronunciation is more common among the educated people of his community.

Dictionaries usually give a full pronunciation which if followed completely would give a person's speech a slow and somewhat stilted sound. In ordinary speech, vowels are often less distinct than most dictionaries indicate, and the stress varies with the position of a word in a phrase.

The only comprehensive survey of American usage in pronunciation is Kenyon and Knott, *A Pronouncing Dictionary of American English*, 1944, available in most college libraries.

48.5 Areas of usage and special labels   Words unlabeled in a dictionary are supposed to belong to the general vocabulary;

other words are labeled *dialectical, obsolete, archaic, foreign, colloquial, slang, British, United States,* or are referred to some particular activity—*medicine, law, astronomy, music, sports, manufacturing, electricity.* These examples illustrate typical use of some labels:

con⁴ (kŏn), *adj., v.,* **conned, conning.** *U.S. Slang.* —*adj.*
1. confidence: *con* game, *con* man. —*v.t.* **2.** to swindle; defraud. [short for CONFIDENCE (GAME or MAN)]

cov·in (kŭv′ĭn), *n.* **1.** *Obs. except Law.* a secret or collusive agreement between two or more to the prejudice of another. **2.** *Obs. or Archaic.* fraud. [ME, t. OF, ult. der. L *convenīre* agree]

pe·dic·u·lo·sis (pĭ dĭk′yə lō′sĭs), *n. Pathol.* the state of being infested with lice. [t. NL, f. s. L *pedīculus* louse + -*ōsis* -OSIS] —**pe·dic·u·lous** (pĭ dĭk′yə ləs), *adj.*

rav·ing (rā′vĭng), *adj.* **1.** that raves; delirious; frenzied raging. **2.** *Colloq.* extraordinary or remarkable: *she's no raving beauty in my opinion.* —*n.* **3.** irrational, incoherent talk.

Reprinted by courtesy of the publishers from *The American College Dictionary,* copyright 1947 by Random House, Inc. (textbook edition by Harper & Brothers).

These labels are rough guides to usage, but a writer should bring his own observation to bear on individual words. Certainly he wouldn't use words marked *obsolete* or *archaic,* but many that carry no label are rarely used (*moot, perforce*) and would mar the writing of young people.

In general the viewpoint of dictionary editors is rather conservative, and many words marked *Dial.* or *Colloq.* (such as *chunky, journalese, highbrow*) would fit perfectly well into both Informal and General English. *Colloq.* means that the word is characteristic of cultivated conversation rather than of Formal writing; *U.S.,* that the word is used in the United States but not in other parts of the English-speaking world.

48.6 Synonyms and antonyms Most dictionaries list words of similar meaning (*synonyms*) with the basic or most comprehensive word of the group and show in what ways they are alike:

—**Syn. 1. See opinion. 2. See feeling. 3.** SENTIMENT, SENTI-
MENTALITY are terms for sensitiveness to emotional feelings.
SENTIMENT is a sincere and refined sensibility, a tendency to
be influenced by emotion rather than by reason or fact: *to
appeal to sentiment.* SENTIMENTALITY implies affected, excessive, sometimes mawkish sentiment: *weak sentimentality.*
—**Ant. 2.** realism, logic.

Reprinted by courtesy of the publishers from *The
American College Dictionary,* copyright 1947 by
Random House, Inc. (textbook edition by Harper
& Brothers).

Often, as above, reference is also made to an *antonym,*
a word of opposite meaning, as *cowardly* would be an
antonym for *courageous.*

48.7 Other linguistic information   Dictionaries give the part
of speech in which a word is generally used and any distinctive forms that a word may assume—the principal parts
of verbs, the plurals of nouns, the comparative and superlative forms of adjectives and adverbs when they are in any
way irregular. They label verbs as transitive or intransitive
and indicate when words are usually capitalized or italicized.

In addition, the *etymology* of the word is given—its origin
and how it got into English. Sometimes this is merely a
statement of the language from which the word came into
English (Italian, Latin, French, Japanese), and sometimes
it is more complicated, as the statement on *scope* in *Webster's
New Collegiate,* tracing the word back through Italian and
Latin, and ultimately to Greek:

scope (skōp), *n.*   [It. *scopo,* fr. L. *scopus, scopos,* fr. Gr. *skopos* a
watcher, mark, aim.]   **1.** *Archaic.* Ultimate intention.   **2.** Room
for free outlook, aim, or action; liberty.   **3. a** Distance within which a
missile carries.   **b** Length; extent; as, *scope* of cable.   **4. a** Range of
view, intent, or mental activity.   **b** The range within which an activity
displays itself; as, the *scope* of Napoleon's genius.   **5.** Short for *oscil-
loscope;* specif., one in the form of a cathode-ray tube with a fluores-
cent screen, constituting the visual indicator in a radar set and sometimes called a *radarscope.*

By permission. From *Webster's New Collegiate Dictionary,* copyright, 1949, 1951, 1953, by G. & C.
Merriam Co.

Whether or not such information helps in the understanding of a word, it often illustrates how word meanings change

from their original to their present-day use and are sometimes interesting in themselves.

48.8 Special dictionaries The general dictionaries—abridged and unabridged—are supplemented by a number of specialized word books which occasionally need to be consulted for material not to be found in general works.

48.8a Historical dictionaries Good college dictionaries are in part based upon scholarly dictionaries made over long periods of time. *The Oxford English Dictionary* (10 volumes and a *Supplement*, 1888-1928) is a historical dictionary of the words and idiomatic phrases of the English language. It traces the various forms and meanings of each word, stating the date of its first appearance in recorded English and giving illustrative quotations from writers to show its typical use at various times in its history (a dozen or more pages are sometimes devoted to a single word). *The Shorter Oxford English Dictionary* (2 volumes), an abridgment of the larger work, may prove easier for the student to use.

The *Dictionary of American English* (4 volumes), made on the same plan as the *Oxford*, gives the history of words as they have been used by American writers from 1620 to 1900. A *Dictionary of Americanisms* (2 volumes) gives the history of words that originated in the United States and brings the record of American English down to 1944.

There are some dictionaries for special periods of English, for particular regions, and for special usage areas, such as slang. Periodicals like *American Speech* and *PADS* (Publications of the American Dialect Society) regularly publish regional and occupational vocabularies.

48.8b Dictionaries in special subjects Most special fields have dictionaries of their specialized vocabularies. It is a good idea to know the one in any field you are going to do much work in. The following titles indicate the range of such books. (Most of them are revised from time to time.)

Abbrevs: (A Dictionary of Abbreviations)
Alsager, C. M., *Dictionary of Business Terms*
Ballentine, J. A., *Law Dictionary*
Chamber's Technical Dictionary
Dorland, W. A. N., *American·Illustrated Medical Dictionary*
English, H. B., *A Student's Dictionary of Psychological Terms*
Good, C. V., *Dictionary of Education*
Hackh's Chemical Dictionary
Henderson, I. F. and W. D., *Dictionary of Scientific Terms* (biological
   sciences)
Rice, C. M., *Dictionary of Geological Terms*

Exercises

1. Write out the following information about your dictionary, for discussion in class or to be handed in if requested.

1) The title, the name of the publisher, and the most recent copyright date. This date may be found on the back of the title page.

2) A list of the sections following the introduction and preceding the dictionary entries (such as "How to Use the Dictionary," "A Guide to Pronunciation," "Usage Levels," and so on).

3) A list of the material in the appendix (if any), such as "Signs and Symbols," "Biographical Names," "Colleges and Universities in the United States."

4) The order of definitions of the words. Does the oldest meaning or the most common meaning come first?

2. Answer the following questions by using your dictionary:

1) Would a man six feet tall weighing *ten stone* be considered underweight or overweight?

2) What relation if any is there between the word *jet* in *jet black* and *jet* in *jet engine*?

3) In what expression is *foots* sometimes used as the plural of *foot*?

4) Is *Welsh rarebit* or *Welsh rabbit* the preferred form for the dish made of cheese and toast? 637

5) Is the population of Milwaukee, Wisconsin, larger or smaller than that of Geneva, Switzerland?

6) When is the term *needle point* hyphened and when is it not?

7) In what sense might the word *guys* be appropriately used in General or Formal English?

8) By what name is *Siam* now known? Thailand

9) Do you have any *siblings*?

10) What distinction, if any, is there between a *golf links* and a *golf course*?

11) Is a *crumpet* something to blow, to eat, or to sit on?

12) Is the California Institute of Technology a coeducational school?

13) A page numbered *lxvi* would be equivalent to what page number in Arabic numerals?

14) In what sense might *crew* be used as a verb in Formal English?

15) Are the islands (or islets) of Langerhans an American protectorate?

3. What information do you find in your dictionary on the spelling of these pairs of words? Are the spellings interchangeable? Which form would you use in writing, and why?

baritone–barytone	inclose–enclose
citrous–citrus	jest–gest
criticise–criticize	oesophagus–esophagus
disfavour–disfavor	practise–practice
employe–employee	rhyme–rime
encyclopaedia–encyclopedia	theater–theatre
gray–grey	veil–vail

4. What form or forms do you find in your dictionary for the plural of these nouns? If there is a choice of forms, which would you use in your own writing?

beau	criterion	medium	ski
bus	gladiolus	phenomenon	stadium
crisis	index	plateau	stratum

5. Read the section in your dictionary that explains the symbols used to indicate the pronunciation of words. Then using the same symbols, indicate how these words are pronounced:

beige	err	gunwale	orgy
boatswain	government	heirloom	salve
ensign	greasy	indict	worsted (yarn)

6. What pronunciations does your dictionary list for each of these words? Is the first pronunciation given the one that you hear most frequently? If not, tell how it differs, including the stress (accent):

address	Don Juan	herb	morale
adult	drama	ice cream	penalize
amateur	economics	idea	pianist
chic	exquisite	isolate	research
coupon	grievous	Los Angeles	rodeo

7. These questions concern the *etymologies* of words—their origins and histories. You can find the answers in the etymological entries either preceding or following the definition of the words in your dictionary.

1) In what respect are the origins of these words similar: *bloomers, fahrenheit, mackintosh, pasteurize, sandwich*?

2) From the combination of what words did the word *nostril* originate?

3) How was the word *what* spelled in Old English?

4) The word *tattoo* has two distinct meanings and two different origins. From what language is each meaning derived?

5) Who coined each of these words: *blurb, kodak, robot, iron curtain*?

8. Consult your dictionary for answers to these questions:

1) What is the meaning of *circus* in an expression such as *Piccadilly Circus* (an area in London)?

2) Would a *Francophobe* be likely to take up permanent residence in France?

3) If you leaf through a magazine quickly and casually, do you *peruse, scrutinize, scan, thumb,* or *study* it?

4) What is a *cartel?* Is more than one meaning given?

5) What is the difference between the American interpretation of *a billion* and that of the British?

6) Which of these words are identical in meaning: *ravel—unravel; childlike—childish; flammable—inflammable?*

7) A very small but perfectly developed American adult would be most exactly described by which of these words: *runt, dwarf, midget, pygmy?*

8) Distinguish between the meaning of the word *monitor* as it is used in grade schools and as it is used in radio. Is the word used as the same part of speech in both instances?

9) You might read the word *billingsgate* in an English publication; express the meaning of it in your own words.

10) How might the title of Robert Burns' well-known poem, "Auld Lang Syne" be expressed in current American usage?

9. Make up two sentences for each of these words—one to show clearly in what sense your dictionary considers the words as *slang* or *colloquial,* and the other to show the word as used in General English. Label each sentence, and after it indicate what part of speech the word is that you have used, as in these examples:

rat: Slang: No kid in the reform school ever *rats* on his friends. (verb)

         General: Like most seaports, the city was infested with *rats.* (noun)

character	cut	ice	junk	shingle
coke	horse	Java	old	tough

49 The reference paper

Planning and writing a reference paper (also called a library, a research, or a term paper) is an important part of most freshman composition courses. This project, usually assigned in the middle or later part of the course, is primarily a record of intelligent reading in several sources—books, magazines, encyclopedias, and other reference works—on a subject either assigned by the instructor or selected by the student.

Since many college courses require reports based upon reading in such sources, standard methods of finding material, putting it together, and presenting it have been developed. Learning these methods is a start on the road of scholarship that leads through advanced courses and graduate study to the work of professional people who constantly add to our knowledge and understanding of the past and the present. For many students the reference paper will also provide practice for various papers they may be called upon to do after graduation as part of a business or professional project.

In addition, this kind of assignment offers more immediate values for college freshmen:

1) Practice in exploring the possibilities of a subject and limiting it so that it can be treated adequately in a paper of a given length—typically from 1500 to 3000 words.

2) An introduction to the resources of the college library, with training in the most efficient ways of locating material.

3) Practice in using source material intelligently—that is, choosing between what is useful and what is not, and organizing and interpreting the information.

4) An opportunity to learn something new about a subject and become something of an authority on it.

Because the reference paper is longer and more complex than the other compositions you are asked to write, it should be handled in successive steps.

49.1 Choosing a topic A good reference paper should begin with your interest in the subject you are going to investigate.

In some courses the subject field is limited by the instructor's assignment (perhaps to various aspects of the United Nations, or to the history of a specific geographic area, or to events in the life of some famous person), but more often the choice of subject will be largely a matter of your personal preference.

In either instance, you should be reasonably certain that the subject you select will be one that you will like to read about, to think about, and then to write about. Since a reference paper may take as much as five or six weeks to prepare, it can easily become a chore and perhaps a waste of time if you do not feel that what you are doing is of some importance.

49.1a Deciding on a field Before making a definite choice of topic, consider your various interests, both inside school and out. These general subjects may suggest others to you:

1) A subject related to one of the courses that you are now taking or that you intend to take. For example, if you are majoring in business administration and you intend to take American economic history next year, you might investigate the beginning of child labor laws or early life insurance companies in the United States.

2) A subject related to your reading interests (biography, history, science fiction, detective stories), or one related to your favorite hobby or sport (4-H clubs, music, mountain climbing, dress design).

3) A subject about which you now have an opinion but little information: Does capital punishment help prevent crime? Are children with high IQ's generally successful in later life? Is hazing in colleges declining? Do rapid readers retain more than slower readers?

4) A subject that has aroused your curiosity but that you have never had time or opportunity to investigate: Why is ROTC a required program in land-grant colleges? Do sun spots actually affect the weather? How has the popularity of TV affected book sales? Can rain be made by aerial cloud seeding?

49.1b Limiting the subject As soon as you know what general field you would like to concentrate on, find a specific topic within that field that can be treated adequately and intelligently in a paper of the assigned length. If you have only a hazy notion about the subject, explore its possibilities by a few hours of preliminary background reading in one or more general or special encyclopedias (see §§49.2c,d), in some magazine articles, and perhaps in newspaper articles, too, if the subject is one of current interest.

Next look through the library card catalog and the guides to periodical literature (see §49.2b) to see how the field you have selected may be broken down into smaller units. A broad subject like *aviation* may first be limited to *commercial aviation,* then to the *functions of the CAA,* and still further limited to *recent safety measures suggested by the CAA.*

Keep these considerations in mind when you are narrowing your subject:

1) Length of the reference paper. A freshman reference paper is not expected to be the last word on a subject; neither is it intended to be a disconnected enumeration of commonplace facts, or a superficial summary of a complex topic. Select a limited subject so that you will feel confident that you can cover it with reasonable thoroughness.

2) Availability of source material. Before you begin to read and take notes, find out whether the more important books and periodicals that you will need are available in the library. Since five or more sources are required for most reference papers, it is important that you know that there are at least this many available before you begin your paper.

3) Complexity of the source material. For some subjects (chemical structures of synthetic rubber, for example), the available material may be too technical for a general audience to understand, and perhaps too complicated for the writer to interpret, too.

49.1c Final definition of the topic   Before you begin to take notes, define your topic as accurately and clearly as possible. Unless you have a reasonably accurate idea of what you are investigating, your reading will be without direction and a great deal of the material you gather may have to be discarded later.

At this early stage a final statement of the central or controlling idea is not expected, but you should certainly know, for example, whether you intend to discuss the growth of rural electrification in the South or changes in farming methods brought about by electricity.

Avoid drastic, last-minute changes in your topic unless it has proved completely unsuitable. A sudden switch, two or three weeks after the paper has been assigned, will not only waste precious time but may also lead to the suspicion that the writer doesn't know or particularly care what he is writing about.

Minor changes within a topic are, of course, permissible and often advisable. As you read further into your material, you may decide to narrow the topic still further, or to shift the emphasis slightly, perhaps changing "sources of pigments for oil painting" to "the process of making oil paints." Consult your instructor about any changes you would like to make before you continue extensive reading.

Thoughtful and early attention to the choice of topic will make all the later stages in the process easier and more profitable.

49.2 Sources of reference   A primary purpose of the reference paper is to acquaint students with the resources of their college library so that they can locate the information they need quickly and efficiently. On most subjects, the material in the library is so extensive and so varied in form (books, periodicals, encyclopedias, newspapers, pamphlets), that a writer about to begin his research would be hopelessly lost unless he knew something about the essential works in his subject, the methods used to index and catalog material, and the quickest way to obtain this information.

This section deals with library facilities and the various aids that will help you find the material that you need for a reference paper. Librarians are always willing to help a student with his research problems, but every student should also be willing to help the librarians, too, by showing some knowledge of the standard sources of reference.

49.2a The library card catalog   The card catalog is an alphabetical index, on cards, of the items in the library. The cards are filed in drawers or trays, and each drawer is labeled to show what part of the alphabet the entries contain (for example: Bank-Bat).

Most card catalogs list the titles of periodicals (and indicate what copies the library has), encyclopedias, the titles of government publications and other works, but most importantly, the card catalog tells what *books* the library has.

All books are listed three ways in the card catalog: by author, by subject, and by title. The cards issued by the Library of Congress, like those reproduced below for *Forty Acres and Steel Mules* by Clarence Herman Nixon, are almost universally used for cataloging.

Subject card (alphabetized by subject)

1 Subject
2 Call number
3 Author
4 Title, facts of publication
5 Pages, Illustrations, height
6 Bibliography
7 Other subject headings
8 Facts for librarians

① AGRICULTURAL ADMINISTRATION

② 309.175 N65f   **Nixon, Herman Clarence,** 1886– ③
④ ... Forty acres and steel mules. Chapel Hill, The University of North Carolina press, 1938.
⑤ vii, 98 p. front., plates. 27 cm.
⑥ "Selected bibliography": p. 97–98.

⑦ 1. Agriculture—Southern states. 2. Southern states—Soc. condit. 3. Southern states—Econ. condit.—1918– 4. Agricultural administration—U. S. i. Title.

⑧ HD207.N5   630.975   38—17363

Library of Congress   ⸢3k⸣

Author card (alphabetized by author's last name)

309.175 N65f   **Nixon, Herman Clarence,** 1886–
... Forty acres and steel mules. Chapel Hill, The University of North Carolina press, 1938.
vii, 98 p. front., plates. 27 cm.

Title card (alphabetized by the title)

Forty acres and steel mules

309.175 N65f   **Nixon, Herman Clarence,** 1886–
... Forty acres and steel mules. Chapel Hill, The University of North Carolina press, 1938.
vii, 98 p. front., plates. 27 cm.

You can save yourself many hours of thumbing through books that are not relevant to your subject by learning to interpret and evaluate the information given in the card catalog.

The *subject* card on page 520, for example, provides answers to these questions:

1) In general, what is the book about? In this instance, agricultural administration. Also listed are the other subject headings under which the book is cataloged.

2) How can the book be obtained for examination? By giving the call number, which is in the upper left-hand corner, to the librarian. In almost all libraries, borrowers are requested to fill out slips with the call number, author, title, and the borrower's name and address.

3) Is the book up-to-date? If you were looking for more recent information on agricultural administration in the South than that compiled in 1938, you would not bother with this book.

4) How extensive is the treatment of the subject? This book is brief—98 pages of text, plus seven (vii) pages of introductory material. Notice, however, that it does contain illustrations (*plates*) that may be useful.

5) Does it have further aids for your research? The two pages labeled "Selected bibliography" might prove helpful.

6) What specific material does it contain that you could use? The subject headings for this book show that it is concerned with agricultural administration problems in the South but also has more general bearing (4. Agricultural administration—U.S.).

The rest of the information on the card is for librarians—the size of the book (27cm—twenty-seven centimeters high), the Library of Congress classification (HD207.N5), and so on. To see what material you should copy on your bibliography cards, consult §49.3, Preparing the working bibliography, p. 528.

49.2b Periodical indexes Next to the card catalog the most important sources of reference are the *Readers' Guide* and the other indexes to periodicals. A great deal of essential material, particularly on current topics, is available only in periodicals, which may range from popular magazines and newspapers to technical journals and learned publications. This material is cataloged in various guides and indexes, some of them published monthly, others annually. Knowing how to use periodical indexes will not only simplify the task of research but it will also make the reference paper more authoritative and up-to-date.

1) *Readers' Guide to Periodical Literature, 1906—* This is the most useful of all periodical guides for the subjects on which most freshmen reference papers are written. The *Readers' Guide* is published monthly in paperbound volumes and later in large cumulative volumes covering one or more years. It indexes the articles in more than 120 magazines of general interest, and gives references up to the preceding month.

The entries in the *Readers' Guide* (like those in the card catalog) are listed alphabetically in three ways: by author, by title, and by subject. The *Readers' Guide* uses many abbreviations—for the titles of periodicals, the month of publication, and for various facts about the article itself. These abbreviations are explained on the first pages of each issue. Here is a reproduction and explanation of seven consecutive main entries:

(1) **EGGEN, Olin Jeuck**
       Tektites: glass from the moon. Sci Digest 33: 53-5 Ja '53
(2) **EGGENSPERGER, Kermit A.**
       Heads up! Flying 52:24-5+ Ja '53
(3) **EGGHEADS.** See Intellectuals
(4) **EGGLESTON, Arthur**
       Labor and civil liberties. Nation 174:647-50 Je 28 '52
(5) **EGGNOG**
       Holiday eggnog; with recipe. il Good H 136:22-3 Ja '53
(6) **EGGPLANT**
              See also
       Cookery—Vegetables
(7) **EGGS**
   (a) Do not blame hen for poor summer eggs. Sci N L
              61:393 Je 21 '52
   (b) Economical egg. J. Nickerson. il tab N Y Times Mag
              p28-9 Ja 6 '52
   (c) Egg and you. Todays Health 29:10 S '51
   (d) Egg encrusted with protoporphyrin. F. B. Hutt and
              J. B. Sumner. bibliog il Science 116:35-6 Jl 11 '52

Reprinted from *Readers' Guide to Periodical Literature,* by permission of H. W. Wilson Co.

Explanation: The headings (1), (2), and (4) are *author* entries. Olin Jeuck Eggen is the author of a three-page article (53-5) titled "Tektites: Glass from the Moon" published in volume 33 of the magazine *Science Digest* for January 1953. The number before the colon in each entry refers to the volume of the periodical; the numbers after the colon refer to the pages of the article. Thus "Heads Up!" by Kermit A. Eggensperger (2) begins on pages 24-5 of *Flying* and is continued elsewhere in the magazine (+).

Entries like (3) and (6) that are followed by *see* or *see also* are cross references. If you wanted to locate articles on the term "Eggheads," for instance, you would look under "Intellectuals."

(5) and (7) are subject entries. In this particular volume of *Readers' Guide* only one article on "Eggnog" (5) is listed —an unsigned, two-page, illustrated (il) article in volume 136 of *Good Housekeeping* for January 1953.

"Eggs" (7), a subject entry, is followed by a list of *titles* on this subject. The wording of the title and the information thereafter are often useful in determining whether an article may be helpful or not in gathering material for a reference paper. The unsigned article (a) in *Science News Letter* (Sci N L) might contain information that a general audience would understand; the article by J. Nickerson (b) in *The New York Times* magazine section, while brief, has a table (tab) that might be consulted; the title of the article (d) in *Science* (written by two authors) suggests that it is a technical discussion that laymen might not understand, but it also includes a bibliography (bibliog) that might lead to sources easier to understand.

2) Other periodical indexes. A number of specialized periodical indexes are often useful for work on a reference paper. Most of these in the following list appear annually (the date after the title shows when they were first published). Those marked with a † are most generally useful.

Agricultural Index, 1916–   Subject index to a selected list of periodicals, books, bulletins, documents

Annual Magazine Subject Index, 1907—   Subject index to a selected list of American and English periodicals and historical society publications

Art Index, 1929—   Author and subject index for fine arts periodicals and museum bulletins

Bibliographic Index, 1937—   Subject index to bibliographies in books and periodicals

†*Biography Index,* 1946—   Subject index to biographical material in books and periodicals

†*Book Review Digest,* 1905—   Author, subject, and title index to published book reviews; gives extracts and exact references to sources

Catholic Periodical Index, 1930—   Subject index to a selected list of Catholic periodicals

Dramatic Index, 1909—   Index to articles and illustrations concerning the American and English theater

†*Education Index,* 1929—   Author and subject index for educational periodicals, books, and pamphlets

Engineering Index, 1906—   Subject index to technical periodicals; transactions and journals of engineering and other technical societies; reports of government bureaus, engineering colleges, research laboratories

Index to Legal Periodicals, 1926—   Author, subject, and book review index for legal periodicals

†*Industrial Arts Index,* 1913—   Subject index to a selected list of engineering, trade, and business periodicals

†*International Index,* 1907—   Author and subject index to periodicals from various countries; devoted chiefly to the humanities and science; supplements *Readers' Guide*

†*Poole's Index to Periodical Literature,* 1802-1906. Subject index to American and English periodicals, many of which are no longer published but are still important; precedes coverage of *Readers' Guide*

†*Public Affairs Information Service,* 1915—   Subject index to books, periodicals, pamphlets, and other materials on economics, government, and other public affairs

United States Government Publications; Monthly Catalog, 1895—   Listing of the various publications of the government in all fields

Ulrich's Periodical Index (5th ed., 1947) lists periodicals under subjects they contain, answering the question: What periodicals are there in this field? It also tells in what guide each is indexed so that it serves as an indirect index to the contents of all magazines.

3) Newspaper index. *The New York Times Index* (1913—)

is a monthly index to articles appearing in *The New York Times,* with annual volumes. This index will help you to find articles of general interest in local papers because it gives the dates of events, speeches, and important documents which would presumably be covered in all papers of the same date.

49.2c General encyclopedias A general encyclopedia is often a good starting place for information. The following encyclopedias, available in all college libraries, are authoritative and include many bibliographies and cross references:

> *Encyclopaedia Britannica,* 24 vols., 1954. Volume 24 contains a general index.
> *Encyclopedia Americana,* 30 vols., 1952. Volume 30 contains a general index.
> *New International Encyclopaedia,* 25 vols., 1922-1930

49.2d Special reference works and encyclopedias The following reference works go further into detail than those in general encyclopedias, and their approach is more specialized. An early acquaintance with those you expect to use will be valuable in your research.

> Architecture: *A History of Architecture* (Bannister-Fletcher), 14th ed., 1948
> Art. *Harper's Encyclopedia of Art,* 1937, 2 vols.
> Biography (American): *Dictionary of American Biography,* 1928-1943, 21 vols.
> *Who's Who in America,* published every two years since 1899. Also a monthly supplement, 1939 to date
> Biography (British): *Dictionary of National Biography,* 1885-1937, 63 vols., and supplement
> *Who's Who,* annually since 1849
> Biography (General): *Current Biography: Who's News and Why,* 1940–
> *International Who's Who,* 1935–
> *World Biography,* 1948, 2 vols.
> Business: *Encyclopedia of Banking and Finance* (Munn), 5th ed., 1949
> Chemistry: *Thorpe's Dictionary of Applied Chemistry,* 4th ed., 1937-1949, 9 vols.
> Education: *Encyclopedia of Educational Research* (Monroe), 1950

History (General): *An Encyclopedia of World History* (Langer), 1940
  Cambridge Ancient History (Bury and others), 2nd ed., 1928-1939,
  12 vols. and 5 supplementary volumes of plates
  Cambridge Medieval History (Bury and others), 1911-1936, 8 vols.
  and supplementary volumes of maps and plates
  Cambridge Modern History (Ward and others), 2nd ed., 1926, 13
  vols. and atlas
History (American): *Dictionary of American History* (Adams), 1940,
  5 vols. and index
Literature (General): *Dictionary of World Literature* (Shipley), 1953
  Columbia Dictionary of Modern European Literature (Smith), 1947
Literature (Classical): *Oxford Companion to Classical Literature*
  (Harvey), 1937
  Oxford Classical Dictionary (Cary and others), 1949
Literature (English): *Cambridge History of English Literature* (Ward
  and others), 1907-1927, 15 vols.
  Oxford Companion to English Literature (Harvey), 3rd ed., 1946
Literature (American): *Cambridge History of American Literature*
  (Trent and others), 1933, 3 vols.
  Oxford Companion to American Literature (Hart), 2nd ed., 1948
  Literary History of the United States (Spiller and others), 1948,
  3 vols.
Music: *Grove's Dictionary of Music and Musicians,* 4th ed., 1954, 9 vols.
  International Cyclopedia of Music and Musicians (Thompson), 5th
  ed., 1949
Philosophy and Psychology: *Dictionary of Philosophy and Psychology*
  (Baldwin), 1910, 3 vols.
  Encyclopedia of Psychology (Harriman), 1946
Quotations: *Bartlett's Familiar Quotations,* 12th ed., 1948
  The Home Book of Bible Quotations (Stevenson), 1949
  The Home Book of Shakespeare Quotations (Stevenson), 1949
  *A New Dictionary of Quotations on Historical Principles from Ancient
  and Modern Sources* (Mencken), 1942
Religion: *The Catholic Encyclopedia,* 1907-1922, 17 vols.
  The Jewish Encyclopedia, 1925, 12 vols.
  Encyclopedia of Religion and Ethics (Hastings), 1911-1928, 13 vols.;
  reissued in 1931 in 7 volumes
Science: *Hutchinson's Technical and Scientific Encyclopedia* (Tweeny
  and Shirshov), 1935-1936, 4 vols.
  Van Nostrand's Scientific Encyclopedia, 2nd ed., 1947
Social Sciences: *Encyclopedia of the Social Sciences* (Seligman and
  Johnson), 1930-1935, 15 vols.; reprinted in 1937 in 8 volumes

See also §48.8b, Dictionaries in special subjects, p. 511.

49.2e Yearbooks and annual publications For information on a wide variety of subjects, particularly those of current interest, these annual publications provide up-to-date facts and figures:

The World Almanac and Book of Facts, 1868— This is one general reference that any student can afford to own (the current price is about $1.10), and one that anyone with a serious interest in current affairs can hardly afford to be without. The index is in the front of each volume.

Information Please Almanac, 1947—

The American Yearbook, 1910— Annual record of events in the United States, with a detailed index and lists of periodicals for further reference

The Americana Annual, 1923— Annual supplement to the *Encyclopedia Americana* with a chronology of events of the last year

The Britannica Book of the Year, 1938— Annual supplement to the *Encyclopaedia Britannica,* with cumulative index

Economic Almanac, 1940— Information about business and government in the United States and elsewhere

The New International Yearbook, 1907— Annual supplement to the *New International Encyclopaedia*

Social Work Yearbook, biennially since 1929. Social work and related fields

Statesman's Yearbook, 1864— Statistical and historical annual publication about political and industrial events throughout the world

United Nations Yearbook, 1946–1947— Activities of the United Nations

49.2f Other reference works Many other specialized reference works can be found by consulting:

Mudge, I. G., *Guide to Reference Books,* 7th edition, revised by Constance M. Winchell, Chicago, American Library Association, 1951, and Supplements

49.3 Preparing the working bibliography A working bibliography is a list—on note cards—of the books, magazine articles, and other published works that you intend to consult when gathering material for your reference paper. This list—compiled from the card catalog, periodical indexes, and other references—is a record of the material available on your topic and the works that will be most valuable in your research.

The number of references you should collect will depend upon the nature of the assignment, but it is always best to get more than you will probably need. If you stop with the minimum number of sources, you will undoubtedly have to take time later to find more: a book you want may already be borrowed from the library; one article on your list may prove to be too technical; another may merely repeat material you have already collected.

49.3a Bibliography cards Use a separate note card for each bibliography entry. The standard size, both for listing references and for taking notes on your reading, is a 3″ x 5″ or 4″ x 6″ card or slip of paper. Cards are suggested for this purpose because they are sturdier and easier to work with than odd slips of paper. With only one reference on each of the cards, they can be rearranged quickly for alphabetizing; new ones can be inserted in the proper places and useless ones discarded.

49.3b What to include on bibliography cards Each bibliography card should include all the facts that you will need to identify the reference and obtain it from the library. Each card should also have the information required for the final bibliography that will appear at the end of the completed paper:

1) *The author's name,* with last name first. If the book is edited, write the editor's name, followed by *ed.* If the article or pamphlet is unsigned, write the title first on the card.

2) *The title* of the book (usually underlined) or the article (in quotation marks)

Sample bibliography cards

for a book by one author

327.73
P719c

Plischke, Elmer
Conduct of American Diplomacy.
New York, Van Nostrand, 1950

for a book, edited

820.9
B326l

Baugh, Albert C., ed.
A Literary History of England
New York, Appleton-Century-Crofts,
1948

for a signed article in an encyclopedia

Reference
room shelf
12

Hamlin, Talbot F.
"Mosaic," Encyclopedia Britannica
14th ed., Chicago, 1949
15: 833-836

for a magazine article

051
For
v.49
pt 1

Harrymon, Maurer
"The M. D's Are off Their Pedestal,"
Fortune, February 1954, pp. 138-142,
176-186

for a newspaper article, unsigned

Periodical
desk

"Mayor Picks Rain-Making Advisers"
The New York Times, March 4, 1959,
p.1, col.2; p.28, col.2

3) *The facts of publication:*

    a) Of a book: the place, the name of the publisher, and the date; also the number of the edition, if given

    b) Of a magazine: the name of the magazine (underlined), the date, volume number, and the pages covered by the article

    c) Of a newspaper story: the name of the newspaper (underlined), the date, the page, and the column number if you wish. Include the name of the section if the pages are numbered separately.

4) *The library call number,* or the location of a reference work in the library—preferably in the upper left corner, just as it appears in the card catalog.

The sample cards on page 529 show how these facts may be listed for different kinds of publications. In addition, it is often helpful to number each bibliography card in the upper right corner so that you can key your notes without having to write out each time the name of the author and the title of the work.

49.4 Taking notes   Accurate and complete notes are essential for writing a good reference paper. You can save time when taking notes if you approach the problem in a workmanlike manner. Don't try to take down on cards everything you read; instead, spend a little time looking over the book, the article, or the pamphlet you have checked out to see if it contains the information that you want.

For example, when examining a book, look first at the index and the table of contents to see in what sections the subject you are writing about is treated. See also if there are any tables, graphs, bibliographies, or further references that might be of use. Skim each chapter, article, or other pertinent reference to find out first what it contains. Then go over it again carefully, taking down the notes you will need.

While the notes you take on your first sources may be fairly extensive, you should be able to summarize or condense subsequent material on a card or two.

Notes should be taken on 3" x 5" or 4" x 6" cards so that you can easily arrange the material according to the plan of your paper.

Each note card should contain these essential parts:

1) The *material*: facts, opinions (summarized in your own words or directly quoted), accurately recorded

2) The *source* (either the number keyed to the bibliography card or enough information, usually author and title, to identify it) and *page number*, accurately noted

3) The *heading* (or "slug") at the top of the card, showing what material it contains

Here is a sample note card indicating how these facts may be put down:

Heading; number keyed to bibliography card	*Senatorial opposition to Alaska purchase* 3
Direct quote in quotation marks	*p. 17 Sen. Fessenden, leader of opposition, said condition of national finances didn't permit "so large an expenditure for so small a consideration."*
Summarized material	*p. 34 Other opponents of treaty apparently more concerned with defeating any proposal of Seward and Johnson than with the purchase itself.*

It is usually a waste of time and effort to try to take notes in numbered outline form since you probably won't know the final plan of your paper until you have finished your reading. What is important is to make each note card accurate, clearly written, and clearly labeled.

Notes that cannot be readily interpreted a week or a month after they have been recorded are obviously of little use to a writer; so too are incomplete or carelessly written notes. You can avoid a good deal of unnecessary work, including rereading and rechecking, by following these simple rules:

1) Use *one* side of each card only. Your material will then be easier to classify and arrange, and you won't run the risk of overlooking a statement on the back of a card.

2) Don't crowd too much information on a card. *One* major point or a few closely related facts from the same source are enough to include on a single card. If the information is too extensive to write on one side of a single card, use two or three cards and number them in sequence.

3) Get all the information accurately the first time you consult a source, so that you won't have to make extra trips to the library.

4) Put all *direct* quotations (statements copied word for word from any published source) in quotation marks. If you omit a word or words in a direct quotation use ellipsis periods (. . .) to indicate the omission.

5) Write your notes legibly in ink (penciled notes may become blurred with frequent handling) so that you won't have to recopy them. When you use abbreviations, be sure that you will know later on what they mean.

It isn't necessary to write out all notes in full sentences; practical shortcuts such as the omission of *a, the, was* and other such words are good for summarizing material. If the method you use for taking notes in lecture courses or on your textbooks has proved successful, use it also for taking notes for your reference paper.

Take as *few* direct quotations as possible, and then only for good reasons such as these: unusually important material that may be vital to your paper; a striking statement that would lose its force in other words; a remark or opinion that might be questioned if put in words other than the author's. Everything else should be *summarized in your own words* so that your paper will sound like your writing throughout, not a patchwork of the different styles of your various sources.

Accurate notes are one of the chief tools of scholarship. Early and careful practice in taking them is excellent training that may be useful in later college courses and in a great many positions after graduation.

49.5 **Evaluating material** Since writing a reference paper is in part an exercise of judgment, it is important that you learn to evaluate the sources you use. "I found a book in the library that said . . ." is a confession of uncritical work; the point is to find the best books and the most recent authoritative material on the subject.

49.5a **Facts to consider in evaluating** A freshman engaged in writing his first reference paper on a subject that is unfamiliar to him is not expected to know offhand that a work by author A is wholly worthless or that author B is considered the foremost authority on the subject. He can, however, arrive at a fairly accurate estimate of the worth of his sources by considering these facts about them:

1) Date of publication: If your subject is one for which recent facts are important, see that the sources are up to date. The most recent edition of a book or an encyclopedia will generally be more useful than an earlier one.

2) Completeness: With magazine articles, it is better to read the original article as it was printed in full instead of a condensation of it. Similarly, an article in a one-volume encyclopedia which the writer may have at home will probably not be as thorough or as reliable as one in the *Britannica* or other major reference works.

3) Facts and opinions: Distinguish carefully between an author's facts and his opinions. Label the opinions "So-and-so thinks. . . ." In general, pay more attention to *facts* (unless your paper is about various opinions), since you will need the facts as a basis for your own opinions.

4) Objectivity of the source: A book or an article based in large part upon an author's opinions or his biases—particularly when the subject is controversial—should not be used as your sole authority on the matter. Read material on the other side of the question before reaching a conclusion.

When you are doubtful about the reliability of a source, a librarian or your instructor can give you advice. Reviews in the more specialized journals evaluate books. After you have worked awhile on your subject, you will be in a better position to evaluate the material yourself.

49.5b Primary and secondary sources A primary source is an original document or a first record of any facts or events. A secondary source is another writer's discussion of such material. For example, the Constitution of the United States is a primary source; an article or a book written *about* the Constitution is a secondary source. A scientist's report of his experiments with penicillin therapy in the *Journal of the American Medical Association* is a primary source; a newspaper or magazine comment on these results is a secondary source.

While most undergraduate reference papers are drawn principally from secondary references, a student should use primary sources whenever they are available so that he can get as close to the facts as possible and form his own conclusions. In preparing a biographical study, for instance, the actual letters, diaries, and other writings of a person provide excellent material and are often more helpful than the comment someone else has written on them. With other subjects you may be able to use lecture notes taken in one of your courses, or you can perhaps get first-hand information through personal interviews with persons who are authorities on the matter—college professors, city officials, or other informed people in the field of your investigation.

49.6 Planning the paper The central or controlling purpose of a reference paper is usually clear in a writer's mind long before he has finished investigating all his sources. He knows, for instance, whether he is trying to reach a conclusion about two opposing viewpoints or to explain an event or situation. When a sufficient amount of material has been gathered, it is time to formulate a sentence that will state this controlling purpose as definitely as possible, and to arrange the material in the order in which the first draft will be written.

49.6a Examining and arranging the notes First read through all your notes to refresh your memory and determine the best order in which to put them. Then arrange the notes in piles according to the headings you have put at the top of each card. If a heading written on a card some time ago now seems inaccurate, you can reword it; if any notes taken earlier don't look useful, put them aside in a tentative discard pile. (Almost anyone engaged in research finds that a certain amount of carefully recorded material has to be discarded, no matter how great the temptation is to put it in the paper.) At this stage you should also note any gaps in your material that will have to be filled in by further reading.

49.6b Making a preliminary outline   When the note cards have been arranged to your satisfaction, make a rough outline showing in what order you intend to present your material. For this purpose a topic outline is generally sufficient; if necessary you can later expand the entries in the outline into complete sentences. Try to group the material so that there are from three to six main divisions—not more, unless your paper is very long. To crystallize the plan and to make it possible for your instructor to examine it and make suggestions, you should write it in standard outline form (see §6, Outlining, p. 65).

Next state in one sentence (not in two or more sentences, nor in the form of a question) the central idea—exactly what you are trying to do in your paper. At this stage, neither the outline nor the thesis sentence needs to be in its final form. It is better, in fact, to make a reasonably flexible outline so that you can make whatever changes prove necessary after writing the first draft of the paper.

On the following page is a thesis sentence (or central idea) and a preliminary outline for a paper on ship launching ceremonies. A specimen page from the completed paper (p. 541) shows how both the central idea and the outline were later revised.

49.7 Writing the paper   The reference paper should represent your writing at its best—in organization, sentence structure,

First draft of outline and thesis sentence

Ship Launching Ceremonies

Thesis sentence: There have been many different kinds of ship launching ceremonies from the earliest times to the present.

I. First recorded ceremonies in 2100 B.C.

II. Primitive man's fear of the sea

    A. Prayers to unseen powers

    B. Humans sometimes sacrificed

III. Evolution of ceremonies can't be traced chronologically

    A. Customs changed from time to time

    B. Some primitive rites practiced today

IV. Customs varied in different countries

    A. Greece and Rome

    B. Religious practices in Middle Ages

    C. First christening of ships

V. English ceremonies and traditions

    A. Elaborate ceremonies of Tudor England

    B. Women first christened ships in 19th century

    C. British war ships first to be christened with wine

VI. Little religious significance to ceremonies today

    A. Fishing fleets sometimes blessed by priests

    B. Most ceremonies strictly traditional

wording, and emphasis. The most convincing proof that you have actually learned something new from your research is the way you have evaluated and organized the material and put it in your own words. Instructions should be followed to the letter about the proper form of footnotes and bibliography; the paper should be as neat as you can possibly make it, with each part in its proper order, and all errors in spelling and punctuation carefully corrected.

49.7a Writing the first draft   Make certain you are thoroughly familiar with your material before you begin to write. You should have the information on your note cards so well in mind that you can write rapidly and with confidence once you start. For this reason, it is a good idea to review your notes one more time—even though you have reread them while planning the paper—just before you begin the first draft.

This draft should be written in the same way you would write the first draft of any other important assignment (see §5, Writing a paper, p. 34), but with ample room left for documentation. You can leave spaces between the lines or at the bottom of the page to insert the necessary footnotes. Some writers put the documentation in the text of the first draft, in this manner:

> Protests about various aspects of bad taste on television involve many kinds of programs. Several years ago one critic objected to televised roller-skating derbies, saying that their purpose was apparently to glorify poor sportsmanship.[5] Since then, wrestling
> [5]Robert Lewis Shayon, "Encouraging Poor Sportsmanship," The Christian Science Monitor Magazine Section, July 1, 1950, p. 13
> matches have drawn censure from all but the

In the first draft, the footnotes may be put all together on a separate page or handled in any other way that will be convenient when you make the final copy.

If a passage seems to need more facts or further documentation, don't stop writing at that point to make an extra trip to the library. Put a question mark or some other notation in the margin, continue with your writing, and look up the necessary material *after* you have finished the first draft.

Most reference papers are written in a Formal and Impersonal style. Usually the writer does not need to refer to himself at all, but if he does, the reference should be brief. Impersonal writing does not have to be flat or lifeless: simply put down the material as compactly and directly as possible. The information itself should provide the interest.

49.7b Revising the paper Revising a reference paper means more than merely putting the footnotes in proper form and order. To do a thorough job—one that will satisfy you as well as your reader—you should examine your paper from these viewpoints:

1) The material or content: See if the main parts in your paper relate directly to the central idea. Omit any sentences or passages that are repetitious or irrelevant, and wherever necessary, make your points clearer by additional illustration, either from your own knowledge or from one of your sources. Examine closely every direct quotation (particularly the longer ones) to see whether you might better put the statement in your own words. Check each technical or unfamiliar term: Is the meaning clear from the context or should you define it?

2) The structure and the expression: First look at the introduction to see if it actually gets the subject started or is just an unnecessary preamble. Then consider the transitions between paragraphs, watching for any abrupt shifts in thought or lack of relationship between the main divisions of the paper. Finally, read the conclusion: Is it as definite and emphatic as the facts will permit? After checking the structure, go over the paper carefully to correct all the errors you can find in wording, punctuation, and spelling (pay particular attention to the spelling of proper names and technical terms).

3) The outline and the central idea: The outline should be an accurate table of contents for the reference paper in its final form. Make certain that it is stated in the way your instructor has requested (either in topics or complete sentences), and that you have followed the conventional numbering system (see §6, Outlining, p. 65). Generally the first outline, made before the first draft is written, contains too many divisions or misleading and overlapping headings; the central idea (thesis sentence) is also likely to be vague or inexact. Both should be revised at this point for greater accuracy. (Compare the first outline and thesis sentence on page 536 with the revision on page 540.)

4) The documentation: When revising your first draft, you should ask yourself whether you have used too many or too few footnotes. A full page without any references needs further examination; on the other hand, a great many footnotes on each page indicate that some of the material might better be combined or rephrased to eliminate unnecessary reference. When you are satisfied that your material is properly documented, check the form of each footnote in detail to make certain that it is complete, accurate, and consecutively numbered. Be especially sure that the abbreviations and punctuation are handled as your instructor directs.

49.8 **Footnotes** Any paper based upon the writings of others should acknowledge each and every source used. In a reference paper the acknowledgments are made by footnotes—numbered notes at the bottom of the page (corresponding to numbers in the text) that show exactly where the information was obtained. The method is illustrated in the portion of a student paper reproduced on pages 541-543.

It is common courtesy to give credit where credit is due and a sign of scrupulousness to tell the sources of specific information, so that a reader can judge them for himself, and perhaps even turn to them if he desires further information. Failure to document (footnote) borrowed information is at best carelessness; at worst, it may suggest plagiarism, which

Final outline and thesis sentence

I Christen Thee . . .

Thesis sentence: Modern ceremonies for launching ships evolved from primitive superstitions and subsequent religious practices.

I. Earliest rites based on superstition
   A. Primitive customs
      1. In pre—Christian era
      2. Among South Pacific tribes
   B. Greek and Roman customs
II. Changes brought about by Christianity
   A. Ships named for saints
   B. Altars on ships
   C. Christening of ships
III. Gradual secularization of ceremonies
   A. Elaborate rituals in Tudor England
   B. British naval customs
   C. First christening by women
IV. Present—day practices
   A. Survival of some religious customs
   B. Conventional naming and launching of naval vessels

Opening pages of the reference paper

I Christen Thee . . .

From watching the newsreels or from
personal experience, most people know that
the launching of ships—commercial as well as
naval vessels—is marked by a good deal of
colorful ceremony. Speeches are made, the
ship is formally christened, and at the
moment she slides down the ways into the sea,
a bottle of champagne is smashed against her
bow. Why are such ceremonies not generally
followed when a new railroad train is
dedicated, or an airplane, or a bus? The
answer is that the traditions and superstitions of the sea and the ships that sail
it are far older and have a far greater hold
on the imagination than any kind of travel
on land or in the air.

The exact date when man first ventured on
the water in his frail craft is unknown, but
the earliest records, dated some 2000 years
before Christ, indicate that the first sailor
knew the danger he faced and offered prayers

to the unseen powers that controlled the wind and the waves.[1] Sometime later, when he had pictured in his mind what these powers looked like, he would fashion an image of the appropriate deity and fix it to his vessel for further protection—a practice that was likely the origin of the figureheads used on the prow of ships up until recent times.[2]

Apparently prayers and pagan images were not considered sufficient safeguards against the perils of the sea, for very early in the history of ship launchings, sacrifices were offered to propitiate the gods. The first sacrifices were often human beings, a barbaric custom that survived until fairly recent times in such out-of-the-way places as the Tonga Islands, where unfortunate natives were used as living rollers on which the ships were launched.[3]

---

[1]Leland P. Lovette, USN, Naval Customs, Traditions, and Usage (Menasha, Wisconsin, 1934), p. 34

[2]Edith Wallace Benham and Ann Martin Hall, Ships of the United States Navy and Their Sponsors, 1797–1913 (Norwood, Mass., 1913), p. 207

[3]Ibid., pp. 207–208

In Western Europe, however, such practices did not long survive. The Greeks sacrificed animals instead of human beings, and they eventually substituted red wine to symbolize the blood of the animals. Today champagne is customarily used in important ceremonies in place of red or other common wine because it is felt that the more expensive wine is more appropriate for the occasion.[4] Both Greek and Roman priests also used water in a ceremony of purification when a new ship was blessed. This custom has been followed at different times in many different countries, but it was common in the United States only during the prohibition era when wine was difficult to obtain legally.[5]

The religion of the middle ages affected ship launching rites. Instead of being named after pagan gods, ships were named after saints. Each ship had its shrine and images. It is believed that these religious statues eventually lead to the custom of figureheads

---

[4]"Ship Christening," Thirteenth Naval District Reserve Bulletin, July 1953, p. 4
[5]Benham and Hall, p. 209

means offering material written by someone else as your own work. Everyone who uses published material has two responsibilities: first, absorbing the ideas into his own thought, and second, giving credit to his sources.

49.8a   Where footnotes are needed   Footnotes are essential in these two situations:

1) After every direct quotation. Each statement taken word for word from a printed source should have a reference number at the end of the quotation, and be properly identified in a footnote. The only exceptions to this rule are well-known expressions, such as those from the Bible ("Thou shalt love thy neighbor as thyself"), famous lines from literature, and proverbs.

2) After all important statements of fact or opinion taken from written sources and expressed in your own words. These include figures, dates, scientific data, descriptions of events and situations about which you have no first-hand knowledge (what happened at a session of the United Nations, how coffee is cultivated in Brazil, the role of Madagascar in World War II, and so on), and all opinions and interpretations that are not actually your own (such as one writer's reasons for the popularity of baseball in the United States or an opinion on foreign policy from a newspaper editorial).

In some publications footnotes are also used for comments or additional information that the writer does not wish to include in the text. In freshman reference papers, however, this practice should be kept to a minimum; if a statement is worth mentioning, it usually belongs in the text.

Footnotes are *not* needed for statements that would pass without question. These include obvious facts ("Certain chemicals cannot be used in the preservation of foods in the United States"), matters of common knowledge ("Hiroshima was devastated by an atomic bomb in August 1945"), general statements and expressions of the writer's own opinion ("Medical science has made unbelievable progress in the last fifty years").

49.8b Numbering and spacing of footnotes   In the text of the paper, the footnote number is placed *at the end* of a quotation, or *after the statement* for which the source is being given; it is never placed before the borrowed material. The number is raised slightly above the line and is placed outside the end punctuation of the statement to which it refers: ". . . nearly 400,000 in 1953."[3]

Footnotes are generally numbered consecutively throughout the paper in Arabic numerals beginning with 1. If the last footnote on the first page is numbered 3, the first footnote on the second page will be numbered 4, and so on. It is impossible to say how many footnotes should appear in a paper of a given length because the number varies with the type of subject and the kind of sources used; however, the typical student reference paper contains from two to four footnotes on a page. Too many footnotes suggest that the paper isn't well organized; too few indicate that the documentation isn't accurate.

In typed manuscript, footnotes are single spaced and the first line is indented as for a paragraph. It is a good idea to separate footnotes from the body of the paper by making a short line (about two inches) from the left margin between the text and the footnotes.

Studying some footnoted articles or books will help you see how the system works.

49.8c Footnote form   Generally, each footnote should contain four essential facts: the author's name, the title of the work, the facts of publication (place and date), and the specific page or pages of the source used.

Practices in footnote form vary, chiefly in punctuation and kinds of abbreviations. This section suggests a simplified form, based upon that used in literature and the social sciences. An alternative system frequently used in scientific papers is given in §49.10 on page 550. Follow carefully any changes your instructor may want you to make in the form described here.

1) Footnotes for books. The *first time* you refer to a book in a footnote, put the information in this order:

The author's name, first name or initials first: Austin Beard, I. A. Richards

The title of the book, underlined: Organic Chemistry

The place and the date of publication in parentheses: (London, 1937)

The number of the page (or pages), using the abbreviations *p.* for *page* and *pp.* for *pages*.

Examples:

[1]Gilbert Highet, *The Classical Tradition* (New York, 1949), p. 315 [one author]

[2]Bernt Balchen and Erick Bergaust, *The Next Fifty Years of Flight* (New York, 1954), pp. 63-68 [two authors]

[3]Harry R. Warfel, ed., *Letters of Noah Webster* (New York, 1954), p. 352 [an edited book]

[4]Harry Levin, "Literature as an Institution," in *Literary Opinion in America,* ed. by Morton Dauwen Zabel (New York, 1951), pp. 658-659 [a signed article in an edited book of selections written by various authors]

[5]Paul Valéry, *Monsieur Teste,* trans. by Jackson Mathews (New York, 1947), p. 47 [a book translated]

[6]*United States Government Printing Office Style Manual,* rev. ed. (Washington, 1953), p. 185 [the revised edition of a book for which no authors are given]

Notice the punctuation in these examples: a comma between the author's name and the title; no comma between the title and the first parenthesis; a comma between the place of publication and the date; a comma after the closing parenthesis. A period is sometimes used at the end of a footnote, but it is not necessary unless the footnote is a complete sentence.

For subsequent references to the same work that do not immediately follow (as for example, footnote 5 on p. 543), a short form should be used: the author's last name only (if not more than one book by the same writer is used), and the page number, thus:

[7]Highet, p. 329

If the book has no author, the title, or a shortened form of a long title, should be used:

⁸*GPO Style Manual,* p. 186

If you are using more than one source by an author, give the title as well as the author's name.

See p. 549 for the use of *ibid.*

2) Footnotes for magazine articles. The first time you footnote a magazine article, give the author's name, the title of the article in quotation marks, the name of the magazine underlined, the date of publication, and the page (the volume number may also be included).

⁹Carroll Kilpatrick, "What Foreign Trade Means to Indiana," *Harper's Magazine,* February 1954, p. 62

If the author's name is not given, begin the footnote with the title of the article:

¹⁰"Mr. Eliot," *Time,* March 6, 1950, p. 22

Later references to the same magazine article may be shortened in the same way as those for books.

When a volume number is used with a magazine, it may be expressed in one of two ways: in Roman numerals, before the date (which is in parentheses):

¹¹Ernest W. Kinne, "Reading Improvement for Adults," *College English,* XV (January 1954), 224-227

Or it may be put in Arabic numbers after the date and set off from the page numbers by a colon:

¹²Ernest W. Kinne, "Reading Improvement for Adults," *College English,* January 1954, 15:224-227

The second form is easier to follow and is the one used throughout this section. Notice that the abbreviations *p.* or *pp.* are not used after a volume number.

3) Footnotes for encyclopedia articles. These are handled in much the same manner as references to books and mag-

azine articles. When the author's name is given, put it first in the footnote. Give the *edition* of the encyclopedia rather than the place of publication:

[13]Talbot F. Hamlin, "Mosaic," *Encyclopaedia Britannica,* 14th ed., 1949, 15:385

If the article is unsigned, begin with the title:

[14]"Roman Architecture," *Columbia-Viking Desk Encyclopedia,* 1953, p. 847

4) Footnotes for newspaper articles. Unless the article is signed, the reference to a news story consists of the name of the paper underlined, the date, and the page.

[15]*The Chicago Tribune,* June 15, 1954, p. 28

When the reference is to a separate section of a paper, that section should be indicated:

[16]Robert Lewis Shayon, "Encouraging Poor Sportsmanship," *The Christian Science Monitor Magazine Section,* July 1, 1950, p. 13

5) Footnotes for pamphlets, government documents, and miscellaneous material. The form is similar to that for a book, but may have added identification taken from the title page of the source, as in the following:

[17]Ella B. Ratcliffe, *Accredited Higher Institutions 1944,* U.S. Office of Education Bulletin 1944, No. 3 (Washington, 1954), pp. 87-88
[18]Wallace Joseph Smith, *The Fur Trade in Colonial Pennsylvania* (unpublished University of Washington Master of Arts thesis, 1950), p. 19

As with a book, when the author's name is not given, the citation begins with the title:

[19]*Higher Education for American Democracy,* Report of the President's Commission on Higher Education (Washington, 1947), 1:26

6) Footnotes for material at second hand. When the material used is taken at second hand from another work, both the original source and the source from which it was taken should be given:

[20]William Caxton, Preface to *Eneydos* (1490), quoted in Albert C. Baugh, *A History of the English Language* (New York, 1935), p. 241

7) Use of *ibid.* in footnotes. *Ibid.* (an abbreviation for the Latin *ibidem*, "in the same place") means in a footnote "in the same book or article as the preceding footnote." It is used to refer only to the work listed in the footnote immediately preceding:

[21]Robert S. and Helen M. Lynd, *Middletown* (New York, 1929), p. 44
[22]*Ibid.*, p. 162

Notice that *ibid.* is always underlined and is always followed by a period. When it stands first in the footnote—and it almost always does—it is capitalized. If footnote 21 in the above example was the last footnote on page ten of a paper, and footnote 22 the first one on page eleven, *Ibid.* would be the proper form just as it would be if both footnotes appeared on the same page.

49.9 **Abbreviations in footnotes**   Standard abbreviations such as those for states (Menasha, Wis.; Norwood, Mass.) are commonly used in footnotes (but *New York* rather than *N.Y.* in reference to the city). The following abbreviations are also used to save space (because they come from Latin, *c.*, *ca.*, and *ibid.* are underlined to represent italics):

anon.	anonymous
c. or *ca. (circa)*	about a given date (*c.* 1490)
ch., chs.	chapter, chapters
col., cols.	column, columns
ed.	edited by or edition (2nd ed.)
f., ff.	the following page ("p. 38f." means page 38 and page 39); the following pages ("pp. 38ff." means page 38 and several following pages). Exact references are generally preferable to *f.* and *ff.*
ibid. (ibidem)	in the same place (explained above)
l., ll.	line, lines

MS, MSS	manuscript, manuscripts (Periods following the letters are optional.)
n.d.	no date given
p., pp.	page, pages. The word *page* is not written out in footnotes.
rev.	revised
trans. or tr.	translated by

The following Latin abbreviations are much less common in current use because they can be just as well expressed in English:

cf. (confer)	compare (usually replaced by the English *see* or *compare*)
et al. (et alii)	and others (used instead of giving all the names when a book has several authors; the preferable form is "C. A. Young and others")
loc. cit. (loco citato)	in the place cited. Use instead the shortened form of reference.
op. cit. (opere citato)	the work cited. Use instead the shortened form of reference.
q.v. (quod vide)	which see (used to suggest consulting a work; now generally replaced by *see*)
vide	see. Use the English word.

49.10 Alternative forms for footnotes   Most scientific publications and some government reports use a slightly different system for footnoting material from that described above. The writer's initials may be used instead of his given name (R. G. Cummings), the place of publication may be omitted, as well as the abbreviation for *page,* and such Latin terms as *ibid.* and *op. cit.* are used sparingly if at all. These sample footnotes show the difference in form:

[1]L. A. Bauer, *Principles of Radio Engineering,* 127–131
[2]H. H. Sisler and C. A. Vander Werf, "Ionization Potentials in the Teaching of Elementary Chemistry," *J. Chem. Educ.,* 22 (1945) 390–396
[3]"The Vitamin Business," *Fortune,* May 1945, 31:140
[4]Bauer, 138
[5]*J. Amer. Chem. Soc.* 57 (1935) 229, 517

You should not of course use shortcuts such as these unless your instructor gives permission. In particular, you should not shift from one system to another in your paper: consistency in form is essential in the use of footnotes.

Any description of footnotes makes their use seem much harder than it really is. If you have good notes with the exact sources of the facts clearly recorded, it is relatively simple to keep track of the necessary sources in the first draft and to place them in the final paper in the proper form.

Reference: For more complex systems and variations in footnotes for different fields, see the works listed in the sample bibliography, page 552.

49.11 **The final bibliography** The finished reference paper concludes with a bibliography of the sources actually used in the paper. This is an alphabetical list of all books, magazine articles, or other publications that have been documented in the footnotes; its principal purpose is to help a reader identify the works used.

Your bibliography cards should contain all the information needed to compile the final bibliography. It isn't necessary to give the page numbers you used in a book or the number of pages the book contains (and don't include the library call number), but you should list the pages for magazine and newspaper articles.

Keep these points in mind when making up the bibliography:

1) All entries are listed in alphabetical order, by the author's *last* name or by the first significant word of the title (disregarding *A* or *The*) when the author is unknown.

2) Don't separate the list according to kinds of publications. Since the bibliography for most freshman papers is short, books, magazine and encyclopedia articles, news stories, and pamphlets should all appear in the same list.

3) The entries are not numbered.

Punctuation varies in different bibliography styles, mainly

in the use of commas, colons, and parentheses. A plain style that gives all the necessary information is usually best. The form shown here illustrates one style that can be followed without difficulty. Be sure to note carefully any different practices your instructor may want you to follow. The sources used for illustration are books, articles, and pamphlets on various aspects of writing and documenting research papers:

Appel, Livia, *Bibliographical Citation in the Social Sciences and Humanities,* Madison, University of Wisconsin Press, 1949

Bleifuss, William W., "Introducing the Research Paper Through Literature," *College English,* April 1953, 14:405-406

Campbell, William G., *Form and Style in Thesis Writing,* Boston, Houghton Mifflin, 1954

Cooper, Charles W., and Edmund J. Robins, *The Term Paper,* Stanford, Stanford University Press, 1934

Hilbish, Florence M. A., *The Research Paper,* New York, Bookman Associates, 1952

A Manual of Style, 11th ed., Chicago, University of Chicago Press, 1949

The MLA Style Sheet, New York, Modern Language Association of America, 1951

Rose, Lisle A., and others, *Preparing Technical Material for Publication,* Urbana, University of Illinois Bulletin, Vol. 50, December 1952

Stewart, Marion F., "The First Footnote Paper," *College English,* April 1953, 14:405-406

Sypherd, W. O., and others, *The Engineer's Manual of English,* Chicago, Scott, Foresman, 1943

Trelease, Sam F., *The Scientific Paper,* Baltimore, Williams & Wilkins, 1947

You will notice from these examples that bibliography form differs from footnote form in that the author's *last* name comes first and that the publisher's name, as well as the place and date of publication, is given.

49.12 The completed paper The reference paper, usually submitted in a manila folder, should contain all the parts in the order your instructor has assigned. Typically, the completed paper has these units:

Title page: The title of the paper should be centered; your name, the date, the course number, and any other information your instructor requests should be put in the lower right-hand corner.

Outline: The thesis sentence and the outline in the form assigned (topic or sentence outline). The revised outline should correspond to the organization of the final paper.

Text of the paper: The final copy of the paper, complete with footnotes, charts, and diagrams wherever needed. The numbering of the text usually begins on the second page, with Arabic numerals centered at the top or at the top right-hand corner.

Bibliography: On a separate page following the last page of the text.

Make certain to include any other material, such as your first outline or first draft, that your instructor calls for.

This extended explanation may suggest to you that writing a reference paper is an impossible task to accomplish in one quarter or one semester's work. It isn't. Done carefully, with due attention to each of the stages outlined in this section, it may be accomplished with no more effort than you would put forth for your other courses. And if your reference paper represents your best work, you will find the assignment a satisfying one and good training for later college work.

Exercises

1. From this list of general fields, select one that you know something about or are interested in, and show how it might be progressively narrowed down to a specific topic suitable for a reference paper of the length assigned in your course. If necessary,

consult the card catalog or one of the periodical indexes to see what subdivisions of the subject are listed.

Agriculture in America	Journalism
Current problems in business	Juvenile delinquency
Child psychology	Literature and its significance
Contemporary music	Medicine
Dancing	Modern art
Fashions in dress	Motion pictures
Foreign diplomacy	Photography
An important figure in history or in religion	Recent contributions of science
	Sports and their importance

2. These are some preliminary subjects submitted by students for reference papers of about 1500 words, before they had begun to investigate their sources. As they are stated here, which ones do you think would be unlikely to result in satisfactory papers, and for what reasons?

1) The Renaissance in Europe
2) Will Hollywood survive television?
3) Nuclear staining of chromosomes and nucleoli
4) The problem of smog in large cities and methods to control it
5) The future of advertising in America
6) Some great moments in American sports
7) Trade unions are undemocratic
8) The Sister Kenny Method for the treatment of polio
9) Napoleon
10) A history of jazz in America

3. Read two articles in general encyclopedias on your topic and at least one other reference—a special reference work (see lists in §49.2d), in a book, or in a periodical. Then contrast or compare these articles as to (1) the most recent dates of publication, (2) completeness of their discussions, (3) emphasis or possible bias, (4) approach, whether popular or technical, (5) the general value of the article for your purpose.

4. After you have decided on a specific topic and have made a preliminary investigation of your sources, prepare brief notes on these topics:

1) Your reasons for choosing the subject

2) Your present knowledge about the subject and what further reading you will have to do

3) The information you assume your readers already have about this subject (consider the members of your composition class as your potential readers)

4) The reference works—general and specialized—that you think will prove most useful to you in finding material

5) The main point or points you hope to make in your paper

5. In what reference works would you look *first* for information on these matters?

1) A speech made by the Vice-President of the United States seven or eight weeks ago in Chicago

2) The college degrees held by a prominent contemporary American

3) The full title of *Don Quixote* as given in the two-volume edition of 1949 translated by Samuel Putnam

4) An extended discussion of the Presbyterian Church in America

5) A good discussion of the first beginnings of opera

6) The paid attendance at last year's World Series games

7) A reliable article on Henry VIII

8) The title and date of an article on the coronation of Queen Elizabeth that appeared in the *New Statesman and Nation,* an English magazine

9) An account of the Whisky Rebellion, an insurrection that occurred in Pennsylvania in 1794

10) A useful summary of an outstanding political event of a year ago

6. If any of these statements appeared in your reference paper,

which would you footnote, and why? Explain why some of the statements would not have to be footnoted.

    1) Pearl Harbor was attacked by the Japanese on December 7, 1941.

    2) In Iraq, military service is compulsory for males between the ages of 18 to 25.

    3) General health rules should be taken very seriously.

    4) Some scientists, however, do not believe that bacterial cells have a nucleus in the strict sense, since they consider the entire cell to be a nucleus.

    5) The boiling point of water at sea level is 212 degrees Fahrenheit.

    6) Discussing the problems of Good and Evil, Dr. Einstein states in his book, *The World as I See It,* that "one does people the best service by giving them some elevating work to do"—a statement with which I agree.

    7) Dorothy Dix, as I will attempt to show in the following pages, was not only the most famous of modern advice-to-the-lovelorn columnists, but she was also an important figure in bringing to the public attention the true nature of mental illness.

    8) Another quotation frequently misquoted is the line by William Congreve, "Music hath charms to soothe the savage breast," a line that many people rephrase as "Music hath charms to soothe the savage beast."

7. Put the following references to source material in consistent footnote form as they would appear in a reference paper. Use the system described on pages 545-549, or one assigned by your instructor. Number the entries consecutively, as they appear here.

    1) To page 143 of a book titled Slang To-Day and Yesterday, written by Eric Partridge and published by the Macmillan Company in New York, 1950.

    2) To pages 42 and 43 of an article in Harper's Magazine for May 1954. The title of the article is Helen Keller, and the author is Van Wyck Brooks. The magazine is published in New York City.

3) To page 527 of this handbook.

4) To pages 147 to 150, inclusive, of the book mentioned in 1.

5) To page 13 of a pamphlet published by the University of Illinois, Urbana, Illinois, in 1952. The title of the pamphlet is Preparing Technical Material for Publication, and three authors are listed on the title page: Lisle A. Rose, Elmer F. Heater, and George R. Foster. The pamphlet is further described as University of Illinois Bulletin Volume 50, Number 32; the price is sixty cents.

6) To a direct quotation by Sir Winston Churchill printed on page 92 of the magazine U.S. News & World Report for July 23, 1954. This is Volume XXXVII, Number 4 of the magazine.

7) To the same source and the same page given in 6.

8) To an unsigned article called Isle of Man in the 1941 edition of the Encyclopedia Americana, a thirty-volume work published in New York and Chicago by the Americana Corporation. The article appeared on page 414 of volume XV.

9) To the same source given in 8, but on page 415.

10) To pages 52 and 59 of a pamphlet titled Raising the School Level Age, published in Paris in 1951 by UNESCO. The author is Isaac Leon Kandel.

8. Make a bibliography using the items given in the preceding exercise.

9. Prepare to write a brief report in class on one of the following topics. Bring your bibliography and note cards with you for reference, if necessary.

1) A summary of your reference paper, giving the essential ideas and the emphasis of the original

2) The sources which you found most useful and why

3) Some problems you encountered in organizing your paper and how you solved them

4) The material you omitted from your rough draft and your reasons for eliminating it

5) What you have learned from the assignment, such as methods of organizing complex material, how to find material in the library, or possible areas for future investigation

Index

Page references in **boldface** refer to important discussions of a topic. The page numbers of appropriate exercises are listed in *italics* after the other references. Abbreviations used in correcting papers are alphabetized as main entries and appear in boldface capitals; for example, **AB.**

Sources for reference papers, 40-41, **519-527**; *ex. 554-557*
availability and complexity of, 518
encyclopedias (listed), 525-526
evaluation of, 533-534
library card catalogs, 519-521
New York Times Index, 524-525
periodical indexes (listed), 521-525
primary and secondary, 534
Readers' Guide to Periodical Literature, 522-523
specialized reference works (listed), 525-526, 527
yearbooks and annual publications (listed), 527
See also Bibliography *and* Footnotes.
SP (spelling), 458
Space, materials arranged by method of, 46-47
Spacing,
footnotes, 545
letters, 93-101
manuscripts, 86-87
Specific words, **257-261**; *ex. 269-271*
Spelling, **458-472**; *ex. 267-269, 472-476*
combined forms, 470-471
compound words, hyphening of, 431-435; *ex. 435*
correction of, on manuscript, 88
dictionary as guide to, 507; *ex. 513*
divided usage in, 471, 472, 507; *ex. 476, 513*
doubling the final consonant, 466-467; *ex. 474-475*
-ei- or *-ie-*, 466; *ex. 474*
final *-e*, dropped or retained, 465-466; *ex. 475*
final *-f*, plural of words ending in, 469; *ex. 475*
final *-o*, plural of words ending in, 468-469; *ex. 475*
final *-y*, changed to *-i-*, 466, 467-468; *ex. 475*

genitive forms, 345-347; *ex. 351*
lists of commonly misspelled words, 462-463, 469-470
methods for improving, 461-464
misspelling, causes of, 458-460
plural forms, **348-350**, 467-469; *ex. 351-353, 475*
possessive pronouns, 363-365
rules for, 464-469
shortened forms, 436, **471-472**; *ex. 476*
similar words, confusion of, 256-257, 459, 469-470; *ex. 473-474*
suffixes, rules for adding, 348-350, 465-469; *ex. 351-353, 474-476*
variant forms, 349-350, **471-472**, 507; *ex. 351-353, 476, 513*
Splice, comma. *See* Comma faults.
Split infinitives, 318
Squinting modifiers, 204-205
Standard English,
defined, 8-9 (table), 16, 17-18
qualities of Good English, 20-27
See also Formal English, General English, *and* Informal English.
Standards for writing, 17-19
States, abbreviations for, 94, 549
Stationery, 92-93, 97
Stilted English, 8
Straight, as adjective or adverb, 312
Street addresses, form for, 94, 448
Stress, shown in dictionaries, 508
Stressed prefixes, hyphen after, 433
Stringy sentences, 213-214
Strong verbs. *See* Irregular verbs.
Study habits, **477-493**; *ex. 493*
attention to material, 477-479
attitude toward material, 480-481
conditions of study, 477-479

(5091)

4 5 6 7 **8** 9 10 11 12 13 14 15 16 17 18 19 20 21 22 23 24 25   65 64 63 62 61 60 59 58 57 56